TECHNIQUE AND IDEAS
IN THE *AENEID*

TECHNIQUE AND IDEAS
IN THE *AENEID*

GORDON WILLIAMS

YALE UNIVERSITY PRESS
NEW HAVEN AND LONDON

Designed by James J. Johnson
and set in Palatino Roman.
Printed in the United States of America by
Halliday Lithograph, West Hanover, Mass.

Library of Congress Catologing in Publication Data

Williams, Gordon Willis.
  Technique and ideas in the Aeneid.

  Bibliography: p.
  Includes index.
  1. Virgil.   Aeneid.   I. Title.
PA6825.W535   873'.01   82–7008
ISBN 0–300–02852–0   AACR2

10   9   8   7   6   5   4   3   2   1

CONTENTS

PREFACE

Two general and related questions confront any reader of the *Aeneid*. These are: first, is the world of the *Aeneid* presented as a part of the world of normal human experience, with a poetic claim to historical reality and separated from us by no more than time and generic conventions; or is it in essence a mythical world, only remotely related to the actual world by means of metaphor and symbol? Second, what ideas are expressed in the epic and how can they be recognised as such? This book originated in an attempt to find a method by which an acceptable answer could be found to these questions. This is a companion volume to *Figures of Thought in Roman Poetry* (New Haven: Yale University Press, 1980). The basic thesis of that book was that Roman poets from Catullus to Horace developed a series of figures of thought that could be used to generate novel relationships between ideas, analogous to the relationships, in general either metaphoric or metonymic in nature, that could be established between single words by figures of speech in accordance with the normal rules of rhetoric. This means that the poet could say one thing but expect his reader to understand also something else, related to what was said by a process of association that was either metaphoric or metonymic.

These figures of thought were mainly used in poems that were small in scale; but, starting with the highly original poem 68 of Catullus, experiments were constantly made in adapting the figures to longer poems. Such experimentation is especially characteristic of the work of Propertius. But the most far-reaching experiments were those of Virgil, first in his *Eclogues* and then, on a very much larger scale, in his *Georgics*; it was the latter poem that supplied the technical model for Horace's *Ars Poetica*.

It is the thesis of this book that the same basic concept can be applied to the interpretation of the *Aeneid*. What is different is due to the vast increase of scale in an epic poem. The figures had to be adapted to that increase of scale. So, for instance, what I called 'thematic anticipation' and 'suspension of judgment' could be used not only as figures of indirection that enabled the poet to say one thing and also mean another, but in addition as a potent means of creating the kind of coherence that is essential to an epic poem. However, the most important figure of thought to the poet trying to write what was in some sense a historical epic was what I have called "the objective framework": the poet appears to be talking about a period of less than ten years in the twelfth century, and yet he is also talking about the history of Rome (only founded in the eighth century) and particularly about the time of composition in the age of Augustus.

But not only were these figures of thought adapted. The poet, when he turned to epic, found himself confronted with a type of composition that had been, over centuries, shaped generically by a series of features (such as the "divine machinery," similes, or apostrophes) that were susceptible of re-interpretation and adaptation both to the new conditions of poetry in Rome and also to the design of this novel kind of epic. In addition to this, there was a feature that characterised all poetry written, whether in Greek or in Latin, under the influence of the great poets (especially Callimachus, Theocritus, and Apollonius Rhodius) who wrote in Alexandria in the third century B.C.: this was what Roman poets called *doctrina* 'learning'; it included abstruse knowledge, learned allusion, unusual words, but (most relevant to the epic poet) it also included the capacity to write in such a way as to require readers to recall the texts of predecessors. The last provided a special opportunity for Virgil to make the texts of his great predecessors active in his own for a variety of purposes, which will be examined in chapter 5.

The basic conviction expressed in this (as in my previous) book is that technique must be prior to meaning both for poet and for interpreter. (Thomas Berger, the novelist and parodist, put it well: "Technical matters are invariably more important than moral purposes in the making of a work of the imagination, but the former are peculiar in that they can usually be studied and identified only after the work has been done.")[1] For this reason, I have always started from questions of technique, asking how a certain feature functions in the narrative, identifying its analogues,

---

1. In an interview with Robert Schickel reported in *The New York Times Book Review*, April 6, 1980, p. 22.

and then considering its usefulness to the poet as a vehicle of meaning. The book is divided into two parts: the first is concerned with features designed to aid the narrative on the large scale by producing movement and coherence and also by connecting the poem with its predecessors, especially Homer (a connexion, however, that enforces dissimilarity as much as similarity). The second part examines features that are adapted in various ways to convey a point of view; here the question is always being raised how the epic poet, without fracturing generic proprieties (especially that of impersonality), can express ideas that may at times bear the overcharge of a personally felt emotion. In all of his works Virgil is most elusive as an individual personality, and never more so than in his epic poem. (Friedrich Leo, writing in 1902, expressed with nice humour the critic's sense of insecurity with this poet: "Man wagt kaum mehr es laut zu sagen, aber ich glaube immer noch, wenn ich Vergil tractire, dass ich es mit einem Dichter zu thun habe.")[2]

Finally, in the Appendix, I have faced the old problem of the poet's changes of mind as they have left marks on the text, particularly in the first half of the poem. It is not intended to present a judicious survey or summation of all the views that have been put forward on this problem, but is a personal account of the way in which the problem has appeared to a reader concerning himself with the questions of technique I have addressed in this book. In that sense the Appendix is retrospective.

The analytic method I have followed has entailed treating the same passages from different points of view in different chapters. I have tried to alleviate the disruption this may cause by cross-references, but the two indexes are intended to provide a ready means of co-ordinating the interpretation of such passages.

The book has been written in the hope that it will reach not just classical scholars and students, but readers who are interested in European literature in general and in the way in which the classical tradition has shaped that literature. Consequently I have translated all Latin and Greek passages. The translations make no claim to elegance; they are as literal as possible so that a reader can work his way through a quoted passage if he wishes. I have quoted generously in order to hold attention focused on the text and to avoid the disruption that would be caused by the need for constant reference to separate texts.

The principle of selection in the Select Bibliography is simple: I have listed there the works that, as far as I am aware, have helped me, in one

---

2. "Vergil und die Ciris," *Hermes* 37 (1902): 22.

way or another, to reach the views expressed in this book. In general that constitutes my sole acknowledgment of indebtedness. This is certainly inadequate in a number of cases: I think particularly of the work of commentators like Roland Austin and R. D. Williams, or of G. N. Knauer's indispensable book which establishes in the fullest detail the relation of the text of the *Aeneid* to those of the *Iliad* and the *Odyssey*. Such works are a ready and constant aid to the interpreter. But this procedure seemed preferable to cluttering the pages with bibliographical footnotes. In fact, footnotes are confined to cross-references, occasional indications of where fuller treatment may be found, and a few modifications of the text, or afterthoughts on it.

I owe much to the generosity and kindness of four friends and colleagues, Thomas Cole, George and Philippa Goold, and John Herington. They all read an earlier draft of this book for me when they had much more urgent calls on their time; they made innumerable suggestions for improvement and I have benefited greatly from their criticisms. This constitutes the only acknowledgment of their help and expression of my heartfelt gratitude. I am also indebted to the readers for the Yale University Press, who made a number of useful observations. I have been most fortunate in my editor, Barbara Folsom, whose perspicacity and sensitivity I must thank for many improvements in the text of this, as of my previous, book.

PART I
FIGURES OF THOUGHT AND STRUCTURE IN THE NARRATIVE

The aim of Part I is to distinguish and analyse a range of devices that are more or less continuously functional in the narrative. They are to be recognised as figures because their significance is not univocal and immediate: in some the poet says one thing but means that something else also should be understood; in others their sense is not complete until more of the text—and in some cases the rest of the poem—has been read. Some of these figures are closely related to the techniques that I analysed in *Figures of Thought in Roman Poetry;*[1] others, however, are peculiar to this poem. But all of them have been conceived and shaped by the poet to meet the unique demands of a full-length epic poem.

The questions to be asked first in each case are questions of poetic technique: How does the poet use this or that figure in the narrative? What special advantage did it offer him? What is its function in key passages? It is important to say this at the outset because many of what are called "figures" here have been treated in the past as if they were really statements of fact or belief by the poet and could be used to discover his own beliefs or even those of Romans of his own time. A typical expression of that ingrained habit is this:[2]

But it would be just as great an error in the opposite direction to regard the gods as mere "reflections" or projections of Aeneas's *psyche*. Virgil really believed in a cosmic fate and a cosmic counter-fate (*ratio* and *furor* on a heavenly scale) and in Rome as much more than a human achievement. . . .

My intention in what follows is to transform all such problems into ques-

1. Williams (1980).
2. Otis (1963), p. 226.

1

tions of technique. This seems to me to be a readier means of analysing certain conspicuous features of the narrative than to make an assumption about the poet's beliefs. This procedure will permit questions about the poet's point of view to be postponed to Part II, after questions about narrative-technique have been considered.

This is not, it must be insisted, to propose a reductive thesis that Fate and the gods are mere figural concepts in the *Aeneid*. It is, on the contrary, to declare a method: to ask questions about technique before trying to discover what ideas are being expressed. This does not in the least exclude the possibility of understanding statements about Fate and the gods also as theological beliefs expressed by the poet. In fact, a major problem to be faced by this book is to decide between two readings of the *Aeneid:* the one regards the world of the epic as a part—even if a distant part—of the real world of human experience, re-created by the poet's historical imagination; the other views the world of Aeneas as mythical and symbolic. In the former view, it is the figure of metonymy that relates the world of Aeneas to ours; in the latter, it is related by a metaphorical mode. Those who take this latter view see statements about Fate and the gods as claiming the same truth-value as statements about the human characters, and so as indicative of beliefs held by the poet. In the former view, however, concepts of Fate and the gods were useful to the poet as a means of locating metaphorically in the narrative certain fixed or constantly recurring features of the human predicament; consequently, they need have no relevance to the poet's beliefs, which then must be sought elsewhere. Of course, equally, their status as figural structures in the narrative need not affect their truth-claims on another level; only deliberate subversion by the poet can do that. The problem is particularly difficult because of this poet's "negative capability," his propensity for the indirect and the indeterminate, which is so powerful an element in his style. That problem will be faced in Part II.

1   THE CONCEPT OF FATE

Chapter 9 of Cyril Bailey's *Religion in Virgil* (Oxford: Clarendon Press, 1935), entitled "Fate and the Gods," begins thus (p. 204): "No account of the religious ideas in Virgil would be complete without a consideration of his conception of Fate and the relation of Fate to the gods; it is indeed in some senses the widest and deepest of his religious ideas." However, it turns out to be very difficult to explain Virgil's conception of Fate in terms of Greek and Roman religious ideas, and the categories devised to accommodate the various meanings suggested by the text are neither very illuminating nor very watertight. Bailey is compelled to decide (p. 232) that "Virgil is using his inheritance of conceptions both Roman and Greek": that is, he was eclectic. But, even so, Bailey is also forced to add (p. 233): "This is perhaps too definite a theology and it is not to be supposed that the poet was at all times conscious of the reconciliation of the many diverse elements he uses, derived from different sources; he is here as always an eclectic. But he is feeling towards a monotheism in which Iuppiter is supreme and, like the Stoic world-god, expresses his will in the decrees of fate. It is perhaps in this conception that we meet Virgil's highest and deepest religious conviction." It is hard to feel persuaded by this. If there is religious conviction as such expressed in the *Aeneid* (and it is far from clear that there is),[1] it is certainly not to be found displayed on the surface of the text.

    In fact, ideas that seem to be religious in origin can also be viewed as figural structures, designed to help in the ordering of the narrative, and it is in this direction that the questions which follow will be aimed. From

---

1. See below, chap. 7, sec. 3, and chap. 9.

that point of view we can ask how the concept of Fate was useful to the poet.

1. Fate as a Figure of Anticipation

One very obvious way in which the concept of Fate is useful can be seen immediately from Lucan, who learned his technique from Virgil. Lucan dispensed with gods in his *Bellum Civile* and so had Fate (or *Fortuna*) as the only superhuman force. As with Virgil, so with Lucan, scholars have tended to ask religious or (slightly more plausibly) philosophical questions about his concept of Fate and to point to its obvious Stoic features. But for the poet, Fate, in one of its more important aspects, is what is going to happen before it happens. The concept allows the author to use his privileged position to create suspense—not the obvious suspense of not knowing what is going to happen, but the suspense that keeps the reader oppressively aware of the future looming ahead. In the *Bellum Civile* the battle of Pharsalia looms over the first six books, and then its shadow falls heavily over the last three.

In the *Aeneid* that use of the concept is to be clearly seen, for instance, on a large scale, in the whole episode of Dido's tragedy and in the anticipation of the death of Turnus throughout the last three books— though that goes even further back. On a smaller scale, it is to be seen, especially in the last six books, in the foreshadowing of many deaths, as for instance, when the poet explains that Juppiter did not allow Pallas and Lausus to meet because (10.438) *mox illos sua fata manent maiore sub hoste* ("soon their fates[2] await them at the hand of a greater enemy"). It is used, with a special adaptation to the character of Aeneas, in the foreboding sense of Troy's imminent destruction in Book 2. That last example can be illustrated by the way in which human characters can use the concept, not so much to explain, as to give suggestive emotional depth to their own tragedies: as, for instance, when Deiphobus in the Underworld explains his horrible death to Aeneas, introducing his account with the words (6.511–12) *sed me fata mea et scelus exitiale Lacaenae / his mersere malis* ("but it was my destiny and the deadly crime of Helen that plunged me in this misery").

In human characters the possibility of this formulation comes from hindsight, but with Juppiter from foresight, as when he comforts Hercules for the death of Pallas by telling him (10.471–72) *etiam sua Turn-*

---

2. Almost equivalent here to "deaths."

um / fata vocant ("Turnus' own destiny is summoning him too"), though, for the reader, that functions as privileged information from the author, foreshadowing the death of Turnus. A very similar situation is when Juppiter sends Mercury down to Carthage to ensure a kindly reception for the Trojans (1.299–300) *ne fati nescia Dido / finibus arceret,* "lest Dido, who knows nothing of Fate, exclude them from her territories." That ignorance on Dido's part will clearly be fatal to her and will lay her open to manipulation. What Juppiter foresees is also a foreshadowing by the omniscient author.

In this way the poet can use the figure of Fate to manipulate the short-range events of the immediate story.

2. *Fate as a Synecdoche for the Historical Process*

There is another closely related use that is original to Virgil. The *Aeneid* is concerned with the events of less than a decade towards the end of the twelfth century B.C., and it is in that period that the poet (and reader) takes his stand. But every now and then the curtain of events in the twelfth century parts and a vista of Roman history is opened up, from the wrong end as it were, toward the shining eminence of the present day—the age of Augustus—in the far distance. The concept of Fate or Destiny can be used to express the privileged sense, derived from hindsight, that, once a series of events has taken place, its unfolding can be seen to have been inevitable: it could not have happened otherwise. The poet seizes on that sense of historical inevitability and transfers it back into the twelfth century by means of the concept of Fate. Consequently, every event is made to have its own special place in a great predestined chain that leads unswervingly to the age of Augustus. But that is a poetic stratagem; the poet is not confessing to a belief in determinism, he is creating a sense of dramatic and significant connectedness, in such a way that a large-scale pattern in history is revealed. What is original is that he has transferred the revelation of that pattern back to the beginning of the period in which it began to be created as a historical reality. Again, this is a poetic figure, not a religious idea.

The sense of a concept that is not just local to its context is evoked early in the epic: (2) *fato profugus,* (18) *si qua fata sinant,* (22) *sic volvere Parcas;* it reaches an early climax in the great speech of Juppiter to Venus (257–96), beginning with the assurance *manent immota tuorum / fata tibi* ("the destiny of your people remains unchanged"). The effect is to make a reader look forward, not just within the poem but far beyond the limits of the poem (defined by the prooemium of Book 1), to a historical continuum that itself extends even beyond the moment at which the poem is actually being written. The reader, that is, in his own day (in the age of Augustus) stands in the same relationship to the future as he does within the limits of the poem, placed in the twelfth century B.C. The ways in which the actual field of the poem is related to fields that are ostensibly outside its scope will be examined later,[3] but the concept of Fate is one of the means the poet uses to make that transfer from the primary to the secondary field.

Determinism, however, would be a poetically boring and dangerous concept, and there are many ways in which any suggestion of that idea is subverted. It is notable that in this poem Virgil uses a technique that is of great importance for the interpretation of the *Aeneid:* a full explanation is not necessarily given by the poet in a context that requires it for complete understanding. Instead, reading the *Aeneid* is more a process of continual modification and re-reading; there operates on a large scale the kind of synecdoche that Quintilian categorizes as *e sequentibus praecedentia.*[4] This virtually means that continuous suspension of judgment is required of the reader from beginning to end of the poem.[5] So ideas that subvert any suggestion of determinism are scattered throughout the poem.

First a distinction is made in a number of ways between events regarded in the short range, for instance by people immediately occupied with them, and the view that can be taken over the long range of history. In 8.398–99 Vulcan makes a surprising assertion to Venus:

> "nec pater omnipotens Troiam nec fata vetabant
> stare decemque alios Priamum superesse per annos."

> "Neither the all-powerful Father [of the gods] nor Fate forbade
> Troy to stand and Priam to survive another ten years."

This compels a re-reading of Book 2 in which it now becomes clear that action by the gods which seemed to tend towards the destruction of Troy was only one level of explanation and not necessarily the one that should matter most in the context; essentially, the human participants were responsible for their own downfall. There could be no doubt about Troy's ultimate fall, and that fact needed the long-term explanation; but there was no necessity that any one occasion should lead to its fall unless the

---

3. chap. 6.
4. See Williams (1980), Index s.v.
5. See Williams (1980), Index s.v.

human actors co-operated in their own destruction. The gap between the two levels of explanation can now be seen to correspond to the gap between the vision to which Venus unsealed Aeneas' eyes (2.604–20) and the poet's reinterpretation of that vision in terms of the physical events that actually meet Aeneas' eyes;[6] it can now also be seen to be significant that Venus enforced that vision in words, leaving it to the reader to understand that the revelation was largely a mental experience as far as Aeneas was concerned. What was real for him was what actually met his eyes (2.624–31); his goddess-mother supplied an explanation that he had to accept on trust, even if he could actually seem to see the gods at work after she told him about them. The essential feature of this, seen in the light of Vulcan's explanation, is that the poet asserts inevitability, expressed in terms of a pre-determined plan, as the way in which history must be viewed as a whole; whereas, in the short term, human beings are fully responsible for their own destiny, since the large-scale pattern is compatible with considerable variation in small-scale events.

The same point is attributed to Juno earlier, in a speech in which she rages at her impotence against Aeneas: she knows she cannot keep him from Italy or prevent his marrying Lavinia (7.313–14), but (315–322):

> "at trahere atque moras tantis licet addere rebus,
> at licet amborum populos exscindere regum.
> hac gener atque socer coeant mercede suorum:
> sanguine Troiano et Rutulo dotabere, virgo,
> et Bellona manet te pronuba. nec face tantum
> Cisseis praegnas ignis enixa iugalis;
> quin idem Veneri partus suus et Paris alter,
> funestaeque iterum recidiva in Pergama taedae."

"I can prolong and delay such important events; I can exterminate the peoples of both kings. At that cost to their peoples let son-in-law and father-in-law come together: the blood of Trojans and Rutulians shall be your dowry, girl, and the goddess of war is ready to be your matron of honour. And the daughter of Cisseus [Hecuba] was not the only wife to conceive a torch and bear fire to be a bridegroom; no indeed—Venus will find her son also a second Paris and the torches will be deadly to a rebuilt Troy."

Juno will take what vengeance she can because in the short term events can still be influenced, though the long-term results are certain and unchanged. That leaves an area for human responsibility as well as

6. See chap. 2, sec. 2.

for divine interference. (The nature and meaning of that divine interference must be examined in the next chapter.) The same idea is expressed by Juppiter to Juno (10.622–27): she can save Turnus for the
moment, but she cannot change the course of the war. Juno herself recognises this fact and realises that her delaying tactics cannot go on
(12.147–50):

> qua visa est Fortuna pati Parcaeque sinebant
> cedere res Latio, Turnum et tua moenia texi:
> nunc iuvenem imparibus video concurrere fatis,
> Parcarumque dies et vis inimica propinquat.

"As far as Fortune seemed to permit and the Fates allowed success to Latium, I
protected Turnus and your walls; but now I see the young man combatting a fate
he is no match for—both the day of the Fates and the violence of the enemy are at
hand".

Here, even in Juno's speech, another gap may be recognised: the
gap between human responsibility and the decrees of Fate. Juno can see
the long-range future, but this is no empty determinism. The author is
not relieving himself from the obligation to write a convincing script in
which the stages of the movement towards the end will be shown and not
just told. Turnus, through his own responsibility and character, carries
his own predicted death within him, and Juno, in asserting the gap between the two, is only helping the poet create a sense of doom and
suspense. That same gap appears in Aeneas' words directed at the absent
Turnus (11.116–18):

> "si bellum finire manu, si pellere Teucros
> apparat, his mecum decuit concurrere telis:
> vixet cui vitam deus aut sua dextra dedisset."

"If he is ready to end the war by violence, to drive out the Trojans, he ought to
have used these weapons in combat with me: that one of us would have survived
to whom God or his own right hand conceded life."

With the same dichotomy Ilioneus swears by Aeneas' "fate and his strong
right arm" (7.234), or Evander asserts that one final deed awaits Aeneas'
"valour and his fortune" (11. 179–80). In an authorial comment on Dido's
death, the poet says (4.696) *nam quia nec fato merita nec morte peribat* ("for
since she perished neither by fate nor by a death she deserved . . .").[7]
What the author denies in the case of Dido is the proposition, "Her fated

7. See p. 217 below.

time had come and she deserved it." To the human actors, however, the general pattern of history is unknown; some of them are vaguely aware that one exists and they acknowledge it, but what they know for certain is only that human qualities are what really count. In special circumstances that distinction can be expressed with full understanding by a human speaker. When Evander realises that Aeneas is the right man to lead the Etruscans, he expresses his view thus (8.475–77):

> "sed tibi ego ingentis populos opulentaque regnis
> iungere castra paro, quam fors inopina salutem
> ostentat. fatis huc te poscentibus adfers."

"But I am ready to join in an alliance with you great peoples and armies rich in the kingdoms they control: an unexpected chance reveals that means of salvation to you; you are arriving here at the bidding of Fate."

Evander sees that Aeneas exactly fits the oracle given to the Etruscans—over the long term this can be interpreted as fulfillment of the demands of Fate; from Aeneas' point of view, however, Evander recognises that the alliance will appear as an unexpected gift of heaven. It is up to Aeneas to make full use on his own initiative of the opportunity offered him. The same point of view will become evident in the treatment of omens and of divinely sent signs (to which this observation of Evander approximates). What is important to notice, however, is that the poet's point of view and that of the gods coincide: this can be put either in the form that the poet sees through the eyes of the gods or that the poet uses the gods to express an authoritative point of view.

3. The Sense of Fate as a Trope for Human Aspirations (and Fears)

A third—and very important—way in which the poet employs the concept of Fate derives from a pattern expressed on the divine level and transferred by analogy to the human level. Juppiter does not create the decrees of Fate, but they are uniquely known to him and are identical with his will. The other gods and goddesses only know of Fate insofar as it is revealed to them by Juppiter. At the beginning of the poem Juno is shown to have heard that a race derived from Trojan blood will overthrow her beloved Carthage (1.19–22). Juppiter reveals "the secrets of Fate" (1.262, *et volvens fatorum arcana movebo*, using a metaphor from mystic initiation) to Venus. She has mistakenly interpreted the Trojan hardships as meaning Juppiter has changed his mind (1.237), but he laughs at her and assures her that it is not so (254, 260). She again uses that convenient rhetoric in her speech to Juppiter in Book 10: If the Trojans have made for Italy contrary to Juppiter's will, they should pay the penalty and he should not help them; but if they have followed oracles from the gods and from the Underworld (which is the case), how can some god (i.e., Juno) subvert Juppiter's will (31–35)? So she regards the various oracles as revelations of Juppiter's will. Juno, in her reply, uses her own rhetoric (67–69):

> Italiam petiit fatis auctoribus (esto)
> Cassandrae impulsus furiis: num linquere castra
> hortati sumus aut vitam committere ventis?

"All right: he made for Italy at the behest of Fate, inspired by the ravings of Cassandra. But it was not I, was it, who persuaded him to desert his army or entrust his life to the winds?"

She undermines the majesty of Fate by equating it with Cassandra's ravings, and then asserts her own innocence—she did not persuade Aeneas to go off to Etruria and leave the Trojan camp vulnerable to Turnus. She is right: it was Evander who was responsible. But her rhetoric consists in confusing the two levels; she ignores the gap between the long-term decrees of Fate and the short-term area in which human freedom operates. It is her desire, however hopeless, to try to subvert the decrees of Fate. Juppiter's reply is that, since the gods are fighting among themselves and there is no end to that in sight (106), he will remain neutral (112) and (113) *fata viam invenient* "Fate will find a way." That is, he reasserts the distinction between events in the short term, which can be influenced, and the long-term pattern of Destiny, which cannot; at some point the troubles that beset the Trojans must cease, and Juno herself will recognise that she has gone far enough in opposition (12.147–50).[8] Juppiter's will cannot be other than identical with Fate, even if he does nothing to assert it.

Transferred to the human level, this concept supplies a potent explanation for a problem of deep interest to the poet. Aeneas is a Homeric hero, but he differs from every other Homeric hero in a number of ways. Most notably, he traversed the Mediterranean world from end to end, undergoing all sorts of hardship, denying himself opportunities for rest and love, in order to found a state far from Troy. What was the driving force in such a man? The concept of Fate supplies the explanation: at the human level, Fate is what converts itself into duty once it becomes known

8. See p. 8 above.

to a man. So the forces of Tarchon wait idly by their ships because an oracle has revealed that they must have a foreign leader. That is what Fate is to them. When Aeneas comes to lead them, the poet says (10.154–56):

> tum libera fati
> classem conscendit iussis gens Lydia divum
> externo commissa duci.

Then, freed from Fate, the Lydian nation, on divine instruction, boards ship, committed to a foreign leader.

That interpretation is a human decision. In the same way, Latinus knows that it is his duty to marry his daughter not to Turnus but to Aeneas; that aspect of Fate was revealed to him by an oracle of Faunus (7.81–106). When he is prevented from doing his duty, he can only take refuge in inaction, foreseeing the inevitable disaster (7.594–600).

Aeneas is driven by that inner sense of duty. He possesses it to an extent greater than ordinary men, and it is to the sense of duty that the adjective *pius* is directed. A typical expression of this sense of inner compulsion is seen in his speech to a delegation that comes to ask for a truce to bury the dead (11.110–14):

> "pacem me exanimis et Martis sorte peremptis
> oratis? equidem et vivis concedere vellem.
> nec veni, nisi fata locum sedemque dedissent,
> nec bellum cum gente gero: rex nostra reliquit
> hospitia et Turni potius se credidit armis."

"You ask peace for the dead and those cut down by the fortune of war. It would have been my wish to concede it to the living as well. I had not come here had not Fate assigned me this region to settle in. And I am not at war with your nation: your king abandoned his ties with me and preferred to entrust himself to the weapons of Turnus."

This is a man whose strength of will comes from his having a compelling vision of the future in a way that he can only explain in terms of Fate, Destiny, the will of the gods; such things, he says, are revealed to him and he has visions in which the dead or gods appear to him. People like Dido mock him, but that is all he can say.[9] Once revealed, a knowledge of the future imposes on a man the obligation of seeing it achieved.

Aeneas is not conceived as a mere instrument of a divine will;[10] the

---

9. For instance, 4.375–80.
10. On this, see further chap. 9.

poet subverts any such suggestion in a number of ways. For instance, Aeneas expresses himself as willingly submitting to his Fate (8.131–33):

> "sed mea me virtus et sancta oracula divum
> cognatique patres, tua terris didita fama,
> coniunxere tibi et fatis egere volentem."

"But it has been my courage and the sacred oracles of the gods and the relationship between our ancestors and your fame extended over the world, that have joined me to you and have driven me here willingly by Fate."

Here there is indeed willing submission to Fate, but included in the compulsion is his own *virtus* as well as divine oracles and also Evander's reputation and ancestry. Not only does he existentially choose his destiny, but the vision he has of it is his own and depends on his own interpretation. There are equally moments when the vision fades before despair. In Book 5, after the partial destruction of the fleet and the desertion of a proportion of his followers, he can even "forget Fate" (5.700–03):

> At pater Aeneas casu concussus acerbo
> nunc huc ingentis, nunc illuc pectore curas
> mutabat versans, Siculisne resideret arvis
> oblitus fatorum, Italasne capesseret oras.

But father Aeneas, shaken by the bitter disaster, turned the immense load of anxiety this way and that in his heart: should he forget Fate and settle in the fields of Sicily or should he make for the shores of Italy?

He is then confronted by Nautes, and his resolution to persevere is confirmed by Anchises' appearance to him at night. He is inspired again, tells his followers about the dream, and goes on.

The questions are now worth asking: What is the basis for Aeneas' vision? How much, in fact, does Aeneas know? The answer must be "very little," and here another gap needs to be reckoned with. This time it is the gap between the knowledge possessed by the privileged reader with access to various sources of information and those to which Aeneas has access. Aeneas seems to be told a lot, but how much is he envisioned as understanding? After the Sibyl in trance has delivered Apollo's prophecy about trials for Italy, the poet remarks (6.98–100):

> Talibus ex adyto dictis Cumaea Sibylla
> horrendas canit ambages antroque remugit,
> obscuris vera involvens

In such words from the shrine the Cumaean Sibyl sang terrifying riddles and
boomed through the cave, wrapping the truth in obscurity.

There is nothing in the prophecy that the reader cannot understand, but
the comment must be authoritative as far as Aeneas is concerned and, in
fact, he hardly refers to what he has heard. More explicit is the authorial
comment after Aeneas has received the shield (8.729–31):

> Talia per clipeum Volcani, dona parentis,
> miratur rerumque ignarus imagine gaudet
> attollens umero famamque et fata nepotum.

Such things upon the shield of Vulcan, a present from his mother, he admires and
ignorant of the facts he rejoices in their representation, lifting on to his shoulders
both the fame and Fate of his descendants.

Here the distinction between *res* and *imago* is that between reality and
representation: Aeneas has not yet experienced what is on the shield and
cannot in any real sense understand it, he has only the second-hand
acquaintance that comes from art, but it gives him pleasure and he senses
the grandeur that is presented. That distinction is translated into slightly
different terms as Evander shows Aeneas over the site of future Rome
(8.306–69); there Aeneas looks, is delighted, and is told about the past. It
is the poet who enters the text from time to time to draw the reader's eyes
to the future.[11] These two scenes compel a re-reading of the journey
through the Underworld in Book 6. There Anchises, privileged by being
dead, has access to an understanding that is not available to the living. He
explains the Roman future to Aeneas (889): "incenditque animum famae
venientis amore" ("and fires his spirit with desire for the fame to come").
Here again Aeneas makes no comment. What does he, in fact, understand? The answer must be found by reading the comment at the end of
Book 8 back into the scene at the end of Book 6. Aeneas can in some sense
be inspired by his father's account, and that will give him heart for the
troubles to come. But he cannot understand since he possesses no historical perspective. Only those who have lived through to 23 B.C. can understand, and they include the poet and his privileged reader. In fact,
Aeneas stands in relation to Fate as the poet (and reader—though the
passing of time has introduced a dimension of irony here) stands in
relation to the future that he foresees beyond the age of Augustus.
Aeneas can apprehend something of the magnitude and splendour of

11. See below, chap. 6, sec. 2.

that future of which he is fated to be the beginning, but he has no knowledge or understanding of it.[12]

What is virtually his own epitaph, spoken by himself (like Dido's, spoken by her),[13] provides a means of retrospective judgment on Aeneas. As he puts on his armour to seek and fight Turnus, he says to Ascanius (12.435–40):

> "disce, puer, virtutem ex me verumque laborem,
> fortunam ex aliis. nunc te mea dextera bello
> defensum dabit et magna inter praemia ducet.
> tu facito, mox cum matura adoleverit aetas,
> sis memor et te animo repetentem exempla tuorum
> et pater Aeneas et avunculus excitet Hector."

"Learn from me, my son, courage and true endurance, but from others what ⟨good⟩ fortune is. For the present my right arm shall be your defence in war and shall lead you to great prizes. Do you, however, when maturity of years shall soon come to you, see that you remember and, as you recall in your heart exemplars from among your people, let both your father Aeneas and your uncle Hector inspire you."

Courage and fortitude are what he sees as the marks of his life, but however much he has that inner sense of a destiny greater than himself, he can only see that the short-term run of events has consistently gone against him, and he wishes better fortune for his son. That melancholy, as characteristic of the poet as of Aeneas, provides a measure of what it is like to be a man driven by Fate, and excludes the satisfaction that a real understanding of Anchises' account in the Underworld or of the pictures on the shield might have provided. Aeneas knows only the inner moral imperative but almost nothing of its purpose, and he is the more interesting character for that perception by the poet—which he often leaves for the reader to deduce from various indications throughout the poem. Suspension of judgment is much needed here.

What caught the poet's imagination in the character of Aeneas was what might be called the frontier spirit: the quality in a man that is brought out by his being in a situation where no *mos maiorum* exists; instead, his sense of right and wrong, of what constitutes civilized behaviour, has to come from within himself. This is the point of view Aeneas is made to express when he says to Dido, in admiration for her

12. For the opposite view, see, for example, Otis (1963), pp. 306–12.
13. See below, chap. 7, sec. 2(b).

achievements and the values that he sees expressed both in her words and in all that he has seen in Carthage (1.603–05):

> "di tibi, si qua pios respectant numina, si quid
> usquam iustitiae est, et mens sibi conscia recti
> praemia digna ferant."

"May the gods—insofar as the divine powers have regard for men of devotion, insofar as there is justice anyway—and your own inner sense of having done what is right, reward you in proper measure."

The gods cannot necessarily be depended upon to reward the devoted (*pii*), but a man's consciousness of having done what is right brings its own rewards.[14] What Aeneas admires in Dido and what he regards as worthy of recognition is a system of values that he can understand, a moral sense that depends on the individual judgment. The same inner compulsion that drove Dido on is what drives him on; the privileged poet understands it as a sense of Fate or Destiny, and on his authoritative level he can explain what Fate is. Aeneas only dimly apprehends, and his conduct must be guided by a light that comes from within. The very similarity between Dido and Aeneas, ironically, will be what drives them apart. The adjective *pius* especially expresses that sense of being devoted to a purpose that lies outside oneself. Unfortunately, it does not include Dido.

When Aeneas in despair thinks of abandoning his aspirations, he expresses this as "forgetting Fate" (5.703)—that is, he would give up his long-term vision and resign himself to the short-term movement of events. This is the temptation he has to resist both in Carthage and in Sicily. Turnus has plans, but they are for himself and his own satisfaction. He has no vision of Fate, except as a boastful offset to the Trojans' dreams; his Fate, he says (9.136–38), is to destroy the whole wicked race that has stolen his wife. The poet uses Turnus' lack of any vision of Destiny to portray his defeatism in the final confrontation with Aeneas. Juno, who now knows the future, sees that he is fighting against a Fate which is too much for him (12.149). Turnus (unlike his sister) has no knowledge of the future, but he senses defeat by Aeneas and expresses this sense in terms of omens (messages from the gods) and the hostility of

---

14. For this interpretation, see R. D. Williams (1972), ad loc. (p. 204). Compare the words of Scipio quoted by Macrobius, *Commentary on the Dream of Scipio* 1.4.3 *sed quamquam sapientibus conscientia ipsa factorum egregiorum amplissimum virtutis est praemium* . . . "But although for wise men the very consciousness of their own outstanding achievements is the fullest possible reward for their nobility. . . ." For the fuller context, see pp. 211–12 below.

Juppiter (12.894–95). Here the poet portrays Turnus' collapse in psychological terms by the absence of a vision of Fate that is his own. He lives only for the moment and for himself.

4. The Gap between the Temporalities of Narrative and Composition

There is a feature that has appeared almost accidentally in the course of analysing the concept of Fate: that is the sense of a gap, and it is very important in the general strategy of the epic. The gap can take many forms: it may be between the perception that participants in the action have of a particular phenomenon and the information available to the reader, expressed by a god or revealed in some other way by the omniscient author; it may be between various levels of explanation; or it may be between the views of events in the short run and the views from a much longer perspective. The gap can take any of these forms—and there are several distinguishable variants of each of those mentioned. But whatever particular form the gap happens to take, it can always be seen to be essentially a variant of an archetypal gap that dominates the whole structure of the epic: the gap between the temporality of the narrative and that of the composition. It is the poet's strategy throughout the poem constantly both to measure and, by various devices, to cancel that gap. This was one solution to the basic problem that he set himself—intimately to connect a decade in the late twelfth century B.C. with the age of Augustus—and the concept of Fate was one important device in that technique.

Virgil had a striking precedent and model for this technique in poem 64 of Catullus—a poet whose influence on him (as on other Augustans), both in style and in figural manipulation of ideas, is hard to overestimate. There, at an early stage, Catullus enters his own text in apostrophe (on which see chapter 7, section 2a) to the heroes who were fortunate enough to be born in the age of the *Argo*'s voyage; he declares that he will often address them in his poetry (21–24). This prepares for the surprising end to the poem (384–408), where the poet starts from the happy picture of the gods still walking on earth among men in that age, and then traces the progressive degeneration that has reached a climax in the crime and civil war of his own age (406 *nobis*). The various uses of apostrophe in the hymns of Callimachus, especially in the *Hymn to Delos*, are quite different; not only are they obviously legitimated by the hymnic form, but they do not have the Catullan feature of measuring a significant gap between the temporality of the narrative and that of the composition. It was this feature that caught Virgil's imagination.

2   THE GODS IN THE *AENEID*

Various attempts to construct a more or less systematic theology of the *Aeneid* have been made;[1] but no such attempt is relevant here. What will be examined in this chapter is the way in which what an atheistical age dubbed "the divine machinery" functions in the rhetoric of the poem. From this point of view the gods will be regarded as figural concepts that operate in an apparently literal way on the surface of the poem but also have another meaning equally relevant to the poet and to the understanding of the poem. In particular, it will be relevant to search for the sort of gap that has appeared, in a number of forms, in the ways in which the concept of Fate is used.

1. *The Gods as a Figure for Authorial Intervention*

Lucan is again useful in showing one advantage the poet won from using a divine machinery. Lucan dispensed with gods in his epic; one result of this is a constant series of authorial invasions on the text to provide explanation or, rather, to ensure that the reader will view the particular events in the same way as the poet does.[2] Of course, Lucan will have regarded the necessity to enter his own text in person as one of the advantages to be gained from excluding divine machinery from his epic. However, the corresponding advantage of showing rather than telling is thereby lost to him.[3] The point can be seen strikingly in the Council of the

1. Bailey (1935) is a fair example.
2. See Williams (1978), pp. 232–34.
3. On this distinction, see Williams (1980), pp. 31, 33–34.

Gods in *Aeneid* 10. A recent writer has said of this:[4] "Virgil's divine Council of War . . . strikes the modern reader as a curiously inadequate prologue to a book which is structurally important and in some respects the finest in the poem." A different point of view is needed.

The Council of the Gods has a number of Homeric precedents, and this should be regarded as establishing its generic legitimacy in an epic poem. More important, however, is that Virgil has made use of the opportunity in quite a different way from Homer. Here the gods do the work of the poet and are in some sense his voice, but they are made to speak with an authority that comes from seeing the whole perspective of history. In its first phase the debate among the gods serves to make clear what has indeed been implicit in the account from Book 7 onward but has not been drawn out in the stark and authoritative contrast that becomes possible here. Wars are sometimes wars of naked aggression, and those are simple enough to judge (and condemn). But sometimes wars arise because two points of view are not only totally incompatible but are also mutually incomprehensible to both sides. So it is with Trojans and Italians. Venus, speaking first, expresses the Trojan point of view: she emphasizes suffering, hardship, and dedicated obedience to divine commands. Juno presents the Italian point of view, emphasising what they see as Trojan brutality and ambition and sheer greed; she equates Venus' talk of Fate with "the ravings of Cassandra," and she arouses sympathy for the Italians defending their native soil against piratical usurpers. It is an arresting contrast and comes as something of a shock to a reader who has become familiar with the Trojan point of view and has seen events through their eyes almost exclusively since the beginning of the poem, with the exception of a major part of Book 4 and some passages in Book 7 that display the attitudes of Amata and Turnus.

After Juno's speech a dramatic new point of view is presented by Juppiter. He declares himself neutral; Fate will find its way. He then sets the war in its widest possible historical context by contrasting it with the real war that is to come—namely, the war with Carthage that will occupy a century of Roman effort and will be a war in which Trojans and Italians fight as one nation for their existence against a common enemy. He regards the present war as totally illegitimate, only made inevitable because of quarrelling among the gods. Juppiter presents a point of view that the poet makes his own in the second half of the *Aeneid*: war between Trojans and Italians is, in fact, virtually a civil war, both because of the

---

4. Quinn (1968), p. 213.

mixture of loyalties (some Italians, including Latinus himself, taking the Trojan point of view), and also because of the large historical perspective in which Carthage is the real enemy and the present war can achieve nothing but weakness. That vision of the war as civil war must be read back into the previous three books so that judgment becomes modified, and it must be allowed to dominate the sense of the hatefulness of war that spreads over the last three books.

The usefulness of the gods in permitting the poet to reveal an authoritative viewpoint in a way that approximates showing rather than telling is clear in other passages also. For instance, in Book 1 Venus appears in disguise to Aeneas and gives an account of Dido.[5] That account thereby becomes authoritative not only for Aeneas but also for the reader; it supplies the essential basis for understanding Dido's motivation and for making an objective judgment about her. Similarly, in Book 11.532–94, Diana, with some implausibility and oddities of narrative form,[6] gives a detailed account of Camilla and her background to the nymph Opis. The importance of the account is that it characterises Camilla as an ideal Italian, with the closest possible relationship to the land and its culture, so that she is shown to embody the essence of the opposition to the Trojans. Camilla, however, betrays that background, or perhaps it would be better to say that she reveals its weaknesses, by indulging a characteristically heroic lust for slaughter (with little motivation on her part other than the blood-lust itself) and an excessive interest in loot.[7] The moral contrast is effectively set up by Diana's description of her earlier years, which, however, includes disturbing details of the reckless and arrogant tyranny exercised by her father before his expulsion. How far is the conduct of the daughter to be explained by the nature of the father?

Putting this account into the mouth of her divine protectress here has a less impressive effect than in the case of Venus and Dido, since here there is no human character involved for whose benefit an authoritative account was needed. Here the technique simply achieves authoritative objectivity without the poet's having to make a digressive intrusion into the narrative in his own person; that would, in a climactic region of the poem, have created an impression of deliberately postponing the climax in an unduly obvious way.

5. 1.335–70.
6. See Appendix, sec. 5.
7. See p. 117 below.

Here, as in the other examples examined above, the deity does the poet's work for him. Consequently there is no immediate question of a gap between two perceptions. Even in the case of Venus' account to Aeneas of Dido's background, Aeneas participates in the incident on the same level as the reader. He is privileged beyond most other characters in the epic since his mother was a goddess, but the incident is in general legitimated by Homeric precedent and by the concept that in the age of heroes gods were thought to visit among mortals on earth. The important feature of the examples of divine participation in the narrative of the *Aeneid* so far considered is that they all exist on only one level: apart from the special exception of Venus with Aeneas, they do not impinge on mortals at all. There are others that immediately fall into the same category: for instance, the conversation between Juno and Venus or the orders given by Juppiter to Mercury in Book 4; the orders of Juno to Allecto in Book 7: the scene between Venus and Vulcan in Book 8; the comfort offered by Juppiter to Hercules as Pallas approaches death in Book 9; or the debate between Juppiter and Juno towards the end of Book 12. All of these incidents, and others, exist on the same level as authorial intrusions;[8] they may ultimately issue in results among human beings, but of the prior scene the men involved know nothing. What gap there is in all such cases is potential: the reader is being supplied with a perspective that is not available to participants in the action (except for privileged individuals) and which essentially derives from the age of Augustus.

2. The Gods as a Trope for Human Motivation

We can move to a different aspect of the divine machinery by means of the ending of the scene between Venus and Aeneas. For, as she departs, she surrounds Aeneas and Achates with a cloud that makes them invisible. The action has Homeric precedent, especially in Athene's concealment of Odysseus at the beginning of *Odyssey* 7, and, as used by Virgil, it is something of a generic gesture. Nevertheless, it has an important dramatic purpose that is carefully exploited, and it consequently goes well beyond its Homeric model. For the fact that Aeneas is concealed

---

8. In many such passages the poet also uses elements of sheer Hellenistic rococo to subvert any suggestion that such divine drama is to be interpreted literally. The fantasy-portrait of Neptune riding over the waves with all his nymphs at 5.814–26, after his conversation with Venus, is paradigmatic for the reader's understanding. See sec. 2 below on the subversion of Mercury's intervention in Book 4 by the descriptions of Mercury himself and of Atlas; see also chap. 6, sec. 1.

from Dido but can see and hear her means that her words have an authoritative sincerity[9] which (like Venus' account to Aeneas) is guaranteed equally to Aeneas and to the reader. A point worth noting is that, in Homer, Odysseus seems quite unaware that he is invisible. The same seems to be true of Aeneas and Achates. When they instinctively hold back to see what happens to their friends, they simply remain shrouded in the mist (1.514–16). Then, after Dido's speech (562–78), the poet says, "they were for long eager to burst from the cloud" (580–81); but that reads as an authorial comment and not a statement that Aeneas shares the author's knowledge of the cloud: that is, the words are explanatory to the reader, not descriptive of Aeneas' perception. The cloud is, in fact, dispersed of its own accord (586–87) and the characters do not comment on any strangeness they have perceived. There is a gap here, then, between the poet's account and what the characters perceive.

That gap is more evident in a series of alleged divine appearances. In Book 5 the Trojan women set fire to the ships (604–99). A heavy authorial intervention forms the introduction (604) *hinc primum Fortuna fidem mutata novavit* ("Then for the first time Fortune changed and broke faith"): here *Fortuna* is the force seen in the short run of events; normally it ought to flow in the same direction as Fate, but here it diverges. The cause, the poet explains, was Juno who, still nursing her long-standing anger, sent Iris to earth (606–08).

Iris takes the form of Beroe, one of the Trojan wives, expresses what the women are feeling (623–40), and sets an example by throwing a burning torch on the fleet. An elder matron recognises that she is not Beroe but a goddess and, as the women hesitate, Iris flies up into the sky. They all then join in burning the fleet. It takes a prayer to Juppiter by Aeneas to bring rain and extinguish the fires; four ships have been destroyed.

The pattern of a god or goddess coming to earth and assuming a particular mortal disguise in order to achieve an object by persuasion is Homeric.[10] But most of the incidents in Homer are casually handled: for instance, in *Iliad* 3.121–45, Iris assumes a disguise to lead Helen to the walls, but the poet only mentions her coming and not her going; so too in *Iliad* 4.86–140, Athene's coming is like a meteor and terrifies everyone, but immediately she assumes disguise as Laodocus, persuades Pandarus

---

9. A dramatic example of the technique is Thais' soliloquy at the end of Act 1 of Terence's *Eunuchus*.

10. On this pattern in epic, see Greene (1963).

to break the truce, and nothing is said of her going nor is any more made of her coming. An incident more like that of *Aeneid* 5 is the passage of *Odyssey* 3.371–94 where Athene has disguised herself as Mentor to help Telemachus in his visit to Nestor; she finishes speaking to them, flies off in the shape of a sea-eagle and is recognised by Nestor as Athene. The passage in *Aeneid* 5 differs, however, because it is characterised by what may be called double motivation: the women are already rebellious and of a mind to end all voyaging (613–17). What Iris does is to transform that psychological state into action. The two lines of motivation converge at the point where the women recognise Iris because they see her rising into the sky as a rainbow (657–58). The gap here is again one between what the omniscient poet reveals and what the human characters perceive. But what do they perceive? Was it really more than a rainbow? It is the poet who reveals what no one else knew.

Another similar incident occurs at the beginning of Book 9, where (in the same words as in 5.607) Juno sends Iris down to put the idea into Turnus' mind of attacking the Trojan camp while Aeneas is away. So the poet tells us. But all that Turnus sees is a rainbow in the sky (14–17), and prays to Iris, accepting the sight as an omen for battle. Again there is a gap between the human perception and the poet's privileged knowledge.

There is a similar double motivation and the same gap in the scene where Venus arranges for Dido to fall in love with Aeneas (1.657–750). What did Dido perceive? The charm of Aeneas' son Ascanius led her by an easy path to fall in love with the father. It is the omniscient poet who tells us that this was not really Ascanius but Cupid in disguise. But Dido never knows that (hence the gap) and no such agency is needed to achieve the much more difficult task of making Aeneas fall in love with Dido and suppress his sense of his destiny.[11]

The war starts in Book 7 with divine intervention. Juno's anger at the Trojans is still with her (286–91) and is expressed in a passionate soliloquy (292–322). She summons the Fury Allecto from the Underworld and sends her to arouse emotions of war (323–40). Allecto secretly infuses Amata with poison (346–56); this gradually creates madness in the queen (354–405) till she rampages like a Bacchante. Turnus is next: she first appears to him in the guise of Calybe as he sleeps (406–34); then, when he is simply rude to her (435–45), she loses her temper, appears in her true form, and raves at him; he wakes when she is gone, terrified and mad for war (458–74). Now Ascanius' hunting arrow wounds a pet deer. This

11. On this, see chap. 3, sec. 2.

enrages the whole countryside; Allecto sounds the alarm-call (511–22) and the first fighting takes place. Juno contemptuously dismisses Allecto (540–71).

The gap is once again clear here: the poet gives one account, the human characters perceive something else. Amata has no sense of the Fury; in fact, she is already anxious and angered to a state of madness before Allecto comes (344–45, 350). She is as unaware that any divine power is involved as Aeneas is in Book 1, when the storm wrecks his ship on the African coast: he says that the tempest drove them to Libyan shores (377) *forte sua*, "by a chance of its own" (that is, "by an unexpected chance that is characteristic of storms"). Double motivation is therefore again to be seen in Amata. This sets the scene for Turnus, since the reader must envisage Turnus in terms of the feelings that have been displayed by his kinswoman and supporter Amata. He is asleep, and Allecto's disguising herself as Calybe has no point except to show authoritatively the basic arrogance and violence of Turnus' nature; for what Calybe says to him represents his own thoughts (421–34). Someone of little authority was needed to bring out Turnus' real character; he feels no need to curb his violent instincts for such a person. In fact, as far as Turnus' perception goes, the whole episode is a dream, from which he awakes in a combination of terror and uncontrollable anger (458–66).

In the incident with Ascanius, there is also clear double motivation: the real explanation lies in Ascanius' ignorance of the circumstances; and when the poet says (498) *nec dextrae erranti deus afuit* ("and a god did not fail his right hand or let it go astray"), he is making special use of a kind of phrase that signifies something like "and luck did not desert him".[12] In other words, the help the poet alleges a god gave, was not needed (the negative *nec* goes with *erranti* as much as with *afuit*).[13] Ascanius knows nothing of what the poet asserts.

Finally, Allecto is not needed to arouse the country-folk. Silvia has already done that (504) and Allecto's supernatural trumpet-call is more double motivation. However, at this point the poet allows the figure to encroach on reality, and he imagines not only the far reaches of the country hearing the terrible sound (that is, echoing it), but terrified moth-

12. The vague *deus* has only the sense of "a divinity," as in 2.632 (see p. 284 below); the poet refuses to specify an identity.

13. Another way of expressing the syntactical structure is to say that *erranti* is proleptic ("nor did a deity fail his right hand so that it went astray"). What is not possible is to understand *erranti* as if it were equivalent to *erraturo* ("certain (otherwise) to go astray"). See Fordyce (1977), ad loc.

ers also; angry Italian farmers and the Trojans gather to its sound. That is, by this stage the poet has enough confidence in the reader's ability to understand Allecto's actions as a trope to indulge in a figural expansion that brings the actions of the Fury to the very border of allegory. For essentially this whole series of scenes is a figure, related to personification and allegory, designed to represent the way in which at times certain emotions seem almost to achieve an independent existence, so that the same pattern of behaviour springs up spontaneously in various places. We must return later to this formulation, but for the moment it is worth noting that the poet carefully drew back from fully admitting allegory or personification, for he makes Juno herself (620–22) come down and open the gate of Janus (Latinus refuses to declare war). It has been questioned why Juno does this and not Allecto:[14] the reason is that if Allecto did it, she would confess to being not merely an externalized figure for *furor* (as she is) but a full personification of it; we should then be in the implausible allegorical world of Statius and his long line of successors.

In fact, any temptation to accept literally the poet's accounts of divine intervention is thoroughly subverted by two passages late in the epic. One of these is the scene where Aeneas, frustrated by Turnus' skill in avoiding a fight with him, gets the bright idea of attacking the city of Latinus; tactically this is perfect, for Turnus would then be bound to come to its defence. The poet first tells this as an inspiration put into Aeneas' mind by Venus (12.554–56). He then traces the way in which Aeneas, pursuing Turnus all over the place, suddenly notices the city "untouched by all the war and at peace, with impunity" (559 *immunem tanti belli atque impune quietam*). "Immediately the idea of extending the battle fires his imagination" (560 *continuo pugnae accendit maioris imago*). These are two parallel accounts of the same thing, the one using the gods as explanation, the other showing a man receiving a flash of inspiration. The poet says it was Venus but goes on to show that, as far as the human character was concerned, that explanation has no validity. The dichotomy measures exactly the same gap as in the scene when Troy is falling and Venus opens Aeneas' eyes to a vision that she is obliged, however, to express in words: the vision of the gods tearing Troy down (2.604–623). Aeneas is speaking and he recounts her words; then he says (621–23):

---

14. Otis (1963), pp. 326–27. His answer is: "The war is too considerable to be left to a subordinate agent entirely; Juno alone must finally declare it and thus take on herself the ultimate responsibility for Allecto's acts."

> "dixerat et spissis noctis se condidit umbris.
> apparent dirae facies inimicaque Troiae
> numina magna deum."

"She had spoken and disappeared in the dense shadows of night. Terrible shapes appear and great godheads hostile to Troy."

His dutiful acceptance of his mother's vision is less impressive than the concrete account of what actually met his eyes which he goes on to give (624–31). Of course, the passage is unfinished (line 623 is a half-line) and Aeneas is privileged where Venus is concerned, but there is a clear gap between what gods are said to do and what the human character perceives.

That gap is presented in a striking form by Nisus in 9.184–87:

> Nisus ait: "dine hunc ardorem mentibus addunt,
> Euryale, an sua cuique deus fit dira cupido?
> aut pugnam aut aliquid iamdudum invadere magnum
> mens agitat mihi, nec placida contenta quiete est."

Nisus says: "Is it the gods who inject such emotion into men's hearts or does each man's terrible ambition become a god for him? For a long time my heart has been agitating to plunge into battle or some great enterprise and is not content with the quiet of peace."

Something of the same idea is expressed by Juppiter, of all people, at the beginning of Book 10 (6–10):

> "caelicolae magni, quianam sententia vobis
> versa retro tantumque animis certatis iniquis?
> abnueram bello Italiam concurrere Teucris.
> quae contra vetitum discordia? quis metus aut hos
> aut hos arma sequi ferrumque lacessere suasit?"

"Great inhabitants of heaven, why has your decision been reversed and why do you fight so among yourselves with purposes at odds. I had forbidden Italy to dash into war with the Trojans. What is this hostility contrary to my ban? What fear is it that has persuaded this and that side to go to war and provoke the sword?"

This almost casts the gods themselves as personifications of the kinds of emotions that lead to war, and Juppiter produces a formulation that comes close to Nisus' but from the opposite point of view: Nisus expresses a human scepticism that knows the stories about the gods but does not really see cause to believe them; Juppiter expresses the poet's view of his own figure of divine explanation in such a way as to close the gap between human and divine. Both passages make the reader reconsider his understanding of earlier incidents and deeply subvert any naive or literal interpretation of them. The sense of both passages is of forces at work in the human world that have a universal application and cannot be expressed except in figural language: Nisus views them from the individual's point of view, Juppiter from that of the omniscient poet. The two points of view are united in the poet's own formulation of the psychological condition of the two armies in 9.717–21:

> Hic Mars armipotens animum virisque Latinis
> addidit et stimulos acris sub pectore vertit,
> immisitque Fugam Teucris atrumque Timorem.
> undique conveniunt, quoniam data copia pugnae,
> bellatorque animo deus incidit.

At this point Mars, powerful in battle, infused new spirit and strength into the Latins and twisted sharp goads deep within their breasts; among the Trojans he released Flight and dark Terror. On all sides they collect as the chance to fight is provided and the War-god fell upon their hearts.

The first formulation (717–19) with allegorical personifications corresponds to that of Juppiter;[15] the second (720–21) corresponds to that of Nisus, with the god made into an emotion or the emotion into a god.

One incident that needs retrospective judgment in the light of these passages is the scene in Book 4 in which Mercury appears to Aeneas. The contemptuous words the god uses to address Aeneas (265–76) are clearly also the voice of Aeneas' own conscience, especially the sneer in (266) *uxorius*. Aeneas' reaction is horror (279–80) and an instant desire to leave (281–82); an agitated tricolon with anaphora (283–84), followed by the concept of a mind divided over various possibilities (285–86), expresses his distraught mental state. But the poet has not shown Aeneas' conscience gradually becoming disturbed from within; he has deliberately chosen to summon the divine machinery, with a prayer from Iarbas to Juppiter (198–218), followed by Juppiter's careful look at the lovers (221) *oblitos famae melioris amantis* "in total disregard of their reputations," and his summons and angry charge to Mercury (223–37). Aeneas' later account of the incident to Dido rouses doubt (356–59):

> "nunc etiam interpres divum Iove missus ab ipso
> (testor utrumque caput) celeris mandata per auras

15. Similar is 10.755–61, which has a close Homeric model in *Iliad* 11.67–83.

> detulit: ipse deum manifesto in lumine vidi
> intrantem muros vocemque his auribus hausi."

"Now even the messenger of the gods, sent by Juppiter himself (I swear by both of our lives), sped orders to me through the swift winds: I saw him with my very own eyes in full daylight entering the walls and I received his voice in these very ears."

Dido's sarcastic reply to this is persuasive, as she even mimics his words (377–80):

> "nunc et Iove missus ab ipso
> interpres divum fert horrida iussa per auras.
> scilicet is superis labor est, ea cura quietos
> sollicitat."

"And now the messenger of the gods sent by Juppiter himself brings terrifying orders through the winds. That, I am to suppose, is what occupies the gods, that is the kind of concern that troubles their tranquil lives?"

And, as if to confirm Dido's subversion of this account, the next time Mercury appears to Aeneas it is in a dream and, again, what he says follows exactly the line of argument that would naturally occur to a man in Aeneas' situation: the Trojans are strangers in a foreign (and probably hostile) land; Dido has nothing now to lose, and so she may well order an attack—for one cannot rely on a woman's feelings (560–70).

The account, however, was already being subverted at an early stage by the way Iarbas was introduced. The poet oddly says (204) *dicitur* "he is reported (to have prayed to Juppiter)." This changes the aspect of the narrative in such a way that the poet disclaims authority for the description of Iarbas and his actions, and merely rehearses a report that reached the ears of Dido and Aeneas. It is only as Juppiter reacts and speaks (223–37) that the poet again seems to take responsibility. It is, of course, an important motivation in Dido's suicide that she knows the threat posed by Iarbas. But, more than that, the form of the account figures the expectations of Iarbas in terms of his own barbaric character and of the superstitions of his age, so that the reader is encouraged to understand Juppiter's reaction also within that same context as the mirror-image of the suppliant's expectation. Then Juppiter, as he takes the long view over the centuries, figures the historical imperative that it is the poet's privilege to reveal (see section 3 below). Here the poet takes advantage of his generic licence to use the divine machinery for the special purpose of measuring and momentarily closing the gap between his own historical insight and the vague, uncertain sense of destiny that motivates Aeneas.

But he has gone further in subverting the surface of his account: he describes Mercury in some detail (238–46)—his magic sandals and the caduceus that he uses in herding the souls of the dead to the Underworld. His journey passes by Mount Atlas, and the mountain is described as if it really were a giant with anthropomorphic features (246–51). Then follows his flight, like a diving bird's (254–55), to Libya. This type of writing is easily recognisable: it is the mannerist fantasy of Hellenistic rococo (a particularised development of certain features of Homeric narrative), and belongs to the world of mythic unreality. This style is used a number of times in the *Aeneid*, always to subvert an incident which, if accepted literally, would tend to relegate the poem to the world of Hellenistic frivolity.[16] The storm with which the poem opens is elaborately arranged by Juno in a scene with Aeolus of pure rococo, and it is followed by another scene of equally pure rococo in which Neptune chides the winds, sends them packing, and rides in his grand chariot over the sea to calm it. Not only are we not being asked to believe; we are being asked not to believe. Such passages establish a connection between the divine machinery and the real world in such a way as to subvert literal interpretation of the former. In a later fantastic scene, the poet actually subverts his own account in advance. When Turnus attacks the Trojan fleet, the ships are transformed into sea-nymphs. The poet prefaces the story with these words (9.77–79):

> quis deus, o Musae, tam saeva incendia Teucris
> avertit? tantos ratibus quis depulit ignis?
> dicite. prisca fides facto, sed fama perennis.

What god was it, o Muses, who averted such cruel flames from the Trojans? Who was it who beat back the fires from the ships? Tell me: belief in what happened belongs to olden days, but the story is eternal.

This is a clear signal to the reader that the following account has an allegoric or symbolic value and is not intended to be accepted literally. (The question why the poet used this form of the account—which he invented—will be discussed below.)[16] Such a warning has retrospective force for the reader, who must call into question here (if he has not already done so) his understanding of earlier incidents of divine intervention.

16. See chap. 6, sec. 1.

Another incident that needs consideration occurs toward the end of Book 10 and has something of the pattern of Mercury's first visit to Aeneas. Juno becomes anxious about her favourite, Turnus, and obtains permission from Juppiter to save him—though only for a short time (606–32). Then, in imitation of a number of passages of the *Iliad* (5.449–59 and 20.443–5), Juno creates a phantom Aeneas who appears before Turnus and, by running away, lures him on board a ship that sails home to Laurentum with him (633–88). In the passages of the *Iliad* the divine intervention is direct and is recognised by the combatants: Apollo saves Aeneas from Diomedes, Poseidon saves Aeneas from Achilles, and Apollo saves Hector from Achilles (only in the first incident is the fake image used; in the second Aeneas is bodily removed, and in the third Hector is enveloped in a mist). There is no psychological dimension and no suggestion that the incidents should be understood in any but a literal way; such things happened in the heroic age when gods still walked the earth among men. But the incident in the *Aeneid* is different.

There is a significant detail as soon as Turnus approaches the facsimile (647–52):

> tum vero Aenean aversum ut cedere Turnus
> credidit atque animo spem turbidus hausit inanem:
> 'quo fugis, Aenea? thalamos ne desere pactos;
> hac dabitur dextra tellus quaesita per undas.'
> talia vociferans sequitur strictumque coruscat
> mucronem, nec ferre videt sua gaudia ventos.

Then indeed, once Turnus believed that Aeneas had turned to run away and excitely drank that vain hope into his heart, he said: "Whither are you fleeing, Aeneas? Do not abandon the marriage that is arranged. My right hand here will give you the land you have sought over seas." So shouting he pursues and brandishes his drawn sword and does not see the winds carry his joy away.

Turnus is afraid of Aeneas but hardly admits it to himself. This is the first sign of his fear. Throughout Book 12 Turnus will avoid Aeneas and will only take courage when he sees him wounded and forced to withdraw (324–25). In fact, what Juno does for Turnus is the emblem of that fear: it mirrors his emotions and produces an ideal situation for him. It is only when he is safe that shame overwhelms him and he contemplates suicide but is again prevented by Juno (680–86). Here is another example of the gap between the divine action and what the human character perceives: Turnus knows nothing of what has happened (666 *ignarus rerum*); he simply realises that he has deserted his forces and cannot explain why (668–79). As far as Turnus is concerned, he thought he saw Aeneas running away but realises that such a story will not carry much conviction. The divine intervention, as in the case of Dido's infection with love, provides mitigation for Turnus at the same time as it suggests the essential cowardice. But Turnus cannot, any more than Dido can, exculpate himself, since his understanding of the situation is on the human level and falls far short of the privileged reader's. In consequence the situation acquires a moral ambiguity that is characteristic of the *Aeneid*.

The actions of Juturna, Turnus' sister, in Book 12 also demand consideration in this context. Juno, in withdrawing her help from Turnus, tells Juturna to do what she can for her brother (142–53). Juturna's first opportunity comes when the Latins begin to feel pity for Turnus, who is obviously terrified at the prospect of single combat with Aeneas; they have no more doubt about the outcome than Turnus has (216–21). Juturna assumes the form of Camers and successfully works on their already existing sympathies (222–43); she then sends an omen (244–65) and the truce is broken. She is next found in action, after Aeneas, recovered from his wound, has returned to the battle; again Turnus and the Latins are terrified (446–48)—so too is Juturna (449 and 468). She now throws Metiscus, the charioteer, from Turnus' chariot, assumes his place and appearance, presumably unnoticed by Turnus, and drives the chariot far from that part of field where Aeneas is engaged. The crisis comes when Aeneas gets the idea of attacking the Latin city (see p. 24 above). Turnus can no longer ignore the burning of the city; he stops the chariot (622) and says, most surprisingly, to Metiscus—as the reader supposes (632–37):

> "o soror, et dudum agnovi, cum prima per artem
> foedera turbasti teque haec in bella dedisti,
> et nunc nequiquam fallis dea. sed quis Olympo
> demissam tantos voluit te ferre labores?
> an fratris miseri letum ut crudele videres?
> nam quid ago? aut quae iam spondet fortuna salutem?"

"O my sister—for I have recognised you for a long time, right from when you cunningly upset the truce and joined in this war; and now, goddess that you are, your deception is in vain. But who was it who wanted you to descend from Olympus and bear all these sufferings? Was it to enable you to witness the cruel death of your brother? For what can I do? What road to safety does Fortune now guarantee me?"

These words enforce a re-reading of the text from line 216. There has been no indication that Turnus suspected anything. He is shown to be as acquiescent in Juturna's guidance as he was in pursuing the phantom

Aeneas. That is, the actions of Juturna are another emblem of Turnus' fear of Aeneas. This time he is forced to admit the fact because his pride can no longer tolerate the swiftly accumulating evidence of his cowardice— the burning city, fewer and fewer of the enemy anywhere near his chariot (615), and his own flagging spirits (614–16). The scene is so striking that it also prompts a retrospective reading of Book 10.645–88: did no thought of the oddity of the circumstances occur to him there? The poet denies it(652 *nec ferre videt sua gaudia ventos*) in such a way as to suggest wishful think- ing on Turnus' part, and incredible lack of perception.

But Turnus' speech holds further surprises (638–42):

> "vidi oculos ante ipse meos me voce vocantem
> Murranum, quo non superat mihi carior alter,
> oppetere ingentem atque ingenti vulnere victum.
> occidit infelix nostrum ne dedecus Ufens
> aspiceret; Teucri potiuntur corpore et armis."

"I saw with my own eyes, right in front of me, Murranus calling me by name, a man than whom there is no other more dear to me; I saw him fall, a mighty warrior laid low by a mighty wound. Poor Ufens fell to avoid witnessing my disgrace; the Trojans have possession of his body and weapons."

This compels a further re-reading of the text, for we have been witnesses to the deaths of Murranus (529–34) and Ufens (460) but nothing in the accounts gave the slightest hint of what Turnus says. Ufens is one of the first killed after Aeneas returns and the Latins (and Turnus) were ter- rified; his name occurs in a brief catalogue of those slain—he was killed by Gyas. In Turnus' view, however, he willed his own death because he realised the cowardice of Turnus and lost the desire to defend himself. The death of Murranus, on the other hand, is described in some detail (529–34):

> Murranum hic, atavos et avorum antiqua sonatem
> nomina per regesque actum genus omne Latinos,
> praecipitem scopulo atque ingentis turbine saxi
> excutit effunditque solo; hunc lora et iuga subter
> provolvere rotae, crebro super ungula pulsu
> incita nec domini memorum proculcat equorum.

Murranus, loudly proclaiming his ancestors and the ancient names of his for- bears, a whole line descended from kings of Latium, ⟨Aeneas⟩ sent flying with a rock, with the whirling crash of an enormous boulder, and laid him low upon the ground; as he fell beneath the reins and chariot-pole, the wheels rolled across him, and hooves speeding with fast-recurring beat, hooves of horses that had no thought for their master, trampled over him.

Turnus' friend had cause to be remembered, but in death even his horses did not heed him. The significant detail strikes home but seems satisfied within its context, until Turnus' words (638–40) are read; then judgment needs to be revised—nor did his close friend, mighty warrior, heed him though he called out to him.

News now arrives of Amata's suicide and the imminent fall of the city. It is only at this point that authorial intervention objectively describes the mixture of emotions in Turnus—shame, grief, madness, love, and self-conscious proud courage (665–68). The whole episode of Juturna is a figural analysis, for the first time, of Turnus' psychology, and it has an organisation that requires a suspension of judgment until the whole passage to line 671 has been taken in.

Turnus is privileged in the same way as Aeneas: he, too, is related to a divinity; and, as Aeneas can recognise his mother Venus, so Turnus can his sister Juturna. For Turnus has a defeatist attitude toward Aeneas and expresses it—using the term that Aeneas would understand—as Fate. It is his destiny, he senses, to fight Aeneas, and he has never had (apart from wishful thinking) any doubt about the outcome.[17] So he says to his sister (676–80):

> "iam iam fata, soror, superant, absiste morari;
> quo deus et quo dura vocat Fortuna sequamur.
> stat conferre manum Aeneae, stat, quidquid acerbi est,
> morte pati, neque me indecorem, germana, videbis
> amplius. hunc, oro, sine me furere ante furorem."

"Now at last Fate, sister, has won: cease to delay it. Let us follow whither God and whither cruel Fortune bid us. It is my resolve to fight Aeneas; it is my resolve to suffer all the bitterness there is in death, and you shall no longer see me disgraced, sister. You must—I beg you—allow me to indulge this madness before ⟨the end⟩."

He then runs off to challenge Aeneas to single combat. This is no objective statement of determinism; he has the horrible feeling that not only must he in honour fight Aeneas, but also that Aeneas is (as he is) the greater warrior, and he expresses his apprehension by using the concept of Fate.[18] But in doing that Turnus does not have access to the privileged

17. On this see chap. 8.
18. See chap. 1, sec. 3.

authorial sense of Fate; he uses the concept as a figure for his fear (as Aeneas uses it as a figure for his vision of duty).

Juturna is forgotten for the moment until Turnus, "out of his mind with terror" (776 *amens formidine*), prays to Faunus to keep Aeneas' spear locked in the wild olive-tree in which it lodged; as Aeneas struggles in vain, "the Daunian goddess [Juturna], changed again into the guise of the charioteer Metiscus, runs out and returns his sword to her brother" (784–85). Meanwhile the scene shifts to heaven (791–868): Juppiter and Juno come to terms about the Trojans and Italians; he then sends a Fury from the Underworld to warn Juturna off. The Fury—on the model of a famous incident from later Roman history—takes the form of a screech-owl and beats her wings against Turnus' shield. He is frozen with terror; he regards it as an omen. But Juturna sees it for what it is and, after a long speech (872–84)—apparently addressed partly to her brother—abandons him. The passage cannot be judged, however, till the lines have been read where Turnus is finally cornered and looks around for help (914–18):

> tum pectore sensus
> vertuntur varii; Rutulos aspectat et urbem
> cunctaturque metu letumque instare tremescit,
> nec quo se eripiat, nec qua vi tendat in hostem,
> nec currus usquam videt aurigamve sororem.

Then various feelings fill his heart: he looks towards the Rutuli and the city and he hesitates in fear and he trembles at the approach of death and he can see no way to escape nor any way to attack his enemy nor can he see his chariot anywhere nor his charioteer sister.

This requires retrospective interpretation of Juturna's departure. She was (869) "far off" when she seemed to address her brother, and it can now be seen that her speech was not an address to Turnus but an apostrophe; he did not hear a word she said. That incident, then, re-establishes the gap, closed since Turnus' recognition of his sister, between what the poet says the gods do and human perception of the same incidents. Juturna's speech, addressed to the reader, is used by the poet to foreshadow, at the same time as it increases tension by postponing, an end now become inevitable. What happens throughout the complex series of incidents from the truce onward is that Turnus' relationship with a goddess is used by the poet to interconnect the two levels of the narrative—the divine and the human—in a way that makes the figural concept of the gods as concrete as possible. This is linked with a feature of Book 12 that will be discussed further below (p. 38).

Several incidents of divine intervention have been seen to have a special feature: there existed throughout the intervention a distinct gap between the poet's account and what the human beings perceived that lasted until the moment when the deity left, was recognised, and thereby re-inforced the idea or emotion, the arousal of which had been the purpose of the visitation. The gap is momentarily closed at that point. Such a motif functions in the same way as an omen, and something should briefly be said about the numerous omens in the *Aeneid*.

Omens seem deterministic, but are not to be interpreted so in this epic. The poet has ensured a retrospective judgment of omens by a striking incident in Book 12. Juturna, having fostered Latin feeling against the truce, sends an omen (244–56). The omen is carefully interpreted by Tolumnius in words that echo the poet's own account of it (248 *litoreas agitabat avis,* 262 *territat invalidas ut avis;* 250 *rapit improbus uncis,* 261 *quos improbus advena bello;* 256 *penitusque in nubila fugit,* 263–64 *penitusque profundo / vela dabit*). It is a convincing interpretation and persuades the audience, but it is in fact mere wishful thinking: Tolumnius could not be more wrong. What this does is to call into question one's reading of the whole range of omens in the *Aeneid:* human beings interpret omens as their circumstances or their wishes suggest. As in the case of divine intervention to inculcate an emotion or an idea, that very idea or emotion already exists in the human being concerned. Both types of incident, far from asserting determinism, demonstrate that it is the individual's character and will that matter: everything comes back to human vision and decision. So in Book 2, the account of the sea-serpents attacking Laocoön (199–227) ends with the creatures taking refuge with Athene; the Trojans interpret this as a judgment against Laocoön for hurling a spear at the wooden horse and they are convinced that the horse must be brought within the walls. The poet does not say whether their interpretation was right or wrong; that question was simply irrelevant—what mattered was that men had made a decision about divine will and that decision led to another decision that certainly was totally mistaken. The gap here is between the point of view of hindsight, which reads determinism or inevitability into events that have already taken place, and that of the immediate circumstances, where men seem to themselves to be free to decide their own fates on the facts as they see them.

To sum up the argument of this section: there are three ways in which the poet drew an advantage from using the divine machinery as a trope for human motivation. First, he could express the often accidental or coincidental element in the way in which emotions or ideas tend to

arise in human beings. Second, the trope conveys the sense that somehow emotions come to human beings at least to some extent from outside
and apart from their volition, and that emotions are far from being completely under an individual's control. Third, the divine machinery suggests the inexplicable mechanism whereby emotions can become con-
tagious, leading to the phenomenon of crowd-hysteria and thereby to acts
that would be unthinkable in single individuals.

3. *The Gods as a Trope for Reconciling Free Will and Determinism*

There is one further function performed by the gods in the *Aeneid*.
Recognition of it explains what were the advantages of constructing an
epic, not on the model of the *Iliad* or the *Odyssey*, in which the gods
actively participate in the action, but one completely sui generis, in which
the narrative movement is on two co-ordinated and simultaneous levels
(though both are not equally continuous)—one divine, the other human.
Events on earth are referable by a process of counterpoint to events on the
divine level, except that this is true only of a selection of the most significant events on earth. Essentially the poet's advantage in this unprece-
dented arrangement lies in the fact that the divine machinery is a figure
for the historical process viewed retrospectively; that figure is a figure of
thought in the mode of synecdoche, and it is also a figure of substitution
which requires the reader to reconstruct the ideas for which it has been
substituted.[19] In the functioning of this figure the concepts of the gods
and of Fate are complementary: Fate is a figure for the idea that the
historical process, when viewed retrospectively, seems made up of an
inevitable series of events; the divine machinery is a figure for the process
by which the series of events that constitutes history came to take place as
they did and so to create the pattern of Fate.

There is normally a gap between the account of an incident given by
the poet on the divine level and the perceptions of the human participants
in that event. This gap, carefully preserved by the poet except for a very
few privileged participants on a very few occasions, enforces the separation between the determinism that is the instinctive reaction of a retrospective viewpoint on the historical process, and the freedom of choice
that human beings feel they have in every set of particular events. The
answer to the essentially deterministic question How could it have happened otherwise? can only come from close scrutiny of particular circum-

19. For this type of figure, see Williams (1980), chap. 4, sec. 1.

stances; but that close scrutiny itself enforces an assumption of free will. What excited the poet's interest was the thought that in the late twelfth century B.C. perhaps only one man had the slightest idea that the events in which he was participating would lead to the Roman empire of the Augustan age, and even he had only the faintest glimmer of the idea, and, without in the least understanding it himself, he had the inner power to endure suffering in contributing his part to a process that extended far beyond himself and his son. Aeneas essentially had freedom of choice to follow that vision or not, and it was the concept of an individual acting freely within what now appears to be a deterministic historical process inevitably leading to the Augustan state that Virgil expressed by the twin concepts of Fate and the gods.

Two minor incidents will illustrate this. When the Trojans reach the future site of Rome, Ascanius, by his comment that they are eating their tables (7.116), draws attention to the fulfilment of an important prophecy destined to signify the future site of the city. In order to "eat their tables" the Trojans had to use bread as plates, and the poet introduces the incident thus (7.107–11):

> Aeneas primique duces et pulcher Iulus
> corpora sub ramis deponunt arboris altae,
> instituuntque dapes et adorea liba per herbam
> subiciunt epulis (sic Iuppiter ipse monebat)
> et Cereale solum pomis agrestibus augent.

Aeneas and the leading commanders and handsome Iulus lay their bodies down beneath the branches of a tall tree. They begin their meal and lay out wheaten pancakes on the grass to hold their food (so Juppiter himself suggested that they do) and they pile the cereal plates with fruits of the countryside.

Here the authorial comment (110) *sic Iuppiter ipse monebat* could be taken literally and in a poet like Ovid or Statius that would be justifiable. But it would then be an idle appeal to the divine machinery, and no indication is given here of any human perception of the god's intervention. The event itself is accidental and inexplicable until Ascanius' comment triggers a memory in Aeneas; it is then the author who intervenes with an explanation of divine intervention. Here again is that gap between the poet's explanation and the human perception. The technique takes an accidental event belonging to a crucial occasion and invests it with significance by using a god's intervention to establish by hindsight the special part it played in what could later be recognised as a meaningful sequence of events. The idea of purposiveness, unknown to any human participant at the time, arises from the reference to the divine machinery.

That same gap[20] is exploited to fine ironic effect at the end of Book 11. Camilla is dead and Turnus, a poor strategist, has taken her bad advice and abandoned his ambush (901–02):

> ille furens (et saeva Iovis sic numina poscunt)
> deserit obsessos collis, nemora aspera linquit.

He [Turnus] mad for battle (and the cruel godhead of Juppiter so requires) abandons the hills he had invested and leaves the rough woodland terrain.

The motivation here does not come from Juppiter; it comes from within Turnus himself—he no sooner hears the bad news than he is *furens*. The comment is authorial and makes the point that Turnus was also thereby co-operating with the requirements of Juppiter which are also those of Fate. Irony resides in the gap between the poet's comment and Turnus' lack of strategic perception.

Beyond being a means of distinguishing between, and simultaneously making use of, both determinism and free will, the gods had a further advantage. There is a generalising power of explanation in using gods and their agents to account for motivation: it asserts the inexplicable existence of irrational but frequently appearing forces in the world that operate on men. It is sometimes said that Juno personifies the forces of evil. But that is not a useful formulation. The concept of a hostile Juno serves to unify what the Trojans see as the forces of evil: that is, the various events that thwart their plans and progress, the elements of "bad luck" (for instance, 5.604 *hinc primum Fortuna fidem mutata novavit*) they endure. She is a narrative device designed both to unify this anti-Trojan tide and to create tension by suggesting disaster before it happens. Her agents are above all natural events and the weaknesses—especially the emotions—of human beings (as, for example, in Dido, Amata, or Turnus) and also their ignorance of circumstances (as, for example, with Ascanius in 7.475–510). Such an account of motivation can serve to unify a series of phenomena that seem at first sight to be fundamentally different but essentially are not.

Finally, a curious feature of the *Aeneid* demands notice. It is in the last book that the frequency of divine intervention is greatest. This seems

---

20. A simpler instance can be seen at 10.689, where Mezentius' entry into the battle is said to be "at the behest of Juppiter" (*Iovis . . . monitis*).

to be deliberate, and its effect is to approximate the human and divine levels as the decisive moment of the epic approaches. What this means is that as events in the twelfth century B.C. reach a climax that will be crucial for the age of Augustus, a millennium ahead, the deterministic view of history that comes from hindsight and the concept of free will that resides in immediate confrontation with single events are made to converge in such a way that the history of Rome, lying far beyond the bounds of the *Aeneid*, is seen to be determined by the *Aeneid*. This poetic concept is useful to the poet, who is far from being a determinist. In fact, as with a number of crucial issues in the *Aeneid*, the poet expresses or tacitly permits to emerge two views that seem to be opposed and cannot be resolved; such ambiguities embody the essential clash of opposite viewpoints. But the divine machinery is really a means of defining and even reconciling the opposition of determinism and free will; for the gods are a synecdoche for both aspects of history. Fate and Juppiter and, to some extent, Juno (because of her support of Carthage) represent the immutability and inevitability that characterise the past as seen from the present, except that the poet uses them to look forward from the origin rather than backward from the end (as he himself does). But the gods also participate in events as they take place in apparently random sequence, and, in doing that, they are a synecdoche for the chaos and lack of pattern that characterise events viewed in the immediate context of their occurrence. Both points of view come together in the final book of the epic.

But the positivisitic optimism that is the danger in such a scheme has already been poignantly undercut. The most affecting treatment of the short-term view of Fate comes at the climax to the review of Roman heroes by Anchises in Book 6. Marcellus, as he appears in contemporary poets, was clearly understood to represent Augustus' hope for a successor to himself.[21] However, he died unexpectedly in 23 B.C., aged twenty-one. Anchises foresees that death, but nothing can be done about it; he can only mourn (882) *heu, miserande puer, si qua fata aspera rumpas!*, "Alas pitiful boy—if only you could break out of your harsh destiny!" Coming as the climax to the grand review of Roman history that reaches its greatest moments with Augustus, this expresses the view through the poet's eyes forward from the very moment of writing: what he sees is that the future has collapsed; there may be some great pattern of Fate stretching into the future, but he cannot see it. There is just the certainty of uncer-

---

21. Especially in Horace *Odes* 1.12. See Williams (1974), and (1980), pp. 13–19.

tainty. Only the view backward inspires confidence; there is no view forward.

4. An Influential Predecessor

Virgil's procedure in handling the divine machinery may well have been influenced by Euripides' sophisticated re-shaping of the Homeric gods in his plays, but there was also a much closer exemplar in a poet whose work frequently comes alive in all Virgil's poetry. Lucretius opened his poem *de rerum natura* with an extensive prayer to Venus (1.1–43). Such a prayer contradicts a fundamental tenet of the Epicurean philosophy which he expounds, and it cannot therefore be understood at face value. Here the goddess functions as a synecdoche that unifies a wide range of forces to be seen at work in the universe; at one extreme they include the sexual drive, at the other the instinct for peace. The poet asks inspiration for himself and peace for the Roman world so that his distinguished addressee, Memmius, may have leisure to attend to his message. Lucretius subverts any literal interpretation by an immediate assertion of the Epicurean doctrine of the total disconnexion of the gods from the human world (44–49). That assertion is repeated from time to time later, and outstandingly at 2.167–83, where the specific example of Venus is used to examine false views of the gods in language which closely echoes that of the opening prayer. In the final book (6.68–79) the correct attitude to the gods is defined by contrast with the false, in an exemplary confrontation.[22]

This poetic and generically legitimate use by Lucretius of divine machinery, subverted and defined by later stages of the text, supplied a model for Virgil's very much more complex and extensive adaptation of his generic inheritance. It is worth noting that Virgil actually provides a simple but exemplary model of the way an artist can use the gods as figural structures when he describes Vulcan's representation of the opposed sides at the battle of Actium on the shield he designed for Aeneas (8.698–706); here, too, the characteristic gap between the human participants and the divine level is carefully observed in the text.

22. For a fuller account of this, see Williams (1968), pp. 143–45.

RETROSPECTIVE
JUDGMENT ENFORCED

A frequent feature of poetry from Catullus to the death of Horace is that its composition requires a reader to suspend judgment on the interpretation of a particular passage or idea until more, or often all, of the poem has been read.[1] The effect is to sustain the energy of a poem by arousing an expectation that is not satisfied in the immediate context. When this figure is transferred to epic, the change in scale dictates a considerable variation in technique. Sometimes it may even happen that the question or doubt is not aroused in the reader's mind until he reaches the point where, had the expectation been in his mind, it would have been satisfied. Such instances compel a re-reading, and a number of examples of the technique have already been noticed.[2] Especially significant is Turnus' speech to his sister Juturna in which he confesses that he has known her identity all along and calls into question the accounts that have been given of the deaths of two of his friends.

1. Irony

Of course, in poetry on the scale of epic, the effect can also be seen, for instance, in certain cases of irony, for the irony cannot be recognised until the situation that will reveal it as such has been reached. Aeneas says, in his first speech to Dido (1.607–10):

> "in freta dum fluvii current, dum montibus umbrae
> lustrabunt convexa, polus dum sidera pascet,

1. On this, see Williams (1980), s.v. "Suspension of judgment."
2. See Index s.v. "Retrospective judgment."

> semper honos nomenque tuum laudesque manebunt,
> quae me cumque vocant terrae."

"As long as rivers shall flow into the ocean, as long as shadows shall move over mountain slopes, as long as clouds shall nourish the stars, for ever shall you be honoured, respected and revered whatever lands call me on."

The hyperbole may suggest a rash formulation, but those words are only dramatically ironic in the light of Book 4 and the particular way in which the tragedy of Dido takes place. For Dido will feel dishonoured by Aeneas' treatment of her to such an extent that she is compelled to suicide.

Another example can be seen in the words of Latinus as he praises his people and his kingdom (7.202–04):

> "ne fugite hospitium, neve ignorate Latinos
> Saturni gentem haud vinclo nec legibus aequam,
> sponte sua veterisque dei se more tenentem."

"Shun not our hospitality and understand that the Latins are the race of Saturn, a race that is not righteous by any compulsion of law, but is self-controlled of its own free will and after the manner of the god of old."

It will turn out that the Latins indeed do exercise free will and are lawless, but not in the way that Latinus intended. They will break the sacred bond of hospitality and they will also break a solemn truce. Full appreciation of the dramatic irony in Latinus' words does not come until well into Book 12. There is something like authorial irony, too, in the case of Latinus. After the second prooemium to the *Aeneid* (7.37–45), we read (45–46):

> Rex arva Latinus et urbes
> iam senior longa placidas in pace regebat.

King Latinus, now advanced in years, ruled over fields and cities that were quiet in a long-standing peace.

This seems to be a statement that is to be taken as authorially objective. But in fact it expresses the conplacent viewpoint of Latinus, and the nature of the peace only becomes clear later. The Latins are at peace simply because Turnus is fighting their war with Etruria for them. Allecto disguised as Calybe says to him in a dream (7.425–26):

> "i nunc, ingratis offer te, inrise, periclis;
> Tyrrhenas, i, sterne acies, tege pace Latinos."

"Go on then, place yourself in dangers that win you no gratitude—they only mock you; go on, lay low the battle-lines of Etruria, keep the Latins safely at peace."

Nor is that all. Tiber reveals later to Aeneas that Evander and his people (8.55) *hi bellum adsidue ducunt cum gente Latina* "have been waging continuous war with the Latin race." It is true that the war turns out to be insignificant, because Evander is old and his forces small; they are simply ignored by the complacent Latinus. His idealism is further undercut by Numanus' boastful words later (9.607–13):

> "at patiens operum parvoque adsueta iuventus
> aut rastris terram domat aut quatit oppida bello.
> omne aevum ferro teritur, versaque iuvencum
> terga fatigamus hasta, nec tarda senectus
> debilitat viris animi mutatque vigorem:
> canitiem galea premimus, semperque recentis
> comportare iuvat praedas et vivere rapto."

"Our youth is inured to toil and accustomed to frugality, and either tames the ground with harrows or makes cities quake with their warfare. All our life is spent with weapons and we use a reversed spear to goad the backs of our oxen. Old age comes late and does not weaken the powers of our spirit or alter its vigour. We cover gray hair with the helmet and it is our delight to haul back ever more loot and to live on what we have stolen."

Numanus is, of course, contrasting his own people with the effeminate Trojans, but the further unspoken contrast with the complacent portrait given by Latinus is shockingly ironic. There is, however, a further powerful dramatic irony in Numanus' words, because it is exactly that desire for loot that will be the immediate cause of Turnus' death (no less than that of the ideal Italian Camilla).[3]

In these passages a suspension of judgment or—what amounts to the same thing—a second reading reveals a hidden dimension in an earlier passage when it is brought into confrontation with a later one. There are several major cases in the *Aeneid*, however, where a reader has to exercise retrospective judgment on a question of real magnitude, in such a way as to be compelled to interpret an earlier stage of the text in the light of a later, or to read what was not said in an earlier stage back into that stage on evidence supplied by a later passage.

3. On judging this portrait of Italians, see especially Horsfall (1978).

2. *Aeneas in Carthage*

It is a remarkable fact that the major focus of Book 4 is on Dido and her emotions, to such an extent that very little information is given about Aeneas and his feelings. Dido's infection with the poison of love is described in detail toward the end of Book 1, and the effect of the poison's spreading is examined and described in the first third of Book 4. But what about Aeneas? The poet briefly states, authorially, that Aeneas is in love with Dido, though he tries hard to conceal it (332 *obnixus curam sub corde premebat* "making an effort, he suppressed the love in his heart")—a selfless concealment of what could harm is characteristic of the man (at 1.208–09 he is shown presenting an optimistic front to his companions and suppressing his anxieties). Full authorial statement of the pain felt by Aeneas because of his love for Dido is made only after she has fainted and been carried away: 395 *multa gemens magnoque animum labefactus amore* "groaning deeply, his heart shattered by his great love." But not the slightest hint is given of how he came to feel that love. In the absence of explanation one is inclined to suppose that love grew from the episode in the cave (160–72) and that it was characterised by physical passion— though the words of *Fama* in 194 (*turpique cupidine captos* "slaves of a disgraceful lust") put the worst possible gloss on the affair.

But how could this man seriously think of staying in Carthage? Throughout the first book the poet, and throughout the next two Aeneas himself, portrayed him as a man driven by a compelling inner sense of purpose, of a destiny that required him to find a particular part of Italy and there to found a state; that inner sense was shown to be constantly reinforced by omens, oracles of the gods, messages from the dead, and never to be out of the forefront of his consciousness since he left Troy. One of the most interesting problems for the poet must have been to show how such a man could be overcome by passion to the extent that he was able to ignore that driving force within. In fact, Dido is Aeneas' first serious test, and he seems to give way without a struggle—or at any rate, the poet seems not to have portrayed him enduring any severe moral struggle.

One reason for this is that the poet has chosen to see the love affair from Dido's point of view; she is the focus of attention throughout the book. This had the advantage of giving the book the unity of a tragedy that is consummated in one individual. But it had the greater advantage of displaying Aeneas, the centre of the poet's focus in Book 1 and the subject of his own autobiographical narrative in Books 2 and 3, from an unexpected angle and through someone else's eyes. The poet seized such an opportunity whenever it was offered: on a number of occasions in Books 7–12 an unflattering view of Aeneas and the Trojans is given through the eyes of the Latins, or of Turnus, or of Juno, and the report of a speech by Diomedes in Book 11 allows the poet the chance for some revisionist history of the Trojan war and the part in it played by Aeneas.[4] But nothing is more surprising and shocking than the sight Aeneas presents as seen through Mercury's eyes (4.259–76):

> ut primum alatis tetigit magalia plantis,
> Aenean fundantem arces ac tecta novantem
> conspicit. atque illi stellatus iaspide fulva
> ensis erat Tyrioque ardebat murice laena
> demissa ex umeris, dives quae munera Dido
> fecerat, et tenui telas discreverat auro.
> continuo invadit: "tu nunc Karthaginis altae
> fundamenta locas pulchramque uxorius urbem
> exstruis? heu, regni rerumque oblite tuarum!
> ipse deum tibi me claro demittit Olympo
> regnator, caelum ac terras qui numine torquet:
> ipse haec ferre iubet celeris mandata per auras:
> quid struis? aut qua spe Libycis teris otia terris?
> si te nulla movet tantarum gloria rerum
> nec super ipse tua moliris laude laborem,
> Ascanium surgentem et spes heredis Iuli
> respice, cui regnum Italiae Romanaque tellus
> debetur."

As soon as his winged feet touched the huts, he saw Aeneas laying down fortifications and building new houses. He had a sword starred with tawny jasper and a cloak hanging from his shoulders gleamed bright with Tyrian crimson—a cloak that wealthy Dido had made as a present for him and had picked out its texture in fine gold. He went straight into the attack: "Are you actually laying the foundations of lofty Carthage and building a beautiful city, infatuated with your wife? Terrible: and what about your kingdom and the concerns that are your own? Have you forgotten them? The ruler of the gods sends me down from bright Olympus, he whose nod makes heaven and earth go round, that very god bids me bring you these orders through the swift breezes: What are you constructing? And what intention makes you idle your time away on Libyan soil? If no interest in glory and greatness stirs you and you spend no effort on your own reputation, at least think

4. 11.252–93.

of the growing Ascanius and the expectations invested in your heir Iulus to whom a kingdom in Italy and the land of Rome is due."

The picture of Oriental luxury and effeminacy objectively legitimates the contempt in the words that follow. This is certainly not the man whose portrait has dominated three books of the epic, and, even if the reader is not persuaded to share Mercury's contempt, at least the scene arouses the question of how this has happened. What change has taken place in this man, previously so conscious of his destiny, to make him forget it and fall to such a degree under the spell and influence of an Oriental woman? The urgency of that question is increased by the immediate collapse of Aeneas. He has no self-confidence: his hair stands on end with horror and his voice sticks in his throat (280). He instantly wants to flee the land, though he loves it (281 *dulcis . . . terras*).

At this point a further advantage can be seen in the concentration on Dido: not only is there the totally new angle from which Aeneas is so surprisingly seen; there is also the advantage of the indirection itself. There is no direct approach to Aeneas' psychology in the lengthy period between the episode in the cave and the arrival of Mercury. The reader has to reconstruct for himself, and the one clue will only come in the course of Aeneas' short and troubled speech to Dido (333–61) after he has lost the initiative because he was afraid to tell her he was leaving and weakly lets her find out for herself (291–94). He explains that, if Fate had given him the choice, he would certainly have rebuilt Troy (340–44); but (345–61):

> "sed nunc Italiam magnam Gryneus Apollo,
> Italiam Lyciae iussere capessere sortes;
> hic amor, haec patria est. si te Karthaginis arces
> Phoenissam Libycaeque aspectus detinet urbis,
> quae tandem Ausonia Teucros considere terra
> invidia est? et nos fas extera quaerere regna.
> me patris Anchisae, quotiens umentibus umbris
> nox operit terras, quotiens astra ignea surgunt,
> admonet in somnis et turbida terret imago;
> me puer Ascanius capitisque iniuria cari,
> quem regno Hesperiae fraudo et fatalibus arvis.
> nunc etiam interpres divum Iove missus ab ipso
> (testor utrumque caput) celeris mandata per auras
> detulit: ipse deum manifesto in lumine vidi
> intrantem muros vocemque his auribus hausi.

>desine meque tuis incendere teque querelis;
>Italiam non sponte sequor."

"As it is, however, Apollo of Grynium and his oracles in Lycia have ordered me to make for the great land of Italy: my love lies there, that is my fatherland. If you, a Phoenician, are kept here by the citadels of Carthage and the sight of your own city in Libya, why ever should you grudge us Trojans our settling in Ausonian territory? It is permissible for us, too, to seek a kingdom in a foreign land. As often as night covers the earth with dank shadows, as often as stars rise in fire on high, the agitated ghost of my father rebukes and terrifies me in dreams; my son, too, and the injury I do his dear being in robbing him of a kingdom in Hesperia and the lands decreed by fate. Now even the messenger of the gods, sent by Juppiter himself (I swear by both of our lives), sped orders to me through the swift winds: I saw the god with my very own eyes in full daylight entering the walls and I received his voice in these very ears. Cease then from enflaming emotion in both of us by your reproaches (360): it is not of my own choice that I am making for Italy."

Apollo and the oracles are exactly what have been conspicuous by their absence so far in Book 4. What now becomes clear is that they were absent from the text, but not from Aeneas' thought. All that time he was busy suppressing his feelings of guilt, but they were getting through to him in dreams about his father—who would indeed be "agitated" by his son's behaviour—and about his son. Mercury's words represent his own suppressed guilty thoughts, and, once they found expression, he felt relief and now eagerly desires what he had with equal eagerness previously suppressed. This reconstruction explains the speed of the reversal once he hears Mercury's words. The indirectness of the poet's approach to this problem and the demand made on the reader for retrospective judgment are far more effective in their "showing" than would have been direct authorial intervention to "tell" of Aeneas' struggles with his moral dilemma. The pathos of his optimistic expectation that Dido will instantly understand and be reasonable is evidence of the effort involved in the suppression and the relief of release, but it shows small understanding on his part of at least one area of human nature. The moral ambiguity of this situation will be discussed later.[5]

3. Aeneas in the Underworld

The journey through the Underworld ends with Aeneas returning to the world above through the Gates of Sleep (6.893–99):

5. In chap. 8.

> sunt geminae Somni portae, quarum altera fertur
> cornea, qua veris facilis datur exitus umbris,
> altera candenti perfecta nitens elephanto,
> sed falsa ad caelum mittunt insomnia manes.
> his ibi tum natum Anchises unaque Sibyllam
> prosequitur dictis portaque emittit eburna;
> ille viam secat ad navis sociosque revisit.

There are twin Gates of Sleep, one of which is said to be of horn, and through it an easy passage out is provided for true shades; the other is said to shine finely wrought of white ivory but the Manes send deceptive dreams to the daylight above. There, with those words Anchises sees his son off together with the Sibyl and sends them out through the gate of ivory. He cuts his path to the ships and rejoins his companions.

That choice of gate comes with a surprise so shocking that resort has been made to emendation (Ribbeck—who also though the lines spurious—wrote *averna* for *eburna* in line 898). The latest editor says: "There is no means of knowing what deeper significance this held in Virgil's mind for Aeneas' experience in the Underworld. . . . The matter remains a Virgilian enigma (and none the worse for that)".[6]

The concept used by the poet here has a model in *Odyssey* 19.562–67. There, immediately after the dramatic scene in which Odysseus is recognised by the nurse whom he silences, Penelope tells the stranger of a dream in which her twelve geese were killed by an eagle; the eagle then revealed itself as Odysseus. She asks him to interpret the dream and he declares it true—the suitors will be killed. But Penelope replies (560–69):

> "ξεῖν', ἦ τοι μὲν ὄνειροι ἀμήχανοι ἀκριτόμυθοι   560
> γίγνοντ', οὐδέ τι πάντα τελείεται ἀνθρώποισι.
> δοιαὶ γάρ τε πύλαι ἀμενηνῶν εἰσὶν ὀνείρων·
> αἱ μὲν γὰρ κεράεσσι τετεύχαται, αἱ δ' ἐλέφαντι·
> τῶν οἳ μέν κ' ἔλθωσι διὰ πριστοῦ ἐλέφαντος,
> οἵ ῥ' ἐλεφαίρονται, ἔπε' ἀκράαντα φέροντες·   565
> οἳ δὲ διὰ ξεστῶν κεράων ἔλθωσι θύραζε,
> οἵ ῥ' ἔτυμα κραίνουσι, βροτῶν ὅτε κέν τις ἴδηται.
> ἀλλ' ἐμοὶ οὐκ ἐντεῦθεν ὀίομαι αἰνὸν ὄνειρον
> ἐλθέμεν· ἦ κ' ἀσπαστὸν ἐμοὶ καὶ παιδὶ γένοιτο."

"Stranger, dreams occur that are certainly troublesome and difficult to interpret.

---

6. Austin (1977), p. 276 (with references to other views).

By no means is everything in them fulfilled for mortals. For there are twin gates of insubstantiate dreams: the one constructed of horn, the other of ivory. And such dreams as come out through the carved ivory cheat us, bringing messages that are not to be fulfilled. But such as issue forth through the polished horn bring their truths to fulfillment for any mortal who sees them. I fear, however, that my grim dream did not come from there, welcome though it would be to me and my son."

The fact that Virgil is so clearly appealing to this passage draws attention to the differences, which are as striking as the similarities. The concepts are identical in the mention of the two gates, their materials, and the false dreams issuing from the ivory. There similarity ends. First, Virgil creates an unbalanced contrast between the purposes of the two gates: "false dreams" should be balanced by "true dreams," not by "true" or "real ghosts." In fact, Virgil, by this formulation, has made it impossible for Aeneas to be sent through the gate of horn. So, a fortiori, he can only return through the gate of ivory. Here an ambiguity in *falsa* needs to be taken into consideration. For *falsus* need not mean "false," that is, objectively untrue; it can also mean "deceptive" or "illusory," and its significance amounts to saying what Penelope says about dreams in general—dreams are in some sense illusory, unreal. In that case, the poet chose to recall the words of Penelope so that the familiarity of his readers with the passage of Homer could be used to suggest rather than state ideas that arise from the differences. The process is synecdochic. Since the verbal formulation forces Aeneas through the ivory gate, the gate of horn becomes unimportant, and the idea suggested is that there is a connexion between the experience that Aeneas has undergone and the gate of ivory. There is something illusory or unreal about the journey through the Underworld. The illusion or unreality, however, need not be authorially guaranteed as affecting Aeneas: the poet is far more likely here to be subverting his own account. Such a subversion does not amount to confessing that the account is unreal or untrue, but, in a manner similar to his subversion of the account of the ships transformed into nymphs (p. 28), by suggesting that interpretation is needed, as with dreams, it signals that the relationship of the account to the truth is not literal. At this point the other major difference from the Homeric passage needs to be taken into account.

For the gates are not, as in Homer, the Gates of Dreams, but the Gates of Sleep. It is that difference that allowed the poet to construct the unbalanced contrast between "real ghosts" and "deceptive dreams." This variation from Homer carries the clear implication that Aeneas' emergence from the Underworld was analogous to waking from sleep, and that, therefore, his journey through the Underworld was in some way analogous to sleeping and dreaming.[7]

This means that the passage on the Gates of Sleep is intended to compel a re-reading and a retrospective interpretation; in fact, the whole concept of a physical journey through the Underworld by a living man is called into question.

The poet began his account with an invocation (264–67):

> Di, quibus imperium est animarum, umbraeque silentes
> et Chaos et Phlegethon, loca nocte tacentia late,
> sit mihi fas audita loqui, sit numine vestro
> pandere res alta terra et caligine mersas.

O Gods who hold sway over the souls, and silent ghosts, and Chaos, and Phlegethon, regions that are hushed on all sides in night, may it be permitted to me to tell of things I have been told, may it be in accord with your will that I should reveal things sunk deep in earth and darkness.

The powers addressed are not the Muses: it is not inspiration that the poet needs. What he needs is permission to reveal things that are not known to living men, so he prays to the powers of the world of the dead, including the souls of the dead themselves. The poet has been told secrets, but he is not saying, as for instance Homer does, that his knowledge is only second-hand report (e.g., *Iliad* 2.485–86); in such cases the poet attributes real knowledge to the Muses (and second-hand to himself).[8] But here there is no distinction between report and real knowledge. What is suggested here is that the poet has been told things which he ought to keep to himself and not make generally known; the situation is that of someone who has information about a mystery cult—publication of such secrets was forbidden by oath. That is, the poet hesitates over a revelation of mysteries; he is not calling into question the truth of what he has heard. However, he is also certainly disclaiming authorial responsibility for the literal truth of what he has heard: thus, for the narrative of the travels and sufferings of Aeneas he is responsible, but the journey through the Underworld is different; at that point the objective narrative of historical realities is suspended.

The language appropriate to profanation of mysteries echoes an

---

7. Thornton (1976), pp. 60–69, argues that Aeneas' passage through the Underworld is a dream.

8. Norden (1927), pp. 208–09, tries to treat the address in terms of traditional commonplaces.

immediately preceding theme. The poet describes an epiphany of the goddess of the Underworld, Hecate (255–58), in terms modelled on a passage of Apollonius Rhodius about black magical ceremonies performed by Jason (3.1191–224)—just before dawn the ground groans underfoot, trees shake, and dogs bark. At that point the Sibyl shouts (258–59) *procul o procul este, profani . . . totoque absistite luco* "keep your distance, keep your distance, all uninitiated . . . and do not come near any part of the grove." Such an order by the presiding priest was normal practice at mystery ceremonies. But it is odd that this is combined with a sacrifice that summons Hecate to the world above. The latter concept goes with the detail of Aeneas ordered to draw his sword (260) to suggest the situation in *Odyssey* 11 where the ceremony is one of necromancy as distinct from one of descent into the Underworld. The detail of the drawn sword (intended in the *Odyssey* to keep irrelevant ghosts from drinking the blood) is often said to be idle here, because at lines 290–94 the Sibyl has to restrain the terrified Aeneas from using his sword to attack some monstrous ghosts by explaining that they are just shadows without substance. Such apparent contradictions are often explained by saying that Virgil has simply combined two accounts (the *Odyssey* and a Golden Bough descent or the *Odyssey* with a *Descent of Herakles*).[9] But that is just to treat the text as a mere patchwork of sources mindlessly stitched together. The detail of the drawn sword should be understood as suggestive of necromancy; but that suggestion itself is subverted by the incident where Aeneas almost attacks the ghosts, an incident that belongs to a physical journey through frightening regions.

The sense of an initiation ceremony is suggested by another important incident. There is no sign of the Golden Bough in literature before Virgil and it seems to be an invention of his. But initiates in the mysteries of Persephone carried a branch of myrtle (similar to the Golden Bough in being from a non-deciduous tree).[10] The special idea of initiation is also conveyed by the detail that only a chosen person could break off the Golden Bough, a man selected by Fate (146–47).

What happens here is that the poet represents the experience of Aeneas in terms that suggest both necromancy and initiation in a mystery cult, but both concepts are then subverted, after the prayer to the powers of the Underworld, by the more traditional concept of a physical descent to Hades. This can be put differently. The poet represents the experience of Aeneas by three concepts which are synecdochically related to it, and

9. For instance, by Norden (1927), pp. 206–07.
10. See ibid., pp. 173–74.

thereby he disclaims a factual account of "what really happened," since each synecdoche is in turn substituted for it.

It may seem as if the journey through the Underworld was "what really happened" to Aeneas, but that too is subverted, in many ways, proportionately to its length. It opens with a general statement that seems to cover the whole journey, and then swerves away into simile (268–72):

> ibant obscuri sola sub nocte per umbram
> perque domos Ditis vacuas et inania regna:
> quale per incertam lunam sub luce maligna
> est iter in silvis, ubi caelum condidit umbra
> Iuppiter, et rebus nox abstulit atra colorem.

They went dimly in the lonely night through the shadow and through the empty houses and insubstantial kingdom of Dis: as is a journey through woods under the grudging light of a fitful moon when Juppiter has shrouded the sky in shadow and black night has robbed everything of its colour.

The impressionistic language suggests the general condition of their journeying in terms that can be apprehended concretely. But the first creatures they see are abstractions: Luctus, Curae, Morbi, Senectus, Metus, Fames, Egestas, Letum, Labos, Sopor, mala mentis Gaudia, Bellum. These creatures—which are followed by monsters of fable—undercut the concrete sense of a physical journey and are more suggestive of a vision, an experience that is totally mental, though it also includes sensations appropriate to a physical situation. But that sense of a vision is itself subverted by Aeneas' abortive attack (290–94). The road then becomes physical (295) to Charon, Palinurus, Dido, and Deiphobus.

It is, however, subversive of a journey in the Underworld that time is not just measured, but perceived, by the travellers in terms of the physical signs of time in the world above. The sacrifice is performed just before the first light of the sun (255), yet it is in a region of darkness (238 *tuta lacu nigro nemorumque tenebris*). Much more striking is that actually in the Underworld and the regions of night, Aeneas' conversation with Deiphobus is interrupted (535–39):

> hac vice sermonum roseis Aurora quadrigis
> iam medium aetherio cursu traiecerat axem;
> et fors omne datum traherent per talia tempus,
> sed comes admonuit breviterque adfata Sibylla est:
> 'nox ruit, Aenea; nos flendo ducimus horas.'

With this exchange of conversation Dawn with her rose-bright chariot had already crossed the midpoint of the sky in her heavenly journey; and perhaps they would have drawn out all the allotted time with such talk, but his companion the Sibyl admonished him and spoke briefly to him: "Night rushes on, Aeneas; we are drawing out the hours in tears."

The description of Dawn's movement across the sky could be attributed to the poet had he not specifically made the Sibyl aware of it and herself measure time by a perception that belongs to the world of day as well as night. This deliberately decreases a reader's sense that they are deep beneath the earth in a region of everlasting night.

Charon is made to explain pontifically (390) *umbrarum hic locus est, somni noctisque soporae* ("this is the region of the shades, of sleep and of drowsy night"), where the pun in *umbrarum* is certainly intended but hard to catch in English—the same word means both "shadow" and "ghost." Yet in this place of shades and sleep and night everyone is not only awake but active; the ghosts make their points with vivid rhetoric. The surroundings are changed but the individuals are as they were in life. The contradictions become more striking when Aeneas reaches the Elysian fields. Here suddenly there is light, and a brighter light than there is in the world above (640–41):

> largior hic campos aether et lumine vestit
> purpureo, solemque suum, sua sidera norunt.

Here a more bountiful sky covers the plains, clothing them with dazzling light, and they enjoy a sun of their own, their own stars.

This is the way Homer and later poets describe the Islands of the Blessed, situated at the end of the earth, removed from the toils of ordinary life. The poet has magically installed the physical properties of those islands in a favoured region of the Underworld. A dreamlike inconsequentiality infuses other features in the region. Aeneas meets his father, is greeted by him, and tries to embrace him (700–02):

> ter conatus ibi collo dare bracchia circum;
> ter frustra comprensa manus effugit imago,
> par levibus ventis volucrique simillima somno.

Thrice then he tried to put his arms around his neck; thrice the ghost, grasped in vain, escaped from his hands, weightless as the light breeze and like nothing so much as a fleeting dream."

The lines are repeated from 2.792–94, where the ghost of Creusa appeared to Aeneas in the burning city. Yet, curiously enough, companions of Anchises have horses that graze on the plain (652–53, 654–55), while they themselves picnic on the grass nearby or sing paeans (656–58). The feasting and singing heroes belong to a different concept of life after death than that which accommodates Anchises: they are in a sort of Valhalla. Some of those in this region bear the shapes they had on earth (645–55); others, however—the Roman heroes—are in the shapes they will assume in the life that awaits them centuries ahead.

There are also frequent contradictions that, for want of a better word, may be called philosophical. Dido appears in the *Lugentes Campi*, not among the suicides. Famous heroes, Greek and Trojan, are in a region of their own, but some Trojans are later found in the Elysian fields (648–50). There is no judge to decide whether a shade should be assigned to the region of punishment.[11] Those who are met by Aeneas on his first arrival in Elysium seem to be permanently there, assigned to a life of bliss. But Anchises introduces a totally new principle of reincarnation (680, 724–51), and Elysium is no longer the paradise of the blessed, but a staging-place on the return to life.[12] This concept then leads into the review of the heroes of Roman history (756–886).

In fact, what happens here is that each stage of the supposed journey is self-contained and has a consistency of its own together with an ancestry that, allowing for considerable Virgilian reconstruction or invention, can be traced in earlier writers and beliefs. It is as if a series of set scenes were passing before Aeneas' eyes rather than that he were making a journey in a region with a defined geography. The verbal signals insist on a journey, but the intellectual organisation suggests more the vivid incoherence of a dream.

Finally, just before Aeneas is sent back to the world above, the poet says (886–87):

> . . . sic tota passim regione vagantur
> aëris in campis latis atque omnia lustrant.

So they wander everywhere throught the whole region in the broad regions of air and they examine everything there.

Servius' comment on this is accurate: "however he has spoken in accordance with those who believe that Elysium is on the plane of the moon." This is yet another eschatology: in this view, the soul moved upwards

---

11. On this feature, see Williams (1968), pp. 390–400.
12. For the purification of souls as located above earth, see Norden (1927), p. 28.

after death towards and beyond the plane of the moon.[13] Allusion to this view clearly subverts the idea of a physical journey under the earth, and enforces a reading of that journey as a synecdoche for an experience that is not described in its own terms.

At this point the expectations of readers need to be taken into account. For, by a ready synecdochic association, thoughts of the Underworld easily evoked ideas of necromancy, initiation ceremonies, and literary treatments of Descents to the Underworld. All three are suggested by the poet at the beginning of his account. But there are two other famous writings on eschatology that the topic would have evoked. The earlier of these is the myth of Er at the end of Plato's *Republic*. Socrates begins the account polemically by denying that he is going to produce a tale of Alcinous; the reference is proverbial since "Ἀλκίνου ἀπόλογοι" signified long and boring stories, but it also has a special reference here to the account of the Underworld in *Odyssey* 11—Socrates, that is, does not intend to indulge in the falsities and nonsense of traditional accounts of the Underworld. Instead, Er's account is of the judging of the souls of the dead, their assignment to the heavenly region or to the place of punishment below, their return after a certain period of expiation, and their choice of a new life on earth. Included also is a certain amount of cosmology and a description of the universe with its eight spheres and the earth stock still at the centre. Er obtained his information during a shamanistic flight of the soul to the regions of the dead; he had been killed in battle, taken up (his body uncorrupted) after ten days, and two days later fortunately awoke on the funeral pyre and told his story. The circumstances that led to his seeing the world beyond are devised to create a dramatic and plausible explanation.

A reader of the *Aeneid* could certainly be expected to think of this famous vision. But even more immediately accessible to the mind of a contemporary of Virgil's was Cicero's imitation of this vision in the sixth book of his *de re publica*. Cicero referred to the myth of Er in the introductory conversation, leading to his own imitation, and asserted that "what was said of the immortality of the soul and of the heavens was not the inventions of dreaming philosophers or the sort of unbelievable tales that the Epicureans mock, but the conjectures of wise men."[14] Cicero's imitation takes the form of a dream which came to P. Cornelius Scipio Africanus the younger when, on campaign in Africa in 149 B.C., he spent an

13. References in Austin (1977), ad loc.
14. Frag. 3, p. 124, Ziegler.

evening with Massinissa, talking about Scipio's grandfather, P. Cornelius Scipio Africanus the elder, the conqueror of Hannibal in the battle that ended the second Punic War. The elder Scipio then appeared to the younger in a dream that night. He first showed him the city of Carthage and predicted its destruction by his grandson in two years' time. The sight of Carthage is "from a lofty place, bathed in starlight, bright and shining" (11. *de excelso et pleno stellarum, illustri et claro quodam loco*); so a journey of some sort is suggested. The old man also predicts the younger's career, even dramatically suggesting his murder; this is done in a way that foreshadows Anchises' words to Marcellus: "you must as dictator restore the state—if only you can escape the impious violence of your relatives" (12. *dictator rem publicam constituas oportet, si impias propinquorum manus effugeris*). At this Laelius cries out and the others groan (and Scipio will indeed be murdered in a few days). Anchises, also foreseeing Marcellus' death, says to him (882) *heu, miserande puer, si qua fata aspera rumpas!*, "Alas, pitiable boy—if only you could break out of your harsh destiny!"

Then Cicero makes the elder Scipio say (13):

"sed quo sis, Africane, alacrior ad tutandam rem publicam, sic habeto: omnibus qui patriam conservaverint, adiuverint, auxerint certum esse in caelo definitum locum ubi beate aevo sempiterno fruantur; nihil est enim illi principi deo qui omnem mundum regit quod quidem in terris fiat acceptius quam concilia coetusque hominum iure sociati quae civitates appellantur; harum rectores et conservatores hinc profecti huc revertuntur."

"But that you may be the more eager to support the state, look at it in this way: for all who have saved, helped, or extended their fatherland there is a special place reserved in heaven where in bliss they may enjoy eternal life; for of all that is done on earth nothing is more pleasing to the supreme god who rules the universe than those assemblies and federations of men associated in justice that are called states. Their rulers and protectors come from this place and to this they return."

This is, as it were, the nucleus of Anchises' review of the heroes of Rome in *Aeneid* 6, and the dominant concepts of patriotism and selfless service to the state are a keynote of both compositions, together with the idea that political achievement (including military victories) is the supreme criterion of real fame. When the elder Scipio goes on to speak of the earthly body as a prison-house, in this Platonic sentiment, too, he is echoed by Anchises (724–51).

The younger Scipio then meets his dead father, L. Aemilius Paullus, who continues the theme of the body as a burden, but one that is imposed

by god and from which a man can only be released by god. Then he says
(16):

"sed sic, Scipio, ut avus hic tuus, ut ego qui te genui, iustitiam cole et pietatem,
quae, cum magna in parentibus et propinquis, tum in patria maxima est; ea vita
via est in caelum et in hunc coetum eorum qui iam vixerunt et corpore laxati illum
incolunt locum quem vides (erat autem is splendidissimo candore inter flammas
circus elucens), quem vos ut a Graiis accepistis orbem lacteum nuncupatis."

"But, Scipio, just as your grandfather here did, as I did who begat you, cultivate
justice, and also devotion (*pietatem*) which, important as it is in the case of parents
and relatives, is of the very greatest importance in the case of one's fatherland. A
life like that is the path to heaven and to this assembly of men who have now lived
out their lives and, released from the body, dwell in the region that you now see
(and it was a circular place blazing among the other [heavenly] fires with the most
glowing brightness) and that you [on earth] call by the name you get from the
Greeks the Milky Way."

Here the nucleus of the review by Anchises takes into itself the Platonic
idea of the souls of the blessed rising into the heavens to find their
Elysium. It is this idea that Virgil intends when he speaks of (887) *aeris in
campis latis* "in the broad plains of air." It is also clear that in his dream the
younger Scipio, though nothing is explicitly said of this, has journeyed
upwards to the Milky Way. From here he looks on the nine spheres
(including the earth) and hears their music. The dream ends with a
lengthy and detailed disquisition on cosmology.

It would certainly be these two closely related visions of the afterlife
that would dominate a reader's expectations, at least from the point
where Aeneas reaches Elysium and meets Anchises. Further, it is clear
that from that point to the end of *Aeneid* 6 the more immediately important of these compositions was that of Cicero—to Virgil as well as to a
contemporary reader. It can also be said that the germinal idea for the
climax of *Aeneid* 6—the review of future Roman heroes by Anchises—was
in Cicero's dream of Scipio and especially in the way in which not only are
the virtues of *iustitia* and *pietas* there valued above all others, but also a
political career in Rome is the foundation for man's greatest claim to fame.

It is consequently of significance that the poet concludes that climax
to *Aeneid* 6 with a phrase that, subverting the idea of a journey deep
underneath the earth which is the supposed framework of the account,
suggests an incorporeal or dreamlike movement through the upper atmosphere, and closely recalls the situation of the younger Scipio in Cicero's
account of his dream. From here there is a metonymic movement of ideas,

for the last book of Plato's *Republic* and the sixth book of Cicero's *de re publica* had made the concept of viewing the souls of the blessed in Elysium (or whatever name was used for the region) contiguous with the idea either of a shamanistic flight of the soul or of a dream. The poet uses that contiguity to move from the words that recall Cicero's *de re publica* even more than Plato's *Republic* (886–87) to a special adaptation of Penelope's portrait of the two Gates of Dreams. The conversion of the Gates of Dreams into Gates of Sleep permits two ideas to be suggested. First, the ending of Aeneas' journey through the Underworld and his return to the world above is analogous to waking from sleep—that is, it is a passing back from the region of Sleep through the Gates of Sleep to the world of real waking experience. Consequently Aeneas' experiences in the Underworld were analogous to dreaming. Second, it is suggested that our knowledge of what happened to Aeneas in the Underworld is analogous to a deceptive dream. This does not mean that what is known is untrue, but that it needs interpretation. If this proposition is looked at from the other point of view, we need a formulation such as that used by Cicero in *de re publica* to characterise the vision of Er as being not "the invention of dreaming philosophers . . . but the conjectures of wise men." The best that can be known about the afterlife is conjecture, and for the purpose one resorts to myth, which is like a deceptive dream or can be framed as a dream that needs interpretation or as a journey beneath the earth or as initiation into a mystery or as a meeting and consulting with souls of the dead or as a shamanistic flight of the soul. Each of these functions as a synecdoche for the actual experience of being dead, and what the poet does in the case of Aeneas' journey is to suggest each in turn and then subvert it; he has used the synecdoche of a journey as the main framework, but he has reserved the moment for subverting that to the very end, where he suggests the experience of a dream.

The poet faced grave danger in sending Aeneas into the Underworld because, if taken literally, the poem—or at least that whole part of it—would be converted into the sort of portentous frivolity that characterises Hellenistic fantasy. It is all very well for the poet to make occasional use of the epic licence that depends on belief in gods walking on earth among men of the heroic age, especially in the case of a man whose mother was attested to have been a goddess; but outside modest use of that licence the poet keeps gods and men far apart, in different worlds. It would be a gross violation of that sensitive principle to bring Aeneas into direct confrontation with the powers of the Underworld. Consequently, not the experience of Aeneas itself but the poet's description of it is constantly subverted so that it can only be viewed through a series of distant synecdoches, and the poet expressly disclaims an account that is vouched for on his own authority. He does not know himself; he only has (266) *audita* "what he has been told," and that is the traditional material by which men have tried to express their conjectures about an afterlife. This the poet constantly undercuts and then ends by giving an explicit injunction for retrospective judgment.[15]

15. See further, p. 210 below.

4 FIGURES OF MOVEMENT AND LINKAGE

The figures considered in this chapter are all designed to keep the narrative moving and to create coherence and arouse expectation. They are thematic figures and are related to the techniques of thematic anticipation used by poets of the period to sustain the energy of short poems.[1] The scale of epic poetry, however, created totally different problems, and the figures are all considerably adapted to meet them. Simile is the figure that is most characteristic of epic poetry. Here Virgil—to some extent following the precedent of Catullus[2]—devised ways to make this traditional figure more energetic in its context by shaping it in such a way that frequently a simile means more than the poet appears to say within the particular context. A figure that contributes both to the arousing of expectation and to coherence is the technique by which a theme that will be of great importance is allowed to make a minor entrance at an earlier stage in the narrative. That was a figure known to rhetorical theorists (who called it *sustentatio*) but, since their interest was in oratory, its effectiveness in poetry escaped their notice. Another figure that is of great importance in the *Aeneid* is ring-composition.[3] Essentially it is a figure that achieves closure, but in an epic poem it can be used in a variety of ways not only to close the poem on the large scale but also to close sections of the narrative. It is a figure of coherence because the early entrance of the theme that will be used to effect closure can be marked by the poet in such a way as to create expectation of that closure. Consequently it is not just a figure

1. For this, see Williams (1980), chap. 5 and Index s.v.
2. Ibid., pp. 45–50.
3. See Williams (1968), Index s.v., and (1980), Index s.v.

of retrospection. Finally, there is the technique of narrative that became very important in later European epic poetry called "interlacing." It is essentially a technique for dealing with more or less simultaneous episodes in the narrative, but it can be used artistically by the poet to create tension by postponement.

1. Similes Over-Adequate in Their Contexts

It is a characteristic of a number of striking similes in Homer that they are over-adequate to their context: that is, the poet adds a detail that is not functional in the context. A good example of this is the simile in which stones thrown by Achaeans and Trojans are compared to a snowstorm (*Iliad* 12.277–89):

> τῶν δ', ὥς τε νιφάδες χιόνος πίπτωσι θαμειαὶ
> ἤματι χειμερίῳ, ὅτε τ' ὤρετο μητίετα Ζεὺς
> νιφέμεν, ἀνθρώποισι πιφαυσκόμενος τὰ ἃ κῆλα·   280
> κοιμήσας δ' ἀνέμους χέει ἔμπεδον, ὄφρα καλύψῃ
> ὑψηλῶν ὀρέων κορυφὰς καὶ πρώονας ἄκρους
> καὶ πεδία λωτεῦντα καὶ ἀνδρῶν πίονα ἔργα,
> καί τ' ἐφ' ἁλὸς πολιῆς κέχυται λιμέσιν τε καὶ ἀκταῖς,
> κῦμα δέ μιν προσπλάζον ἐρύκεται· ἄλλα τε πάντα   285
> εἴλυται καθύπερθ', ὅτ' ἐπιβρίσῃ Διὸς ὄμβρος·
> ὣς τῶν ἀμφοτέρωσε λίθοι πωτῶντο θαμειαί,
> αἱ μὲν ἄρ' ἐς Τρῶας, αἱ δ' ἐκ Τρώων ἐς Ἀχαιούς,
> βαλλομένων· τὸ δὲ τεῖχος ὕπερ πᾶν δοῦπος ὀρώρει.

And as thick as flakes of snow fall on a winter's day when Zeus the Planner has roused himself to snow, revealing his weaponry to mankind; after lulling the winds he snows continuously till he can cover the peaks of the high mountains and the jutting headlands and the clover meadows and the rich fields of men; and even upon the inlets and shoreline of the grey sea he pours down, but the waves washing in keep it back; but everything else is buried from above when the storm of Zeus falls upon it. So thick were the stones as they flew from those throwing on both sides, some against the Trojans, others from the Trojans against the Achaeans, and the din arose above the length of the whole wall.

Here the details of the sea-coast and the waves stemming the advance of the snow are not active in the context. Similes provide the opportunity for the poet to bring to momentary life a totally different scene from that of the context in which it appears; and the very distance of the field of the simile from that of the context is one important criterion of its success.[4]

4. On similes, see further chap. 7, sec. 1.

Here the non-functional details allow the poet to proceed just a little further in creating the momentary independence of a remote scene before he retraces his steps to return to the context by picking up an earlier element in the simile.

Another example is the simile in *Iliad* 4.141–47, where a wound stains Menelaus' white thighs and legs:

'Ως δ' ὅτε τίς τ' ἐλέφαντα γυνὴ φοίνικι μιήνῃ
Μῃονὶς ἠὲ Κάειρα, παρήϊον ἔμμεναι ἵππων·
κεῖται δ' ἐν θαλάμῳ, πολέες τέ μιν ἠρήσαντο
ἱππῆες φορέειν· βασιλῆϊ δὲ κεῖται ἄγαλμα,
ἀμφότερον, κόσμος θ' ἵππῳ ἐλατῆρί τε κῦδος·   145
τοῖοί τοι, Μενέλαε, μιάνθην αἵματι μηροὶ
εὐφυέες κνῆμαί τε ἰδὲ σφυρὰ κάλ' ὑπένερθε.

As when a woman, a Carian or a Maeonian, stains ivory with scarlet to be a cheek-piece for horses; and it is laid in a store-room and many horse-drivers have desired to take it; but it waits there to be the adornment of a king—in two ways, both as an ornament for his horse and as a mark of distinction for his driver. So, Menelaus, were your shapely thighs stained with blood and your shins and your trim ankles below them.

The alternative specification of the woman's origin is characteristic of the poet's desire to give concreteness and particularity to a simile, and that motive is then sustained by extension of the simile's life into a field that has nothing to do with the context—the future life of the carved ivory as it waits for the coming of a worthy purchaser. The poet has then, having gone too far, to reach back over the final details for a means of returning to his context.

Virgil imitates the shape of the Homeric simile and often seems to allow himself the wealth of non-functional detail that Homer does. But this impression is generally false: Virgilian similes tend to have many more detailed elements of correspondence with the context than Homeric similes do, and in some cases Virgil can be shown actually to have engineered the context in order to produce more correspondences.[5] Sometimes, however, there is an element in a simile—characteristically it belongs to the expansion where, in Homer, non-functional details would be expected—that is not on the surface of the context but needs to be read into the context by the reader. Normally a sense of over-adequacy in the simile is the only signal to the reader to enlarge the context by an other-

5. See West (1969), pp. 42–47.

wise unspoken element. The analogue to that unspoken element is anticipated in the simile.

The comparison of Dido to Diana in *Aeneid* 1 is an example of this
technique (498–504):

> qualis in Eurotae ripis aut per iuga Cynthi
> exercet Diana choros, quam mille secutae
> hinc atque hinc glomerantur Oreades; illa pharetram
> fert umero gradiensque deas supereminet omnis
> (Latonae tacitum pertemptant gaudia pectus):
> talis erat Dido, talem se laeta ferebat
> per medios instans operi regnisque futuris.

Just as Diana appears when she leads the dancing on the banks of Eurotas or
along the ridges of Cynthus, and a thousand Oreades follow her and crowd round
her on all sides; she wears a quiver on her shoulder and as she walks she towers
above all the goddesses: feelings of joy clutch the silent heart of Latona. Even so
was Dido, even so she carried herself rejoicing ⟨among her people⟩, pressing on
with her task and the kingdom to be.

The detail of Diana's mother and her pleasure at the sight of her daughter
seems non-functional in the context—except that there is what has been
called an "irrational" correspondence in (503) *laeta*.[6] But it is exactly this
pleasure in the onlooker at the sight of Dido that needs to be read into the
context, and especially in Aeneas, an onlooker whose name opened the
description of Dido's approach (494) and who is named again (509) at the
dramatic interruption as the arrival of the lost Trojans disrupts Dido's
calm dispensation of justice. That selfless pleasure that she inspires in
others is the basis of the scene with the Trojans, of the scene with Aeneas,
of the banquet-scene, and it is a thread in the tragedy of her affair with
Aeneas. For the selfless pleasure that she inspires in others has its correla-
tive in her own selflessness, for which her love of fairness and justice and
civilized behaviour (507–08, 562–64) is a symbol; it is a quality recognised
by Aeneas (603–05), whose characteristic it is also.

When Amata has been infected by Allecto she goes wild (7.376–84):

> tum vero infelix ingentibus excita monstris
> immensam sine more furit lymphata per urbem.
> ceu quondam torto volitans sub verbere turbo,
> quem pueri magno in gyro vacua atria circum
> intenti ludo exercent—ille actus habena

6. Ibid., p. 44.

> curvatis fertur spatiis; stupet inscia supra
> impubesque manus mirata volubile buxum;
> dant animos plagae—non cursu segnior illo
> per medias urbes agitur populosque ferocis.

Then the unfortunate woman, crazed with enormous fantasies, rages maddened and unrestrained throughout the huge city. As at times a top, sent flying by an oft-plied whip when boys, absorbed in their game, drive it in a great circle around empty halls; driven by the lash it races in a curving path; looking down at it, a crowd of naive children gape in astonishment at the whirling boxwood; the blows give it spirit. Speeding no more slowly than it, Amata sweeps through the midst of cities and uncivilized peoples.

There are many correspondences between the simile and its context,[7] but it remains over-adequate in the detail of the crowd of onlookers who do not understand what is happening and can only gape in amazement. That detail, however, needs to be read into the context, for it expresses the helplessness of the husbands, and especially of Latinus, at this extraordinary outburst on the part of their womenfolk. The simile has another function. Already the terms in which Amata's madness is described (376–77) suggest orgiastic excitement. The poet then describes how she careers into the woods (385) "in the pretence of Bacchus' inspiration," attracting many other women to accompany her. The section ends (404–05):

> talem inter silvas, inter deserta ferarum
> reginam Allecto stimulis agit undique Bacchi.

Such was the queen in the woods, in territory inhabited only by wild beasts, as Allecto drove her in all directions with Bacchic goads.

This is authorial comment. The queen thought that she was pretending Bacchic inspiration; in fact, the experience she was undergoing was completely out of her control and was, in effect, Bacchic. That deliberate movement of ideas actually resides in the simile and is anticipated there, because the top was one of the sacred emblems of Bacchus and therefore could be used as a metonymy for Bacchic frenzy.

When Hercules finally storms the cave of Cacus and tears its roof off, the interior is revealed (8.241–46):

> at specus et Caci detecta apparuit ingens
> regia, et umbrosae penitus patuere cavernae,

7. Ibid., p. 49.

non secus ac si qua penitus vi terra dehiscens
infernas reseret sedes et regna recludat
pallida, dis invisa, superque immane barathrum
cernatur, trepident immisso lumine Manes.

But the cave and great palace of Cacus was uncovered and exposed, and the
shadowy caverns deep within lay open to view, not otherwise than if the earth
were to gape wide open through some violence and unbar the infernal abodes and
open up the ghostly kingdom, hated by the gods, and the enormous abyss be
seen from above, the souls of the dead would tremble at the light cast in on them.

Here again there are many points of correspondence with the context, but
the simile is over-adequate in the final detail of the frightened souls of the
dead. But that too needs to be read into the context. At Hercules' first
onslaught (222–24) Cacus is said to be frightened, but that is all. There is
no mention of fear in the account of the fight that follows: he is a terrifying monster and he fights desperately, but the fear (and a certain sympathy for that desperation) needs to be transferred from the simile to the
context.

Sometimes a simile goes much further in suggestion than the poet
does explicitly in the context (or in the narrative at all up to that point).
When Turnus attacks the Trojan camp at the beginning of Book 9, the
Trojans stay behind their ramparts and Turnus becomes frustrated
(57–66), like a ravening wolf.[8] This goes far beyond any wolf simile in
earlier epic in portraying the sheer naked savagery of the animal in contrast to the soft gentleness of its intended prey.[9] What will become ob-
sessively important in the portrait of Turnus will be his blood-lust, his
sheer love of slaughter. This simile conveys the sense of a psychopath
who has for too long been deprived of the chance to kill. This has nowhere been said by the poet but needs to be read into the context from
this simile.

Sometimes a simile is substituted for a description that is therefore
omitted in the context. For instance, when Camilla is well embarked on
her path of slaughter, she is lured out of her chariot by the son of Aunus
who then drives off himself, hoping to escape, but she runs and catches
up with him and kills him (11.720–24):

. . . poenasque inimico ex sanguine sumit:
quam facile accipiter saxo sacer ales ab alto

8. On this simile, see further chap. 7, sec. 1.
9. For text and commentary, see pp. 173–75 below.

> consequitur pennis sublimem in nube columbam
> comprensamque tenet pedibusque eviscerat uncis;
> tum cruor et vulsae labuntur ab aethere plumae.

. . . and exacts the penalty on his enemy blood as easily as a hawk, a sacred bird, swoops from a high pinnacle on a dove winging high in the clouds, and, catching it, holds it tight and disembowels it with hooked talons; then blood and plucked feathers fall down from the sky.

There is no description of the death of Aunus; the horrible details of the dove's suffering convey it.

That procedure becomes quite frequent in poets from Catullus to Horace, but Virgil greatly expanded the capacity of a simile to suggest something that was therefore omitted from the immediate context. A good example is the simile that describes Aeneas' landing after he has returned from Etruria. The Italians suddenly see the whole sea moving with ships (269). Then (10.270–75):

> ardet apex capiti cristisque a vertice flamma
> funditur et vastos umbo vomit aureus ignis:
> non secus ac liquida si quando nocte cometae
> sanguinei lugubre rubent, aut Sirius ardor
> ille sitim morbosque ferens mortalibus aegris
> nascitur et laevo contristat lumine caelum.

His helmet burns upon his head and fire is shed from the crest at the top and the golden shield-boss shoots out vast flames: not otherwise than when at times blood-red comets glow balefully in the clear night or the fire of Sirius rises—he who brings drought and disease to weak mortals—and makes the heavens mournful with his sinister light.

So Aeneas is like the Dog-Star or a comet. Turnus is delighted and tells his men (279) "what you have been wishing in your prayers has happened." Here the simile, with its authorial prognostications of disaster in the details that are clearly over-adequate to the supposed context, sets up a point of view in which Turnus' words can be understood with dramatic irony. The simile has, in fact, expanded the context to take in the rest of the epic, and in that wider context Turnus' words are deeply ironic.

Sometimes a simile changes direction when it is only half-completed. In several striking instances this is achieved by moving from one model to another. For instance, in the catalogue of troops in Book 7 the great contingent of Messapus sing as they march together (691–98). Then a simile based on a Homeric model (*Iliad* 2.459–65) illustrates their singing by means of a picture of swans collecting along the river Cayster in Asia; this is followed by a shift in the point of view from the sound to the impressions of mass movement, and the poet uses Apollonius Rhodius (4.238–40) for a picture of a great cloud of birds sweeping in from the sea. There is a similar shift both in point of view and from one model to another in a scene on the banks of the river Styx as Aeneas approaches (6.305–14):

> huc omnis turba ad ripas effusa ruebat,
> matres atque viri defunctaque corpora vita
> magnanimum heroum, pueri innuptaeque puellae,
> impositique rogis iuvenes ante ora parentum:
> quam multa in silvis autumni frigore primo
> lapsa cadunt folia, aut ad terram gurgite ab alto
> quam multae glomerantur aves, ubi frigidus annus
> trans pontum fugat et terris immittit apricis.
> stabant orantes primi transmittere cursum,
> tendebantque manus ripae ulterioris amore.

Hither the great crowd in a mass rushed to the banks, mothers and husbands, and bodies of great-hearted heroes devoid of life, boys and girls unwed, and young men laid on pyres before the eyes of their parents: as many as are the leaves that in the woods flutter down and fall at the first chill of autumn, or as many birds as crowd in landwards from the deep ocean when the chill season makes them retreat across the sea and sends them off to sunny lands. They stood there begging to be first to make the crossing and stretched out their hands in longing for the further shore.

In the corresponding passage of Homer (*Iliad* 6.146–49), Glaucus, answering Diomedes' inquiry about his ancestry, asks what lineage matters anyway: the generations of men are like leaves that die and then come to life next spring. The tone is optimistic. The emphasis in Virgil is altered; what matters is not the successive generations of leaves, but the death of every leaf when its time comes. The following simile of the birds has no predecessor; what is extraordinary is that it converts the pessimism of the leaf simile into optimism: the birds, when winter comes, have a long, arduous flight, but at the end is sunshine and that is the driving force that makes them undertake their journey. The idea of Elysium and the life of the blessed in their bright sunshine has no relevance here. The apparent shift in the simile from pessimism to optimism is delusive and ironic; it is parallel to a shift in the context from the crescendo of pain that the list of the dead achieves (in the most poignant form of premature death) to their longing to get across the river. They feel *amor* for the further bank; but what an irony it is to feel *amor* for that region as it will be described by the poet. The forces that move both birds and the souls of the dead are the same: the winter that expels them—the one from home, the other from life—and the longing that makes them want to get to the other side of the water. In the case of the birds that longing is justified and will be rewarded; but the condition of the souls of the dead will not be improved, in spite of the eagerness of each to be first (313). The irony of that vain love is not even hinted at in the context; it is pre-enacted in the second simile and has to be read into the context from there.

2. Thematic Anticipation

When Aeneas and Dido have exchanged speeches and Dido welcomes him to her palace, Aeneas sends Achates to the ships to fetch Ascanius (1.646 *omnis in Ascanio cari stat cura parentis* "all the affection of a beloved parent is concentrated on Ascanius") and presents for Dido. Both missions have a sinister aspect. Not only will Ascanius be the agent for infecting Dido with fatal love for Aeneas, but the degree of his love for Ascanius will be the deciding factor in his decision to abandon Dido (4.354–55, motivated by what Mercury says in lines 274–76): that is, the completeness of his love for Ascanius excludes the possibility of real love for Dido. That sinister element in his love for his son does not become evident till the tragedy of Dido is inevitable. But the gifts, too, foreshadow doom. One of them is a beautiful outfit that had belonged to Helen (650–52):

> quos illa Mycenis,
> Pergama cum peteret inconcessosque hymenaeos,
> extulerat, matris Ledae mirabile donum.

which she had brought—a wonderful present from her mother Leda—from Mycenae when she was setting off for Pergamum and a marriage that was forbidden.

The other present was (653–55):

> praeterea sceptrum, Ilione quod gesserat olim,
> maxima natarum Priami, colloque monile
> bacatum, et duplicem gemmis auroque coronam.

Besides, a sceptre that Ilione had once carried, the eldest of the daughters of Priam, and a necklace of pearls and a double crown of jewels set in gold.

It is bad enough to give Dido something from Helen; that the gift should be specified as connected with her absolutely illegal marriage to Paris is a clear anticipation of the theme, very important in Book 4, that Dido regards her liaison with Aeneas as marriage (which she—no less than he— in some saner moments knows to be illegitimate).[10] The mention of Ilione is as foreboding, though in a way that is more immediately appreciable; for her husband murdered her brother and she either committed suicide or murdered her husband or both. The tragic history of Ilione coincides sufficiently with Dido's, even as it is known to the reader at this point, to project the possibility of tragedy for her. The gifts, of course, also have an immediate function in recalling the unbroken series of tragic events that forms Aeneas' own background and that does not augur well for his happiness.

There are constant parallels to this use of thematic anticipation to foreshadow events. It is a frequent feature of the use of this figure in the *Aeneid* that it is not recognised until the later passage has been read. So, for instance, the description in 9.164–67 of the arrogant debauchery indulged by the Italians within sight of the besieged Trojan camp anticipates the theme of disaster: for their drunken stupor will make them easy victims to be slaughtered by Nisus and Euryalus. This is related to a type of thematic anticipation that is particularly frequent in the war-books, by which the poet deliberately suggests in advance a tragic outcome to a particular scene or event. A simpler type of thematic anticipation is designed to achieve a particular tone in advance of the theme for which that tone is particularly appropriate. So the tone of the journey through the Underworld is set right at the beginning of the book by various scenes wrought by Daedalus on the temple-doors (20–33), and this tone is further amplified by the death and funeral of Misenus (149–82 and 212–35). These are more or less local uses of the figures, but there are some anticipations of themes whose effect pervades the whole epic.

The last figure that Aeneas sees in the pictures of Troy is that of Penthesilea (1.490–93):

> ducit Amazonidum lunatis agmina peltis
> Penthesilea furens mediisque in milibus ardet,
> aurea subnectens exsertae cingula mammae
> bellatrix, audetque viris concurrere virgo.

10. See Williams (1968), pp. 377–89.

Penthesilea, blazing with battle-zeal, leads her Amazon ranks with their crescent shields, and shines out in the midst of thousands, a warrior-queen, with one breast left bare and a golden band beneath it, and though a virgin she is ready to do battle with men.

The feminine details balance the male character in her, especially in the word-play *viris . . . virgo*. She is a man in every way, except that she is a woman: the paradox is striking. The theme seems to be satisfied as Aeneas lifts his eyes from her and sees Dido, whose beauty is taken up in a simile comparing her to the warrior-queen Diana; and indeed Dido seems to behave in every way like a man, and so like Penthesilea—except that, in her, statesmanship takes the place of love of fighting. But the apparent similarity has already been foreseen in Venus' account of Dido and her passionate love of her husband. In that account also she behaved like a man—(364) *dux femina facti*—but in an enterprise that demanded intelligence and skill and determination, not the qualities of a warrior. Yet in that context, too, a significant figure appeared. Venus, disguised as a huntress, is compared to a Spartan girl or to Harpalyce (314–17):

> cui mater media sese tulit obvia silva
> virginis os habitumque gerens et virginis arma
> Spartanae, vel qualis equos Threissa fatigat
> Harpalyce volucremque fuga praevertitur Eurum.

His mother proceeded to meet him in the middle of the wood, with the features and dress of a virgin and the weapons, too, of a virgin, a Spartan perhaps or such as Harpalyce appears when in Thrace she tires out horses or outstrips the swift East wind.

Harpalyce is not known elsewhere, but the commentary of Servius Auctus asserts that her father was a king, driven out by his people and killed; she then lived in the woods, fending for herself, until she was also killed. Hyginus adds the detail that her father brought her up in the woods after he mother's death, and taught her the use of weapons. This is, then, another woman, like Penthesilea, in all other respects like a man. But her likeness to a man is in a sphere that is totally removed from Dido's. Both figures contrast with Dido in a most important respect. But the story of Harpalyce is precisely that of Camilla,[11] and, in her close combination with Penthesilea—as in the contrast of both with Dido—this portrait an-

11. See Austin (1971), ad loc. (pp. 118–19).

ticipates the theme of the warrior-maid that forms the climax of Book 11. But Camilla also appears at the climax of the catalogue of Italian forces at the very end of Book 7. There, like Penthesilea, she is (805) *bellatrix* and (806–07) *proelia virgo dura pati* ("a virgin, she endures hard-fought battles"); like Harpalyce, she (807) *cursuque pedum praevertere ventos* ("with speed of foot she outstrips the wind").[12] This is a detailed (803–17) and romantic portrait of a warrior-maid. There is a further anticipation of her appearance when, in Book 11, Turnus, answering Drances' sensible arguments, lists the forces that will ensure a hard fight for the Trojans; among them is Camilla (432–33):

> est et Volscorum egregia de gente Camilla
> agmen agens equitum et florentis aere catervas.

And there is too Camilla from the famous clan of the Volsci, leading a squadron of cavalry and companies aflower with bronze.

His words repeat 7.804, and draw especial attention to the striking metaphor in *florentis*—the armour of her troops is so brilliant that the effect of the bronze is like a tree in flower. Her long anticipated coming begins with a detailed account of her background put into the mouth of her patron Diana; the episode ends in a tragedy that she brings on herself. With her death, a moment of climax that brings the end of the *Aeneid* clearly in sight is achieved.

It is true of this thematic anticipation, as it is also true of most uses of this figure in poetry from Catullus to the death of Horace, that the more frequently the poem is read the more striking becomes the anticipation already in Book 1 of the figure of Camilla. Thereby the irony of Venus' disguising herself not just as a virgin, but as a warrior-maid like Camilla, is sharpened in the contrast that is aroused between Venus and the virgin huntress Diana.

Another thematic anticipation of the greatest importance in judging the poet's attitude to his own times also starts in Book 1. As Neptune calms the storm, the poet moves out into a striking simile (148–56):

> ac veluti magno in populo cum saepe coorta est
> seditio saevitque animis ignobile vulgus;
> iamque faces et saxa volant, furor arma ministrat;

---

12. The MSS give *Hebrum* at 1.317. But the emendation of Jan Rutgers, *Eurum*, seems certain. There is the same error of the MSS at Horace *Odes* 1.25.20 (see the commentary of Nisbet and Hubbard, ad loc.). The imitation by Silius Italicus *Punica* 2.75 merely shows that the error was in MSS of the *Aeneid* by about A.D. 80.

> tum, pietate gravem ac meritis si forte virum quem
> conspexere, silent arrectisque auribus astant;
> ille regit dictis animos et pectora mulcet:
> sic cunctus pelagi cecidit fragor, aequora postquam
> prospiciens genitor caeloque invectus aperto
> flectit equos curruque volans dat lora secundo.

And as often, when amongst a great crowd a civil disturbance arises and the common people lose control of their anger and soon firebands and rocks are flying, their insanity provides weapons; then, if by chance they catch sight of a man who is distinguished for his selflessness and public services, they fall silent and stand there with ears pricked; he wins over their spirits with his words and soothes their breasts. In the same way did the roar of the ocean totally fall silent after the father, looking out over the waters and riding across the clear sky, steered his horses, and, flying along, gave rein to his speedy chariot.

This simile is remarkable in its departure from the normal epic technique of using nature and natural phenomena to illustrate human behaviour and emotion. But it is even more remarkable in being totally Roman in its details and, more generally, in the assumptions that it makes about the social and political situation. On this Servius quotes from Cicero's *de re publica* 6 on the meaning of *seditio;* Cicero was concerned with that topic in this section of his dialogue, and a further fragment, quoted by Nonius (p. 519, 17), illustrates his attitude: *et vero in dissensione civili, cum boni plus quam multi valent, expendendos civis, non numerandos puto* ("and indeed when there is civil strife and men of moral worth are of more value than crowds, my opinion is that citizens should be weighed not counted"). That is essentially the sentiment behind the simile, though it expresses it in a dramatic portrait, and the situation that both writers are thinking of is civil war, the pernicious ailment that destroyed the Republic, just within Cicero's experience, well within Virgil's.[13]

The figure of the man of duty, to whom the state meant more than personal ambitions (*pietate gravem*) and who quells the disturbance simply by the *auctoritas* that resides in him, is reminiscent of Cato, admired both by Cicero and by Virgil as the exemplar of the man of principle. The simile looks forward to a theme that dominates the second half of the *Aeneid*. This is the idea that the war between Trojans and Italians is morally wrong, not just because war is wrong in itself (though that idea is clear in the *Aeneid*), but because it amounts to civil war. Juppiter declares it a war

13. Cicero ends his *Brutus* with a dire warning of the consequences to the Republic of Caesar's victory in the civil war.

forbidden by him (10.8 *abnueram bello Italiam concurrere Teucris* "I had forbidden that Italy should clash in war with the Trojans"). This is sometimes thought contradictory with 1.263 *bellum ingens geret Italia* ("he shall wage a great war in Italy") where Juppiter reveals the future to Venus. But the apparent contradiction is merely the distinction between the long-term and the short-term views:[14] Juppiter absolutely forbade enmity between Trojans and Italians, though in the short term he knew that there would be war before his ban took full effect. The basic attitude expressed is to be seen in a prayer spoken by the poet as the last mutual slaughter of Trojans and Italians begins (12.500–04):

> Quis mihi nunc tot acerba deus, quis carmine caedes
> diversas obitumque ducum, quos aequore toto
> inque vicem nunc Turnus agit, nunc Troius heros,
> expediat? tanton placuit concurrere motu,
> Iuppiter, aeterna gentis in pace futuras?

What god can tell me in poetry of all the bitterness, the variety of slaughter, the fall of leaders whom over the whole plain in turn now Turnus, now the Trojan leader pursues? Was it really a decision of yours, Juppiter, that two peoples destined to live in eternal peace should clash with such violence?

The poet begins as if he were addressing a god concerned with poetry (Apollo or one of the Muses) and asking for inspiration, but he is deflected into a bitter question to Juppiter which, on the basis of the future unity of the two peoples, views the war as having the quality of a civil war. The same theme comes out in deliberate authorial comment as the war starts (7.583–84):

> ilicet infandum cuncti contra omina bellum,
> contra fata deum perverso numine poscunt.

Thereupon everyone one of them demands war, a war that is unspeakably wrong[15] and contrary to the omens, contrary to the oracles of the gods and against their will.

The immorality of the war rests on the exchange of hospitality and pledges between Latinus and Aeneas, symbolising the union of the two peoples.

    That is Juppiter's point of view in the council of the gods at the beginning of Book 10, but there he links it with another potent idea. The

---

14. See chap. 1, sec. 2.
15. Juppiter, too, condemns the war in the same terms in 12.804 *infandum . . . bellum.*

two peoples are and ought to be joined in a close bond, but the dissension (analogous to civil war) among the gods disrupts that situation. That is wrong; the gods should wait (10.11–15):

> "adveniet iustum pugnae, ne arcessite, tempus,
> cum fera Karthago Romanis arcibus olim
> exitium magnum atque Alpis immittet apertas:
> tum certare odiis, tum res rapuisse licebit.
> nunc sinite et placitum laeti componite foedus."

"A legitimate time for war shall surely come (do not hasten it), when proud Carthage shall loose great destruction and the breaching of the Alps upon the citadels of Rome: then it will be legitimate to set your hatreds against one another, then you can plunder one another. Till then leave it alone and with joyful spirits compound the union that I have decreed."

The idea here is that war between these two peoples, destined by Fate to be one, is wrong because they will have to fight a real, legitimate war (*iustum bellum*) together in the future against Carthage. That idea neatly reverses the historical viewpoint. To Virgil and his contemporaries, civil war was a crime (*scelus*) because it was fought by Romans against Romans who had been mixed as one nation in the crucible of history—and that included the Carthaginian wars. As put by Juppiter, the idea is that war between Trojans and Italians is a crime in the twelfth century because the two peoples will be made one in such wars as those against Carthage.

The wars against Carthage are also a theme anticipated from an early stage in the *Aeneid.* Juno's anger against the Trojans is explained at the beginning of the epic (1.12–22) as in the first place attributable to her love of Carthage and the rumour that a race descended from the Trojans would destroy it. The poet then sets the first four books in Carthage. But all is peace; there is not a hint of the troubles to come—the Roman wars against Carthage are carefully omitted from Juppiter's great prophecy to Venus (1.257–96). The change comes suddenly when Dido is rejected and in most dramatic language hopes for a successor to avenge her (4.624–29):

> ". . . nullus amor populis nec foedera sunto.
> exoriare aliquis nostris ex ossibus ultor
> qui face Dardanios ferroque sequare colonos,
> nunc, olim, quocumque dabunt se tempore vires.
> litora litoribus contraria, fluctibus undas
> imprecor, arma armis: pugnent ipsique nepotesque."

"Let there be no love between our peoples, and no treaties. Arise some avenger from my bones and harass the Dardanian colonists with fire and sword, now, in the future, at whatever time the power shall be at hand. My curse is that shore clash with shore, waves with waves, weapons with weapons: may they themselves and all their descendents always be at war."

She foresees her avenger Hannibal, and this future crisis for Romans hangs over the rest of the epic to make war between Trojans and Italians criminal.

The theme of civil war, conceived in the terms of Virgil's own time, is suggested at an early stage of the epic in the simile of a riot quelled. But it also emerges at the climax of Juppiter's prophecy to Venus: cessation of civil war is the crowning achievement of the age of Augustus (294–96). It appears again in the review of Roman heroes in Book 6, when Anchises gives a peremptory order to Julius Caesar to be the first to throw away his weapons (835). Julius Caesar is then accompanied by his son-in-law, Pompey, and both are told in very blunt terms (they are addressed as *pueri*) "and do not turn your mighty powers against the vitals of your fatherland" (833 *neu patriae validas in viscera vertite viris*). That is a sharply outspoken condemnation of civil war and especially of the adoptive father of Augustus. The theme finally forms the climax to the review of Roman history on the shield made by Vulcan. There it is in the form of a celebration of Augustus' part in the battle of Actium, which brought an end to the civil war (8.675–713). There, however, civil war is viewed in a special light: Antony is indeed portrayed, but as having allied himself with Cleopatra, a foreign enemy of Rome, and that is used to give the battle legitimacy.

This is the concept that supplies the background to the Italian wars, characterised by treachery and broken truces, of the last six books. The selfless figure of authority in the early simile is envisaged as a modern analogue to the qualities discovered in Aeneas in the succession of unexpected and cruel crises that he faces in dealing with what are treated as outbreaks of civil war. That thematic contrast, so important in the twenties of the age of Augustus, between the crime of civil war and the inspiring crusade against threatening external enemies of Rome,[16] lies at the basis of the *Aeneid* and is signalled by anticipatory appearances of those themes. It is figured in the relationship established between the Italian wars fought reluctantly by Aeneas (and viewed as a type of civil war) and the great life-and-death struggle with Carthage, the external enemy (analogous to the Parthians of Augustan times). The Italian wars, too, are

16. On this, see Williams (1980), Index s.v. "Crusade against Parthians as expiation for civil war."

foreseen: first by Juppiter (1.263–64), then in a horrible curse laid on Aeneas by Dido in which, allowing that Fate decrees his arrival in Italy, she wishes on him all the horrors that actually do befall him (4.612–21):

> "si tangere portus
> infandum caput ac terris adnare necesse est,
> et sic fata Iovis poscunt, hic terminus haeret:
> at bello audacis populi vexatus et armis,
> finibus extorris, complexu avulsus Iuli
> auxilium imploret videatque indigna suorum
> funera; nec, cum se sub leges pacis iniquae
> tradiderit, regno aut optata luce fruatur,
> sed cadat ante diem mediaque inhumatus harena.
> haec precor, hanc vocem extremam cum sanguine fundo."

"If it is unavoidable that his accursed head should reach harbour and swim to shore, if the Fates of Juppiter so demand and this conclusion stands firm, yet, harassed in wars by the weapons of an impetuous people, an exile from his territories, torn from the embrace of Iulus, may he beg for help and witness the cruel deaths of his people; and, when he has submitted to the conditions of an unjust peace, may he not enjoy his kingdom or the loved light of life, but die before his time and lie unburied in the midst of sands. This is my prayer, these last words I pour forth with my blood."

This is a hostile reading of what actually happens in the last six books and of what is not contained in the *Aeneid* (the legend that Aeneas drowned). The prophecy that he will live only three years after the Italian wars has already been made by Juppiter to Venus (1.265–66), and this fact simply confirms the power of those anticipated themes on Dido's lips. Something of the same pessimistic picture of the wars to come is picked up and repeated in the prophecy which the Sibyl gives to Aeneas (6.86–94)— though she ends with encouragement (95–96). In this way, both the wars to come and their peculiarly unpleasant nature are made to loom over the struggles of the first six books.

3. Ring-Composition

Ring-composition in an epic poem is virtually thematic anticipation used for structural purposes. Some examples are hard to classify exactly. For instance, several prophecies are given in Book 3 that do not find their completion until Books 7 and 8. The prophecy delivered by the Harpy Celaeno in 3.250–57 is not fulfilled until 7.107–34, when Ascanius re-

marks that the Trojans are eating their tables; the prophecy given by
Helenus in 3.388–93 about the future site of Alba Longa is fulfilled in
8.42–48 and 81–85. The effect in both cases is to arouse expectation of
fulfilment from the moment each prophecy is delivered; both prophecies
concern events that are terminal in the sense that, once they are fulfilled,
the Trojans will have attained the site of future Roman history. Here the
nature of the expectation is so clear at first delivery that the fulfilment
functions as a closure for a large section of the narrative.

Similar to these in the deliberate arousal of expectation is the ring-
composition between Book 10 and the end of Book 12.[17] When Turnus
has killed Pallas, he strips the body of a belt with remarkable gold engrav-
ing on it and delights in the loot he has taken (495–500). The poet then
enters his own text in person to condemn Turnus' folly and to predict that
the day will come when Turnus will mightily regret that act (501–05).
Pallas' body is carried away and attention shifts to Aeneas' reaction. The
scene these words anticipate occurs in the very last lines of the *Aeneid*
(12.930–52), where the three characters involved in that scene in Book
10—Turnus, Pallas, and Aeneas—come together. The effect of this particular ring-composition lies, not just in the expectation created by the poet's
words in Book 10, but in the way in which the killing of Turnus by Aeneas
is thereby legitimated as the closure of the epic as a whole. The deliberately aroused expectation of Turnus' day of reckoning is made to dominate the narrative from that particular entrance of the poet to the end of
the poem. Events beyond that ending have already been sufficiently foreseen at an earlier stage.

In many cases ring-composition does not involve the arousal of
expectation at the first stage and the figure is only recognised as such
when the ring is completed. For instance, Book 5 is self-contained and
something of a digression. It is marked as such by ring-composition on
the figure of Palinurus: the book begins with his guiding Aeneas' ship
through the storm away from Carthage and ends with the drowning of
Palinurus. That drowning, in turn, is itself a thematic anticipation of his
meeting with Aeneas in the Underworld in 6.337–83.[18]

A large ring-composition of this type encloses the epic as a whole,
with Juno angry at the very beginning of Book 1 and Juno appeased in the
penultimate scene of Book 12 (791–842). That theme of Juno's anger
which began the poem, with the poet's question (11) *tantaene animis*

17. See pp. 87–92 below.
18. On the difficulties involved in this connexion, see Appendix, sec. 4.

caelestibus irae? ("is there really such anger in heavenly hearts?") is taken up in Juppiter's resignedly humorous reproach to Juno (12.830–31):

> "es germana Iovis Saturnique altera proles,
> irarum tantos volvis sub pectore fluctus."

"You truly are indeed a sister of Juppiter and a second child of Saturn, so great are the waves of passion you allow to surge in your heart!"

Juno then agrees to what Juppiter says: (841) *adnuit his Iuno et mentem laetata retorsit* "Juno nodded assent to this and joyfully changed her attitude." The word *laetata* marks the changed Juno, no longer *irata*.

The more important, but parallel, element in this ring-composition is between Juppiter's interchange with Venus in Book 1 and his dialogue in Book 12 with Juno. The ring-composition is marked by detailed links between Juppiter's speech in Book 1 (257–96) and his and Juno's speeches in Book 12.[19] Aeneas will become a god (1.259–60 and 12.794–95); the name of the people will be *Romani* (1.276–77 and 12.827); their dress will be the toga (1.282 and 12.825); finally, and most important, Juppiter prophesies to Venus that angry Juno will change her attitude and will join Juppiter in becoming the patron deity of Romans. The relationship between these two impressive passages at the beginning and at the end of the epic has a further particular function. Understood together, they look beyond the end of the *Aeneid* not just to the distant future of Rome but to the events that will take place immediately after the death of Turnus. Aeneas and Lavinia will be happily married (12.822); Aeneas will rule both peoples for three years and then will die (1.265–66); he will become a god, and, in particular, that type of god known to Romans as a *deus indiges* (1.259–60 and 12.794–94); thereafter Ascanius will rule for thirty years and will found Alba Longa, transferring the capital thither from Lavinium (1.267–71).

This is a particularly satisfactory use of ring-composition in solving a problem peculiar to the *Aeneid*. Although the ending of the epic with the death of Turnus is structurally and dramatically justified, it is an historical epic and purports to be the story of Aeneas, so the question naturally arises as to what happens to the hero after his victory. Yet if the narrative were to continue after Aeneas kills Turnus it would be intolerably anticlimactic. That difficulty is ingeniously solved by indirection, by letting the details of what will happen immediately after the end of the epic

19. On this, see chap. 6, sec. 2.

emerge as if by accident in passages that are directed to a different purpose. Those passages are then marked by an emphatic ring-composition,
so that closure of the epic is achieved in effect by two structures of ring-
composition: one that spans all twelve books but concludes, sym-
metrically with its opening, some way before the end of the epic; and
another that spans the final action, which is thereby endowed with a
striking dramatic unity, from Book 10 to the last line of Book 12.

4. Interlacing

Ostensibly, interlacing of threads in the narrative allows the poet to
keep in chronological focus simultaneous events that happen in different
places. However, Virgil used the technique, even where it was not necessary, for artistic—especially dramatic—purposes. The technique itself can
be seen used strikingly in the *Odyssey*. There the poem opens with a
council of the gods that serves to introduce the plight of Odysseus, who is
still trying to reach home after ten years. After that, the first four books
tell the story of Telemachus' attempts to gather news about his father.
The sub-plot of Penelope and the suitors is introduced in Book 2, and at
the end of Book 4 the narrative returns to reveal the suitors planning to
ambush Telemachus on his return. The next ten books concentrate on
Odysseus: his leaving Circe, his arrival in Phaeacia, his meeting with
Nausicaa, his reception by Alkinoos, his stories, and his arrival in Ithaca.
By Book 16 all the threads in the story have come together. But this
structure is awkward, especially in the ten-book concentration on Odysseus that makes one lose sight of Telemachus.

Virgil clearly learned from the difficulties of his predecessor and at
first even seems to have been nervous about allowing a two-book account
of his own wanderings by Aeneas.[20] These two books in which Aeneas
becomes the narrator are in danger of disrupting the sense of Dido's being
present and continuously infected with passion for Aeneas; at any rate, in
Book 3 one loses all sense of Dido's presence, though the poet has made
some attempt to bring the audience alive to the reader in Book 2.

The interlacings where Virgil's artistry shows itself are all on a much
smaller scale and occur throughout the whole epic. In Book 1 there is the
harrowing separation of Aeneas from many of his company by the storm,
which leads to a corresponding split in Aeneas as he tries to encourage
the survivors (198–207) while feeling serious doubts himself (208–09). The

20. On this, see Appendix, secs. 1 and 2.

scene changes to heaven for the dialogue between Venus and Juppiter (223–304), and returns to Aeneas to find him still awake and worried (305). This keeps the thought of those lost companions in the forefront of the text. Aeneas' meeting with Venus follows, and the two threads of narrative are brought together by a finely dramatic use of divine mist that keeps Aeneas hidden as the lost friends enter (509–12) and reveal that they have been suffering the same worries as Aeneas (544–58).

There is a more contrived interlacing in Book 2. The wooden horse is found, there is debate, and Laocoön throws the spear that sticks in its side (31–56). With the sound made by the spear still echoing, the scene changes to the capture of Sinon, who tells his story vividly in three speeches (57–198). Then attention returns to Laocoön (the spear is still in the side of the horse) and his killing by the sea-serpents (199–231). This interlacing was deliberately chosen to make a dramatic postponement of Laocoön's death; it was not necessary, but it succeeds because the brilliance of Sinon's narrative presents a convincing explanation for the Wooden Horse and one parallel to what the reader knows to be true. The issue of credibility is only solved by Laocoön's death. A closely similar use of the technique occurs in Book 6. There the death and funeral of Misenus is interlaced with Aeneas' search for the golden bough: 149–82, death of Misenus and felling of trees for the pyre; 183–211, Aeneas helps, he also searches for and finds the golden bough; 212–35, funeral of Misenus. Here the effect of the interlacing is to avoid an episodic movement from the death and funeral of Misenus to the plucking of the golden bough (or vice versa). As with the episode of Sinon, the narrative is kept moving by the arousal of expectation. But here the expectation is aroused by the Sibyl's introduction of both themes, first the golden bough (136–48), second, the death of Misenus (149–55). That death has an element of mystery since the Sibyl does not mention a name, and this fact leads to the partial treatment of the Misenus-theme first, followed by that of the golden bough before the final return to the Misenus-theme. In this way, the sombre tone of the Misenus-episode is injected into the finding of the golden bough, in anticipation of the atmosphere in which the journey through the Underworld takes place.

Both of these interlacings were deliberately sought. Often, of course, some interlacing is inevitable. For instance, in Book 5, while the games are still going on the women burn the ships, so that the narrative of that event has to be inserted. But that is done at a point where the last event (the *lusus Troiae*) of the games seems to be completed; then attention is shifted back to the scene of the games by the arrival of a message, and connection with the previous episode is neatly contrived by making Ascanius, still on horseback, the first to react (667–74). In general, the particular use of the divine machinery made by Virgil in such a way that action is often taking place on the two levels of human and divine required the constant interlacing of those two levels of narrative.[21] But it is in the last six books that the artistry of interlaced narrative was made authoritative for later European literature. The fact itself of there being two sides in the war made interlacing to some degree essential, and action on the divine level complicated this still further. Here action among the gods is often used to break off human actions at a crisis or climax. So, in Book 7, the embassy to Latinus has been successful in an unexpected and dramatic way; they start off to take the news back to Aeneas (284–85) and the narrative turns to Juno. What happens in the episodes that follow, concentrated on Amata, Turnus, and Ascanius, closely concerns Latinus, as war breaks out against his will. Of course, it also concerns the Trojans, but only passively; they are hardly mentioned, and Aeneas not at all. The end of the book comes after the long catalogue of Italian forces. Even at the beginning of Book 8 the focus is on Turnus as he prepares for war (1–17). Then, at last, with the words (18) *talia per Latium*, attention focuses on the troubled state of mind of Aeneas. Here strategic use is made of the end of the book, so that Turnus is a link between the end of Book 7 and the beginning of Book 8, as he will not appear again until the beginning of Book 9. (Very similar to this deliberate spanning of an end of a book is the postponement of the second *prooemium* of the poem (7.37–45) until the movement of the Trojans from Cumae (end of Book 6) to the Tiber (beginning of Book 7) has been completed.)[22] The rest of Book 8 is taken up with

---

21. Recognition of this would remove a problem that has troubled commentators in Book 5. After the burning of the ships, Aeneas loses heart but is strenthened by Nautes and the ghost of Anchises (680–745); then arrangements for the founding of Segesta are made (746–61); the funeral rites and feast are completed and Aeneas sets sail (762–832). Here a scene between Venus and Neptune is inserted (779–826), which the poet uses to motivate the drowning of Palinurus (827–71) and to look forward to Book 6. There is a storm during the divine episode (817–21) which Neptune quells; but it is calm, with following winds, when Aeneas sets sail. R. D. Williams (1960), for instance, says (p. xxvi): "It seems highly likely that 5.779–871 was composed a good deal later than Book VI and probable that it was later than the rest of Book V. . . . This would also explain one awkwardness in the present version of Book V, namely that the weather seems to be calm when Aeneas sets out (774 f.), yet Neptune, at Venus' instigation, drives away the storm-clouds and stills the waters (820 f.)." That the passage is a late composition is probable, but the weather is no evidence of that. Venus' interview with Neptune must be understood to take place during the preparations for founding Segesta (779 *interea*).

22. On this, see Fraenkel (1945).

interlacing of the human (Aeneas and Evander) and divine (Venus and Vulcan) levels. The narrative becomes divided into three strands at 8.541–53, where Aeneas sends a large part of his force back to fortify and hold the camp by the Tiber. The action of Book 9, consequently, takes place without Aeneas, whose absence is constantly in the forefront of awareness. Book 10 brings these three strands gradually together after the council of the gods (1–117) and the return of Aeneas (260–75), but the distinctness of the three strands is maintained in order to allow the poet to focus on various parts of the battlefield, and this device is used to keep Aeneas and Turnus apart. In Book 11 the narrative separates again into three strands with the return of Pallas' body to Pallanteum, but the book is mainly composed of the two Trojan and Latin strands, with one diversion to the divine level (532–96); the book ends with Camilla's death, Turnus' foolish abandonment of the ambush, and night. Book 12 is the most complex, with constant interlacing of four strands: Turnus, Aeneas, Latinus and the city, and the gods. Here the technique of moving between the three human strands, with divine interventions that are often enacted on the human level, is used with one aim in view—to maintain suspense to the last few lines of the poem, with increased psychological pressure making itself felt to some extent on Aeneas but especially on Turnus. In this structure, the strategy by which the dialogue between Juppiter and Juno (791–842) is made to interrupt the fight between Aeneas and Turnus, not immediately after its first stage but only after both have been re-armed for the final stage, considerably increases the impact of the dialogue as a means of looking at the immediate future beyond the epic after the fight has ended, and marks it as an authorial intervention by means of the gods.

5   CONNEXIONS WITH PREDECESSORS: *imitatio exemplorum*

The *Aeneid* is filled with echoes of the language and ideas of Virgil's predecessors, and that sense of the poem as a late product of a very long poetic tradition is an important dimension in its interpretation. But a distinction needs to be made here. The majority of such echoes are inactive in the text: that is, the reader's understanding is not affected by his recognising or being unable to recognise the nature of the poet's relationship to a specific passage of a predecessor. Such echoes, in fact, add to the intellectual biography of the poet without affecting understanding of the poem.[1] There are, however, echoes and imitations that are to a greater or lesser extent active in the text, and to that extent they must modify understanding.

For instance, a simile of a stallion illustrates the eagerness of Turnus for battle after he has put on his armour (11.492–97). That simile had been used by Homer to describe Paris, delighted with his own handsome appearance in armour (*Iliad* 6.506–11); he is on his way to meet Hector, who has armed and has just come from one of the most moving scenes of the *Iliad*, that in which his wife Andromache expresses her mixture of love and foreboding. The simile emphasises the contrast between the vanity and frivolity of Paris and the brave seriousness of Hector. Ennius had adapted the same simile to a heroic purpose (unknown to us) by adding the detail of foam around the stallion's mouth. Virgil, however, went back to Homer and altered the impact of the simile merely by a skillful rearrangement.[2] There is a certain irony simply in realising that a simile

---

1. On this distinction in Virgil's *Ecologues*, see Williams (1980), p. 226.
2. See Williams (1968), pp. 695–96.

designed to reflect the lady-killer Paris has been used to describe the grim Turnus, a lover indeed but no Paris. But Homer can provide unwelcome surprises. That sense of irony is somewhat diminished when a reader realises that in *Iliad* 15.263–68, Homer used the same simile in exactly the same words to express the eagerness of Hector for battle after he has regained consciousness (he had been struck by a rock thrown by Ajax) and has been encouraged by Apollo. What one can say of this is that the oral poet here demonstrates the essential weakness of his technique: the re-used material was much more appropriate in the earlier context. Consequently, one can still judge the Homeric material on the basis of its more appropriate occurrence in *Iliad* 6. A reader can therefore derive a sense of irony from Virgil's use of the simile in a way that unexpectedly enforces a certain sense of vanity and self-admiration in Turnus, and the idea is thereby conveyed that Turnus is more like Paris than he is like Hector in one very important respect—his interest in battle is utterly self-centred and self-regarding. In that respect he is also strongly contrasted with Aeneas.

A sense of irony is perhaps the most frequent result of the poet's calling attention to a context in a predecessor. This can be seen again in the moving simile that bridges the departure of Vulcan from Venus and his starting work on the weapons intended for Aeneas (8.407–15). This simile has no close model in a predecessor, though its strongest appeal is not to Homer but to a passage of Apollonius Rhodius. There the poet compares the sudden flare-up of love in Medea to the sudden blaze of kindling-wood as a woman lights it in order to start working while it is still night (*Argonautica* 3.291–96). There is a nice irony in the use of that material to illustrate the devoted Vulcan leaving his beloved wife, and it underlines a complex relationship between Virgil's use of the simile and its context.[3]

There are many passages that can be interpreted along these lines, but the concern of this chapter is with instances where a connexion with a predecessor is made to work within a wide context on a much larger scale and in such a way that a reader's understanding is substantially modified by the recognition.[4]

3. See further below, chap. 7, sec. 1.
4. The rest of this chapter is much indebted to the work of Knauer (1964) for the details of the relationship between Virgil and Homer. He has also thoroughly explored the possibilities for deliberate structural imitation (even on the large scale of sequences of scenes) by Virgil of Homer, and that aspect of the relationship is not considered in this chapter.

1. ~ Used to Shape a Framework for Judgment

Behind the portrait of Dido and the shaping of her story the Homeric figure of Calypso from *Odyssey* 5 is visible, and the visit of Hermes to her prefigures the visit of Mercury to Aeneas; also to be seen is something of the figure of Circe from the story told by Odysseus in *Odyssey* 10, and also something of Catullus' portrait of Ariadne abandoned by Theseus on the island of Naxos. In various ways the reader thinks of all three women as the story of Dido unfolds; the effect is to create a depth of analogy against which a reader can test his perception of Dido. She is none of them; yet she clearly belongs in their company.

But no narrative was more continuously in the consciousness of the poet at this point than that of Medea's love for Jason. Servius, with his accustomed exaggeration and love of the unqualified statement, recognised the truth when he said in the introduction to his commentary on *Aeneid* 4: "Apollonius Rhodius wrote the *Argonautica* and in the third book he introduces the figure of Medea in love; from there the whole of this book was derived." The imitation can be traced even in detailed correspondences. For instance, Aphrodite, to persuade Cupid to enflame Medea with love for Jason, promises him a present of a wonderful ball that had been a toy of the young Zeus. Cupid, with childish delight, throws away all his toys and asks for it immediately (3.145–50). But Aphrodite swears an oath (151–53): "Be my witness this loved head of yours and my own, I shall give you the present and shall not cheat you, if you will implant an arrow in the daughter of Aietes." Virgil remembered that strange oath when he made Aeneas swear to Dido that what he had said was true: Mercury really had come with a message to him (356–59)— *testor utrumque caput* "I call both our heads to witness." The journey of Cupid as he flies down to earth (3.156–66) contributes, together with Hermes' flight in *Odyssey* 5.43–58, to the picture of Mercury's flight down to Carthage (*Aeneid* 4.238–61).

Dido has the same thoughts of Aeneas and his appearance (10–12, 80–85) that Medea has of Jason (3.451–58). Just as striking is the curse with which Chalciope threatens Medea if she does not keep their pact a secret (3.701–04): "I beg you by the blessed ones and by yourself and by your parents not to see them [my sons] pitifully destroyed by an evil fate. Otherwise, dead with my dear sons, may I come as a hateful Fury to haunt you from Hades." Medea threatens a similar haunting of Jason if he forgets her (3.1109–17). Virgil used that thematic material to construct Dido's curse on Aeneas (4.382–87): she will haunt him from the grave and the news of his laments will reach her in the Underworld. Aeneas, when he first met Dido, promised her everlasting gratitude and remembrance for her generosity (1.607–10) and that theme is echoed in his speech explaining the necessity for his departure (4.333–36); there is deep irony in the tonal contrasts between the two passages. A similar irony resides in two speeches of Jason to Medea: in the first (3.990–96), he promises remembrance and fame to Medea throughout Greece if the Argonauts return safely; in the second (3.1079–81), he says: "And assuredly never by night nor by day shall I forget you, once I escape death and flee safely to Achaia." Those confident assurances will prove ironic in the long run; the similar assurances of Aeneas are found to be explicitly ironic in the text. Finally, both poets apostrophise Love at crucial points in their texts: Apollonius, when Medea tricks her brother Apsyrtus into allowing himself to be captured by Jason (4.445–51), by whom he will be murdered; Virgil, when he depicts the feelings of Dido as she sees Aeneas and his men making hasty preparations for departure (408–15).[5] The contrast between the two apostrophes symbolises the contrast between the external narrative drama of Apollonius' text and the inner drama of Dido's tragedy.

The effect of this use of the earlier poet's framework is to construct an extensive context for viewing and judging the relationship between Dido and Aeneas, but it is a context whose differences are at least as important as its similarities. For instance, both Jason and Medea always think of their relationship in terms of marriage; nothing else occurs to them, and Medea—by her own assertion—remains a virgin to the moment of her marriage; so she explains to Arete (4.1014–28) that it was not lust that compelled her to help Jason and that she is still as much a virgin as she was in her father's house. Jason promises to marry her if she will accompany him to Hellas (3.1120–30 and 4.95–98). What this does is to establish the reader's horizon of expectation: marriage is the natural expectation of a woman in such circumstances, especially if the woman is a virgin—which, technically, Dido is not, though her chastity and faithfulness to her first husband come close to being the equivalent of a state of virginity, and this is suggested in the simile that compares her to Diana (1.496–504). Consequently, Dido is shown debating the possibility of marriage to Aeneas and reluctantly rejecting it in the interest of her faithfulness to Sychaeus (4.9–29), while Anna urges marriage and chil-

5. On this, see further chap. 7, sec. 2(a).

dren upon her (4.31–53). But the real equivalence of the situation in the *Argonautica* and in the *Aeneid* is set up by the agreement between the two goddesses—Athene and Hera in the earlier, Juno and Venus in the later— to contrive love between the couples. Juno explicitly speaks in terms of marriage: 4.103–04 *liceat Phrygio servire marito / dotalisque tuae Tyrios permittere dextrae* "let her, then, be a slave to her Phrygian husband and place her Tyrians in your control as a dowry." When Jason and Medea wed, it has to be in a hurry, since the Colchians are present and will be allowed by Alcinoos to arrest Medea and take her back to her father unless she is married. The marriage takes place in a cave, and Hera sends the nymphs to officiate (4.1128–60, 1192–1200). The next day all the people gather to celebrate the wedding, "for Hera had sent out a true rumour among them" (4.1184–85). This supplied the basic pattern for the *Aeneid*, where the marriage takes place in a cave under the auspices of Juno, and the nymphs officiate (4.168 *summoque ulularunt vertice Nymphae*). The expectation of marriage, then, is fully confirmed, and the poet can now shockingly subvert it with his own comment: 172 *coniugium vocat, hoc praetexit nomine culpam* "she calls it marriage, with this word she concealed her sin." The surprising authorial assertion reveals that Dido is mistaken: she is not married. The assertion is underlined by the contrast that follows; for, whereas in the *Argonautica* a "true" rumour spread news of the wedding abroad, in the *Aeneid* the grotesque figure of Fama spreads a very different report of a couple (194) *regnorum immemores turpique cupidine captos* "forgetful of their kingdoms and enslaved to a disgusting lust." Here is the reverse of the purity of Medea's relationship with Jason.

This parallel focuses the reader's attention on Aeneas; for, though Dido is quite content, indeed ecstatic, to be a Medea, Aeneas is no Jason. Partly, that is because Dido is really no Medea either and cannot be carried off home by Aeneas. But mainly it is because Aeneas is an Odysseus rather than a Jason: his one thought has to be how to leave his Calypso. The situation that seems to be a marriage to Dido can be nothing of the sort to Aeneas. Jason did not want to marry until he returned home to his father's house (4.1161–64), but he was quite prepared to put that wish aside in order to save Medea from the Colchians. This fact serves to bring out both the parallelism of Aeneas' situation and also the total impossibility of his marrying in Carthage. At the same time as the expectations aroused by the close connexion with Apollonius Rhodius are systematically defeated, so are the means also supplied for understanding the various ways in which the circumstances of Dido and Aeneas differed from those of Medea and Jason. The grounds for moral judgment of the actions of Dido and Aeneas are thus provided within the framework which Virgil took from the earlier poet and used to structure his own narrative.

There is another similar large-scale use of a structural connexion with a famous predecessor that needs to be considered in this context. It is the figuring of the contest between Aeneas and Turnus in terms of that between Hector and Achilles in *Iliad* 16–22. The connexion is made before the fight between Pallas and Turnus, when Juppiter comforts Hercules for the approaching death of his favourite Pallas and recalls how painful the death of his own son Sarpedon was to him; that death and Zeus' grief are recounted in *Iliad* 16.419–553. Sarpedon is killed by Patroclus not long before Patroclus himself is killed by Hector (*Iliad* 16.818–63). Thus a corresponding relationship is set up between Hector's killing of Patroclus and the killing of Pallas by Turnus. The importance of this connexion is marked by the poet's entering his own text to comment on Turnus' appropriation of the dead Pallas' belt (10.501–505):

> nescia mens hominum fati sortisque futurae
> et servare modum rebus sublata secundis!
> Turno tempus erit magno cum optaverit emptum
> intactum Pallanta, et cum spolia ista diemque
> oderit.

O minds of men ignorant of fate and of the vicissitudes to come and of the need for moderation when uplifted by success. The time will come for Turnus when he shall long to purchase even at great price an unharmed Pallas and when he shall loathe those spoils and this day.

These words echo closely what Zeus says as he sees Hector stripping the body of dead Patroclus (*Iliad* 17.198–208):

> Τὸν δ' ὡς οὖν ἀπάνευθεν ἴδεν νεφεληγερέτα Ζεὺς
> τεύχεσι Πηλεΐδαο κορυσσόμενον θείοιο,
> κινήσας ῥα κάρη προτὶ ὃν μυθήσατο θυμόν·   200
> "ἆ δείλ', οὐδέ τί τοι θάνατος καταθύμιός ἐστιν,
> ὃς δή τοι σχεδὸν εἶσι· σὺ δ' ἄμβροτα τεύχεα δύνεις
> ἀνδρὸς ἀριστῆος, τόν τε τρομέουσι καὶ ἄλλοι·
> τοῦ δὴ ἑταῖρον ἔπεφνες ἐνηέα τε κρατερόν τε,
> τεύχεα δ' οὐ κατὰ κόσμον ἀπὸ κρατός τε καὶ ὤμων   205
> εἵλευ· ἀτάρ τοι νῦν γε μέγα κράτος ἐγγυαλίξω,
> τῶν ποινὴν ὅ τοι οὔ τι μάχης ἐκ νοστήσαντι
> δέξεται Ἀνδρομάχη κλυτὰ τεύχεα Πηλεΐωνος."

When Zeus the cloud-gatherer saw him from afar clothing himself in the armour of the godlike son of Peleus, he shook his head and addressed his own heart: "Ah fool! death does not occur to your mind, though it now comes close to you. But you don the armour of a great hero at whom all others tremble. His lovable and brave friend you killed and rudely stripped the armour from his head and shoulders. Yet for the moment shall I guarantee you great power as recompense for the fact that you will not return from the battle and Andromache shall not receive from you the glorious armour of the son of Peleus."

As often, the differences here are even more significant than the similarities. The effect of the poet's taking over in his own voice what Homer had attributed to Zeus is complex. First, it means that the author specifically asserts a connexion between his own text and that of Homer at this point. Second, his words are a promise that their message will be fulfilled in his own text. Third, when Zeus asserted the folly of Hector, he meant that Hector had not properly taken into consideration the consequences of his own action, since it will inevitably arouse Achilles to avenge his friend. But in the *Aeneid* the poet asserts an entirely un-Homeric morality that calls for the exercise of restraint and moderation precisely when the temptation is greatest to regard those virtues as irrelevant. That moral principle has universal validity, and in breaking it Turnus is merely behaving in a way that is typical of mankind in general. (We shall need to return to this question later from a different direction.)[6]

This intervention by the poet looks forward to the ending of his narrative in a powerful ring-composition, and it dominates the rest of his text. Consequently, odd touches here and there are sufficient to keep the Homeric framework active. So the detail of human sacrifice at the end of *Aeneid* 10 (517–20) and at the beginning of Book 11 (81–82) relates Aeneas to the Homeric portrait of Achilles; but, again, here the differences are more significant than the similarities (see below p. 115). The connexion had already been signalled in the simile illustrating the effect the appearance of Aeneas as he landed had upon those who witnessed it (10.270–75); Homer used the same simile to portray the effect Achilles rushing angrily toward Troy had upon the defenders, and especially upon Priam (*Iliad* 22.25–32).

The connexion is fully exploited in *Aeneid* 12. The various devices by which the Italians seek to avert a single combat between Turnus and Aeneas (12.217–65) recall the vain attempts of Priam and Hecuba to persuade Hector not to remain outside the walls to fight Achilles (*Iliad* 22.33–92), while Hector's soliloquy and inward debate (98–130) are improved upon in Turnus' self-condemnation and final decision (631–96).

6. Pp. 117–18 below.

Here, too, the differences are important. Homer can risk allowing Hector to run away from Achilles after his inner debate with himself (137–247). But Turnus' cowardice is deeply engrained in his character; he has to recognise and reject it before he can fight Aeneas, and so—unlike Hector—he runs away before events force him to stand and conduct his own inner debate. He runs away again after his sword has shattered (731–33), until he is given back his own sword. The final stage of the fight takes place with Turnus armed, like Hector, with a sword, and Aeneas, like Achilles, with a spear.

Throughout this whole episode the poet makes many connexions with the Greek text, even down to details. So, as Aeneas pursues Turnus, the poet comments (12.764–65):

> neque enim levia aut ludicra petuntur
> praemia, sed Turni de vita et sanguine certant.

For no unimportant or playful prizes were being contested; it was for the life and blood of Turnus that they were fighting.

This closely echoes Homer's comment as Achilles chases Hector round the walls of Troy (*Iliad* 22.159–161):

> ἐπεὶ οὐχ ἱερήϊον οὐδὲ βοείην
> ἀρνύσθην, ἅ τε ποσσὶν ἀέθλια γίγνεται ἀνδρῶν,   160
> ἀλλὰ περὶ ψυχῆς θέον Ἕκτορος ἱπποδάμοιο.

Since it was not for a sacrificial animal or an oxhide shield, such as are the prizes for men's fleetness of foot, they were contesting; but they were racing for the life of horse-taming Hector.

Another striking motif is re-used by the Roman poet. As Achilles chases Hector, Zeus declares his favour of Hector and wonders whether to save him (167–76); Athene is indignant (177–81) and Zeus denies that he really meant to save Hector (182–85). Then as the chase rounds the walls for the fourth time, Zeus holds up a balance (209–13):

> καὶ τότε δὴ χρύσεια πατὴρ ἐτίταινε τάλαντα,
> ἐν δ' ἐτίθει δύο κῆρε τανηλεγέος θανάτοιο,   210
> τὴν μὲν Ἀχιλλῆος, τὴν δ' Ἕκτορος ἱπποδάμοιο,
> ἕλκε δὲ μέσσα λαβών· ῥέπε δ' Ἕκτορος αἴσιμον ἦμαρ,
> ᾤχετο δ' εἰς Ἀΐδαο, λίπεν δέ ἑ Φοῖβος Ἀπόλλων.

And then the father laid out a golden scales and on it he placed two lots of death that lays out at length, the one for Achilles, the other for horse-taming Hector.

Holding it by the centre, he lifted it up. The fateful day of Hector weighed it down; he went to the house of Hades and Phoebus Apollo deserted him.

This motif is used by Virgil while the first clash is taking place between Turnus and Aeneas (12.725–27):

> Iuppiter ipse duas aequato examine lances
> sustinet et fata imponit diversa duorum,
> quem damnet labor et quo vergat pondere letum.

Juppiter then lifted up a pair of scales with the beam levelled and placed upon it the diverse destinies of the two men to decide which the struggle should doom and on which side death should weigh it down.

In the Greek, a real decision is being made, and it is then acted upon by Athene, who encourages Achilles (214–23). But, in the Roman poet, the motif is a piece of generic symbolism and its effect is twofold. First, it makes direct appeal to the framework constituted by Homer's account of the combat between Achilles and Hector. But, second, its difference is underlined: no decision is involved and no result is announced; the poet uses the motif to assert the gap between his privileged account of action on the divine level and the totality of human responsibility. In the Homeric account the gods intervene directly in the human actions; but in the *Aeneid* no act on the part of the gods is allowed to infringe on the area of human responsibility. If Juturna brings Turnus his sword, then Venus frees Aeneas' spear from the sacred tree-root (760–87). The balance is simply restored.

A further structural feature which Virgil imitates from *Iliad* 22 is the digressive scene among the gods (166–87). In Homer the scene is used to bring to a close the chase round the walls of Troy, though the chase is prolonged until Zeus weighs the fates of the two men. In the *Aeneid* not only is the scene longer (791–842) and very much more important (it is, in fact, one of the crucial scenes of the whole epic), but it interrupts the fight in a way that marks it as deliberately digressive and sets it apart on a totally different level. It comes at the point where both warriors are re-armed and refreshed and start the battle anew; the poet introduces the digression with (791) *interea.*

There are other parallel features in both accounts. For instance, Juturna, recognising the Dira (869–86), abandons Turnus just as Phoebus Apollo deserts Hector after the weighing-scene (*Iliad* 22.213). Furthermore, the narrative in the *Aeneid* is bracketed by two very striking similes (749–57 and 908–14); they correspond to the two less striking and briefer similes in *Iliad* 22 (189–93 and 199–201) which closely follow one another. Once again, here the differences are more significant than the similarities (see pp. 168–73 below).

These differences culminate in the final scene when Turnus is wounded; here the close similarities with the Homeric scene invite the reader to understand and weigh the differences. Hector is fatally wounded in the throat, but in such a way as to allow him to speak (*Iliad* 22.329). So in reply to Achilles' refusal of burial (331–36), Hector pleads (337–43):

> Τὸν δ' ὀλιγοδρανέων προσέφη κορυθαίολος Ἕκτωρ·
> "λίσσομ' ὑπὲρ ψυχῆς καὶ γούνων σῶν τε τοκήων,
> μή με ἔα παρὰ νηυσὶ κύνας καταδάψαι Ἀχαιῶν,
> ἀλλὰ σὺ μὲν χαλκόν τε ἅλις χρυσόν τε δέδεξο,   340
> δῶρα τά τοι δώσουσι πατὴρ καὶ πότνια μήτηρ,
> σῶμα δὲ οἴκαδ' ἐμὸν δόμεναι πάλιν, ὄφρα πυρός με
> Τρῶες καὶ Τρώων ἄλοχοι λελάχωσι θανόντα."

Hector of the shining helmet addressed him, his strength all spent: "I beg you by your life and by your knees and by your parents, do not leave me by the ships of the Achaeans for the dogs to devour; but accept both bronze and gold in sufficiency, gifts that my father and my queen mother will give you. Give them my body to take back home so that the Trojans and wives of the Trojans may give me my due of fire when I am dead."

Achilles addresses him as (345) "dog" and refuses. Then Hector says (356–60):

> "ἦ σ' εὖ γιγνώσκων προτιόσσομαι, οὐδ' ἄρ' ἔμελλον
> πείσειν· ἦ γὰρ σοί γε σιδήρεος ἐν φρεσὶ θυμός.
> φράζεο νῦν, μή τοί τι θεῶν μήνιμα γένωμαι
> ἤματι τῷ ὅτε κέν σε Πάρις καὶ Φοῖβος Ἀπόλλων
> ἐσθλὸν ἐόντ' ὀλέσωσιν ἐνὶ Σκαιῇσι πύλῃσιν."   360

"I know you well and see my fate, nor had I any chance to persuade you. Indeed you have a heart of iron within your breast. Consider, however, lest you find that I become a cause of wrath to the gods on that day when Paris and Phoebus Apollo shall destroy you, magnificent as you are, by the Scaean gates."

Hector dies and Achilles replies defiantly (361–66).

Turnus' wound, however, is not fatal; it is in his thigh and brings him to his knees at Aeneas' mercy (924–27). The poet then reports his words (930–38):

> ille humilis supplex oculos dextramque precantem
> protendens "equidem merui nec deprecor" inquit;
> "utere sorte tua. miseri te si qua parentis
> tangere cura potest, oro (fuit et tibi talis
> Anchises genitor) Dauni miserere senectae
> et me, seu corpus spoliatum lumine mavis,
> redde meis. vicisti et victum tendere palmas
> Ausonii videre; tua est Lavinia coniunx,
> ulterius ne tende odiis."

He beseechingly turns humble eyes to him and a right hand in entreaty; and says "I have deserved it and I do not beg off; exercise your good fortune. If any feeling for a pitiable parent can affect you, I beg you (you too had a father like him in Anchises) take pity on the old age of Daunus and restore me, or, if you prefer, my body deprived of life, to my people. You have defeated me and the Ausonians have seen me defeated stretching out my hands to you. Lavinia is your wife; do not go any further in hatred."

Aeneas hesitates, is moved and inclined to spare Turnus when he suddenly catches sight of the belt taken from Pallas; he erupts in anger and kills Turnus, with these words (947–49):

> "tune hinc spoliis indute meorum
> eripiare mihi? Pallas te hoc vulnere, Pallas
> immolat et poenam scelerato ex sanguine sumit."

"Are you to be saved from me, adorned as you are with things taken from my friends? With this wound Pallas sacrifices you, Pallas exacts the penalty from your accursed blood."

This situation has been deliberately created by the poet's varying a detail from the Homeric account. For it is the fact that Turnus' wound is only disabling and not fatal that makes possible both his appeal for his life and Aeneas' decision after weighing the two courses open to him. Turnus is unlike Hector in that he pleads for his life, and Aeneas is unlike Achilles in that he is tempted to grant the request. The moral dilemma on both sides is carefully presented in its most extreme form. Both men's acts are made perfectly understandable, but neither is morally unscathed: it may be easier to feel sympathy for the sudden blinding rage of Aeneas than for Turnus' pleading, but it is impossible to make a clear-cut distinction between them.[7]

7. See further chap. 8.

Here, then, as in the story of Aeneas and Dido, the poet has defined a moral situation by assimilating it closely and deliberately to a famous situation in a great predecessor. Thereby he has provided the means of analysis and judgment by measuring the various ratios of distance between the famous exemplar and his new creation.

2. ~ Used for Irony

As can be seen from the Homeric framework used to structure the end of the *Aeneid*, there is an underlying suggestion that the war between the Italians and the Trojans is, to some extent, a repetition of the war between the Greeks and the Trojans. This concept is thematically anticipated in the paintings Aeneas sees on the temple of Juno in Carthage (1.441–93).[8] This is only partly done by selecting events from the *Iliad* that will be used by the poet to structure various stages in his account of the Italian war. A striking detail, briefly described (1.479–82), shows the Trojan women offering a peplos to Athene and praying, but Athene (482) "kept her face averted and her eyes fixed on the ground." The scene is based on *Iliad* 6, where Hector, coming back from battle, tells Hecuba to offer sacrifice and a peplos to Athene (269–79); this Hecuba and the other women do, but Athene rejects their prayer (286–311). The incident is reshaped in *Aeneid* 11.475–85. There Turnus excitedly renews the fight (459–68); but Latinus is deeply troubled (469–72), and the Italian women take gifts and sacrifice to Minerva; their prayer to her (482–85) closely follows the prayer of Theano in *Iliad* 6.305–10. The poet gives no hint of a result; in fact, just as with Juppiter's weighing-scene (see above), he enforces the gap between the levels of divine explanation on the one hand and of human action on the other by conspicuously omitting the Homeric touch of commenting on Athene's reaction (which he did, however, reproduce in the scene on the temple walls). Instead he immediately turns to the scene of Turnus arriving (486–97).

The scenes in Juno's temple reach a climax with a portrait of Penthesilea (490–93). The appropriateness of that painting lies in the fact that Aeneas' gaze moves from the portrait of the warrior-maid to the sight of Dido making her entrance (p. 69). But the portrait also anticipates the account of Camilla, who is described as an Amazon (11.648–52). This scene is not from the *Iliad*, which supplied no model for the figure of Camilla. Straight from the *Iliad*, by contrast, is the scene of the night foray

8. See Knauer (1964), pp. 349–50.

made by Diomedes (and Odysseus) that with vast slaughter robbed Rhesus of his horses (*Aeneid* 1.469–73). The details selected here to emphasise sleep and slaughter thematically anticipate the poet's reconstruction of the scene from *Iliad* 10 in the ninth book of the *Aeneid*. It is especially significant that only Diomedes (471 *Tydides*) is mentioned in the scene as Aeneas sees it in Juno's temple, since Diomedes will play an important role in Books 8 and 11 of the *Aeneid*.

Another scene that is not from the *Iliad* follows immediately (*Aeneid* 1.474–78), treated in some detail. It is that of Troilus clashing with Achilles (475) *infelix puer atque impar congressus Achilli* "unlucky boy who fought with Achilles though no equal for him." The pathetic details make a strong impression and thematically anticipate the impression that will be created by Pallas' conflict with Turnus. The connexion is signalled by the word *impar*. The poet describes Pallas as being the first to throw his spear (10.457–59):

> hunc ubi contiguum missae fore credidit hastae,
> ire prior Pallas, si qua fors adiuvet ausum
> viribus imparibus, magnumque ita ad aethera fatur:

When he thought that ⟨Turnus⟩ could be reached by a spear-throw Pallas went first in the hope that chance would aid his daring in the face of strength he was not equal to, and thus he addressed the great sky above. . . .

There is a nice irony here, for, just as Pallas is no equal for Turnus, so Turnus will be perceived by the Italians to be no match for Aeneas (12.216–18):

> At vero Rutulis impar ea pugna videri
> iamdudum et vario misceri pectora motu,
> tum magis ut propius cernunt non viribus aequos.

But in fact the Rutuli had long seen that contest to be unevenly balanced and their hearts were troubled with a range of feelings—the more so as they see at closer range that they were unequal in strength.

The irony is underlined by the connexion between the scene of Troilus and Achilles and that of Pallas and Turnus, for Turnus views himself as Achilles. Nor is he alone in this point of view. The Sibyl is also made to present a thematic anticipation of the Italian war in terms of the Trojan war, and in so doing she reinforces the connexion between the scenes on Juno's temple and the events of the Italian war. These are her words to Aeneas (6.83–97):

> "o tandem magnis pelagi defuncte periclis
> (sed terrae graviora manent), in regna Lavini
> Dardanidae venient (mitte hanc de pectore curam),
> sed non et venisse volent. bella, horrida bella,
> et Thybrim multo spumantem sanguine cerno.
> non Simois tibi nec Xanthus nec Dorica castra
> defuerint; alius Latio iam partus Achilles,
> natus et ipse dea; nec Teucris addita Iuno
> usquam aberit, cum tu supplex in rebus egenis
> quas gentis Italum aut quas non oraveris urbes!
> causa mali tanti coniunx iterum hospita Teucris
> externique iterum thalami.
> tu ne cede malis, sed contra audentior ito
> qua tua te fortuna sinet. via prima salutis,
> quod minime reris, Graia pandetur ab urbe."

"You who have finally weathered the severe dangers of the sea (but worse await you on land), the Trojans shall reach the kingdom of Lavinium (put any worry on that score out of your mind), but they will not also be glad to have reached it. Wars, terrible wars, I see and the Tiber foaming with floods of blood. You shall not find lacking a Simois or a Xanthus or a Greek army; a second Achilles has been acquired by Latium, himself also born of a goddess; nor shall Juno fail to harass the Trojans at any point, while you, in desperate straits, what tribes of the Italians, what cities will you not beg on your knees for help! The cause of that trouble to the Trojans will once again be a foreign bride and once again an alien wedding. Do not give way to these hardships, but confront them the more boldly in the way that Fortune will allow. Little though you think it, a path to salvation will first be opened for you from a Greek city."

The Delphic prophecy gave the poet a perfect opportunity to prefigure the events of the Italian war in terms of the Trojan war and so to pick up the thematic anticipation that had been constructed from the pictures on Juno's temple. The theme of Helen will be taken up by Amata as she tries to persuade Latinus to marry Lavinia to Turnus (7.359–64):

> "exsulibusne datur ducenda Lavinia Teucris,
> o genitor, nec te miseret nataeque tuique?
> nec matris miseret, quam primo aquilone relinquet
> perfidus alta petens abducta virgine praedo?
> at non sic Phrygius penetrat Lacedaemona pastor,
> Ledaeamque Helenam Troianas vexit ad urbes?"

"Is Lavinia really to be handed over in marriage to the exiles from Troy, sire, and are you to feel no twinge of pity either for your daughter or for yourself? No pity either for her mother whom at the first sign of a north wind that treacherous pirate will desert, abducting her daughter and making out to sea? But was it not exactly like that the Phrygian shepherd wormed his way into Sparta and carried off Helen daughter of Leda to the city of Troy?"

This is hostile in a way that the Sibyl's portrait is not, and so the emphasis is placed, rather, on Aeneas as a Paris than on Lavinia as a Helen. It is the situation with which Juno threatens Venus in 7.317–22 (see p. 7). This is a theme which, because of its close connexion with the Trojan defeat by the Greeks, is easily related to the theme of Trojan effeminacy. That aspect of the theme is vituperatively expressed by Iarbas in his prayer to Juppiter (4.215–18):

> "et nunc ille Paris cum semiviro comitatu,
> Maeonia mentum mitra crinemque madentem
> subnexus, rapto potitur: nos munera templis
> quippe tuis ferimus famamque fovemus inanem."

"And now that Paris, with his unmanly crew, who ties an Asiatic bonnet over his oily locks and under his chin, has possession of what he raped—while we, as you see, bear gifts to your temples and foster your fame in vain."

Iarbas is jealous of this new Paris who has stolen his Helen. That theme of contempt for Trojan unmanliness recurs on the lips of Numanus in 9.598–620:

> "non pudet obsidione iterum valloque teneri,
> bis capti Phryges, et morti praetendere muros?
> en qui nostra sibi bello conubia poscunt!   600
> quis deus Italiam, quae vos dementia adegit?
> non hic Atridae nec fandi fictor Vlixes:
>
> . . . .
>
> vobis picta croco et fulgenti murice vestis,
> desidiae cordi, iuvat indulgere choreis,   615
> et tunicae manicas et habent redimicula mitrae.
> o vere Phrygiae, neque enim Phryges, ite per alta
> Dindyma, ubi adsuetis biforem dat tibia cantum.
> tympana vos buxusque vocat Berecyntia Matris
> Idaeae, sinite arma viris et cedite ferro."   620

"Are you not ashamed to be pent in once again by a siege and a rampart, twice-captive Phrygians, and to use walls to defend you from death? Just look at the people who demand brides from us in battle! (600) What god, what insanity drove you to Italy? It is not the Atridae you find here or a Ulysses clever at talking. . . . You wear clothes gaudy with saffron and shining scarlet; idleness is your joy and indulging in dances (615); your tunics have sleeves and your bonnets have ribbons. O truly women not men of Phrygia, process on high Dindyma where the pipe provides a doubled note to devotees; the cymbals and Berecynthian boxwood of the Idaean mother are calling to you. Leave weapons to men and keep away from the steel."

Here the idea that the Italians are tougher than the Greeks is linked with the effeminacy of the Trojans. That, too, is the theme of Turnus' prayer as he rushed out to combat with Aeneas (12.95–100):

> "nunc, o numquam frustrata vocatus
> hasta meos, nunc tempus adest: te maximus Actor,
> te Turni nunc dextra gerit; da sternere corpus
> loricamque manu valida lacerare revulsam
> semiviri Phrygis et foedare in pulvere crinis
> vibratos calido ferro murraque madentis."

"Now o spear that never failed to heed my call, now has the time come. The great hero Actor once, now the right hand of Turnus hefts you. Grant me to lay low the body and with my strong hand tear the breastplate off the effeminate Phrygian and foul in the dust his locks crimped with hot curling-iron and soaked in perfume."

These themes come together in an exemplary way that also defines Turnus' view of himself in the speech he makes after his army has been shaken by seeing Aeneas' ships turned into nymphs. He starts with a re-interpretation of the omen (9.126–36):

> at non audaci Turno fiducia cessit;
> ultro animos tollit dictis atque increpat ultro:
> "Troianos haec monstra petunt, his Iuppiter ipse
> auxilium solitum eripuit: non tela neque ignis
> exspectant Rutulos. ergo maria invia Teucris.
> nec spes ulla fugae: rerum pars altera adempta est,
> terra autem in nostris manibus, tot milia gentes
> arma ferunt Italae. nil me fatalia terrent,
> si qua Phryges prae se iactant, responsa deorum:
> sat fatis Venerique datum, tetigere quod arva
> fertilis Ausoniae Troes."

But the self-confidence of the rash Turnus was not shaken; unasked he lifts their spirits with these words and unasked rebukes them: "This omen is aimed against the Trojans: by it Juppiter has actually deprived them of their usual escape-route.

They cannot abide Rutulian weapons and fire. So the sea is no longer open to the Trojans and they have no possibility of running away: one part of the world is now denied them, but the land is in our control, the tribes of Italy—so many thousands of them—are under arms. I am completely unmoved by any fateful prophecies of the gods that the Phrygians bandy about: satisfaction has been done to Fate and to Venus in that the Trojans have landed in the fields of fertile Ausonia."

So the only success the cowardly Trojans have had has been in using their ships to run away. He now avails himself of different terms to establish his own position in relation to the Trojans (136–45):

> "sunt et mea contra
> fata mihi, ferro sceleratam exscindere gentem
> coniuge praerepta; nec solos tangit Atridas
> iste dolor, solisque licet capere arma Mycenis.
> "sed periisse semel satis est": peccare fuisset
> ante satis, penitus modo non genus omne perosos
> femineum. quibus haec medii fiducia valli
> fossarumque morae, leti discrimina parva,
> dant animos, at non viderunt moenia Troiae
> Neptuni fabricata manu considere in ignis?"

"And I too have Destiny on my side—to cut to pieces with the sword that wicked race for having stolen my wife from me; it is not only the Atridae who feel that pain and it is not given to Mycenae alone to take up arms. 'But it is enough to have suffered destruction once': it ought to have been enough to commit that crime once and feel deepest repugnance for almost all womankind. And these are people to whom confidence in the rampart in between and the delaying ditches— tiny gaps from death—supply courage; yet did they not see the walls of Troy, built under Neptune's hand, sink into the flames? But who of your heroic band is ready to tear down the rampart with steel and at my side break into the terrified camp?"

Right is on Turnus' side: Lavinia is his wife and his Helen; he must teach the Trojans the lesson they did not learn from the Greeks—keep away from women. Here the theme of Helen again casts Turnus and the Italians as the victorious Greeks. He now expands that equation (148–55):

> "non armis mihi Volcani, non mille carinis
> est opus in Teucros. addant se protinus omnes
> Etrusci socios. tenebras et inertia furta
> [Palladii caesis summae custodibus arcis][9]

---

9. Line 51, closely repeated from 2.166, should probably be regarded as an interpolation: see R. D. Williams (1973), ad loc. (p. 289).

ne timeant, nec equi caeca condemur in alvo:
luce palam certum est igni circumdare muros.
haud sibi cum Danais rem faxo et pube Pelasga
esse ferant, decimum quos distulit Hector in annum."

"Against Trojans I do not need weapons made by Vulcan nor a thousand ships. All the people of Etruria can join them as allies immediately. They do not have to be afraid of darkness and unwarlike tricks, for we shall not hide in the black belly of a horse: it is our unalterable resolve to surround their walls with fire in broad daylight. I shall see to it that they do not complain of dealing with Greeks and the Pelasgian youth that Hector held off for ten years."

Here the theme is clear that in fact the Italians are far more formidable than the Greeks and do not need the sort of stratagems that the Greeks used to trick the Trojans. But most important is the way in which Turnus casts himself, not just as Achilles but as greater than Achilles, and treats Hector as an enemy who will not be able to survive as Homer's hero did.

For herein lies the irony. As the whole structure that the poet has devised for the end of the epic shows, the greatest sympathy that he can show toward Turnus is to portray him as a Hector defending his native land. But Turnus' own view of himself is exactly the opposite. When he exchanges words with Pandarus before killing him, that irony is openly expressed in answer to the real irony of Pandarus (9.735–42):

tum Pandarus ingens
emicat et mortis fraternae fervidus ira
effatur: "non haec dotalis regia Amatae,
nec muris cohibet patriis media Ardea Turnum.
castra inimica vides, nulla hinc exire potestas."
olli subridens sedato pectore Turnus:
"incipe, si qua animo virtus, et consere dextram,
hic etiam inventum Priamo narrabis Achillem."

Then huge Pandarus darts forward and blazing with rage at his brother's death, says: "You are not here in Amata's palace, her wedding-gift to you, nor is Ardea surrounding Turnus and protecting him with its ancestral walls: you see around you the camp of the enemy; there is no possibility of your getting out of here." His spirits unmoved, Turnus smiles at him: "Come on, if you have any courage in your heart, and join battle with me. You will be able to tell Priam that you found an Achilles here too."

Turnus answers the overt irony of Pandarus with what he thinks is also overt irony—Pandarus will meet Priam in the Underworld and the news will be no news to Priam, but a repetition of what Trojans had already experienced in Troy. However, in picking up the words of the Sibyl (6.89–90), dramatic authorial irony reveals Turnus' fatal mistake—his analogy is not only foolishly optimistic; it is false. This cannot be a second Trojan war for the Trojans, as the reader is aware.

The false analogy is also taken up by other Italians; not just by Numanus, but also by Liger on his chariot as he faces Aeneas (10.580–83):

> cui Liger:
> "non Diomedis equos nec currum cernis Achilli
> aut Phrygiae campos: nunc belli finis et aevi
> his dabitur terris."

To him spoke Liger: "You are not looking at the horses of Diomedes or the chariot of Achilles or the plains of Phrygia: on this day and in this territory an end shall be made to the war and to your life."

The latter mockery refers specifically to an incident in *Iliad* 20.273–352 in which Poseidon saves Aeneas from Achilles by casting a mist over Achilles' eyes and carrying Aeneas off to the edge of the battlefield. The former incident is in *Iliad* 5, where Aeneas fights Diomedes and is saved by Aphrodite, but she is wounded by Diomedes and forced to drop him (297–343). Phoebus Apollo then comes and completes the rescue (344–46 and 431–48). The folly of this mockery is not revealed just by the immediate result, but also by the speech of Diomedes to the Italian embassy, where his refusal to help and his advice not to fight against the Trojans allows the poet an opportunity for some revisionist history. Diomedes demonstrates at length (11.255–78) that the Greeks were unjustified in warring against Troy and thereby incurred the wrath of the gods. He does not recall or take the least pleasure in those old miseries (280). Aeneas is a terrifying warrior whom Diomedes has experienced and he wishes no repetition; in fact, if Troy had had two more such, it would be Greece, not Troy, that would now be in mourning. Aeneas and Hector alone kept the Greeks off for ten years—and Aeneas was the stronger in *pietas* (281–92). That revisionist history, in the most authoritative mouth, is enough to bring out the dramatic irony in the analogies that Turnus and the other Italians rely on. Latinus instantly recognises the truth.

3. ~ Used to Measure the Distance from a Conventional Heroic World

When Patroclus is killed Achilles goes on a rampage of wild slaughter and Xanthus runs red with blood. Finally he tires (*Iliad* 21.26–32):

... ὁ δ' ἐπεὶ κάμε χεῖρας ἐναίρων,
ζωοὺς ἐκ ποταμοῖο δυώδεκα λέξατο κούρους,
ποινὴν Πατρόκλοιο Μενοιτιάδαο θανόντος.
τοὺς ἐξῆγε θύραζε τεθηπότας ἠΰτε νεβροΰς,
δῆσε δ' ὀπίσσω χεῖρας ἐϋτμήτοισιν ἱμᾶσι,   30
τοὺς αὐτοὶ φορέεσκον ἐπὶ στρεπτοῖσι χιτῶσι,
δῶκε δ' ἑταίροισιν κατάγειν κοίλας ἐπὶ νῆας.

But when his hands grew weary with killing, he selected twelve living young men from the river, as payment for the death of Patroclus, son of Menoetius. He drove them, dazed like fawns, on to the bank and bound their hands behind their backs with fine-cut leather thongs that they wore on their woven tunics, and he turned them over to his companions to take to the hollow ships.

The scene is used as a model for Aeneas' behaviour when he hears of the death of Pallas (10.510–20):

Nec iam fama mali tanti, sed certior auctor
advolat Aeneae tenui discrimine leti
esse suos, versis tempus succurrere Teucris.
proxima quaeque metit gladio latumque per agmen
ardens limitem agit ferro, te, Turne, superbum
caede nova quaerens. Pallas, Euander, in ipsis
omnia sunt oculis, mensae quas advena primas
tunc adiit, dextraeque datae. Sulmone creatos
quattuor hic iuvenes, totidem quos educat Ufens,
viventis rapit, inferias quos immolet umbris
captivoque rogi perfundat sanguine flammas.

No longer is there just a rumour of so terrible a disaster, but a trustier messenger flies up to Aeneas: his men are only a hair's breadth from death, it is time to assist the Trojans who have been put to flight. He lays low everything within reach of his sword and, raging, drives a broad lane with the steel through the enemy line, seeking you, Turnus, arrogant from your latest slaughter. Pallas, Evander are the only things he sees before his eyes, the hospitality that first greeted him as a stranger, the right hands joined in solemn pledge. Four young men begotten of Sulmo, the same number brought up by Ufens he takes alive to sacrifice as an offering to the shades and to soak the flames of the pyre with their captive blood.

Then follows the killing of Magus (521–36) modelled—but in a skillfully abbreviated form—on the account of Achilles' refusal to spare the life of Lycaon, which immediately succeeds the taking of the sacrificial captives (*Iliad* 21.34–135). The structural connexion between the episodes is clear, and the Homeric situation must be reckoned to be active here in the text of the *Aeneid*.

What it does is to bring out to the full, in authorial comment with the poet entering his own text in apostrophe (514), the irony of Turnus' view of himself as an Achilles. It is Aeneas who is Achilles, and this connexion forshadows the final moments of the epic. But the poet also invites the reader to measure the distance between Aeneas and Achilles.

When Patroclus is killed, Ajax orders Menelaus to search the battlefield for Antilochus, son of Nestor, and to give him the task of taking the news to Achilles (*Iliad* 17.651–701). Achilles has a presentiment of bad news (18.1–14) but collapses when Antilochus tells him, and his hands have to be held to prevent his committing suicide (15–35). He mourns so extravagantly that Thetis hears him, comes, and promises him new armour (35–147). The whole episode is an elaborate scene of mourning, self-reproach, regret, self-abasement, and threats. Achilles can do nothing (except shout) since he cannot wear anyone else's armour.

This lengthy, self-indulgent scene is transformed into a few lines in the *Aeneid*. Nothing is made of the news-bringing (510–12). Aeneas immediately makes for Turnus (513–15), and the poet leaves the emotion to be expressed in his own brief apostrophe to Turnus. The battle with Turnus had been viewed by Pallas in very particular terms (449–51):

> "aut spoliis ego iam raptis laudabor opimis
> aut leto insigni: sorti pater aequus utrique est.
> tolle minas."

"I shall win fame either for gaining the *spolia opima* or for dying with distinction—my father is ready for either event. Cease your threats."

The important Roman concept here is that of the *spolia opima:* a battle could be decided by single combat between the two commanders. If the Roman won, he was awarded the *spolia opima;* it happened only three times in Roman history. But it is this concept that puts Turnus under such moral pressure to fight Aeneas—a pressure equally felt by Aeneas. The moral pressure felt by Aeneas throughout the last two books is, consequently, not primarily the Homeric one of vengeance; it is the sense that he can assume the whole burden of the war. Pallas should not have taken—or been allowed to take—that duty upon himself, since he was only the subordinate commander of his own troops. The duty was Aeneas', and it is that particular recognition of his duty that sends him immediately searching for Turnus. Achilles reproached himself for allowing Patroclus to take his place. He was the best fighter on the Greek side and it was anger that kept him in his tent while Patroclus risked his life. The situation is similar to that between Aeneas and Pallas, but it is also significantly different in its inclusion of the Roman concept of the surrogate single combat.

And there is another Roman element in the immediate situation. The poet describes no emotion in Aeneas; he only gives a concrete account of his thoughts (515–17). That account points directly back to a very important scene. Evander had the good idea that Aeneas should lead the forces of Etruria, who are awaiting a leader designated by fate. Evander explained that he himself was too old; then he said (8.511–19):

> "tu, cuius et annis
> et generi fata indulgent, quem numina poscunt,
> ingredere, o Teucrum atque Italum fortissime ductor.
> hunc tibi praeterea, spes et solacia nostri,
> Pallanta adiungam; sub te tolerare magistro
> militiam et grave Martis opus, tua cernere facta
> adsuescat, primis et te miretur ab annis.
> Arcadas huic equites bis centum, robora pubis
> lecta dabo, totidemque suo tibi munere Pallas."

"You, whose years and descent are favoured by fate, and whom the gods demand, go forward, bravest commander of both Trojans and Italians. Besides I shall send Pallas here, my one hope and consolation, along with you. Let him learn under your tutelage to endure warfare and the grim work of Mars and to watch how you behave; I want him to model himself on you from his earliest years. I shall give him two hundred Arcadian cavalry, the chosen flower of our young manhood, and Pallas shall give you the same number in his own name."

Soon after this Evander bids a very emotional farewell to his son, collapses at the end, and has to be carried indoors (572–84). There is no Homeric model for this dramatic situation. The closest analogue is the scene in Apollonius Rhodius' *Argonautica* where Lycus sends his own son to accompany the Argonauts (2.799–805):

> τῷ νῦν ἥντιν' ἐγὼ τῖσαι χάριν ἄρκιός εἰμι,
> τίσω προφρονέως. ἦ γὰρ θέμις ἠπεδανοῖσιν   800
> ἀνδράσιν, εὖτ' ἄρξωσιν ἀρείονες ἄλλοι ὀφέλλειν.
> ξυνῇ μὲν πάντεσσιν ὁμόστολον ὔμμιν ἕπεσθαι
> Δάσκυλον ὀτρυνέω, ἐμὸν υἱέα· τοῖο δ' ἰόντος,
> ἥ τ' ἂν ἐυξείνοισι διὲξ ἁλὸς ἀντιάοιτε
> ἀνδράσιν, ὄφρ' αὐτοῖο ποτὶ στόμα Θερμώδοντος.   805

"Whatever kindness in recompense I can pay, I shall pay gladly. For that is the law for weak men when stronger men begin to help them. So I am ordering my son Dascylus to go along with all of you in your company. With him accompanying you, you will find that all men are well-disposed to you all along the sea-coast right to the mouth of the river Thermodon itself."

The difference between this situation and that in the *Aeneid* is clear. Lycus sends his son as a way of thanking the Argonauts for their services to him, and his son will be of considerable assistance to them. But Evander sends his son with Aeneas for the benefit of his son: it is Aeneas who can help him, not the reverse. In fact, the poet is here making use of the Roman practice of *contubernium*, whereby an aristocratic father would put his son in the care of an army commander on active service; the young man would live in the general's tent and learn the business of war from him; the general would be in loco parentis to him for the period of his service. What Evander does is to entrust Pallas to Aeneas as his *contubernalis*. A picture of this relationship in action is given in 10.159–62:

> hic magnus sedet Aeneas secumque volutat
> eventus belli varios, Pallasque sinistro
> adfixus lateri iam quaerit sidera, opacae
> noctis iter, iam quae passus terraque marique.

Here sits great Aeneas and turns over in his mind the varied happenings in the war, and Pallas, glued to his left side, questions him at one time about the stars and their course through the dark night, at another about all his experiences both by land and by sea.

A son—that is what Pallas has become, and the fact is signalled by the use of the patronymic as Aeneas receives Pallas from Evander (8.521) *Aeneas Anchisiades* (the same patronymic later indicates his remorse at killing Lausus, so loyal to his father Mezentius—10.822). What Pallas is doing on the voyage is what the child in *Eclogue* 4 will do when he can read (26–27):

> at simul heroum laudes et facta parentis
> iam legere et quae sit poteris cognoscere virtus.

But as soon as you will be able to read about the famous deeds of the heroes and the exploits of your father and come to know the real nature of courage. . . .

But Pallas has the advantage of being tutored by a hero. The same advantage and the same advice are given to Aeneas' son in 12.438–40, where Aeneas specifically adds the protection (436–37) that he failed to give

Pallas. This is the other element in Aeneas' emotions when he hears that Pallas has been killed by Turnus: not the regret and remorse of Achilles but the sense of a solemn duty neglected—he had allowed himself to be drawn away by the battle and to forget his obligation of protecting Pallas and initiating him in warfare. It was Aeneas' duty both to fight Turnus and to look after Pallas: he had neglected both. Aeneas, then, is deliberately linked by the poet with Achilles, but in order to draw out the differences between them, by making the text of the *Iliad* active in the text of the *Aeneid*.

But, this distance from Achilles once established, the poet proceeds to approximate them again both in the theme of human sacrifice and in Aeneas' behaviour. For Aeneas, frustrated by his inability to reach Turnus, embarks on an orgy of killing that is worthy of Achilles himself and echoes Homeric details in many respects. There are two other such reversions by Aeneas to heroic standards of behaviour. The first occurs when he sees that the Greeks have taken Troy and virtually destroyed it (2.314–17):

> "arma amens capio; nec sat rationis in armis,
> sed glomerare manum bello et concurrere in arcem
> cum sociis ardent animi; furor iraque mentem
> praecipitat, pulchrumque mori succurrit in armis."

"Out of my mind, I take up arms; and yet there is no real sense in arms, but my spirits are afire to collect a band for fighting and join with comrades in occupying the citadel. Madness and rage hurl down reason and the beauty of death in battle fills my mind."

The marks of the condition are absence of reason and excess of *furor* and *ira*—a man cannot kill without the latter.[10] Aeneas comes to his senses when he is deserted and alone after witnessing the murder of Priam (559–66) and when, after Venus has opened his eyes to the divine level of explanation (604–23), he can see the reality for himself (624–33). The *furor* recurs when Anchises refuses to budge (671–79), but is then dissipated by Anchises' recognition of omens that recommend departure. It recurs again when Creusa is lost (735–70), but finally disappears when Creusa's spirit appears and reveals a goal beyond Troy that is decreed by Fate (771–95). What is shown happening here is that a man who has a mind capable of and receptive to ideas beyond pride in self and fame still keeps

---

10. See Index s.v. *"furor* and *ira,"* and Thornton (1976), appendix A.

reverting to the heroic ideal of self-aggrandizment and glory achieved through slaughter when he is frustrated by external events from following the course he senses as his duty.

That essentially non-heroic sense of duty (*pietas*) is made objective in this context by a remarkable dream (2.268–97):

> "Tempus erat quo prima quies mortalibus aegris
> incipit et dono divum gratissima serpit.
> in somnis, ecce, ante oculos maestissimus Hector   270
> visus adesse mihi largosque effundere fletus,
> raptatus bigis ut quondam, aterque cruento
> pulvere perque pedes traiectus lora tumentis.
> ei mihi, qualis erat, quantum mutatus ab illo
> Hectore qui redit exuvias indutus Achilli,   275
> vel Danaum Phrygios iaculatus puppibus ignis;
> squalentem barbam et concretos sanguine crinis
> vulneraque illa gerens, quae circum plurima muros
> accepit patrios. ultro flens ipse videbar
> compellare virum et maestas expromere voces: 280
> 'o lux Dardaniae, spes o fidissima Teucrum,
> quae tantae tenuere morae? quibus Hector ab oris
> exspectate venis? ut te post multa tuorum
> funera, post varios hominumque urbisque labores
> defessi aspicimus! quae causa indigna serenos   285
> foedavit vultus? aut cur haec vulnera cerno?'
> ille nihil, nec me quaerentem vana moratur,
> sed graviter gemitus imo de pectore ducens,
> 'heu fuge, nate dea, teque his' ait 'eripe flammis.
> hostis habet muros; ruit alto a cumine Troia.   290
> sat patriae Priamoque datum: si Pergama dextra
> defendi possent, etiam hac defensa fuissent.
> sacra suosque tibi commendat Troia penatis;
> hos cape fatorum comites, his moenia quaere
> magna, pererrato statues quae denique ponto.'   295
> sic ait et manibus vittas Vestamque potentem
> aeternumque adytis effert penetralibus ignem."

"It was the time when the beginning of peacefulness commences for wretched mortals and by the kindness of the gods creeps over them most delightfully. Suddenly, then, in a dream right before my eyes I saw Hector present himself to me most mournfully and pour out a flood of tears, as he had been once after being dragged by the chariot, blackened with bloody dust and his swollen feet pierced with thongs. Alas! what a sight he was, how changed from that Hector who came back clad in the armour stripped from Achilles or after throwing Trojan fire on the Greek ships. His beard was filthy and his hair matted with blood and he had those many many wounds that he had received defending his ancestral walls. It appeared to me that I spoke to him first, weeping myself, and that I poured out sad words (280): 'O salvation of Troy, o most reliable hope of us Trojans, what has delayed you for so long? From what shores, so long looked for, do you come? How glad we are to see you, wearied as we are after many deaths among your people, after varied disasters both to our men and to our city! What cruel cause has disfigured your calm countenance? And why do I see these wounds?' He said nothing in answer nor did he heed my foolish questions, but drew deep sighs from the bottom of his lungs: 'Alas! make your escape, son of a goddess, and save yourself from the flames. The enemy occupies our walls; Troy is collapsing from its tallest towers (290). Your duty to the fatherland and to Priam has been discharged; if Troy could have been defended by a sword-arm, it would still have been defended by mine. To you Troy entrusts its sacred objects and its Penates: take these to accompany you in your destiny; for these seek a city, a great city which you shall found after you traverse the whole ocean.' So he spoke and in his hands he brought out from the innermost shrine Vesta in whom power resides, with her garlands, and the everlasting fire.''

Dreams in Homer and Virgil are usually mere repetitions of real life: that is, they are narrative devices that function in the immediate context. That is true even of the remarkable dreams that Dido experiences when she realises that Aeneas is going to leave her (4.465–72); the poet does not describe them but simply lists a series of visions. The function of those dreams is to show Dido's state of mind and the extent of her sufferings. But the vision of Aeneas in Book 2 has no function in the context. He does not even wake up till later (302), and he then only slowly discovers that the Greeks have captured Troy. Here is a duplicated motivation: the dream could have revealed the truth to Aeneas, but the poet does not use it in that way; instead he allows the physical reality around the sleeping man to make a gradual impact on him. This is somewhat like the duplicated motivation later in the same book (604–23 and 624–33) where Venus opens Aeneas' eyes to an explanation on the divine level but it does not have a physical effect on him;[11] instead the poet shows Aeneas affected by the actual physical ruin taking place all around him. This analogy shows that the experience represented by the dream is on a different level from that of ordinary reality and that the level on which it operates is analogous to that of the gods. What Aeneas describes is an authentic mystical experience, and it is marked as authentic by the sharp dichotomy

11. See pp. 24–25 above.

between fantasy and reality. In his description, lines 272–73 are authorial comment, or rather (since Aeneas is the "author" here), an explanatory comment that derives from hindsight. In reality Aeneas knows that Hector is long since dead, but in his dream he does not know that. In reality he knows what the disfigurements on Hector mean, but he has no idea in his dream. He thinks that Hector has been delayed for a long time from reaching Troy. This authenticating dichotomy between the fantasy of the dream and reality is parallel to the dichotomy between the *quies* that is so enjoyable and the reality outside which only gradually breaks through sleep to Aeneas after the dream is over.

This highly authentic dream functions as the first indication (chronologically, not textually) of the fundamental difference between Aeneas and the usual heroic character: Aeneas has a sense of mission that transcends his own personality, and it is to his devotion to the goal that lies outside himself that his reputation for *pietas* is owed. The dichotomy between dream and reality here is maintained after the dream has ended so that Aeneas' reaction to the Greek treachery can be conventionally heroic (and so realistic). The two levels of his being, as it were, are drawn together in the scene with his goddess-mother and again in the scene with the ghost of his dead wife, but they are not united so that the goal becomes a reasonable object in real life until some way into Book 3. These two books lay the foundation for the poet's exploration of the psychology of a new type of man in the heroic world, and what the poet shows in this early stage is Aeneas' realisation of the power of that inner vision. Then the first really serious test of his *pietas* comes with his love of Dido and the temptation to stay in Carthage.

The final occasion on which Aeneas goes berserk in conventional heroic style is recounted in Book 12. Turnus has been running away from him after promising to fight, the treaty has been broken again, and Aeneas has just recovered from being treacherously wounded. His indignation is expressed in his words to Latinus (579–82):

> ipse inter primos dextram sub moenia tendit
> Aeneas, magnaque incusat voce Latinum
> testaturque deos iterum se ad proelia cogi,
> bis iam Italos hostis, haec altera foedera rumpi.

Aeneas himself in the front line extends his right hand to the walls and at the top of his voice indicts Latinus and calls on the gods to witness that he is for a second time being compelled to fight, that for a second time the Italians are his enemies and that this is the second treaty that is being broken.

But it takes a long time for Aeneas' anger to be roused. He recovers from his wound (383–429), arms himself (430–32), addresses his own epitaph to his son (435–40), and rushes out to battle (441–45). Turnus and the Italians are terrified (446–50), and Aeneas collects the Trojans and leads them into battle (451–63). But Aeneas does not kill (12.464–67):

> ipse neque aversos dignatur sternere morti
> nec pede congressos aequo nec tela ferentis
> insequitur: solum densa in caligine Turnum
> vestigat lustrans, solum in certamina poscit.

He does not deign to lay low in death either those who turn from him or those who meet him foot to foot nor does he pursue those who brandish weapons; Turnus alone in the dense cloud ⟨of battle⟩ he tracks down while scouring the ground, him alone he demands to fight with.

The motive of Aeneas is to settle the war by single combat with Turnus (that was the substance of his promise to Ascanius—436–37); otherwise he avoids fighting. The poet shows this resolve breaking down as Juturna succeeds in keeping Turnus well out of the way (468–85). Aeneas is baffled and frustrated (12.486–87):

> heu, quid agat? vario nequiquam fluctuat aestu,
> diversaeque vocant animum in contraria curae.

Alas! what is he to do? He is vainly tossed on a shifting tide ⟨of anxiety⟩ and different preoccupations draw his heart in opposite directions.

At this moment Messapus treacherously attacks him from a distance with a spear-throw; he hits Aeneas' helmet and Aeneas loses his temper (12.494–99):

> tum vero adsurgunt irae, insidiisque subactus,
> diversos ubi sensit equos currumque referri,
> multa Iovem et laesi testatus foederis aras
> iam tandem invadit medios et Marte sucundo
> terribilis saevam nullo discrimine caedem
> suscitat, irarumque omnis effundit habenas.

Then finally his anger was aroused and, compelled by the treacherous attack (after he realised the horses and chariot were being driven in the opposite direction), calling often on Juppiter to witness and the altars of the violated treaty, he finally charged into the midst of the enemy and, terrifying in his success, he stirred up a pitiless and indiscriminate slaughter and flung off all restraint to his rage.

The poet has shown Aeneas' high sense of duty and purpose being gradually eroded by frustration until at last he reverts to the natural state of the Homeric hero. The poet condemns what follows, in his own voice (500–04), treating it as a form of civil war (12.503–04):

> tanton placuit concurrere motu,
> Iuppiter, aeterna gentis in pace futuras?

Was it your decision, Juppiter, that peoples destined to live in eternal peace should clash in an uprising of such magnitude?

What follows is slaughter on a Homeric scale, with the poet noting first killing by Aeneas (505), then by Turnus (509), both introduced by name but thereafter taken up in a series of alternating movements by *ille* (Aeneas) and *hic* (Turnus). In the midst of this the poet links both men uniquely in the same pair of similes (521–26); both are Homeric battle similes, the one of fire started in a parched forest (*Iliad* 11.155–57 and 20.490–92), the other of a river in flood (*Iliad* 4.452–55, 11.492–95, and 16.389–92). The two men are virtually indistinguishable, except in one telling detail: Turnus displays the enjoyment he finds in killing for its own sake (511–12):

> curruque abscisa duorum
> suspendit capita et rorantia sanguine portat.

and cutting off the heads of the pair, he hung them from his chariot and carried them away dripping with blood.

Aeneas kills everyone he meets, with savage anger, but there is no sign that he enjoys it. And soon he regains control of himself sufficiently to devise a tactic to force Turnus to fight him—the attack on the city (554–64); he has again a firm grasp of his real purpose: to end the war by fighting a duel with Turnus. The killing by Aeneas ceases as he tries to force the surrender of the city by agreement (579–82) and, failing, then sets fire to it (587–92). The Homeric hero has once again given way to the new kind of man. He will again become Achilles during the duel and will again give way, when the outcome is decided, to the new kind of man but will end as a modified Achilles.

  We can now return to Aeneas berserk after hearing of the killing of Pallas. The whole scene (10.510–605) is structurally modelled on *Iliad* 21.1–210, and there are many detailed imitations (though there are also many small-scale echoes of other battle scenes in the *Iliad*); this is the scene where Achilles in his new armour goes on an orgy of killing until the river Scamander rises up against him. Aeneas is clearly figured as Achilles, as much in his cruel speeches as in his ruthless killing. There is, however, one touch that measures the distance from Achilles. Aeneas meets the two brothers Liger and Lucagus in their chariot (575–79); Liger promises him immediate death in Italy (580–83—see p. 100 above); Aeneas kills Lucagus without answering (583–90) and then speaks bitterly. The poet introduces his words thus (591): *quem pius Aeneas dictis adfatur amaris:* ("Him the dutiful Aeneas addressed with bitter words"). Here the word *pius* marks that side of Aeneas' character that is not heroic; it recalls not just the devotion to Pallas that was the immediate cause of the slaughter but also the devotion that has brought the Trojans to Italy (treated with contempt in the words of Liger), and it leads to the fact with which the poet concludes this scene. Aeneas has never lost sight of the purpose for which he returned from Etruria—to relieve the besieged garrison of Trojans. The scene ends with these lines (10.602–05):

> talia per campos edebat funera ductor
> Dardanius torrentis aquae vel turbinis atri
> more furens. tandem erumpunt et castra relinquunt
> Ascanius puer et nequiquam obsessa iuventus.

Such deaths the Dardanian leader dealt out over the field, raging like a torrent of water or like a black tornado. Finally Ascanius and the ⟨rest of⟩ the young men, besieged to no purpose, burst forth and abandon the camp.

Achilles had no such tactical purpose in his assault on the enemy, but that aspect of Aeneas is kept alive in the surprising placement of (591) *pius:* even in his battle-rage he is thinking not of himself but of others and of a purpose that lies beyond personal ambition.

At this climax the scene shifts to the divine level and Juno is given permission by Juppiter, in an Iliadic episode, to delay (though not alter) Fate by removing Turnus from the battlefield (see pp. 29–30 above). This episode is followed by a return to the fighting; but now the poet's gaze is on the Italian side and he recounts the slaughter wreaked on the Trojans by Mezentius. The account is Homeric in style, but no single passage of the *Iliad* has been imitated; instead there are echoes of many Homeric scenes, and there are four Homeric battle similes. Mezentius is Virgil's creation, but his character and outlook are typically heroic. The climax, long anticipated, comes when he meets Aeneas. He has been characterised several times (7.648, 8.7) as *contemptor divom* and his speech displays his attitude (10.773–6):

> "dextra mihi deus et telum, quod missile libro,
> nunc adsint! voveo praedonis corpore raptis
> indutum spoliis ipsum te, Lause, tropaeum
> Aeneae."

"Now let my right hand that is my god, and the weapon that I poise to throw, come to my aid. I vow you, Lausus, as a *tropaeum,* over Aeneas, clothed in armour stripped from the body of that bandit."

The blasphemy of worshipping his own right hand is equalled both by the vow and the metaphor of treating his son as a living *tropaeum* because he will wear Aeneas' armour. This theme will recur later in a totally different form. Aeneas is contrasted with him by the single word *pius* (783). But the poet tells of their battle from Mezentius' point of view, until he is wounded and Aeneas is delighted (787 *laetus*) at the sight of his blood and rushes in for the kill. Here Lausus comes forward to protect his father and the poet enters his own text to promise him a memorial in his poem (791–93: see p. 204 below). Aeneas is held off by Lausus and over-whelmed by a storm of spears (796–809). Then he warns Lausus (10.811–12):

> "quo moriture ruis maioraque viribus audes?
> fallit te incautum pietas tua."

"Why are you rushing to your death and daring a feat beyond your strength? Your loyalty is making you rash and leading you astray."

Lausus persists; Aeneas becomes angry and kills him. Then (821–32):

> at vero ut vultum vidit morientis et ora,
> ora modis Anchisiades pallentia miris,
> ingemuit miserans graviter dextramque tetendit,
> et mentem patriae subiit pietatis imago.
> "quid tibi nunc, miserande puer, pro laudibus istis,
> quid pius Aeneas tanta dabit indole dignum?
> arma, quibus laetatus, habe tua; teque parentum
> manibus et cineri, si qua est ea cura, remitto.
> hoc tamen infelix miseram solabere mortem:
> Aeneae magni dextra cadis." increpat ultro
> cunctantis socios·et terra sublevat ipsum
> sanguine turpantem comptos de more capillos.

But when the son of Anchises saw the face of the dying youth and his features tinged with unearthly pallor, he groaned deeply in pity and stretched out his right hand and the picture of his own loyalty to his father came into his mind: "What shall loyal Aeneas now give you, piteous boy, to match such a glorious deed, what shall be given that will be worthy of such a nature as yours? Keep your weapons and armour of which you were proud; and I send you back to the shades and ashes of your ancestors, if that regard means anything to you. This fact, in spite of your disaster, shall console you for your pitiful death: you lie dead by the hand of great Aeneas." He then actually reproved Lausus' friends who held back, and he lifted him up from the ground where blood was staining his well-kempt hair.

The emphasis on *pietas* picks up a theme that has persisted in Aeneas' battle-fury and shares it with an enemy; the patronymic (822) *Anchisiades* points to the analogy with Pallas (8.521: see p. 104 above) and consequently calls attention to the differences between this scene and Turnus' treatment of Pallas, the cause of all (and more) that followed. The scene and the values it expresses are almost totally non-heroic; the one detail that finds a Homeric echo is the refusal to take the weapons as spoils. Andromache recalls in *Iliad* 6.413–20 that when Achilles sacked her city and killed her father, he had such respect for him that he did not strip off his armour but gave him burial. The connexion with Achilles is subtly maintained, but the detail of forbearing to strip the body and giving it burial, uncharacteristic of the Homeric hero and mentioned with surprise by Andromache, is built into a major incident in the Virgilian scene to influence the reader's judgment.

The book ends with Mezentius killed by Aeneas. The tyrant has been presented as totally unsympathetic not only as *contemptor divom* but also as a ruler whose excesses of violence and cruelty brought about his expulsion from his own country (8.481–95); he is a prototype of the Tarquins. Nevertheless, the poet shows a memorable nobility in this hated creature before his death, in a scene that has various minor echoes with very small Iliadic passages but is basically original. The words spoken to his dead son (846–56) are an act of contrition for his past, in which he admits his guilt and repents communicating it to his son. He then addresses his horse (860–66). There are two Homeric precedents for this. In one, Hector urges his horses on to a special effort (*Iliad* 8.184–97). In the other, Achilles reproaches his horses for letting Patroclus be killed (*Iliad* 19.399–403); one of the horses then replies (404–17) and warns Achilles that his own death is drawing near. Neither incident provided Virgil with a model—except for words being addressed to a horse. The noble speech of Mezentius is more of a soliloquy than an address, and the only response from the horse is that he allows Mezentius to mount him (Mezentius would otherwise be unable to move since he has been disabled by his earlier wound). In fact, the poet adapts the Homeric motif to allow Mezentius to speak and to use the horse as addressee in order to express his unwavering opposition to the Trojans (865–66). That makes the end inevitable: Mezentius must die. But the poet does everything to make that death as morally intolerable as possible. The two brief speeches of Mezentius to Aeneas, which express bravery, defiance, disregard of death and the gods, and anguish at his son's death, decisively tip the balance of sympathy in Mezentius' favour. His final speech is especially important (10.900–06):

> "hostis amare, quid increpitas mortemque minaris?
> nullum in caede nefas, nec sic ad proelia veni,
> nec tecum meus haec pepigit mihi foedera Lausus.
> unum hoc per si qua est victis venia hostibus oro:
> corpus humo patiare tegi. scio acerba meorum
> circumstare odia: hunc, oro, defende furorem
> et me consortem nati concede sepulcro."

"Implacable enemy, why mock me and keep threatening death? There is no crime in killing, and I did not come to war on those terms, nor was it conditions like those that my Lausus arranged with you on my behalf. This one request I beg in the name of any humanity felt towards conquered enemies: permit my body to be buried in the earth. I know that the bitter hatred of my people surrounds me: keep that insane fury from me and allow me to share a grave with my son."[12]

This speech, strategically placed at the end of Book 10, is intended as a standard by which to judge the parallel speech of Turnus at the end of Book 12. What the speech does is to express the conditions of war in the twelfth century; they are absolutely accepted by Aeneas and he immediately kills Mezentius. That is, when it comes to war, the only framework of behaviour Aeneas can use is that of the Homeric hero. The moral qualities of Mezentius that emerge in this scene and win sympathy for him underline this fact: the values that good men normally live by are completely subverted by war. This is a constant theme of the poet.[13] Commentators often say, as the latest does: "Virgil does not tell us

---

12. The theme of the tyrant's grave being desecrated by his enraged people has a contemporary echo in the case of Nicias, tyrant of Cos (who was probably deposed immediately after the battle of Actium); the incident was the subject of an epigram by Crinagoras (*Anth. Pal.* 9.81). See Gow and Page (1968), 2:230–31.

13. See pp. 196–99 below.

whether Mezentius' request was granted."[14] But this is a striking difference between Homer and Virgil—perhaps it is really the difference
between oral and literary epic: Virgil trusts a reader to make judgments
where nothing is explicitly said. If there is the slightest temptation to
doubt whether Mezentius was allowed burial, it is totally dispelled in
retrospective judgment by the speech of Aeneas to the Latin delegation
that comes to request a truce to bury the dead (11.106–19). Here Aeneas
exhibits both hatred of war and generosity toward his enemies; there is
nothing of this in the corresponding scene in *Iliad* 7.379–420, and no
doubt is left about the treatment of Mezentius.

There are two further important motifs that carry over from Book 10
to Book 11. The first goes back to 10.517–20 where Aeneas captured eight
young men to sacrifice at the funeral pyre of Pallas. The latest commentator says of the motif:[15] "The passage is based on Hom. *Il.* 21. 27f.,
23.175 f., where the human sacrifice is a horrifying act of barbarity; in the
gentle Virgil it seems worse still. Nothing would have been easier than for
Virgil to omit this ghastly act of Achilles in his reworking of the story;
therefore the fact that he has included it must be accorded its full significance. The anger and passion for vengeance which overwhelms Aeneas is
terrible enough to cause even such an act of savagery as this!" But the
"anger and passion" belong to the battlefield and Aeneas' first hearing
the news of Pallas' death. The poet could have dropped the motif after
that, but he did not. It is picked up again as the procession bearing the
body of Pallas to Evander is formed (11.81–82):

> vinxerat et post terga manus, quos mitteret umbris
> inferias, caeso sparsurus sanguine flammas.

And he had bound behind their backs the hands of those he designed should be
sent as funeral offerings to the shades, intending to sprinkle the flames with their
slaughtered blood.

That is, the poet shows Aeneas continuing in cold blood the act he had
conceived in rage. When Achilles sacrifices young men at the pyre of
Patroclus there is condemnation (*Iliad* 23.173–83):

> ἐννέα τῷ γε ἄνακτι τραπεζῆες κύνες ἦσαν,
> καὶ μὲν τῶν ἐνέβαλλε πυρῇ δύο δειροτομήσας,

---

14. R. D. Williams (1973) on 10.905 (p. 379).
15. Ibid. on 10.519 (p. 356).

δώδεκα δὲ Τρώων μεγαθύμων υἱέας ἐσθλοὺς   175
χαλκῷ δηϊόων· κακὰ δὲ φρεσὶ μήδετο ἔργα·
ἐν δὲ πυρὸς μένος ἧκε σιδήρεον, ὄφρα νέμοιτο.
ᾤμωξέν τ' ἄρ' ἔπειτα, φίλον δ' ὀνόμηνεν ἑταῖρον·
"χαῖρέ μοι, ὦ Πάτροκλε, καὶ εἰν Ἀΐδαο δόμοισι·
πάντα γὰρ ἤδη τοι τελέω τὰ πάροιθεν ὑπέστην.   180
δώδεκα μὲν Τρώων μεγαθύμων υἱέας ἐσθλοὺς
τοὺς ἅμα σοὶ πάντας πῦρ ἐσθίει· Ἕκτορα δ' οὔ τι
δώσω Πριαμίδην πυρὶ δαπτέμεν, ἀλλὰ κύνεσσιν."

The prince [Patroclus] had nine dogs that attended his table; two of them he [Achilles] flung on the pyre after slitting their throats and twelve fine sons of great-heared Trojans, killing them with the sword—it was an evil deed that he conceived in his mind. Then he let loose the steely power of fire to feed upon them. Thereafter he groaned and called his dear friend by name: "All hail, I say, Patroclus, even in the halls of Hades. Now I am bringing to pass all the things that I promised you: twelve fine sons of great-hearted Trojans, all of whom the fire is consuming together with you; but Hector, son of Priam, I shall not give to the fire to consume, but to the dogs."

Here the poet's parenthetical comment condemns the cold-blooded slaughter. There is no such condemnation in the *Aeneid*. But there is a difference. Achilles slaughters dogs and human beings alike with his own hand. The poet keeps Aeneas away from the funeral of Pallas in words that express Aeneas' hatred of war (11.96–98):

> 'nos alias hinc ad lacrimas eadem horrida belli
> fata vocant: salve aeternum mihi, maxime Palla,
> aeternumque vale.'

"The same grim destiny of war calls us away to different tears. Hail for ever, I say, great Pallas, and forever farewell."

Aeneas is kept away by the necessity to conduct the funerals of his own men. What this motif signifies is that the poet deliberately represents Aeneas as conforming, in his guise as Achilles, to a barbaric twelfth-century ritual; though, equally deliberately he shows him as not participating personally in that ritual. When it comes to war, Aeneas is capable of becoming like everyone else and has only one pattern of behaviour.

However, that pattern can be varied, and this is what the other motif shows. At the beginning of Book 11 Aeneas is shown paying the gods "their dues" (4 *vota deum*), and especially he uses the armour of

Mezentius to construct a *tropaeum* (5). This custom was not Homeric,[16] but it passed from later Greek practice to Rome; and here Aeneas is again anticipating a practice of later Romans. The motif contrasts sharply with the behaviour of others: with Mezentius' grandiose metaphor of making Lausus a living *tropaeum* of victory over Aeneas (10.773–76) as much as with Turnus' greedy self-aggrandizement (10.495–500). The act of Aeneas is precisely *pietas* in action—that devotion to the gods which later Romans thought responsible for their universal military success throughout the world.[17] The normal heroic instinct was to strip loot from a dead enemy as personal gain and adornment. But the poet's explicit condemnation, in general terms of the type of action represented by what Turnus did, calls attention to a moral theme of some importance. The idea that restraint should be observed in success (10.502) is not heroic and condemns not only Turnus but, retrospectively, Euryalus (and Nisus, to some extent). His preoccupation with loot not only caused fatal delay (9.359–66) and is the object of reproval by Nisus (9.354–55), but his wearing of the looted helmet gives him away to the enemy in the dark. Prospectively, Camilla is also condemned; for it is her interest in loot as she concentrates on an unworthy enemy distinguished only for the richness of his apparel (11.768–806), that provides Arruns with the opportunity to kill her. The poet enters the text to condemn her (11.778–82):

> hunc virgo, sive ut templis praefigeret arma
> Troia, captivo sive ut se ferret in auro
> venatrix, unum ex omni certamine pugnae
> caeca sequebatur totumque incauta per agmen
> femineo praedae et spoliorum ardebat amore.

The girl, whether to dedicate Trojan equipment in the temples or to parade herself as a huntress in looted gold, blindly pursued him over the whole of the battlefield and, unguardedly along the length of the battle-line, was on fire with a female lust for loot and spoils. . . .

Here the possibility of temple-dedication is half-hearted and immediately subverted in the outspoken comment on Camilla's foolish lust.[18]

16. Quite different is the incident at *Iliad* 10.458–68, where Odysseus holds up the spoils stripped from Dolon to Athene for her to appreciate as he asks for her further help; he then hides them in a bush and marks them so that he and Diomedes will not miss them in the dark when they return. He intends them as an offering to Athene (570–71).

17. See Cicero *de natura deorum* 2.8 and the various parallels collected by A. S. Pease (1958), ad loc. For Horatian expression of the concept, see Williams (1969), pp. 44, 63.

18. Numanus considers Italian greed for loot as a virtue—9.612–13.

A moral viewpoint is expressed in these passages that contradicts the heroic ideal of self-aggrandizement, and they provide the means for judging Aeneas. He is again in this motif presented as a new kind of man in the twelfth century, whose values anticipate Roman history. The contrast with Camilla is particularly emphasized when Aeneas kills the priest Haemonides, whose apparel is magnificent (like that of Camilla's intended victim); Serestus takes away his armour for Aeneas to set up a *tropaeum* to Mars (10.537–42). The small incident is a thematic anticipation of the much more important episode with Mezentius' armour, and symbolizes that *pietas* which is a part of Aeneas' nature even when circumstances compel him into the conventional heroic role.

What happens in the second half of the *Aeneid*, then, is that the poet makes continuous use of the figure of Achilles and a whole range of Iliadic episodes (many of which are related to Achilles, though some are not) to measure the distance between the greatest of Homeric heroes and the new type of twelfth-century man that the poet has conceived as the progenitor of the Roman state. In the first six books the same effect is achieved by using the figure of Odysseus and a range of episodes from the *Odyssey*. The distance between Aeneas and Odysseus is much easier to measure than that between Aeneas and Achilles. This is largely because the essentially Homeric character of the battles that occupy most of the last six books compels Aeneas into a much more sustained approximation to Achilles compared with the distance that is constantly measured from Odysseus on the single central issue of purpose. Odysseus travels in the hope of reaching home, but he is also a born traveller with an interest in the exotic for its own sake and a readiness to be prodigal with time: he spends a year with Circe feasting and enjoying the delights she has to offer;[19] he spends seven years with Calypso (though more reluctantly). There is nothing in Odysseus corresponding to what Aeneas describes as the compulsion of Fate that makes him search through constant hardships for the designated site of the future state. The likeness consists in the inner driving force, the sense of a goal—well known in the case of Odysseus, unknown but increasingly clearly apprehended in the case of Aeneas; the contrast is largely between the characteristically heroic self-centredness of Odysseus and the *pietas* of Aeneas, the devotion to others (including unborn generations).

That concern for others appears in various ways: for instance, Aeneas after the storm puts a brave face on things and speaks encour-

19. *Odyssey* 10.466–71.

agingly (1.198–207) but conceals his serious worries (208–09). The speech is modelled on one of Odysseus (12.208–12), with telling variations, and the dissimulation of feeling, not intended to deceive[20] but in the interest of others, measures the distance from Odysseus. Again, when Odysseus' companions are seduced by lotus-eating into forgetting the bringing of news and the returning home (*Odyssey* 9.95), he has them seized, dragged back to the ships, and chained there (9.98–102). However, in the parallel incident in Sicily where the women burn the ships so that there may be no more sea-voyaging, Aeneas falls into despair but is persuaded to found a settlement for the disaffected that will one day be the historical city of Segesta, an ally of Rome (*Aeneid* 5.700–18 and 746–61). Here the interests of the disaffected are served; but also, by means of the revelations made by Anchises to Aeneas in a dream (719–45), the connexion of the settle-ment with Aeneas' sense of destiny, as well as with the past history of Troy and the future history of Rome, is made clear. The distance from Odysseus is even greater when Aeneas leaves Dido and the reader thinks of Calypso; Odysseus has spent every day (apparently) of seven years weeping on the sea-shore, longing to go home. As in the time spent with Circe and the leaving of her after a year, sexual pleasure is casually treated as pleasant but unimportant. There is nothing of the tension found in *Aeneid* 4 between Love (sexual pleasure is hardly mentioned) and Aeneas' sense of destiny.

Finally, the distance is easily measured (and the similarities taken into account) between the experiences of Odysseus and Aeneas in their very different (yet at times oddly similar) Underworlds. At all of these and at many other points, Aeneas is being defined through similarities and contrasts with Odysseus. The unusual quality of this new man of the twelfth century is now and again startlingly brought out, as in his words to Dido implying that, in spite of the gods, one's real reward comes from the sense of having done right (1.603–05).[21] There is nothing like this in Homer; it is characteristic of the frontier spirit of a man trying to create a new society and recognising in Dido a kindred spirit.

20. As is Dido's motive at 4.477.
21. See p. 15 above.

PART II
THE POINT OF VIEW

The aim of Part II is to analyse various techniques used by the poet to communicate a point of view that does not emerge immediately from the surface of the narrative. The techniques examined here are sometimes techniques of indirection, by which the poet says one thing but at the same time means something else. A technique of major importance in this respect is what I have called "the objective framework,"[1] whereby the poet connects with the surface of his texts another field, or series of fields, of ideas; these are linked to the primary field generally by modes of contiguity, though the mode may at times be one of similarity. The relationship between the two fields is consequently synecdochic, and the reader is left to apprehend the secondary field, and to some extent to reconstruct it, by means of indexes of proportionality. The technique is closely modelled on the procedures that Virgil had already used in *Eclogues* and *Georgics*, but they are here adapted to the great increase in scale in epic. Another technique that is used to allow a point of view to come through indirectly from the narrative is that of appearing to permit the poet's own voice to be heard, sometimes by direct intrusion into the narrative, at others by leaving ambiguities to the reader's judgment or by using what seem to be traditional generic features of epic in a way that deliberately raises questions. In these latter techniques the problem of discerning the aspect or the tone of a passage becomes very important, and, given the traditional impersonality of epic, it is not easily solved. For that reason these are potent techniques of poetic indirection. The problem of the way in which what may be called general ideas are somehow incorporated into the weave of the epic and are gradually made evident to a reader will also be considered.

1. See Williams (1980), chap. 7.

6   INDEXES TO OTHER FIELDS (*imitatio vitae*)

Objective framework is the technique to be analysed here. Within the primary or ostensible field constituted by the surface of the text, there are indexes of proportionality that enable a reader to apprehend a secondary field; these indexes function as a means of understanding the relationship of the two fields and even of sensing something of the constitution of the secondary field, at least in outline. Thus the poet, in talking of the primary field, is also to some degree focusing attention on the secondary field.

Epic—at least Virgilian epic—is so complex and extensive a literary form that there is no one unified secondary field; instead, the secondary field changes from one area of the epic to another, though all of the secondary fields are related to one another by associations of contiguity as they all are to the primary field. This fact does not, however, exclude the possibilities that there are also associations of similarity to be recognised in the relationships between the primary and the secondary fields and that these too have been deliberately exploited by the poet.

When the *Aeneid* is viewed in this way, an answer is provided to the old question of the extent to which Aeneas is portrayed by the poet as a symbol of Augustus, and this question will be taken up in a later chapter.[1] It is one aspect of the problematic relationship between events said by the poet to have taken place within less than a decade in the twelfth century, and the events that took place over the whole course of Roman history in general, especially those that belong to the era of Augustus and the Roman world contemporary with the poet.

---

1. Chap. 9.

1. *Indexes from Hellenistic Rococo*

It is exactly that crucial connexion between the epic world of what would ordinarily be regarded as myth and the concrete political realities of the poet's own day that created a particular difficulty for a poet working within the conventional generic forms of epic. How was he to treat scenes in which poetical fantasy was allowed free range? The problem especially concerned scenes that purported to give a factual account of dramatic events among the gods or that showed the divine level intersecting with the human. Many of the latter have already been discussed in chapter 2, "The Gods in the *Aeneid*," and it seems clear that a certain degree of generic licence was claimed by the poet, and that this itself could be regarded as subverting any over-factual interpretation. But a number of passages remain, and the poet, in fact, faced the problem right at the beginning of his epic by introducing two scenes, one exclusively among gods, the other involving active intervention by a god on the human level. Both scenes are treated by the poet with exemplary rhetorical verve and pleasure.[2]

The first portrays Juno's anger at seeing the Trojans happily sailing along (1.34–49). The scene is modelled on that in *Iliad* 14 where Hera tricks Zeus (though Juno's angry speech and its setting also have elements that recall Poseidon's anger in *Odyssey* 5.263–90, when he sees Odysseus sailing his raft away from Calypso). There Hera adorns herself (153–86) and obtains from Aphrodite a special belt that induces love and desire (187–223). Next she bribes the god of Sleep to put Zeus asleep as soon as he takes her in his arms; but Sleep is frightened and refuses the bribe, which Hera has to increase from a chair and footstool to something more enticing (267–69):

> ἀλλ᾽ ἴθ᾽, ἐγὼ δέ κέ τοι Χαρίτων μίαν ὁπλοτεράων
> δώσω ὀπυιέμεναι καὶ σὴν κεκλῆσθαι ἄκοιτιν
> Πασιθέην, ἧς αἰὲν ἐέλδεαι ἤματα πάντα.

"But come, and I shall give you one of the beautiful Graces, Pasitheë, to marry and to call your wife, whom you are always desiring, all the time."

Sleep is attracted by that bribe and agrees. The scene of Zeus' seduction and sleep follows. The account of the gods' behavior is witty and scandalously anthropomorphic.

---

2. The element of poetic fantasy in such passages of drama among the gods has the important function of subverting any literal claims to have truth in the poet's treatment of the divine machinery. See p. 20, no. 8.

This tone is missing in Virgil's account of Juno's approach to Aeolus—except perhaps in the detail that her opening address to him (65) *Aeoli (namque tibi . . .)* uses a prayer-formula. Basically the tone is serious, and Aeolus instantly obeys. What he has been offered is this (71–75):

> "sunt mihi bis septem praestanti corpore Nymphae,
> quarum quae forma pulcherrima, Deiopea,
> conubio iungam stabili propriamque dicabo,
> omnis ut tecum meritis pro talibus annos
> exigat et pulchra faciat te prole parentem."

"I have seven nymphs with lovely bodies, and the most beautiful in figure, Deiopeia, I shall join with you in eternal marriage and shall make her yours, so that for your services to me she may spend all of her time with you and make you the father of handsome children."

This is totally Roman in tone, with solemn phrases that emphasise the dignity of Roman marriage in the old style; and she expresses the basic ideals of Roman marriage—the eternal nature of the bond, the control of the husband, the devotion and obedience of the wife, and the purpose of marriage (for the final line is a poetic rendering of the antique Roman phrase *liberum quaesundorum causa* "for the purpose of begetting children").[3] This passage anticipates an important theme in the epic—the concept of the ideal Roman marriage: it will appear in the portrait of Dido and in the scene between Venus and Vulcan (see below). What the element of Roman reality does in this passage of poetic fantasy is to provide an index that measures the distance from the world of imagination or fantasy (which generic licence makes available to the poet) to the actual world that human beings inhabit. The poet thereby subverts his own account and claims relief from any guarantee of literal truth. The divine drama is to be treated as a trope.

The storm-scene ends with a piece of pure Hellenistic rococo (124–56), as Neptune raises his head above the waves, berates the winds, and then rides magnificently in his chariot over the seas, calming them. Such rococo has its precedent in Homer; for instance, in *Iliad* 13.10–31, where Poseidon is described travelling from Samothrace to Troy. But this type of composition was greatly extended by Hellenistic poets. Here the poet exploits the opportunity for poetic fantasy but provides an index to the world of reality by using the striking simile of a Roman statesman quieting a riotous crowd (148–53: see p. 71 above). This index also func-

---

3. See Williams (1958), pp. 23–25.

tions as a thematic anticipation of the concept of the civil wars that disfigured Virgil's own generation; that concept is a leit-motiv of the epic.

The narrative of *Aeneid* 8 contains the remarkable scene of the seduction of Vulcan by his wife Venus, followed by Vulcan's journey to his
Cyclopean forge under the volcano Aetna (370–453). The Homeric model
for the seduction is once again the seduction of Zeus by Hera in *Iliad* 14;
with that is combined the persuading of Hephaestus by Thetis in *Iliad*
18.369–467 and the opening of the account of the making of the shield
(18.468–82). These various scenes have been totally re-worked by Virgil,
and this is not a case where the models are operative in the new context—
with the exception of one detail. Both scenes in the *Aeneid*—the seduction
of Vulcan and, even more, the portrait of Vulcan's forge—are perfect
examples of Hellenistic rococo: the poet has fully exploited the opportunity for poetic fantasy, especially in the latter scene.

Linking the two scenes is a remarkable simile (407–15):

> Inde ubi prima quies medio iam noctis abactae
> curriculo expulerat somnum, cum femina primum,
> cui tolerare colo vitam tenuique Minerva
> impositum, cinerem et sopitos suscitat ignis
> noctem addens operi, famulasque ad lumina longo
> exercet penso, castum ut servare cubile
> coniugis et possit parvos educere natos:
> haud secus ignipotens nec tempore segnior illo
> mollibus e stratis opera ad fabrilia surgit.

Then when the first quiet of night, her chariot now beyond the midpoint of her
course, had driven off sleep, at the very time when a lady, on whom has been
imposed the burden of making life bearable by spinning and fine-drawn weaving,
rakes the ashes and damped fires to life, adding night to her working hours, and
sets the maidservants to their long work by the firelight, so that she may preserve
chaste her husband's bed and bring up her small children: in the very same way
and no later in time than she, the Lord of Fire rose from his soft bed to his
craftsman's work.

The simile has predecessors in Homer and Apollonius Rhodius. The Homeric analogue is very remote. The battle of Trojans and Greeks is as
evenly balanced "as when an honest working-woman holds up a weigh-
ing-scales, balancing the weight and the wool on either side so that she
may gain a wretched pittance for her children" (*Iliad* 12.433–35). There is
little in common here except the hard labour and the wish to benefit
children. There are two analogues in Apollonius Rhodius. In the first, the
sudden blaze of love in Medea's heart is compared to a fire (*Argonautica*
3.291–95):

ὡς δὲ γυνὴ μαλερῷ περὶ κάρφεα χεύατο δαλῷ
χερνῆτις, τῇπερ ταλασήια ἔργα μέμηλεν,
ὥς κεν ὑπωρόφιον νύκτωρ σέλας ἐντύναιτο,
ἄγχι μάλ᾽ ἐγρομένη· τὸ δ᾽ ἀθέσφατον ἐξ ὀλίγοιο
δαλοῦ ἀνεγρόμενον σὺν κάρφεα πάντ᾽ ἀμαθύνει·   295

As a working woman, whose preoccupation is with the spinning of wool, heaps dry tinder round a burning log so that she may provide a light at night under her roof, after waking up very early; and an extraordinary flame aroused from the little log consumes all the tinder together . . .

The second simile also concerns Medea. She is in Phaeacia but is afraid of a deputation of Colchians; in spite of assurances by the warriors that they will protect her, she cannot sleep (4.1062–65):

οἷον ὅτε κλωστῆρα γυνὴ ταλαεργὸς ἑλίσσει
ἐννυχίη· τῇ δ᾽ ἀμφὶ κινύρεται ὀρφανὰ τέκνα
χηροσύνη πόσιος· σταλάει δ᾽ ὑπὸ δάκρυ παρειὰς
μνωομένης, οἵη μιν ἐπὶ σμυγερὴ λάβεν αἶσα·   1065

As when a wool-working woman whirls her spindle through the night; and around her weep her children orphaned because she is widowed of her husband. A tear drips down her cheek as she reflects how dreary a lot has overtaken her.

There are touches of all three similes in the Virgilian figure. The Homeric treatment shares with that in *Argonautica* 3 the figure of the working-woman (the same word is used in both—χερνῆτις). In the later simile of Apollonius, there is little sense of the woman's status; and in Virgil (408) *femina* by itself suggests a woman of respectable status, and only she—of these epic working-women—has maidservants to help her. In Virgil, then, the portrait is of a woman who lives in a house of some substance. There can be no doubt whatever, even apart from *Argonautica* 4.1062–65, that the reader must understand her to be a widow. What is entirely new in Virgil is the moral judgment implied in (412) *castum . . . cubile*. The concept expressed here is purely Roman; it is the ideal of the *univira* who regards herself as still married to her dead husband—Dido's attitude as she expresses it in *Aeneid* 4.24–29 and 552 is paradigmatic. Another marriage is an unthinkable (as *in-castum*) as prostitution. In the Roman context, the wool-working, too, has the symbolic significance of virtuous toil.

This simile, therefore, is a clear index of proportionality that measures the distance from poetic fantasy to a Roman reality that was of particular importance at the time Virgil was writing, since Augustus was trying to bring back these ideals of marriage by legislation. But the simile also works powerfully within its context. The similarities with Vulcan reside in the early hour of rising and the urgency to be at work, and the simile also anticipates in its mention of the woman's maidservants the spectacular helpers that figure in the subsequent description of Vulcan's forge. But there is one further significant detail. Vulcan is like the hard-working woman and, by implication, he shares her virtue; but the bed from which he rises is very different from her *castum . . . cubile*. He rises (415) *mollibus e stratis* and from the side of a very different woman. Venus has actually urged her request for arms for Aeneas with the words (383) *genetrix nato* "a mother for her son"; but that mother is Vulcan's wife, yet he is not the father—that was Anchises. Venus' use of her charms to win over Vulcan is described in words that underline deception: (393) *sensit laeta dolis et formae conscia coniunx* "his wife perceived it [Vulcan's sexual interest], rejoicing in her deceit and keenly aware of her physical charms." Finally, when Vulcan says that she could have got the request earlier while Troy still stood (396) *similis si cura fuisset* "if your interest had been the same," the words are ambiguous between Venus' interest in her request and in her husband. Venus is no honest woman; her bed is not chaste; and her life is luxurious. She is unlike both the woman in the simile and her own husband; but both the simile and the portrait of Vulcan make a significant thematic connexion with the earlier scene in which the frugal, honest, virtuous life of Evander and his people were portrayed (306–69).

One of the purest pieces of Hellenistic rococo is the transformation of the ships in *Aeneid* 9.77–122. Conington says of this incident:[4]

At the opening of the attack a portent occurs, the transformation of the Trojan ships into sea-nymphs, just at the moment when they are threatened with con-flagration. This as Sir G. C. Lewis remarks, is evidently an echo of the story in the Fifth Book, the burning of the ships by the Trojan women. Virgil was doubtless glad to put the legend to a double use, whether the form which it takes on this second occasion was invented by him or borrowed from tradition. In any case he was likely to regard the metamorphosis as part of the supernatural machinery which is an epic poet's property. Even in Servius' time however the incident provoked question as being without precedent: and modern criticism will be more disposed to account for it than to justify it.

The reference here to the burning of the ships in Book 5 is hardly relevant. What does need to be recognized is that there is no sign that the transfor-mation of the ships was in the legend before Virgil's time, and it may be assumed that he deliberately invented it. Servius comments adversely on

4. Introduction to Book 9.

the incident (on line 81): "Although this is a poetic fiction, it is nevertheless condemned by critics because it lacks precedent: for that reason it is excused by a long introduction. For the reason why ⟨the poet⟩ says that the transformation of ships into nymphs was accomplished in a way to be explained by early religion and the kindness of Juppiter was to enable it to have verisimilitude to some extent." By "long introduction" he means lines 77–79, and he is worried by the incident's lack of verisimilitude, in spite of the fact that (as he shows in his comments on line 78) the "long introduction" can be interpreted in a way that dissociates the poet from any claim to verismilitude.[5] The latest editor says:[6]

This is the most incongruous episode in the whole *Aeneid,* and has been censured from the time of Servius onwards . . . the Argo and the Phaeacians belong wholly to a heroic world, in contrast with Aeneas' fleet which is entering a proto-Roman world. Virgil is aware of this incongruity when he says (line 79) *prisca fides facto, sed fama perennis.* Why then did he introduce the story?

We may understand his motives best if we consider the context. The passage which has just preceded (47–76) has given a chilling and terrible picture of violence unleashed: irresistibly, it seems, the Rutulians fall in wild frenzy upon the ships, and yet they *are* resisted, supernaturally. Virgil snatches us away from the awful inevitability of unopposed military might into the pastoral world, where violence and destruction is avoided by supernatural power, where fire cannot burn nor brute force prevail, where at the moment of annihilation there is intervention, escape, transformation from the mortal world.

Here the reference to "the pastoral world" is irrelevant; there can be no question of a generic explanation involving the influence of pastoral poetry on this part of the *Aeneid.* Nor is Virgil likely to be saving his readers from too much horror and violence; he shows no such scruples throughout Books 10 to 12.

The lack of precedent together with the lack of verisimilitude to which Servius objects are more powerful considerations. But he is asking for an exact precedent, preferably in Homer, and so he overlooks the fact that many such magical moments of divine intervention are to be found in *Iliad* and *Odyssey* as well as in the *Argonautica* and in Hellenistic poetry. What characterises Homer and distinguishes him from Virgil is his complete acceptance of all kinds of direct divine intervention in human action—an intervention recognised and also accepted without question by the human participants. What Virgil does is accept a certain degree of

5. See pp. 28–29 above.
6. R. D. Williams (1973), pp. 283–84.

generically licenced divine intervention but subverts its truth-value in various ways so that it becomes a device of the narrative to be interpreted as a trope in each context. This is what happens here. The introductory lines 77–79 are a warning to the reader not to accept what follows as literal truth; it is in some sense *allegoria*. That is, the introductory appeal to the Muses functions as an index that measures the distance of what follows from historical reality. The poet is saying one thing and meaning something else: whatever actually happened to the ships is irrelevant; what the reader needs to understand is the meaning in the context of what the poet has substituted for the (unknown) historical facts—and that is complex.

The loss of the ships, regarded simply as a loss, symbolises the severance of the last tie with the life in Troy; not only can there be no going back, but the Trojans are now decisively located on Italian soil. This allows the portrayal of two opposed attitudes, one unexpressed. Turnus is made to understand the loss of the ships as an advantage to him. But he is wrong on two counts: first, he views the Italian war as a repetition of the Trojan war and himself as greater than the Greeks;[7] second, he has not taken account of the way the ships have been lost. This is dramatic irony, for the reader has privileged knowledge about the nature of the divine intervention. The encouragement of the Trojans is unexpressed, but it is latent in lines 114–15, where the supernatural voice says: "Do not be anxious, Trojans, to defend my ships or take weapons in your hands; Turnus will be allowed to burn the ocean before those sacred ships." The transformation of the ships is not, as Turnus views it, a sudden response to danger, but the fulfilling of a promise made by Juppiter to Cybele years before (98–106). The reader knows that; the Trojans can feel encouragement; Turnus is wilfully wrong. A factual account of the loss could only have described physical destruction, with no opportunity for a dramatically ironic anticipation of the war to come.

Another important advantage also would have been lost. The poet uses the transformation of the ships to move onto the divine level. Cybele's revelation of the origin of the ships functions retrospectively over the whole of the preceding narrative and, taken with Juppiter's words, adds an element of drama and even pathos to the loss of the ship in the storm of *Aeneid* 1 and to the burning of the ships in *Aeneid* 5. But Juppiter's words also have a much wider significance. Cybele asked Juppiter to use his power as king of the gods to guarantee the preservation of the ships (83–92) He replies (94–103):

7. See chap. 4, sec. 2.

> "o genetrix, quo fata vocas? aut quid petis istis?
> mortaline manu factae immortale carinae
> fas habeant? certusque incerta pericula lustret
> Aeneas? cui tanta deo permissa potestas?
> immo, ubi defunctae finem portusque tenebunt
> Ausonios olim, quaecumque evaserit undis
> Dardaniumque ducem Laurentia vexerit arva,
> mortalem eripiam formam magnique iubebo
> aequoris esse deas, quales Nereia Doto
> et Galatea secant spumantem pectore pontum."

"How, mother, are you trying to influence Fate? or what are you asking on their behalf? Are ships fashioned by mortal hand to possess the right to immortality? Is Aeneas to pass through uncertain dangers certain of safety? What god is allowed power like that? No: when they have completed their duty and shall in time reach the goal and ports of Italy, I shall free all ships that have escaped the waves and have carried the Dardanian leader to the Laurentian fields from their mortal shape and bid them be goddesses of the great ocean, like Doto, daughter of Nereus, and Galatea, who cleave the foaming waves with their breasts."

A retrospective survey of the *Aeneid* is enforced by these words so that the Trojan ships are seen metaphorically as human beings subject to the lottery of chance: some will survive, some will not. What was the unknown future in Juppiter's words is now history, and the reader knows what has happened to various ships and can sense the pathos of the few survivors now made immortal. More important is the retrospective judgment enforced by Juppiter's words about Aeneas. He has got safely to the shores of Italy and, consequently, it can now be seen to have been his destiny to do so; but divine protection did not bring him through. A rereading of the earlier books is compelled by those words: each human being has only himself to rely on. What this speech does for the *Aeneid* as a whole is to enforce the separation of the divine and human levels; the divine level is a narrative stratagem of the poet. This passage is an index to the reading of the whole *Aeneid*.

Finally, there is an index here to historical Rome in the figure of Cybele, whose worship was very important—especially in aristocratic circles—from the time of its introduction to Rome in 204 B.C. The cult became so prominent during the second century B.C. that the poet could leave this index from the twelfth century (where it belongs to the sphere of poetic fantasy) to late historical Rome unexpressed. That kind of pointer forward from the twelfth century is frequent in the *Aeneid* and will be considered further in the following section.

In all of these passages of Hellenistic rococo (and in others besides those analysed here) the poet can be seen to have deliberately subverted some ostensible truth-claims of his own text. In each case he draws a clear distinction, at the same time as he measures the distance, between a world of poetic fantasy and a reality that is present to his mind and is made present to the reader's mind by means of at least one index of proportionality. Beneath the surface of the text there is more or less dimly apprehended another field of ideas; the index not only points to that other field but allows the reader to sense the relationship or proportionality between that field and the field that is represented by the surface of the text. Very often critics have been offended by what is presented by the surface of the text and have asked why Virgil chose to depart so widely from truth to reality; it is characteristic of this difficulty that, unlike other applications of the objective framwork to be considered later, it is easier to express the indexes of proportionality that appear in passages of Hellenistic rococo in relation to their origin—that is, to the primary field from which they point—than to their object—that is, the secondary field, which is unexpressed. The reason for this is that such passages of traditional poetic artifice are most remote from the secondary field and that the constitution of the secondary field in the reader's imagination depends primarily on many other types of poetic expression; in the passages of poetic fantasy it was enough for the poet to subvert any tendency to literal interpretation and point briefly in the direction to which the whole epic otherwise alludes. Most of these passages of Hellenistic rococo serve to establish the gap between the divine level, which is exclusively the domain of the poet, and the human level, where truth-claims are admitted and substantiated.

2. *Indexes to Historical Rome and the Age of Augustus*

The poet has so composed the *Aeneid* that a reader, aware that he is set among events that took place within a few years in the latter part of the twelfth century B.C., is nevertheless always conscious of the historical Rome, whose remote origin is at least four centuries later. This relationship between events of the late twelfth century B.C. and the actual history of Rome can usefully be analysed in terms of the "objective framework." The poet in his relationship to the immediate events of his narrative constitutes the primary field of ideas; to that is related synecdochically the secondary field of the poet in his relationship to the history of Rome and especially to the age of Augustus in which he himself lives. That latter element in the secondary field is of the greatest importance and will be analysed shortly. First, the way in which indexes are constantly provided to the history of Rome can be briefly demonstrated.

The indexes to the historical field begin in the prooemium with the words (6–7)

> genus unde Latinum
> Albanique patres atque altae moenia Romae.

from whom [i.e., Aeneas] the Latin race and the city-fathers of Alba and the walls of lofty Rome took their origin.

The gap spanned by *unde* is the considerable gap between the primary and secondary fields. The epic begins with the wrath of Juno and the hardships she imposed on the Trojans (12–32); the account is closed by a sentence that is self-contained within the metrical unit (33) *tantae molis erat Romanam condere gentem* "Such was the effort it took to found the Roman race." Quintilian (8.5.11) quotes the line as an example of *epiphonema:* "an exclamation attached as a climax to a narrative or demonstration." This is the voice of the poet advancing a surprising thesis: Aeneas was the founder of Rome, and the events of the poet's narrative that took place in the late twelfth century B.C. are to be viewed as the essential events that led to the foundation of Rome. Here the secondary field is brought clearly within the privileged reader's view. The gap between the two fields is skilfully measured in the poet's voice when he takes the generic opportunity to indulge Hellenistic *doctrina* (1.108–11):

> tris Notus abreptas in saxa latentia torquet
> (saxa vocant Itali mediis quae in fluctibus Aras,
> dorsum immane mari summo), tris Eurus ab alto
> in brevia et syrtis urget, miserabile visu . . .

Three ships the South wind seized and hurled onto hidden rocks (these rocks, out in the middle of the ocean Italians call "The Altars," a huge spine just below the sea's surface), three the East wind drove from the deep into shallows and sand bars. . . .

The "Italians" and the present tense belong to the secondary field but point to a time-scale that includes a period far earlier than the poet's own age.

Soon after this comes the passage of Hellenistic rococo with Neptune's chariot calming the waves. The index here is the simile (148–53) of the Roman statesman quelling a riot. The simile describes a situation from a period far later than the twelfth century, and the reason why this is not simply disruptive is that, in similes in epic, the voice of the poet is heard directly.[8] That is, a simile automatically measures a distance from the surface of the context. Here the fact that it is the poet's voice locates the simile not just in Roman history in general but in the period of civil war that preceded the age of Augustus. The simile, therefore, not only anticipates a theme of importance in the epic; it also functions as a striking index to the secondary field at a point that approaches the age of Augustus.

This constant succession of indexes to the secondary field is more or less typical of the epic as a whole—the poet was naturally concerned to create a special impression of the technique in the first book—and does not need detailed demonstration. Instead a few examples will be considered. In *Aeneid* 3 the Trojans are made to land at Actium (276–88); the "little town" is mentioned (276) and they celebrate games (280–82). In the legend the Trojans built temples and celebrated games at Zacynthus, but Virgil has transferred those activities to Actium to create an index to his own time. The "little town" points to Nicopolis, which was re-founded by Augustus from a number of surrounding towns.[9] The games point to the Greek quinquennial games that Augustus re-established at Actium soon after his victory there in 31 B.C., and Aeneas' dedication there of spoils taken from Greeks at Troy forms a link with the trophies that Augustus dedicated there after the battle. What happens here is that the two fields are linked in such a way that events in the twelfth century take their analogues in recent historical events that are located in the secondary field and need no mention to remind the privileged reader, as they are contemporary with him.

A similar technique is used in *Aeneid* 5 where, during the funeral games of Anchises, a larger number of individual Trojans is paraded than anywhere else in the first six books. The poet takes the opportunity, when naming a Trojan, to trace the line of descent to a historical Roman family. So, at 116, Mnestheus is named—*mox Italus Mnestheus, genus a quo nomine Memmi* "soon to be the Italian Mnestheus, from which name descends the family of Memmius"; at 121, Sergestus—*domus tenet a quo Sergia nomen* "from whom the house of Sergius takes its name"; and at 123, Cloanthus—*genus unde tibi, Romane Cluenti* "from whom you, Roman Cluentius, derive your name." A special opportunity was created by the

8. See chap. 7, sec. 1.
9. Strabo *Geographica* 325.

poet when he made the *lusus Troiae* the climax of the games. This eques-
trian manoeuvre was a spectacle that is attested in the time of Sulla;[10] it
was revived by Julius Caesar,[11] and was instituted as a regular perfor-
mance, put on by young aristocrats, by Augustus, who took a special
interest in all aspects of education. What the poet does here is analogous
to his linking of family origins; he reveals the *lusus Troiae* to be one of
thoes Trojan customs that were brought to Italy and preserved to be
handed on to historical Rome. The occasion gave the poet a further opportunity. Among the leaders he mentions (568–69):

> alter Atys, genus unde Atii duxere Latini,
> parvus Atys pueroque puer dilectus Iulo.

The second was Atys, from whom the Latin Atii have derived their descent, little
Atys, a boy much loved by Iulus, himself a boy.

The mention of Atii is skilfull. Julius Caesar's sister married M. Atius
Balbus and their daughter, Atia, who married C. Octavius, was the mother of Augustus. It is appropriate that he should be specially loved by
Iulus, who was the founder of the *gens Iulia*, since the two are destined by
remote descent to be close kinsmen. The poet can afford not to explain a
detail that would instantly come alive in the secondary field for contemporary readers.

Similarly, when the disaffected are being settled with Acestes in
Sicily, their city has a significant name—(718) *urbem appellabunt permisso
nomine Acestam* "they shall call their city—if the name be allowed—
Acesta." The city will be called Egesta by Greeks and Segesta by Romans.
When Aeneas lays it out (756–57) *hoc Ilium et haec loca Troiam / esse iubet* "he
bids this be Ilium and this region Troy." This picks up an important
theme from the earlier omen of Acestes' arrow catching fire; the poet
anticipates the omen with portentous words (522–24):

> hic oculis subitum obicitur magnoque futurum
> augurio monstrum; docuit post exitus ingens
> seraque terrifici cecinerunt omina vates.

Here was presented to their eyes an unexpected omen and destined to be of great
portent in time to come; the grand outcome showed it so in later times and
awesome prophets sang of omens still to be fulfilled.

---

10. Plutarch *Cato Maior* 3.
11. Suetonius *Julius Caesar* 39.

The gap here between the primary field, in which Aeneas and his people do not understand what they see, and the secondary field is spanned by the voice of the omniscient poet. He understands but does not explain. The passage has to be retrospectively judged after the foundation of Acesta. The significant theme here is one that pervades the *Aeneid:* it is the concept that the great trial Rome will face will be the wars with Carthage. Segesta immediately surrendered and joined the Roman side in the first war against Carthage, and it is to Segesta's fame as a Roman ally that the omen alludes. The very allusiveness enforces a suspension of judgment on the reader till the passage on the founding of Acesta has been read. The connexion of ideas here is evidence of the constant presence of the secondary field in the imagination of the poet, and by these devices it is constantly brought to the mind of the reader.

Another opportunity for a wide-ranging index to the secondary field is created by the poet in his account of the beginning of the Italian war. A complex ecphrasis opens the scene (7.601–17):

> Mos erat Hesperio in Latio, quem protinus urbes
> Albanae coluere sacrum, nunc maxima rerum
> Roma colit, cum prima movent in proelia Martem,
> sive Getis inferre manu lacrimabile bellum
> Hyrcanisve Arabisve parant, seu tendere ad Indos   605
> Auroramque sequi Parthosque reposcere signa:
> sunt geminae Belli portae (sic nomine dicunt)
> religione sacrae et saevi formidine Martis;
> centum aerei claudunt vectes aeternaque ferri
> robora, nec custos absistit limine Ianus: 610
> has, ubi certa sedet patribus sententia pugnae,
> ipse Quirinali trabea cinctuque Gabino
> insignis reserat stridentia limina consul,
> ipse vocat pugnas; sequitur tum cetera pubes,
> aereaque adsensu conspirant cornua rauco.   615
> hoc et tum Aeneadis indicere bella Latinus
> more iubebatur tristisque recludere portas.

There was a ritual in Hesperian Latium, that the Alban cities thence forward observed as sacred and so now too does Rome, greatest state of all, as soon as they stir Mars to battle, whether they prepare to visit tearful war violently upon the Getae or the Hyrcanians or the Arabs, or to make an expedition against the Indians (605) and follow an Eastern course and demand back the standards from the Parthians: twin gates of War there are (that is the name they give them), sanctified by religious awe and fear of cruel Mars; one hundred bars of brass close them and the eternal strength of steel, and Janus never moves his guardianship from their threshold (610). These, when the decision for battle is decided by the senators, the consul, decked in his Quirinal cloak and the cincture of Gabii, with his own hand unbars the creaking doors, and in his own person announces war; then follow the rest of military age as the brazen horns breathe out in unison their raucous assent (615). By means of this ritual even at that time Latinus was bidden declare war against the people of Aeneas and open those grim gates.

Here is an all-inclusive ecphrasis on the traditional epic pattern from (601) *mos erat* . . . to (616–17) *hoc . . . more . . .* ;[12] within this there is a subsidiary ecphrasis of the same pattern from (607) *sunt geminae Belli portae* . . . to (611) *has.* . . . The tense change from (601) *erat* to presents, with the imperfect picked up again as the poet moves from ecphrasis back to the narrative context in (617) *iubebatur*, spans the gap from the late twelfth century of Latinus to the present contemporary with the poet, and the present tenses also universalise the ritual as being continuously observed throughout that period.

Servius knew that the poet had invented the existence of the ritual in the twelfth century and criticises him for it (on line 601): "His assertion that this custom was ancient is false; for it was first instituted by Numa Pompilius. But, as usual, he mingles history with his poetry." Here the gap between the primary and secondary fields is momentarily closed by a potent index invented by the poet for that purpose. The index points forward across the gap that separated the twelfth century from historical Rome (601–02 *quem protinus urbes / Albanae coluere sacrum*) and is then directed to the present day by (602) *nunc*. The potential enemies of Rome that are named were among those that most concerned Augustan policy in the twenties, and various expeditions were launched against most of them (Indians are often a metonymy for Parthians). In fact, however, what concerned Augustus far more was the closing of the gate of Janus not its opening, and the poet had witnessed that event in 29 B.C. and again in 25 B.C. On both occasions the closing followed military victories; as Augustus said in his *res gestae* (13) "after peace had been created on land and sea by victories throughout the whole empire of the Roman people." That is, peace was a sign of military victories and supremacy. The gate was shut in Latinus' time (presumably because Turnus had taken on the war with Etruria) and Latinus' reluctance to open it is paradigmatic of Augustus' eagerness to shut it. The ritual of closing the gate was presumably similar to that for opening it, which is what the poet is

12. On this pattern, see Williams (1968), Index s.v. *"est locus . . . and similar formulas."*

forced to describe (611–15) in response to the context. But the index here
leads the reader to apprehend a very important element in Augustan
ideology—that peace and military supremacy are virtually interchange-
able terms.

There is also another element here that is brought out in the contrast
between the roll-call of Roman enemies and Latinus' reluctance (which is
applauded by the poet): the only war consistent with the traditions of the
Roman state is a war against external enemies; Latinus would have to
break a treaty and bonds of hospitality to declare what would consequently be more or less a civil war. The metonymically related idea that
Augustus had ended civil war and directed Roman energies against external foes is suggested. This idea is a leit-motiv of the *Aeneid:* it goes back to
the associations of the early simile of the statesman quelling a riot
(1.148–53); it is then taken up in one of the major indexes of proportionality to the secondary field—Juppiter's great speech to Venus in
Aeneid 1.257–96.

The way in which the index of the gates of Janus is invented and
used by the poet points to a difficulty he had to face. There was a considerable paradox in treating Aeneas as the founder of Rome since even the
name did not exist in the twelfth century and the founder of the city was
normally reckoned to be Romulus, who lived some four centuries later.
The speech of Juppiter functions as a large-scale historical framwork that
not only looks to the future immediately beyond the ending of the *Aeneid*
but also serves to define the chronological relationship between the primary and the secondary fields. Juppiter assures Venus that Aeneas will
found the city of Lavinium and will then be assumed to the heavens by
her (258–60). That looks just beyond the end of the *Aeneid,* and at that
point Juppiter goes back and, using a metaphor from initiation (262 *et
volvens fatorum arcana movebo*), initiates Venus in the events to come from
present to future. He begins with Aeneas (263–66):

> "bellum ingens geret Italia populosque ferocis
> contundet moresque viris et moenia ponet,
> tertia dum Latio regnantem viderit aestas,
> ternaque transierint Rutulis hiberna subactis."

"He shall wage a great war in Italy and shall crush its arrogant peoples and shall
establish codes of behaviour and walls for them until the third summer shall find
him still reigning in Latium and three winters shall have passed after the subjection of the Rutuli."

Aeneas' death has already been dealt with; it will be a form of apotheosis

(259–60), and that does not need tactless repetition. But, in fact, Aeneas will only live for three years beyond the end of the *Aeneid*. Then (267–71):

> "at puer Ascanius, cui nunc cognomen Iulo
> additur (Ilus erat, dum res stetit Ilia regno),
> triginta magnos volvendis mensibus orbis
> imperio explebit, regnumque ab sede Lavini
> transferet, et longam multa vi muniet Albam."

"Then the boy Ascanius who now has the cognomen Iulus added to his name (it used to be Ilus as long as the Ilian kingdom stood firm), shall complete in his reign thirty great circuits as the months fulfill their cycles, and shall transfer his kingdom from the city of Lavinium and shall build the powerful city of Alba Longa."

The story is thus carried on thirty years, and Ascanius, by the change in his name, is designated the ancestor of the *gens Iulia*; like his father, he too shall found a city. The connexion with Rome, however, has been established in the explanation of the name Iulus, which will be echoed later (288). At this point comes the period of difficulty; for only thirty-three years have passed since the end of the *Aeneid*. Juppiter makes the transition with aplomb (272–77):

> "hic iam ter centum totos regnabitur annos
> gente sub Hectorea, donec regina sacerdos
> Marte gravis geminam partu dabit Ilia prolem.
> inde lupae fulvo nutricis tegmine laetus
> Romulus excipiet gentem et Mavortia condet
> moenia Romanosque suo de nomine dicet."

"Here for a full three hundred years shall the rule of kings be maintained derived from Hector's race, until Ilia, the regal priestess, pregnant by Mars shall give birth to twins. From that source, Romulus, taking pleasure in the tawny skin of his wolf-nurse, shall inherit the family-line and shall found walls of Mars and shall name the people Romans after his own name."

After three hundred years of kings at Alba, there at last appears the founder of Rome in his most familiar iconographic pose. The ordering of events is deliberately used to limit his importance; here, he is only a stage in the progress from Aeneas to Augustus. But he established the Roman state as such, and a striking prophecy that looks into the farthest future is attached to the achievement of Romulus (278–83):

> "his ego nec metas rerum nec tempora pono:
> imperium sine fine dedi. quin aspera Iuno,
> quae mare nunc terrasque metu caelumque fatigat,

> consilia in melius referet, mecumque fovebit
> Romanos, rerum dominos gentemque togatam.
> sic placitum."

"To them I set no limit of power or time: an empire without boundary have I assigned to them. In fact, hostile Juno, who now exhausts sea and land and sky with dread, shall alter her ideas for the better and shall join me in supporting the Romans, the toga-clad race and masters of the world. That is our decision."

This part of the prophecy alludes to, but slides tactfully over, another theme of great importance in the *Aeneid*—the wars against Carthage. It would preempt the drama of the Trojan visit to Carthage if Juppiter were allowed to recall what actually happened to Carthage; but the form of his words is an assurance of success that will transcend all opposition. Instead Juppiter's thoughts turn more opportunely to Greece (283–85):

> "veniet lustris labentibus aetas
> cum domus Assaraci Pthiam clarasque Mycenas
> servitio premet ac victis dominabitur Argis."

"As the half-decades slip by, the time shall come when the house of Assaracus shall oppress with slavery Phthia and famous Mycenae and shall be lord in conquered Argos."

The concept of Greece enslaved by Rome comes well at a point between the Greek triumph over Troy and Aeneas' despairing envy of those Trojans who had died fighting the Greeks at Troy (1.94–101). There is a fine ironic contrast between Aeneas' depression and the terrible enslavement of Troy, on the one hand, and the historical fact of later Roman domination over Greece. From that conquest, which closely accompanied the final destruction of Carthage, in the second century B.C. the prophecy leaps to the time contemporary with both poet and reader (286–96):

> "nascetur pulchra Troianus origine Caesar,
> imperium Oceano, famam qui terminet astris,
> Iulius, a magno demissum nomen Iulo.
> hunc tu olim caelo spoliis Orientis onustum
> accipies secura; vocabitur hic quoque votis.
> aspera tum positis mitescent saecula bellis;
> cana Fides et Vesta, Remo cum fratre Quirinus
> iura dabunt; dirae ferro et compagibus artis
> claudentur Belli portae; Furor impius intus
> saeva sedens super arma et centum vinctus aënis
> post tergum nodis fremet horridus ore cruento."

"There shall be born Caesar, a Trojan in his splendid ancestry, a Julian, his name handed down from his ancestor Iulus, destined to limit his empire only by ocean, his fame by the stars. One day you shall welcome him happily in heaven, loaded with rich spoils of the East; him too shall men call upon in prayer (290). Then shall ages once harsh put aside war and grow civilized: grey-haired Trust and Vesta and Quirinus with his brother Remus shall deal out justice. The gates of War, threatening with their close-fitting steel fastenings, shall be closed, and within them impious War-Madness, seated on a pile of cruel weapons, his arms bound behind his back with a hundred brazen fetters, shall roar dreadfully from his blood-spattered mouth."

The climax of the prophecy breaks in without a particle of transition or connexion, and so marks itself as the climax also of Roman history. Doubts about the identity of the person designated go back to Servius. Is he Julius Caesar or Augustus? Champions have been found down through the ages for each candidate, and our age has produced the characteristic compromise that the passage is ambiguous and that both are meant.[13] But there can be no doubt that the poet intended Augustus. There is not only the reference to Eastern conquests, to the end of the civil war, and to ideals that were characteristic of the twenties; there is, to clinch the matter, (289) *olim* "at some time in the future." The only reason for adding *olim*, which would be simply redundant in a prophecy in which the precise facts were known to the privileged speaker, was tact: Augustus is still alive at the moment of writing and it is hoped that he will continue to live for a long time. The adverb expresses the embarrassment of the poet who has to mention the death at some time in the future of a great man, known to all his readers and himself also a potential reader. What this forcefully brings home is that the god Juppiter is also a trope for the poet's voice. The poet knows by hindsight, looking back over Roman history from the twenties; the god can speak for the poet, using foresight as he looks forward over Roman history from the twelfth century.

Juppiter's speech functions as an index to the secondary field, and it is composed as a ring-composition that itself reflects the poet's thesis about the history of Rome. It begins with Aeneas and it reaches its climax, in the poet's day, with Augustus. The thematic links between the two are clear: Aeneas will be taken up to the heaven by Venus (259–60) and so will Augustus (289–90); and the phrase (288) *Iulius, a magno demissum nomen Iulo* resumes the wording of Juppiter's account of the significance attached to Ascanius' change of name. Aeneas, like Augustus, will crush

13. See the discussion by Austin (1971), pp. 108–10, with references.

his enemies; but he will also, when the wars are over, set a moral example and a standard of behaviour for all men (263–64). That aspect of Augustus' regime is given great prominence in the theme of the cessation of war and the growth of civility (291), in the concept of straight-dealing (*Fides*) of which Romans were proud; in the figure of Vesta symbolising the eternity of the city; in the junction of Romulus with Remus—for their fratricidal quarrel was a frequent symbol of civil war; and in the basic Roman valuation of the rule of law (293 *iura dabunt*). The closing of the gates of Janus anticipates the theme of *Aeneid* 7.601–17, but the *Furor* that will be locked behind those gates is *impius*—that is, not War-Madness in general but the specific *Furor* of civil war. Those lines summarize the basic ideals of Augustan Rome, and the strategy of the poet is to draw a parallel between Aeneas at the very beginning of Roman history and Augustus at its climactic present. Thereby he created a synecdoche of his thesis that Aeneas was the founder of Rome.

The emphasis is different in the final scene between Juppiter and Juno in Book 12. 791–842. There Aeneas retreats into the background. The scene is thematically so closely related to the speech of Juppiter in Book 1 that the two passages form a ring-composition that opens and closes the epic. Aeneas appears in 12.794–95 again as destined to become a god, but he is not otherwise mentioned. Instead the ideas concentrate on the blending of the two peoples, Trojans and Italians, into one, in such a way that the two fields are momentarily redefined. For here the poet presents a point of view that appears hardly at all in the rest of the epic. Aeneas is at the centre of the *Aeneid* and "Trojan" in most of the epic is defined by the reader in terms of him. But he is a most unusual individual in the heroic world of the twelfth century, and other, more disturbing, associations of the designation "Trojan" appear from time to time. For instance, not only does Iarbas in Book 4 (215–17) regard the Trojans as effeminate, but Numanus (9.602–20) contrasts the sturdy virtue and bravery of the Italians with the womanish foppery and luxury of the Trojans, and Turnus (12.99–100) expresses the same view.[14] Aeneas himself is shown, as he builds Carthage for Dido, arrayed in oriental finery: that is, one could assume, when he is not being himself but indulging his love for Dido, he reverts to being a conventional Trojan. The speakers are enemies; but it is the poet who describes Aeneas at Carthage, and the view of an Eastern people as being effeminate came easily to Romans. But this view is also borne out by odd glimpses of Trojans such as Chloreus the priest, whose finery excites Camilla's lust for loot (11.768–77).

14. See chap. 3, n. 3.

What the poet does in the exchange between Juppiter and Juno is to look at the Trojans as a people and to contrast them somewhat unfavourably with the Italians. Here the two fields are consequently modified into a form not otherwise used in the *Aeneid:* the primary field concerns the contrasted natures of Trojans and Italians in the twelfth century; the secondary field is that of Roman civilization as a whole, regarded from the cultural aspect of name, dress, morals, customs, and language. Aeneas, who is unique and uncharacteristic, can be allowed in Book 1.264 to set standards of behaviour for Trojans and Italians. But when the poet takes the long view of Roman history in Book 12, then (834) *sermonem Ausonii patrium moresque tenebunt* "the Italians shall keep the tongue and customs of their ancestors"; of course, under *mores* the poet thinks partly of *mores* such as that of the gates of War (7.601–15), but the word cannot escape the connotation also of character. And Juppiter's declaration here responds to Juno's request (827) *sit Romana potens Itala virtute propago* "Let the Roman line owe its strength to Italian manliness." Juppiter goes on to limit severely the Trojan contribution (835–37):

> "utque est nomen erit; commixti corpore tantum
> subsident Teucri. morem ritusque sacrorum
> adiciam faciamque omnis uno ore Latinos."

"and as their name is, so it shall be in the future. Mingling in stock only, the Trojans shall only merge into ⟨the Italian nation⟩. I shall add their custom and rites of sacrifice and shall make all of them Latins with a single language."

The Trojans (in the most probable view) are to contribute religious customs and rites. Juppiter then promises Juno (838–40):

> "hinc genus Ausonio mixtum quod sanguine surget,
> supra homines, supra ire deos pietate videbis,
> nec gens ulla tuos aeque celebrabit honores."

"The race that shall rise from this [Trojan] origin, mixed with Italian blood, you shall see outdo all mankind, even the gods, in devotion, and no people shall be their equal in showing you honour."

The poet is thinking in general terms of national characteristics and so the quality that is most specifically Aeneas' is not here attributed to him; but it is clear that the outstanding Roman quality of *pietas* will nevertheless be the legacy of Aeneas.

A retrospective judgment on the *Aeneid* as a whole is invited by this surprising readjustment of the primary and secondary fields. The essential loneliness of Aeneas becomes clear; he was not a typical Trojan. It was he alone who had the vision of the future and the will to pursue it. The occasions when he was in despair and was strengthened by one of his company are virtually confined to the one instance of Nautes speaking with the authority of a prophet in *Aeneid* 5.704–18, and perhaps the eagerness of the Trojans to leave Carthage (4.294–95). The helplessness of the Trojans in Book 9 when Aeneas is away needs to be taken into account here (despite Nisus and Euryalus); Turnus recognises them as easy game in the absence of Aeneas. The great warriors are all non-Trojan: Pallas, Lausus, Mezentius, Turnus. Hector, who is dead, is an exception, but in fact the Trojans as such in the *Aeneid* are nothing without Aeneas and have few positive qualities to recommend them. When Diomedes is asked to join the Latins against the Trojans, it is only Aeneas whom he considers (if there had been one more Aeneas at Troy, the Greeks would have failed).[15] What is enforced by this scene between Juppiter and Juno is the uniqueness of Aeneas (which is, of course, shared by his son Ascanius—though he is too young to be portrayed seriously). Aeneas can found the future state of Rome and can contribute to the qualities that underlie Roman history; the Trojans as such cannot. Juppiter's words (12.835–36) *commixti corpore tantum / subsident Teucri* are devastatingly dismissive. This same point of view, probably influenced by this scene, is powerfully expressed by Horace in *Odes* 3.3, where the virtues that stand as Italian in contrast to Trojan mirror those of Aeneas and are also projected onto Augustus (1–12).

The next great index—the review of Roman heroes by Anchises in the Underworld (6.756–892)—has a different structure and takes a different point of view, though themes of the earlier speech are echoed. Juppiter's speech has a strict chronological framework, and that framework functions as an important index of the proportionality between the primary and secondary fields. But Anchises' review is not ordered chronologically, except here and there where it suited the poet. It begins with Aeneas and defines his relationship to Silvius, who will be king of Alba Longa in succession to Ascanius (760–66); Silvius will be a late-born son of Aeneas by Lavinia. At the time of that birth, Aeneas will be (764) *longaevus*, a surprising statement since he will only live three years beyond the end of the *Aeneid*; but the adjective is as emotional as it is descriptive. It expresses that sense of Aeneas as not only advanced in years but also worn out by his sufferings. That is a constantly recurring theme (cf. e.g., 3.710; 5.725), and its weariness infects his final speech to Ascanius

15. 11.285–93.

(12.435–40). In fact, Anchises' description gives an unexpected glimpse of a man of at least middle age; nowhere else in the *Aeneid* is a sense of Aeneas' age conveyed, and it is characteristic of the poet that it is so unobtrusively suggested.

There follow various Alban kings who function as a way of separating Aeneas and his son from his grandson Aeneas Silvius. The poet uses this character as a means of passing the qualities of Aeneas down the generations (768–70):

> "et qui te nomine reddet
> Silvius Aeneas, pariter pietate vel armis
> egregius, si umquam regnandam acceperit Albam."

". . . and Aeneas Silvius who shall reconstitute you in name, equally distinguished for his devotion and his skill in arms, if ever he shall get the chance to rule Alba."

The *pietas* of Aeneas thus survives the generations at Alba Longa to be transmitted to Romulus, whose mother was the daughter of Numitor and so, by descent from Aeneas, a Trojan (778). Romulus is then celebrated as the founder of Rome (781–84):

> "en huius, nate, auspiciis illa incluta Roma
> inperium terris, animos aequabit Olympo,
> septemque una sibi muro circumdabit arces,
> felix prole virum."

"See, my son, under his [Romulus'] auspices that far-famed state of Rome shall equate its empire with the world, its spirits with Olympus, and, blessed in its progeny of heroes, though but a single city, shall surround seven citadels within its wall."

The definition of the greatness of Rome here (782) echoes what was said in Juppiter's speech of Augustus (1.287) *imperium Oceano, famam qui terminet astris.* That is no accident: Rome's achievement is identical with its ruler's achievement, whether he be the original founder, Romulus, or the second founder, Augustus.[16]

Augustus, in defiance of any chronology, now follows, and the structure of the review is clearly designed to show a direct movement from the Trojan founder, Aeneas, to the actual founder of Rome and then to the second founder, Augustus. More space is given to Augustus

16. Suetonius *Augustus* 7.2.

(788–807) than to anyone else in the review of heroes, with the exception of the young Marcellus (860–86). The pattern—as with the speech of Juppiter—shows Augustus and the present day to be the most important element in the secondary field; or, to put it differently, the primary and secondary fields are so proportioned that the age of Augustus is shaped as the result and climax of preceding history back to the twelfth century. That point of view is strongly expressed in Anchises' words that form a climax to his introduction of Augustus (806–07):

> "et dubitamus adhuc virtutem extendere factis,
> aut metus Ausonia prohibet consistere terra?"

"And do we still feel any hestiation about enlarging our valour by our deeds or does fear still keep us from taking our stand on the soil of Ausonia?"

The unspoken argument moves from the primary to the secondary field, which is possible for the privileged Anchises (he is privileged by being dead): there is a direct connexion between the course that Aeneas feels destined to follow and the greatness of the age of Augustus. The latter depends on the accomplishment of the former. The nature of the trope involved is defined by an introductory remark of Anchises—(759) *et te tua fata docebo* "and I shall teach you your Destiny." The destiny of Aeneas is comprised not just by the events of his own personal life; it is co-extensive with the whole of Roman history down to the poet's own time.

Augustus is treated as the leading figure of the *gens Iulia* and is destined, with its other members, to become a god (789–90). In the sheer covering of territory he will outdo both Hercules and Bacchus; they are often used as figures for benefactors of mankind in this period, but the nature of Augustus' benefaction to mankind in general will not be defined till later (848–53). The direct link between the twelfth century and the age of Augustus is further established by Anchises' assertion that prophecies of Augustus' coming are at this moment terrifying the peoples of the Caspian region (mainly the Parthians but also the Scythians) and of Egypt (798–800). This link is strengthened by another prophecy: Augustus will re-establish in Latium the golden age of Saturn (792–94). This is a significant thematic anticipation of that most attractive character, Evander; he gives a description of the golden age in 8.314–32. The marks of that age were a settled society, law and order, and peace (8.321–25). Those are the ideals of the age of Augustus; they refer to the cessation of civil war, his moral reform of society, and "peace obtained by military victories" (*res gestae* 13). This motif in Book 6 should probably be regarded as another example of the need for retrospective judgment: only after 8.314–32 has been read does it become clear what exactly the implications of the idea that Augustus will re-establish the age of Saturn are.

After the climax of Augustus there is a significant movement of ideas. Anchises returns to pick up the history of Rome after Romulus. He selects the figure of the great religious founder and law-giver, Numa (808–12), a Roman king (810–11) *primam qui legibus urbem / fundabit* "who will be the first to establish the city on a basis of laws." Tullus Hostilius follows, who is lauded for military exploits (812–15). Both figures echo important Augustan themes. He then makes an odd choice: Ancus Marcius is condened for boastfulness and excessive interest in popularity (815–16). He is a figure, therefore, for refusal to take unpopular measures and so for an attitude opposite to Augustus', but perhaps also anticipating the theme of civil disorder and of men like Pompey, and even more Julius Caesar, struggling for support. But the immediate political movement is decline into the tyranny of the Tarquins and the foundation of the republic by Brutus—a figure who is treated with some ambiguity (see p. 215 below). Four individuals or families important in earlier Republican history follow.

There is a pause here and a new start (marked by 826 *autem*). There is a surprising leap forward again, as with the move to Augustus, out of chronological sequence, to the period of civil war between Pompey and Caesar (826–35). They will be in harmony as long as they are in the Underworld (827), but what devastation they will cause when they reach the light (828–31)! The condemnation is severe and outspoken (832–35):

> "ne, pueri, ne tanta animis adsuescite bella
> neu patriae validas in viscera vertite viris;
> tuque prior, tu parce, genus qui ducis Olympo,
> proice tela manu, sanguis meus!—"

"Do not, my children, allow wars like that to be habitual to your spirits and do not direct your mighty powers against your country's heart. Do you be first to refrain, who derive your descent from Olympus, throw the weapons from your hand, blood-kin of mine!"

This is the antithesis of Augustus, placed to bring out the contrast; and the condemnation of Julius Caesar is the sharper precisely because he is a member of the *gens Iulia*. This is war gone mad, not waged against external foes as are the wars of Augustus (his part in civil war is overlooked), but against the vitals of the fatherland. This kind of war is to be the

analogy to the wars between Trojans and Italians in the second half of the
Aeneid; but there Aeneas, despite every effort on his part, will have no
choice but to fight.

Now follows abruptly a series of characters who represent the wars
that destroyed Greece (a list of significant names sharpens the pleasure of
revenge for the ravages of *Aeneid* 2) and Carthage (836–46); the first writes
a conclusion to the Trojan themes of Books 1–6; the second picks up a
theme from Book 4 that will form a basis for condemning the Italian wars
in Books 7–12.

The coda (847–53) provides the rationale for the Roman mission in
the world and explains the nature of Augustus' benefactions to mankind.[17] The arts of Rome will be those of firm government by law; the
imposition of a settled pattern of behaviour on a condition of peace (852
pacique imponere morem); the exercise of clemency for those who submit,
but the subjection by force of those who show arrogance. That combination of *pax* and *mores* was Aeneas' gift to Italy (1.263–64), and it is also
Augustus' gift to the conquered world. It is important that these sentiments are addressed by Anchises not to Aeneas—to whom they would
mean nothing—but to (851) *Romane,* a creature not to be seen in the world
for four more centuries.

The review seems to be over, but Anchises makes an unexpected
addition. He points to the great M. Claudius Marcellus, consul four times
at the end of the third century B.C., conqueror of Gauls and Carthaginians
(here is a thematic connexion with the last figures in the review). But he is
accompanied by the young Marcellus who died in 23 B.C., to the great
misery of Augustus and the shattering of his hopes for a successor. Anchises' thoughts concentrate on the disappointed hopes, with a fine expression of the varied racial origins of Rome that are relevant to the *Aeneid*
(875–77):

> "nec puer Iliaca quisquam de gente Latinos
> in tantum spe tollet avos, nec Romula quondam
> ullo se tantum tellus iactabit alumno."

"Nor shall any son descended from the race of Ilium so greatly exalt the hopes of
his ancestors, nor shall the land of Romulus ever pride itself so much on any other
nursling."

Troy, Italy, Romulus—the lines link the primary field of the *Aeneid* with
its great associated secondary field of the whole panorama of Roman
history. Further, Marcellus' qualities are significant (878–81):

17. See further, pp. 208–09 below.

> "heu pietas, heu prisca fides invictaque bello
> dextera! non illi se quisquam impune tulisset
> obvius armato, seu cum pedes iret in hostem
> seu spumantis equi foderet calcaribus armos."

"Alas for ⟨the loss of⟩ a devotion and an honour characteristic of olden times, and a right hand unconquerable in war. No one in the world would with impunity have confronted ⟨Marcellus⟩ as a warrior, whether he were attacking the enemy on foot or pricking the sides of a foaming steed with his spurs."

The combination of moral qualities with greatness as a warrior picks up the theme by which Aeneas Silvius carried on the inheritance of Aeneas: (769–70) *pariter pietate vel armis / egregius*. These are the qualities of Augustus too (1.286–96).

But the portrait of Marcellus, in which Anchises speaks as if he were actually conducting the funeral of the young man and delivering his *laudatio,* makes the optimism of the review of heroes collapse into pessimism—the great hope for the future has been totally destroyed (see pp. 213–14 below).

The dramatic function of the review of Roman heroes is protreptic. Anchises several times expresses this intention: (718) *quo magis Italia mecum laetere reperta* "so that you may rejoice the more in having discovered Italy, as I do," and in 806–07 (see p. 146 above). Then the poet describes Anchises' purpose: (889) *incenditque animum famae venientis amore* "and he fires his spirits with a passion for the glory that is on its way." Consonant with that purpose, the review expresses a thesis about Roman history: the great achievements of Rome and the benefits it has brought to mankind in general have been laid on a foundation of military superiority. What is true in the primary field—that there are wars that have to be fought, such as the war Aeneas will be forced, against his will, to fight against the Latins and Rutulians—is true also in the secondary field: the wars that must be condemned are those fought for personal advantage against one's country's interest—namely, civil wars (826–35); but (853) *parcere subiectis et debellare superbos* is a principle that benefits mankind—as the war forced on Aeneas will ultimately benefit Italians. This interpenetration of the primary and the secondary fields constitutes the relationship between the age of Aeneas and the age of Augustus; it does so by assuming the essential continuity of Roman history from the twelfth century to the first. Aeneas is not shown as understanding any of this; he is simply filled with wonder (854). The reason is clear: Anchises addressing Aeneas is also a trope for the poet addressing the reader.

The next major index is constituted by a particularly happy invention: Evander, a most sympathetic and attractive character (a strong contrast with the far more powerful Latinus), is portrayed as inhabiting, with his people, the site of the future city of Rome. A whole range of details, therefore, become available to the poet in such a way that their location in the primary field could not fail to evoke their corresponding location in the secondary. This is simply a concentrated form of the technique used throughout the *Aeneid:* the outline of the secondary field is evoked by features that naturally belong to it but are deliberately located by the poet in the primary field of the twelfth century. In the index of Anchises' review of the heroes that technique is represented by two historical Roman customs: the headless spear given as a reward for bravery in action (760), and the civic crown of oak, awarded to one who saved a citizen's life in war (772). This latter was awarded to Augustus in the special circumstances in which he saved the citizen-body from civil war and showed clemency after winning the war (*ob cives servatos* appears with the oak leaves on contemporary coins). This fact is partly echoed in the concept (853) *parcere subiectis;* as Augustus said of himself (*res gestae* 3.1) *victorque omnibus veniam petentibus civibus peperci* "and after winning, I showed mercy to all citizens who asked for pardon." This was a concept of considerable political importance in the twenties when a society that had been divided against itself needed to be brought into harmony. But Augustus goes on to widen his claim to clemency so that it accords closely with Anchises' advice (*res gestae* 3.2) *externas gentes, quibus tuto ignosci potuit, conservare quam excidere malui* "It was my preference, where foreign peoples could safely be pardoned, to save rather than exterminate them."

The indicative details in the episode with Evander (8.102–369 and 454–584) are mainly place-names that became famous with the growing fame of the city of Rome and aetiological legends that establish the existence in the twelfth century of ceremonies well known to living Romans. But there is one theme of major importance that serves as an index to the proportionality of primary and secondary fields. This is the theme of the moral excellence of simplicity and moderation.

It enters almost immediately in the phrase, ending a list of those present at the sacrifice, (105) *pauperque senatus.* The adjective is hard to translate because, unlike the English "poor," it conveys no tinge of pity or contempt; nor does it generally carry a sense of deprivation. It is a positive word suggesting moderation, moderate means, and even an implication of virtue. "The frugally living senate" is being recommended by the poet. For throughout the whole scene the secondary field is constituted in the voice of the poet. Evander is not privileged like Anchises and can therefore know nothing of the future. His gaze is backward to the past; but so lively is the sense of the secondary field throughout the scene that Evander is actually made to say (268–69):

> ex illo celebratus honos laetique minores
> servavere diem.

"Ever since that time this festival of honour has been celebrated and later generations have been glad to observe this day."

Evander has just described how Hercules rid the community of the monster Cacus; he himself witnessed the event, and so the phrase "later generations" looks at the celebration of the festival far more readily from the viewpoint of the Augustan age than from Evander's. The poet's eagerness to relate the primary and secondary fields here by means of a major festival seems to provide a more acceptable explanation of the oddity than the supposition that the words were intended to refer to Evander's younger contemporaries. But a stark choice should probably not be presented in those terms. Rather, Evander's words are ambiguous in such a way as to mean one thing in the immediate dramatic context but to suggest something else to an Augustan reader. This is confirmed by Evander's next words (269–72):

> primusque Potitius auctor
> et domus Herculei custos Pinaria sacri
> hanc aram luco statuit, quae maxima semper
> dicetur nobis et erit quae maxima semper.

"Potitius was the originator of the cult of Hercules (and the house of Pinaria was its guardian) and set up in the grove this altar which shall always be called Maxima by us and which shall in fact always be the greatest."

Evander is allowed to look forward into the remote future (of the Augustan age) and to assert the existence of the cult in an identical form even then. Here his voice almost merges with that of the poet to connect the primary and secondary fields.

As Aeneas and Evander walk back from the festival, they pass various places that were to have great significance for the historical city of Rome. Here the poet takes over in his own voice at once to connect the scene in the twelfth century immediately with present reality in Rome (337–61). The theme of moral excellence in surroundings characterised by frugality and a proper respect for the gods reaches a climax in these words (359–61):

talibus inter se dictis ad tecta subibant
pauperis Euandri, passimque armenta videbant
Romanoque foro et lautis mugire Carinis.

With such conversation they came up to the dwelling-place of the frugally living
Evander and they saw cattle lowing everywhere throughout the Forum of Rome
and in wealthy Carinae.

The poet's voice connects the twelfth century immediately with the age of
Augustus as he sees the Forum and the elegant quarter of Carinae taking
shape out of Evander's cattle pasture. The index of proportionality between the two fields is provided by the contrast between (360) *pauperis*
and (361) *lautis*. The implicit criticism of the age of Augustus for ignoring
a moral value that was known to the twelfth century provides the basis
for the following words of Evander (362–65):

ut ventum ad sedes, "haec" inquit "limina victor
Alcides subiit, haec illum regia cepit.
aude, hospes, contemnere opes et te quoque dignum
finge deo, rebusque veni non asper egenis."

As they reached his house he said: "This was the doorway that Hercules entered
as a victor, this was the palace that received him. Be bold, my friend, to despise
wealth and shape yourself also to be worthy of godhead and approach our strait-
ened circumstances without criticism."

The ruler of the twelfth century is allowed to preach the sermon that is
needed by the age of Augustus, and that sermon is directed at the poet's
own age by the index spoken just before in his own voice. There is a nice
ambiguity in *te quoque dignum / finge deo* since it can mean "shape yourself
to be worthy of the god, Hercules" (which is Evander's meaning in the
dramatic context); but the words can also mean "shape yourself to be
worthy of being a god," and that dramatically ironic meaning is made
available to the privileged reader by his knowledge of Aeneas' destined
apotheosis (1.259–60 and 12.794–95). There is another nice irony in the
words that is heightened in the following scene of divine luxury and
immortality, as Venus displays a very different aspect of a god's behaviour—even though her husband more closely resembles Evander.

The function of the whole scene with Evander is to provide a moral
framework that will anticipate and contain the ideals of the Augustan age
(as the poet interpreted them). That interest in morality continues
through the poetic simplicity of the scene of dawn and birdsong and
waking and dressing (454–67), and it dominates the final great index, the

scenes on the shield made by Vulcan. The point of view of this long description (626–728) differs from its Homeric model (*Iliad* 18.478–617). Homer's interest lay in the skill of the divine craftsman, and so he describes the actual making, as scene after scene takes shape under the artist's hands. Virgil's interest, on the other hand, concentrated on the eye of the human observer; the craftsman's skill is not ignored, but the making is firmly relegated to the past by pluperfect tenses, and the human recipient is shown, in present tenses, examining the artistry with wonder and admiration (617–25 and 729–31). There is a gap, however, between the poet's decipherment of each scene, vividly in his own voice, and the uncomprehending pleasure of the recipient; this is the gap between the privileged reader in the age of Augustus, with his framework of Roman history, and Aeneas in the twelfth century, sensing a great future but knowing nothing of it. The gap is emphasised by the poet's direct apostrophe at several points to a reader contemporary with himself. The reader is told (650) *aspiceres* "you could have observed" (Porsenna's anger) or (676) *videres* "you could have seen" (Actium ablaze with war) or (691) *credas* "you would think" (the ships to be islands). The poet lives in two periods—the twelfth century and the age of Augustus—and with these apostrophes he spans that gap. At two other points he intervenes with comment on his decipherment. As he is describing the horrifying dismemberment of Mettus, he apostrophises him parenthetically (643) *at tu dictis, Albane, maneres!* "but, man of Alba, you should have stood by your word." The particle *at* here responds to a supposed protest by Mettus (speaking, as it were, for the revolted reader) at his barbaric punishment, and the poet's exclamation emphasises the enormity of the crime without condoning the barbarity. Another personal appearance is an apostrophe to Catiline (668) which has the effect of underlining the enormity of his crime against the state. Finally, the poet comments on the climactic detail in Antony's disgrace: (688) *sequiturque (nefas) Aegyptia coniunx* "and there follows him (a crime indeed) his Egyptian wife." Here Antony's disgrace is the greater in that he is portrayed as actually married to Cleopatra. In all of these ways the poet distances himself to stand in the age of Augustus. The same gap is spanned by the poet's voice, in line 348, by the contrast between *nunc* ("nowadays") and *olim* ("in former times").[18]

---

18. Cf. *quondam . . . nunc* at 7.411–13 *locus Ardea quondam / dictus avis, et nunc magnum manet Ardea nomen, / sed fortuna fuit* "the place once called Ardea by our ancestors; even now the great name of Ardea lasts, but its glory is gone."

The index of the shield, like the speech of Juppiter and the review of heroes, purports to be a survey of Roman history (626–29):

> illic res Italas Romanorumque triumphos
> haud vatum ignarus venturique inscius aevi
> fecerat ignipotens, illic genus omne futurae
> stirpis ab Ascanio pugnataque in ordine bella.

Upon it the Lord of Fire, not uninformed by prophets or ignorant of the age to come, had represented the history of Italy and the triumphs of the Romans, upon it, too, the whole lineage of the stock that would derive from Ascanius and the wars in order as they were fought.

Vulcan as a god shares the privileged knowledge of the poet which is not available to Aeneas, but the poet's account that follows gives only a selection from Roman history—though here, unlike the review of heroes, a chronological succession is observed. As before, in fact, the poet here presents a particular theory about the history of Rome. This final great index to the secondary field is most potent in not starting from the context of the *Aeneid* (as the two earlier did), but from some four hundred years later, at the point that Romans would normally assume to be the beginning of Roman history—the birth of Romulus and Remus. The connexion with the *Aeneid* is then made in a series of thematic links, mainly with the scene between Evander and Aeneas. In general, the opening description of the twins nursed by a wolf (630–34) recalls the setting of Pallanteum in sylvan simplicity. The twins are (630) *Mavortis in antro;* "the cave of Mars" was the Lupercal, seen by Aeneas (342–44). A connexion here looks foward, because the cave was restored by Augustus (Suetonius *Aug.* 31.4). Later the Capitol is depicted (653), which had also been pointed out to Aeneas (347–48). Still later, the Salii and Luperci are represented (663–65); both had been mentioned previously, the Salii in the celebration of Hercules' festival (285–86), the Luperci as associated with the Lupercal, the name of which was explained by the poet in lines 342–44. Finally, Romans are referred to as (638) *Romulidis* "sons of Romulus" in the second vignette; later, however, they are called (648) *Aeneadae* "descendants of Aeneas" in the important context of the establishment of the Republic (646–51).

These thematic links establish a continuous connexion between the earlier scene at the future site of Rome in the twelfth century and the actual existence of Rome as a political and cultural entity from the eighth century onward. But there is a further striking connexion with Evander. The thesis expressed by the poet's treatment of the shield is moral: it is that certain virtues are basic to the explanation of Roman success, and these virtues can also be seen to have existed in Evander's society.

The rape of the Sabine women was (635) *sine more*, with *mos* expressing the idea that the basis for moral behaviour lies in observance of tradition. The importance of *mos* was made clear by Evander (314–32), and that too was the basis for Roman morality. The Cures are characterised as (638) *severi*, a word that combines the virtues of morality and frugality. The end of the Sabine vignette (639–41) extols the related values of *foedus* and *pax*; it was Turnus' disregard for the former that led to the breaking of the latter. The story of Mettus (642–45) illustrates the value of *fides*. The attack of Porsenna (646–51) shows the political value of *libertas* and (in the persons of Horatius and Cloelia) the quality of *virtus*. The attack of the Gauls, betrayed by the geese that the Romans refused to eat (652–62), shows the necessity of *pietas*. This topic is further expanded by a portrait of Salii and Luperci, further exemplars of *pietas*, and of *matronae* riding in their carriages. This latter detail is neatly linked by metonymy to the story of the Gauls, since the women were given the right to use carriages because of their loyalty to the state during that attack. The matrons are characterised as (665) *castae:* that is, they are a further example of that potent symbol of *univiria* so important in the Augustan moral legislation. A strange vignette follows of Catiline tortured in the Underworld and of Cato dispensing justice (*dantem iura*) among the blessed (666–70). Each of the major indexes in the *Aeneid* contains a reflection on civil war. That is clearly the function of this vignette. The dispensing of justice by Cato is a metonymy for the stand he took for *res publica et libertas* and his suicide rather than surrender those principles to Caesar: that is, the act of *iura dare* is a symbol both of *res publica* and of *libertas*. Cato is selected as the most outstanding champion of the cause of constitutionality and freedom. His enemy was Julius Caesar, but the poet has chosen a more extreme example of a man's readiness to subvert the state for private ambition and so bring about civil war. Cato and Catiline are here used as anticipatory figures for Augustus and Antony.

A portrait of Augustus comes as the climax to the decipherment of the shield. The rest of Roman history from Romulus occupies forty-one lines (630–70); the portrait of Augustus takes fifty-eight (671–728). The climax of the portrait is a highly poetic treatment of the triple triumph of 29 B.C. (714–28). Augustus can be seen in this portrait to embody all the virtues that have appeared in the earlier scenes: *pax*, imposed by his victories; *fides*, as contrasted with the *perfidia* of Antony (for whom Mettus is an anticipatory figure) who brought foreigners into a Roman civil war;

castitas, in the contrasting of his marriage to a Roman woman (for whom the *matres* are an anticipatory figure) with the marriage (no less) of Antony to a foreign woman; *libertas*, as contrasted with the tyranny of Cleopatra (for whom Porsenna is an anticipatory figure); *pietas*, both to country and gods; *virtus* in his military achievements; and *res publica et libertas* through his metonymic connexion with Cato. A final important relationship is made clear in line 679 *cum patribus populoque, penatibus et magnis dis*, which is almost repeated from 3.12 *cum sociis natoque penatibus et magnis dis*, where it is applied to Aeneas. Augustus is figured as a direct descendant from Aeneas, both in bloodline and in character. One is reminded of Augustus' words at the end of *res gestae* (34.1–2):

in consulatu sexto et septimo, postquam bella civilia exstinxeram, per consensum universorum potitus rerum omnium, rem publicam ex mea potestate in senatus populique Romani arbitrium transtuli. quo pro merito meo senatus consulto Augustus appellatus sum et laureis postes aedium mearum vestiti publice coronaque civica super ianuam meam fixa est et clupeus aureus in curia Iulia positus, quem mihi senatum populumque Romanum dare virtutis clementiaque et iustitiae et pietatis caussa testatum est per eius clupei inscriptionem.

In my sixth and seventh consulships [28–27 B.C.], after I had extinguished civil war, and when I was in supreme control by universal consent, I transferred the state from my control to the dominion of the senate and people of Rome. For this service I was named Augustus by decree of the senate, the door-posts of my house were wreathed with laurel at public expense, a civic crown was placed above my door, and a golden shield was set in the Curia Julia which the inscription on it affirmed was given to me by the senate and people of Rome in recognition of my courage, my clemency, my justness and my devotion.

With the exception of clemency, these virtues are prominent in the decipherment of the shield, and they all go back to the twelfth century,[19] where they are exemplified not only in the portrait of Aeneas but also in that of Evander and his people.

3. Indexes to the Human Condition

It would be an inadequate analysis to suggest that the secondary field of the *Aeneid* is confined to the history of Rome. The poet also keeps alive a sense that his characters are not just Trojans, Greeks, or Romans

---

19. The symbolism of the shield of Augustus (the virtues inscribed on it were the best defence of the state) is reproduced by the shield of Vulcan, but with explicit historical illustrations.

who act in a particular historical framework. They are also human beings placed in a universe that is not of their own making. So there constantly recurs an expansion of the reader's apprehension of the secondary field, such that the action of the immediate context is set within a framework that embraces mankind in its relationship to the conditions imposed by the nature of the universe itself. In many ways, Virgil's use of this technique reveals a deep-seated pessimism, and this will be considered later (see chap. 7, sec. 3); here a few examples of the technique will be briefly examined.

When Aeneas begs the Sibyl to let him visit his father in the Underworld he explains (6.110–14):

> "illum ego per flammas et mille sequentia tela
> eripui his umeris medioque ex hoste recepi;
> ille meum comitatus iter maria omnis mecum
> atque omnis pelagique minas caelique ferebat,
> invalidus, viris ultra sortemque senectae."

"I carried him out on my own shoulders amidst flames and a thousand pursuing weapons and snatched him from right among the enemy; he was my companion on my journey, enduring, weak as he was, all that ocean and all the dangers of both sea and sky, ⟨hardships⟩ beyond the powers and the lot of old age."

In those words (114) *viris ultra sortemque senectae*, whose allusiveness is hard to translate, appeal is made to a standard of measurement that consists in recognising the limitations which the human condition imposes on old age. The universality increases the pathos. When the Sibyl replies, she takes up the basis of Aeneas' appeal (125–31):

> "sate sanguine divum,
> Tros Anchisiade, facilis descensus Averno:
> noctes atque dies patet atri ianua Ditis;
> sed revocare gradum superasque evadere ad auras,
> hoc opus, hic labor est. pauci, quos aequus amavit
> Iuppiter aut ardens evexit ad aethera virtus,
> dis geniti potuere."

"Trojan son of Anchises, born of divine blood, the way down to Avernus is easy—every night and every day the gateway to black Dis is wide open. But to retrace one's step and come up to the breezes above, this is the task, this the difficulty. A few, born of the gods, whom impartial Juppiter loved or whom blazing courage elevated to the sky, have been able."

Here the unemphatic concept of the ever-open gate and the ease of descent is an irony with more than a tinge of bitterness, an index that appeals beyond the immediate dramatic context to the secondary field.

When Aeneas and Achates return from the Sibyl, they find Misenus dead: (6.163) *vident indigna morte peremptum* "they find him laid low in an undeserved death." His background and bravery are then briefly recounted (164–70) before the poet returns to tell of his death (171–74):

> sed tum, forte cava dum personat aequora concha,
> demens, et cantu vocat in certamina divos,
> aemulus exceptum Triton, si credere dignum est,
> inter saxa virum spumosa immerserat unda.

But then, as by chance he made the waters echo to a hollow conch-shell—he must have been mad—and challenged the gods to a contest in music, a jealous Triton had caught him—if this deserves belief—and drowned him in the tide foaming among the rocks.

The second parenthesis undercuts the capacity of the myth to explain a death. The index to the secondary field is provided by the contrast between (163) *indigna* and (173) *dignum*. There is no explanation at first for "a death he did not deserve," nor does the myth, when it comes, account for it, since the judgment of whether he did or did not deserve to die could depend on whether or not one thinks it wrong (or mad) to arouse the jealousy of gods. But (173) *si credere dignum est* tends to dismiss the myth,[20] and the pathos arises from a realisation that death comes to a good man (164–70) without being deserved; there is no explanation.

A contrast with Homer is possible in lines 467–72 of Book 10. These are modelled on *Iliad* 16.433–38. There Zeus sees that his own son Sarpedon is going to be killed and addresses Hera:

> "ὢ μοι ἐγών, ὅ τέ μοι Σαρπηδόνα, φίλτατον ἀνδρῶν,
> μοῖρ' ὑπὸ Πατρόκλοιο Μενοιτιάδαο δαμῆναι.
> διχθὰ δέ μοι κραδίη μέμονε φρεσὶν ὁρμαίνοντι,   435
> ἤ μιν ζωὸν ἐόντα μάχης ἄπο δακρυοέσσης
> θείω ἀναρπάξας Λυκίης ἐν πίονι δήμῳ,
> ἢ ἤδη ὑπὸ χερσὶ Μενοιτιάδαο δαμάσσω."

"Alas for me since I see it is fated for Sarpedon, to me most loved of men, to be killed by Patroclus son of Menoetius. My heart is divided in two directions as I

20. See Stinton (1976), p. 65, for an excellent examination of this type of phrase. But when he claims that *si credere dignum est* here is merely "a story-teller's device for heightening the discourse, like 'mirabile dictu,'" this seems to me to compel the Virgilian text into conformity with a wide range of parallels both Greek and Latin, but unconvincingly, because the subtlety of tone in this poet resists the stereotype of parallels.

debate it in my mind whether I shall snatch him alive from tearful battle and set him down in the rich land of Lydia or condemn him now to the violence of the son of Menoetius."

Hera is outraged at the suggestion of saving a mortal whose time has come. In the passage of the *Aeneid*, Hercules has heard the prayer of Pallas to him and weeps (since he knows what must happen). Juppiter addresses him (467–72):

> "stat sua cuique dies, breve et inreparabile tempus
> omnibus est vitae; sed famam extendere factis,
> hoc virtutis opus. Troiae sub moenibus altis
> tot nati cecidere deum, quin occidit una
> Sarpedon, mea progenies: etiam sua Turnum
> fata vocant metasque dati pervenit ad aevi."

"For each man his day is fixed; short and irrecoverable is the span of life for all men. But to increase one's fame by deeds, that is the task of valour. Beneath the high walls of Troy so many sons of gods fell, among them there even fell Sarpedon, my own son. His own doom is calling Turnus too and he has reached the limits of his allotted life."

The contrast with Homer here lies in the Latin poet's sense of the secondary field; the words go far beyond the immediate context of warriors in the twelfth century—the human condition is harsh in the same way for all men at all times. The scope of vision is similar to that expressed by the poet through Mezentius' words to his horse (10.861–62):

> Rhaebe, diu, res si qua diu mortalibus ulla est,
> viximus.

"Rhaebus, a long time have we enjoyed life—if mortals have anything for a long time."

Here—as often—a note of bitterness (and helplessness) is mixed with the pathos.

Sometimes a recognition of the secondary field can settle a point of interpretation by opening a wider point of view. The first quarter or so of *Aeneid* 11 concentrates on the burial of the dead on both sides. Among the rites is this (193–96):

> hic alii spolia occisis derepta Latinis
> coniciunt igni, galeas ensisque decoros
> frenaque ferventisque rotas; pars munera nota,
> ipsorum clipeos et non felicia tela.

At this point others fling spoils stripped from slaughtered Latins on the flames, helmets and emblazoned swords and bridles and chariot wheels that glow; others ⟨fling on⟩ well-known offerings, their own shields and weapons that had not brought them luck.

This is one of the customs that were Roman in historical times and that, by being projected back into the twelfth century, constitute an index to the historical aspect of the secondary field. But the wider field is also drawn in. Conington says of (195) *ferventis* "the epithet is an awkward one here, as they were so soon to glow from another cause" and the latest editor comments, "the epithet is applied to chariot wheels glowing hot from their speed . . . and is a standing epithet not applicable here."[21] Both editors quote Servius' comment "wheels that do not glow now, but normally do." There is a parallel difficulty often expressed over *nota*: does (195) *munera nota* mean "well-known offerings" in the sense of "traditional at such times" or does it mean "well-known things as offerings" in the sense of "well-known to the former owners"? There is a similar difficulty at 6.221 where similar language is used (220–22):

> fit gemitus. tum membra toro defleta reponunt
> purpureasque super vestis, velamina nota,
> coniciunt.

Then they duly placed the body they had wept over on the bier and over it they fling scarlet robes, well-known vestments.

Here Servius comments on *nota* "loved by him" [i.e., Misenus]. This is certainly right, rather than "traditional at such times," which would convey only antiquarian lore and no pathos. In the passage in *Aeneid* 11 the epithets are not ornamental or "standing"; they work for their places. None is otiose: *decoros, ferventis,* and *nota* all serve to reconstruct a world that is now gone, a world in which these objects all had a vital function; the passing of that world is driven home by the final epithet *non felicia*— they did not serve their function. The epithets are a synecdoche for the condition of human beings faced with the finality of death and for the essential futility of human hopes. The only comment needed on *nota* is to contrast 12.734 *ut capulum ignotum . . . aspexit* "when he noticed the unfamiliar hilt" with 12.759 *notumque efflagitat ensem* "and demanded his well-known sword." Turnus in his haste picked up his charioteer's sword and it broke in his hand; he calls for his own, the one he knew and cherished. This is the emotion that resides in *nota*.

21. R. D. Williams (1973), ad loc. (p. 394).

The world of this part of *Aeneid* 11 is dominated by the universalising sense of the human condition. It is remarkably expressed in a portrait of the dead Pallas (67–71):

> hic iuvenem agresti sublimem stramine ponunt:
> qualem virgineo demessum pollice florem
> seu mollis violae seu languentis hyacinthi,
> cui neque fulgor adhuc nec dum sua forma recessit,
> non iam mater alit tellus virisque ministrat.

Then they place the young man high upon his rustic bed: like the flower either of the gentle violet or of a drooping hyacinth, nipped off by a maiden's thumb, not yet has either its brightness or its beauty left it, nor however does mother earth still nourish it and give it strength.

The simile is modeled on the comparison in Catullus' wedding hymn (62.39–47) between the plucking of a flower and the marriage of a girl. The index of association between the two passages is the bed, but while the girls use the image polemically in Catullus 62, the contrast is here transformed into one between appearance and reality. The gentle plucking of the flower, the gentleness of the flower itself, the appearance of life and beauty, the reality (as yet ungrasped) of its being cut off from the source of life—here is a scene of peace and gentleness; no reminder here of the violence of Pallas' death or the murderous rage he displayed in battle. Death leaves only the appearance of gentleness and beauty.[22] The unspoken contrast expressed by the simile draws that concept into the secondary field as a universal feature of the human condition.

A final example from the same context is worth comparing with its Homeric model. A frequent coda to a scene of burial or instructions for burial is the phrase τὸ γὰρ γέρας ἐστὶ θανόντων "for that is the proper tribute to the dead." It is said, for instance, by Zeus as he gives instructions to Apollo to rescue the corpse of Sarpedon (*Iliad* 16.457). When Aeneas, in *Aeneid* 11, gives instructions to bury the dead he says (22–23):

> "interea socios inhumataque corpora terrae
> mandemus, qui solus honos Acheronte sub imo est."

"Meanwhile let us commit our friends and their unburied corpses to the earth, for that is the only rite that means anything beneath deepest Acheron."

This not only means more than the conventional words of Homer, it

---

22. Cf. the flower-simile that transforms the bloody violence of Euryalus' death (9.433–37).

means more than it actually says. First, its universality transfers it from the immediate context to the secondary field. But, second, it is spoken by a man who should have a claim to authority and it suggests a retrospective judgment on what Aeneas appeared to see in the Underworld. Its pessimism suggests that there is no ground for belief in an afterlife; this world is the only one. That idea is expanded in his following words (24–28):

> ite" ait, "egregias animas, quae sanguine nobis
> hanc patriam peperere suo, decorate supremis
> muneribus, maestamque Euandri primus ad urbem
> mittatur Pallas, quem non virtutis egentem
> abstulit atra dies et funere mersit acerbo."

"Go," he said, "honour with the final rites those splendid souls, who with their blood bought this for us as our fatherland, but first to the mourning city of Evander let Pallas be returned whom, not lacking in valour, the black day carried off and drowned in bitter death."[23]

The sentiment is frequent throughout the *Aeneid* that the only mitigation of death is honourable accomplishment in life; it is that alone which lives on.

4. Conclusion

This technique of implying an all-embracing field, constantly but unobtrusively brought alive to a reader, has a most important function. The celebration of Rome's greatness could easily acquire a tone of facile jingoism; and that sense of an elitist pride which focuses on Rome and excludes consideration of the rest of the world (whose existence, consequently, only has reality in relation to—and dependence on—Rome) is to be detected in other Augustan poets. But in the *Aeneid* the field of Roman history and the age of Augustus is subsumed within the greater field of the human condition. It is in relation to this field that the voice of the poet is most unambiguously heard. This enables him to distance himself to a greater or lesser extent from the voices to be heard in Juppiter's prophecy in Book 1, Anchises' review in Book 6, and Vulcan's artistry in Book 8. The only time when the poet allows his own voice to be heard unequivocally in relation to the field of Roman history and the age of Au-

---

23. This is to be read as an epitaph (or *laudatio*) on Pallas, spoken by Aeneas; the poet himself has already spoken one over him at 10.507–09. See chap. 7, sec. 2(b).

gustus is significant: it is when Evander shows Aeneas the future site of Rome and expresses his own moral viewpoint. The technique allows the fundamental ideas, underlying but not made explicit in the *Aeneid*,[24] to be generated by the tension between the fields of the human condition as such, and of Roman history and the age of Augustus. Certain ideals implicit in Augustan ideology achieve expression in the *Aeneid*, but they do not represent the ultimate judgment of the poet on the world in which he found himself. That judgment only emerges indirectly.

24. See chap. 9.

7   THE POET'S VOICE

Epic poetry is generically impersonal; the poet does not intrude on his own text except within strictly prescribed limits and by means of traditionally recognised structures.[1] The most obvious of these is the prayer for inspiration with which the poem opens or which prefaces a major section of the poem or a section the poet wishes to distinguish as being particularly difficult for the composer. In spite of the fact that Hellenistic Greek poets somewhat loosened the form of these structures to accommodate a more revealing exhibition of the poet's own personality, they still remained generically cramping. Virgil, however, exploited the Hellenistic licence somewhat further, so that the prooemium to the *Aeneid* begins with seven lines of personal declaration defining his subject matter before he appeals to the Muse (8–11). Moreover, this appeal to the Muse is not for help or inspiration in general but only for revelation that will enable the poet to give explanations on the divine level; the human level, he implies, is his own concern. That divided work-load parallels the way in which the poet uses the gods in his text as an explanatory trope (see chapter 2).[2]

His technique is even more surprising in the second prooemium (7.37–45) prefacing the Iliadic half of his epic, the account of the wars in Italy. This address, purporting to be a prayer to the Muse Erato, is phrased throughout in self-assertive future tenses in the first person singular; the only concession to the Muse is a centrally placed phrase, mark-

1. In this respect, Lucan (and to some extent Valerius Flaccus and Statius) is an exception: see Williams (1978), pp. 233–34, 291.

2. That is, the prooemium to the *Aeneid* itself prefigures the gap that characterises the work as a whole: see chap. 1, sec. 4.

ed by its form as a parenthesis (41) *tu vatem, tu, diva, mone* "you, goddess, you remind your poet." The explanation is given in the final assertion (44–45) *maior rerum mihi nascitur ordo, / maius opus moveo* "a more important series of events is coming to birth for me, I am entering on a more important task." The verb *nascitur* is surprising. The poet could say of the coming of the Golden Age, in *Eclogue* 4.5, *magnus ab integro saeclorum nascitur ordo* "a great series of centuries begins anew"; here the idea of birth supports the concept of novelty. But in *Aeneid* 7.44, *maior rerum . . . ordo* refers to what the poet claims to be history. Here the verb masks a deliberate ambiguity that is inherent in the idea of a poet's embarking on a particular area of subject matter. Insofar as that area is new to him, it goes through what is like a process of coming to birth; but that coming to birth also covers the poet's own vision and invention, and supports the idea that he had no real poetic predecessor, with the exception, perhaps (to a very limited extent), of Ennius. Much more depends on the poet's own invention in the second half of the *Aeneid*, and the *Iliad* is a much less direct predecessor here than the *Odyssey* in the first half of the epic.

In both of these cases, then, the poet has used a traditional epic form to make a personal statement that goes much further than the surface meaning of the words. But he has also elsewhere adapted other traditional features of epic, never before used for the purpose, in such a way that they echo the poet's own voice and express a point of view that can be seen to be his. The most important of these techniques will be analysed in this chapter. But first an element that may seem slightly different needs attention: the technique by which Virgil used one of the most traditional formal features of epic to vary the direction of the reader's point of view and thereby to manipulate his judgment.

1. *The Problem of Aspect in Similes*

The classical epic simile carries the voice of the poet in a special way: he turns aside from events in the far past to develop an image that belongs to an entirely different context both of ideas and of chronology. In fact, in terms of chronology he may be shifting from the twelfth century to the late first century B.C., a span of more than a thousand years. In respect to subject matter, too, there may be very wide disparity between that of the context and that of the image, and an important criterion of the effectiveness of a simile is the very extent of that disparity. Quintilian puts this in characteristically practical terms when he says (8.3.74): "The more remote the field of the simile ⟨from that of the context⟩, the more novelty it confers and the greater is its unexpectedness." So for instance, in the simile of the statesman calming a riot (*Aeneid* 1.148–53), the distance from the Hellenistic rococo picture of Neptune riding over the waves to the concrete reality of a Roman political situation that belongs to the lifetime of the poet is not measurable.

This example demonstrates two important features of the epic simile. First, the simile measures the gap between two aspects of the poetic text: on the one hand, the narrative in which the poet imagines himself engaged (along with his reader) in events of the twelfth century as they actually take place; on the other hand, the persona—by no means to be regarded as identical with the poet's personal identity as an individual—in which he is a poet occupied with poetic problems in the age of Augustus. Second, in virtue of the textual establishment of that gap, the simile represents the voice of the poet speaking in the authentic tones of a man of the Augustan age, redressing the events of the twelfth century B.C. by appeal to a timeless world which includes the age contemporary with the poet.

This distance between context and simile is easily regarded as constituting a claim to objectivity, and such objectivity toward the context is certainly one aspect of similes that can be traced back to the Homeric models. It is the poet who claims to see and to establish the similarities between the context and the simile; there is no suggestion that the characters in the narrative context would have viewed the situation in the terms of the simile. In this sense, the simile is authorial, impartial, objective. Yet even in Homer there is an element in some similes that is not entirely covered by this formulation. For instance, in *Iliad* 4 the poet recounts how Agamemnon went around encouraging the Greeks who were demoralised after Menelaus was wounded. Finally he comes to the two Ajaxes (273–83):

> ἦλθε δ' ἐπ' Αἰάντεσσι κιὼν ἀνὰ οὐλαμὸν ἀνδρῶν·
> τὼ δὲ κορυσσέσθην, ἅμα δὲ νέφος εἵπετο πεζῶν.
> ὡς δ' ὅτ' ἀπὸ σκοπιῆς εἶδεν νέφος αἰπόλος ἀνὴρ   275
> ἐρχόμενον κατὰ πόντον ὑπὸ Ζεφύροιο ἰωῆς·
> τῷ δέ τ' ἄνευθεν ἐόντι μελάντερον ἠΰτε πίσσα
> φαίνετ' ἰὸν κατὰ πόντον, ἄγει δέ τε λαίλαπα πολλήν,
> ῥίγησέν τε ἰδών, ὑπό τε σπέος ἤλασε μῆλα·
> τοῖαι ἅμ' Αἰάντεσσι διοτρεφέων αἰζηῶν   280
> δήϊον ἐς πόλεμον πυκιναὶ κίνυντο φάλαγγες
> κυάνεαι, σάκεσίν τε καὶ ἔγχεσι πεφρικυῖαι.
> καὶ τοὺς μὲν γήθησεν ἰδὼν κρείων Ἀγαμέμνων,

As he proceeded through the crowd of men he came to the Ajaxes. They were arming and a cloud of infantry followed with them. As when from a lookout place a goatherd has seen a cloud approaching over the sea ⟨driven by⟩ the roaring West wind. Distant as he is from it, it seems to him blacker than pitch as it moves over the sea and brings a great storm with it. He shudders when he sees it and drives his flock into a cave. Just like that did the dark densely packed ranks of strong heroes move with the Ajaxes into deadly battle, bristling with shields and with spears. And King Agamemnon rejoiced when he saw them. . . .

Virgil used this simile as a model in the scene where Aeneas has armed and, accompanied by his troops, rushes out to battle. Turnus, the Italians, and Juturna are terrified at the sight (12.450–58):

> ille volat campoque atrum rapit agmen aperto.
> qualis ubi ad terras abrupto sidere nimbus
> it mare per medium (miseris, heu, praescia longe
> horrescunt corda agricolis: dabit ille ruinas
> arboribus stragemque satis, ruet omnia late),
> ante volant sonitumque ferunt ad litora venti:
> talis in adversos ductor Rhoeteius hostis
> agmen agit, densi cuneis se quisque coactis
> adglomerant.

He flies ahead and races his dark line over the open plain. Just as when a cloud, cutting off the light of the sun,[3] makes for land over the middle of the sea (pitiable farmers, alas! far off feel their hearts trembling, knowing what is to come—it will bring ruin to trees and destruction to crops, it will lay low everything far and wide); the winds fly before it and carry its roar to the shores: just like that the Trojan commander led his line against the enemy arrayed against them, close-packed they crowd themselves together in serried ranks.

The differences from the Homeric model here are striking. First, Homer did not fully exploit the range of the simile. Two elements in it have little explicit support from the context: the force of the tornado's movement and the fear of the goatherd. There is little sense of movement in the context and everything seems to stop while Agamemnon makes his speech and moves on to the next battalion; nor is there a sense of a Trojan presence in the context—they do not appear for another 150 lines (433)— and the goatherd's fear is reduced almost to an ornamental detail. Virgil has made use of the tornado's speed with (450) *volat* in the context and (455) *volant* in the simile. He has also fully exploited the fear induced by

3. Here *abrupto sidere* must carry the sense (demanded by the context) of sudden darkness; consequently, *sidus* refers to the sun (a meaning in which later poets imitate Virgil). See R. D. Williams (1973), ad loc. (p. 468).

the tornado, by first describing the fear of Italians, Turnus, and Juturna (446–49). He has then expanded this element within the simile by entering into it himself and, in an exclamatory and explanatory parenthesis, sharing the pitiable fear of the farmers. In fact, the aspect of the Virgilian simile is different from the Homeric. Whereas Homer is impartial and assesses the impact of the massed troops on his own sensibility, Virgil surprisingly takes the side of the Italians and, seeing the advance of Aeneas through their eyes, pities them at the same time as he forebodes the destruction to come (while the Greek goatherd merely saves himself and his flock). There is an element here which—as is often the case—must be read from the context into the simile: the threatening blackness of the cloud. In Homer it is introduced by the comparison to pitch, but in Virgil it exists only in the epithet (450) *atrum* applied to the column of Trojans; it is then echoed in the simile in the sinister shutting off of the light of the sun. That element supports the sense of ruin that is coming to the Italians, not just from Aeneas but from the Trojans in general, and they are now as helpless in the situation (albeit created by their own actions) as are the farmers. Previously the narrative had elicited sympathy for Aeneas, wounded and frustrated in all his good intentions; but this simile wins sympathy for his enemies. This constant redressing of the balance of sympathy is an important feature of the poet's attitude to the events of Book 12.

One simile is crucial in this respect. It is modelled on a Homeric simile from the scene of Achilles chasing Hector (*Iliad* 22.188–93):

> Ἕκτορα δ᾽ ἀσπερχὲς κλονέων ἔφεπ᾽ ὠκὺς Ἀχιλλεύς.
> ὡς δ᾽ ὅτε νεβρὸν ὄρεσφι κύων ἐλάφοιο δίηται,
> ὄρσας ἐξ εὐνῆς, διά τ᾽ ἄγκεα καὶ διὰ βήσσας·   190
> τὸν δ᾽ εἴ πέρ τε λάθῃσι καταπτήξας ὑπὸ θάμνῳ,
> ἀλλά τ᾽ ἀνιχνεύων θέει ἔμπεδον, ὄφρα κεν εὕρῃ·
> ὡς Ἕκτωρ οὐ λῆθε ποδώκεα Πηλείωνα.

But the swift Achilles relentlessly pressing on him pursued Hector, as when on the mountains a hound pursues a fawn, rousing it from its lair, on through the glades and through the valleys; and even if it should take cover crouching beneath a thicket, yet ⟨the hound⟩ runs on tracking it without pause until it finds it. So Hector did not find cover from the swift-footed Achilles.

A simile of Apollonius Rhodius must also be taken into account. It comes in the scene of the Harpies chased by the sons of Boreas (2.278–83):

> ὡς δ᾽ ὅτ᾽ ἐνὶ κνημοῖσι κύνες δεδαημένοι ἄγρης
> ἢ αἶγας κεραοὺς ἠὲ πρόκας ἰχνεύοντες

θείωσιν, τυτθὸν δὲ τιταινόμενοι μετόπισθεν 280
ἄκρης ἐν γενύεσσι μάτην ἀράβησαν ὀδόντας·
ὡς Ζήτης Κάλαΐς τε μάλα σχεδὸν ἀίσσοντες
τάων ἀκροτάτῃσιν ἐπέχραον ἤλιθα χερσίν.

As when on the shoulders of a mountain hounds skilled in hunting run tracking down horned goats or deer; straining a little distance behind, they clash their teeth at the very tip of their jaws—in vain. So Zetes and Calais, racing along very close, just touched them with the very tips of their fingers—in vain.

The Virgilian simile is this (*Aeneid* 12.746–62):

Nec minus Aeneas, quamquam tardata sagitta
interdum genua impediunt cursumque recusant,
insequitur trepidique pedem pede fervidus urget:
inclusum veluti si quando flumine nactus
cervum aut puniceae saeptum formidine pennae
venator cursu canis et latratibus instat;
ille autem insidiis et ripa territus alta
mille fugit refugitque vias, at vividus Vmber
haeret hians, iam iamque tenet similisque tenenti
increpuit malis morsuque elusus inani est:
tum vero exoritur clamor ripaeque lacusque
responsant circa et caelum tonat omne tumultu.
ille simul fugiens Rutulos simul increpat omnis
nomine quemque vocans notumque efflagitat ensem.
Aeneas mortem contra praesensque minatur
exitium, si quisquam adeat, terretque trementis
excisurum urbem minitans et saucius instat.

No less does Aeneas (though his knees slowed by the arrow often let him down and refuse to run) pursue and hotly press with his foot upon the foot of the frightened man: just as when on occasion a hunting dog, having come upon a stag hemmed in by a river or trapped by the scare of scarlet feathers, presses after him, running and barking; he, however, terrified by the trap and by the high bank, races backward and forward a thousand ways, but the lively Umbrian keeps close to him, mouth agape, and he is ever on the point of catching him and, as if he has caught him, he clashes his jaws and is frustrated by an empty bite; then indeed does an uproar arise and both banks and waters echo around and all the heavens thunder with the tumult. He [Turnus] at every single moment as he runs away does not cease upbraiding all of the Rutuli, calling each by his name, and demands his own trusty sword. Aeneas, on the other hand, threatens death and instant execution should any come near, and terrifies them already frightened, threatening to destroy their city, and though wounded presses after.

Commentators seem confident of the meaning of this simile; for instance: "Turnus has become only the frightened stag, Aeneas its vicious hunter—a hound who has taken to himself all the violence he has felt for others."[4] What is justified in this, as in many similar comments, is that the simile enforces sympathy for Turnus; but the rest is without basis. One element in the simile is denied by the context: that is, it produces a clash between the persona of the poet as engaged in events of the twelfth century and as a detached observer in the age of Augustus. This detail is the dog, the *vividus Vmber*; it is ludicrous to see Aeneas authorially portrayed as the lively dog—the author has explicitly denied the equation by insisting on Aeneas' lameness (746–47 and 762), which every now and then prevents him from running. This detail makes it clear that the aspect of the simile is not impartial and objective: the simile sees the situation through Turnus' eyes and the image of the dog shows how he (not the poet) regards Aeneas. This aspect is confirmed by other details. The hound is made more terrifying by the sound of its clashing jaws as it thinks it has got its prey; this comes from Apollonius Rhodius, the impact of whose dogs is weakened by their plurality, forced on him by the context (there Homer is more powerful and Virgil follows), and also by the unconvincing idea of "the tips of the dogs' jaws," contrived to provide a parallel to "tips of their fingers."

But another important element missing in Apollonius and only hinted at in Homer becomes a major feature of the Virgilian simile: the stag's fear. The tone of the simile is dominated by that fear, and it enforces an element that only gradually emerges from the context. In line 742 Turnus is *amens*, in 748 he is *trepidi*; it is not until line 776 that the poet forthrightly describes him as *amens formidine* "out of his mind with terror." In the simile, the terror that is also Turnus' and his view of Aeneas in terms of a savage hunting-dog are used by the poet to win sympathy for Aeneas' enemy. In Homer, sympathy for Hector is resident in the context rather than in the simile, and in Apollonius Rhodius the impartiality of the simile conceals the poet's actual hostility toward the pursued no less than his sympathy for the pursuers. The slanting of the Virgilian simile by contrast is remarkable.

Here, therefore, a contextually inappropriate element in a simile is an indication that the aspect of the simile is not to be interpreted as objective or authorially impartial. This technique can be seen in another

4. Putnam (1965), p. 189.

important simile. At the beginning of Book 12 Turnus realises that the Latins have been defeated (1–9):

> Turnus ut infractos adverso Marte Latinos
> defecisse videt, sua nunc promissa reposci,
> se signari oculis, ultro implacabilis ardet
> attollitque animos. Poenorum qualis in arvis
> saucius ille gravi venantum vulnere pectus   5
> tum demum movet arma leo, gaudetque comantis
> excutiens cervice toros fixumque latronis
> impavidus frangit telum et fremit ore cruento:
> haud secus accenso gliscit violentia Turno.

When Turnus realised that the Latins, broken by a war that had gone against them, had collapsed, that he was being required to make good his promises, that he was being marked by all eyes, he flew into an implacable rage and exalted his spirit. Like the lion in the territory of the Carthaginians who, disabled by a grave wound in his breast from hunters, then at last takes up arms and exults, tossing the heavy muscles along his neck and fearlessly breaks the brigand's spear buried in his flesh and roars with a blood-stained mouth: not otherwise did violence catch fire within the flaming Turnus.

The two wounded-lion similes in Homer (*Iliad* 5.136–43 and 20.164–73) are not significant in judging the Virgilian effect, mainly because neither Diomedes nor Achilles (to whom the similes are limited) is wounded. But the wounding has real meaning in the case of Turnus, disabled by the death of Camilla and so many Italians. The immediately surprising detail in the Roman simile is the noun *latro* "brigand," for this is a distinctly un-epic word. Many recent commentators interpret it as meaning that the poet is condemning Aeneas, and they point to the fact that on three earlier occasions Aeneas was called a *praedo*, which also means "brig-and."[5] But this is to ignore the speakers: the first time it is Amata, poisoned by Allecto and cursing Aeneas as a prospective son-in-law (7.362); the second time it is Mezentius as he prays to kill Aeneas (10.774); the third time it is the Italian matrons as they pray to Diana to break the weapon of Aeneas in his hand (11.484). In all instances an enemy is giving a hostile appraisal of Aeneas. No reader should for a moment be deceived into thinking that the poet here condemns Aeneas with the word *latro*. The very contradiction indicates that the aspect of the simile is not that of the impartial poet. Here the situation is seen through Turnus' eyes. Fur-

5. For example, ibid., p. 154.

thermore, the surprising lexical correction of the description of the perpetrators of the lion's wound from (5) *venantum* to (7) *latronis* marks the shift in the lion's attitude from being hunted to itself becoming an attacker. That movement also represents the psychological change that takes place in Turnus as soon as he feels himself isolated (1–4): he flies into an implacable rage. Homer describes the lion lashing itself with its tail to work up its rage (*Iliad* 20.170–71); in Virgil that act of self-stimulation does not form part of the simile, but it is in the context and must be read into the simile (as part of the shift from *venantum* to *latronis*). In fact this simile commences as if it were authorial and objective in aspect, but changes, as the lion's rage grows, into accepting the colour and aspect of that rage. It is in the first part of the simile that an authorial detail is introduced: for (4) *Poenorum* serves to pick up the theme of the Carthaginians as the real enemies of Rome.

This simile is not sympathetic to Turnus; it simply sees the situation through his eyes, and sympathy is denied in the word (9) *violentia*. Sympathy for Turnus only comes later, and it reaches a climax in the last formal simile of the *Aeneid*. When Turnus, like a Homeric hero, tries to fell Aeneas with a huge rock, he fails to make it carry far enough (903–14):

> sed neque currentem se nec cognoscit euntem
> tollentemve manus saxumve immane moventem;
> genua labant, gelidus concrevit frigore sanguis.
> tum lapis ipse viri vacuum per inane volutus
> nec spatium evasit totum neque pertulit ictum.
> ac velut in somnis, oculos ubi languida pressit
> nocte quies, nequiquam avidos extendere cursus
> velle videmur et in mediis conatibus aegri
> succidimus—non lingua valet, non corpore notae
> sufficiunt vires nec vox aut verba sequuntur:
> sic Turno, quacumque viam virtute petivit,
> successum dea dira negat.

But neither as he ran nor as he moved did he recognise himself nor as he lifted the huge rock in his hand nor as he impelled it; his knees gave way, his blood chilled and congealed with cold. Then the rock too, whirled through empty space, did not cover the whole distance or carry its blow home. And as in dreams, when relaxing peace at night has overwhelmed our eyes, we perceive ourselves desperately wanting to run on farther, but in vain, and in the midst of our attempts we are faint and collapse; our tongue has no strength, the normal powers are not available in our body and neither voice nor words issue forth: so whenever Turnus exerted his valour to find a way, the terrible goddess denied him success.

This has a brief Homeric analogue in the immediate context of the analogue to the simile of the stag and hound (*Iliad* 22.199–201):

ὡς δ' ἐν ὀνείρῳ οὐ δύναται φεύγοντα διώκειν·
οὔτ' ἄρ' ὁ τὸν δύναται ὑποφεύγειν οὔθ' ὁ διώκειν·   200
ὡς ὁ τὸν οὐ δύνατο μάρψαι ποσίν, οὐδ' ὃς ἀλύξαι.

But as in a dream one cannot catch up with a man who is running away; neither can the one escape away nor the other catch him up; so the one could not catch him by ⟨speed of⟩ foot, nor the other reach safety.

Here the Homeric simile is a mere suggestion. The Virgilian simile is unique in using verbs in the first-person plural to appeal to a common experience the reader must have shared. This technique is characteristic of didactic poetry, where the poet poses as teacher to readers who are pupils and shares his experience with them, but is alien to the impersonal persona of an epic poet. Consequently, a special effect is being sought here. The simile has multiple correspondences with the context,[6] and its aspect is such that it views the situation through the eyes of Turnus. But here the poet goes further and appeals for a sympathetic attitude toward Turnus, who is now paralysed by fear and by a self-defeating sense that death is near (916). The figure or emblem of that fear is the trope of the *dea dira*. The call for sympathetic understanding is made by a momentary shift from epic to didactic persona in a direct appeal to readers.

Here an earlier simile concerning Turnus is worth considering—since its tone is totally different, and its difference is a useful indicator of the degree to which the poet has manipulated the reader's sensibilities in favor of Turnus toward the end of Book 12. Turnus is inspired to attack the Trojan camp at the beginning of Book 9, but he is frustrated because the Trojans stay within the walls (57–66):

huc turbidus atque huc
lustrat equo muros aditumque per avia quaerit.
ac veluti pleno lupus insidiatus ovili
cum fremit ad caulas ventos perpessus et imbris
nocte super media: tuti sub matribus agni
balatum exercent, ille asper et improbus ira
saevit in absentis, collecta fatigat edendi
ex longo rabies et siccae sanguine fauces:
haud aliter Rutulo muros et castra tuenti
ignescunt irae; duris dolor ossibus ardet.

6. West (1970), pp. 268–69.

Wildly he ranges the walls at this point, then at that, and searches for an approach
through the pathless region; and as when a wolf, laying ambush to a crowded
sheepfold, howls at the chinks ⟨in the fence⟩, enduring wind and rain beyond
midnight; safe beneath their mothers lambs engage in bleating, but he, cruel and
beside himself with rage, savages them in imagination; a craving to eat, long pent-
up, and his throat unslaked with blood do not let him rest. Not otherwise did rage
kindle within the Rutulian as he surveyed the walls and camp, and anger blazed
within his flinty bones.

The Homeric analogues to this simile are not close; here again Apollonius
Rhodius provided a more immediate model. Polyphemus hears the cry of
Hylas as he is drawn beneath the waters (1.1243–49):

> βῆ δὲ μεταΐξας Πηγέων σχεδόν, ἠύτε τις θὴρ
> ἄγριος, ὅν ῥά τε γῆρυς ἀπόπροθεν ἵκετο μήλων,
> λιμῷ δ᾽ αἰθόμενος μετανίσσεται, οὐδ᾽ ἐπέκυρσεν   1245
> ποίμνησιν· πρὸ γὰρ αὐτοὶ ἐνὶ σταθμοῖσι νομῆες
> ἔλσαν· ὁ δὲ στενάχων βρέμει ἄσπετον, ὄφρα κάμησιν·
> ὣς τότ᾽ ἄρ᾽ Εἰλατίδης μεγάλ᾽ ἔστενεν, ἀμφὶ δὲ χῶρον
> φοίτα κεκληγώς·

And he went rushing along, near Pegae, like a beast of the wilds to whom the
bleating of sheep has come from afar; blazing with hunger he follows it but does
not reach the flocks, for the shepherds have penned them within the steadings.
And groaning, he roars fearfully till he becomes tired. So did the son of Eilatus
groan greatly, and he went about crying out.

Several important differences from the Virgilian simile are clear. The
groaning and roaring of the animal are emphasised to give the poet a
lead-out from the simile. The hunger of the beast is only slightly operative
either in simile or in context, and its fatigue has no point. Nor is the single
cry convincingly picked up by the bleating of sheep. In fact, the simile is
poorly integrated with its context and creates an impression of superficial
and hasty composition.

The Virgilian simile concentrates its effort on psychology, moving
from objective facts to feelings. At first the simile seems to be authorially
objective, but there is one detail that points to a different aspect: the
Trojans are as lambs only to Turnus; they are, in fact, following the orders
of Aeneas, although they want to go out and fight (44), and they are
armed, ready to repulse the enemy (38–39 and 45–46). The one element
here that works in the context is *tuti*—they are safe in the camp. That
draws attention to another feature. The adjective *turbidus* leads into the
simile and *irae* leads out; that double link with the context corresponds to

asper et improbus ira / saevit inside the simile. But the simile reaches its climax in details that do not operate in the context. The wolf here is tired not by its immediate sufferings (as in Apollonius) but by its long-denied lust for blood. The simile is terrifying, but the Trojans are not terrified because they do not yet know their man. Blood-lust will have become a familiar characteristic of Turnus by the end of the epic; he lives to kill, and as the wolf has long been denied blood so has Turnus. It is he who views the Trojans as a wolf does lambs and, in a most imaginative phrase, savages them though they are absent (that is, he imagines the sensation of tearing them)—their blood will sate his lust. So the aspect of this simile, appearing at first to be objective, is in fact subjective and sees the world from Turnus' point of view, the psychology of which is here revealed for the first time. (This is, therefore, a highly significant instance of thematic anticipation.) In this respect the simile can be contrasted with the one at lines 339–41 (a starving lion falls upon sheep) or at lines 791–96 (a lion gives way under pressure, but without turning tail), both of which are authorially objective in the Homeric style and have close Homeric analogues.

   Another wolf-simile that has a clear model in the *Iliad* can be seen to have something of the same aspect, in contrast with its model, as the simile of Turnus and the wolf. It is the simile that compares Arruns to a wolf after he has killed Camilla. The Homeric model is used of Antilochus who, urged by Menelaus to kill a Trojan, ran out in front of his own troops, threw his spear, and killed Melanippus. Hector then came running up to avenge the death and Antilochus fled back to his own ranks (*Iliad* 15.585–91):

> 'Αντίλοχος δ' οὐ μεῖνε θοός περ ἐὼν πολεμιστής,   585
> ἀλλ' ὅ γ' ἄρ' ἔτρεσε θηρὶ κακὸν ῥέξαντι ἐοικώς,
> ὅς τε κύνα κτείνας ἢ βουκόλον ἀμφὶ βόεσσι
> φεύγει πρίν περ ὅμιλον ἀολλισθήμεναι ἀνδρῶν·
> ὣς τρέσε Νεστορίδης, ἐπὶ δὲ Τρῶές τε καὶ Ἕκτωρ
> ἠχῇ θεσπεσίῃ βέλεα στονόεντα χέοντο·   590
> στῆ δὲ μεταστρεφθείς, ἐπεὶ ἵκετο ἔθνος ἑταίρων.

And Antilochus did not wait, active warrior though he was, but ran away like a beast that has done an evil deed, that, having killed a dog or a herdsman among his cattle, flees before a crowd of men can collect: so did the son of Nestor run away and upon him did the Trojans and Hector, with deafening cries, shower down lethal weapons. But as soon as he reached the group of his companions, he stood and faced about.

Here little is operative in the context except the running away—and that
is only temporary. Antilochus has no reason to feel guilt. The poet objectively sees his hasty retreat in terms of an animal that has done something
outrageous (though Antilochus has not).

This is the Virgilian simile (11.805–15):

> concurrunt trepidae comites dominamque ruentem
> suscipiunt. fugit ante omnis exterritus Arruns
> laetitia mixtoque metu, nec iam amplius hastae
> credere nec telis occurrere virginis audet.
> ac velut ille, prius quam tela inimica sequantur,
> continuo in montis sese avius abdidit altos
> occiso pastore lupus magnove iuvenco,
> conscius audacis facti, caudamque remulcens
> subiecit pavitantem utero silvasque petivit:
> haud secus ex oculis se turbidus abstulit Arruns
> contentusque fuga mediis se immiscuit armis.

Her terrified companions run to her and support their collapsing mistress. But
Arruns, more terrified than any, runs away in delight mixed with fear, and he no
longer dares trust his spear or face the maiden's weapons. And just as a wolf,
before enemy weapons can pursue him, immediately hurries himself, avoiding
paths, up into the high mountains, after killing a shepherd or a great ox, fully
aware of his outrageous act, and drooping back his tail he tucks it in terror under
his belly and makes for the woods: not otherwise did Arruns wildly take himself
out of sight and, happy to run away, hid himself in the middle of the army.

Here the adjective (812) *audacis* draws *facti* into the sense of *facinus* which
is an un-epic word, so that "crime" is nearer to the meaning than "deed."
The word *conscius* completes the idea that Arruns has good reason to have
a guilty conscience. Why? What has he done wrong? There is nothing in
the immediate context to answer that, but as he prepares to throw his
spear he prays to his patron god, Apollo of Soracte, and ends his prayer
with these words (789–93):

> "da, pater, hoc nostris aboleri dedecus armis,
> omnipotens. non exuvias pulsaeve tropaeum
> virginis aut spolia ulla peto, mihi cetera laudem
> facta ferent; haec dira meo dum vulnere pestis
> pulsa cadat, patrias remeabo inglorius urbes."

"Permit, omnipotent father, that this disgrace be wiped out by my weapons. No
spoils or trophy over the beaten maiden or plunder of any kind do I seek, all my

other deeds will win me fame; provided this deadly plague fall beaten by a wound from me, I shall return inglorious to the cities of my fathers."

Apollo heard but granted only half the prayer (794–95). The odd formulation emphasises Arruns' desire not to be known as the author of this deed. He will, in fact, not only not return home; he will be denied all recognition (fulfilling 793 *inglorius*) and his death will be ignored (865–66):

> illum exspirantem socii atque extrema gementem
> obliti ignoto camporum in pulvere linquunt.

As he expired and groaned his last, his companions forgot him and left him in the unknown dust of the plains.

The epitaph[7] shows that his body lay unburied and unmarked, for *ignoto camporum in pulvere* means "in an unknown part of the dusty plains." Arruns' act is militarily useful but cowardly and thus inglorious. His own consciousness of the fact only emerges in the simile which views the world through his eyes: the wolf has done something so dastardly that it knows retribution will follow. The killing of a shepherd or an ox is not fitting for a wolf to do—the fact creates guilt in the animal in the same way as the killing of Camilla, which the cowardly Arruns had no right to do.

Other similes, however, have a different aspect: in them the subject—the main figure in context and simile—is viewed from his opponents' point of view. In Book 7 the people of Latinus demand war and press Latinus to declare it (585–90):

> certatim regis circumstant tecta Latini;
> ille velut pelagi rupes immota resistit,
> ut pelagi rupes magno veniente fragore,
> quae sese multis circum latrantibus undis
> mole tenet; scopuli nequiquam et spumea circum
> saxa fremunt laterique inlisa refunditur alga.

Vying with one another they surround the palace of King Latinus; he stands against them like a rock unmoved by the sea, like a rock that, when the roar of the sea grows great, holds firm by its own mass as the waves bark all around: in vain its crags and its foam-covered reefs roar and sea-weed battered on its side is poured back over it.

7. For the form, see sec. 2(b) below.

The simile is surprising because even by this point an impression of Latinus is beginning to form quite clearly—he is someone who always wants the easy way out, who is unwilling to face unpleasant reality, who knows what he should do but cannot stand firm. The picture of the rock is the opposite of such a character. The explanation comes in what follows (591–600):

> verum ubi nulla datur caecum exsuperare potestas
> consilium, et saevae nutu Iunonis eunt res,
> multa deos aurasque pater testatus inanis:
> "frangimur heu fatis" inquit "ferimurque procella!
> ipsi has sacrilego pendetis sanguine poenas,
> o miseri. te, Turne, nefas, te triste manebit
> supplicium, votisque deos venerabere seris.
> nam mihi parta quies, omnisque in limine portus
> funere felici spolior." nec plura locutus
> saepsit se tectis rerumque reliquit habenas.

But when no possibility is given him of overcoming their blind counsel and events are proceeding at the will of cruel Juno, the father, loudly calling on the gods and the empty breezes to witness "Alas!" he cries, "we are being shattered by fate and carried out of control by the storm. It will be you yourselves, pitiful creatures, who will pay the penalty for this with your sacrilegious blood. It is for you, Turnus, that the crime, for you that the bitter punishment will be waiting, and your prayers to the gods will be too late. For I have won my repose and, right at the mouth of the haven, I am ⟨only⟩ robbed of a happy death." Saying no more, he shut himself inside his palace and relinquished the reins of state.

The image Latinus uses for himself is that of a ship shattered by the seas and driven helplessly before a storm. He has no feeling whatever of being a rock standing firm against the breakers. The poet has here made use of the two related Homeric similes. In *Iliad* 15 the Trojans, led by Hector, storm the Greek ships. But at first the Greeks stand firm against the assault (618–29):

> ἴσχον γὰρ πυργηδὸν ἀρηρότες, ἠύτε πέτρη
> ἠλίβατος μεγάλη, πολιῆς ἁλὸς ἐγγὺς ἐοῦσα,
> ἥ τε μένει λιγέων ἀνέμων λαιψηρὰ κέλευθα   620
> κύματά τε τροφόεντα, τά τε προσερεύγεται αὐτήν·
> ὣς Δαναοὶ Τρῶας μένον ἔμπεδον οὐδ' ἐφέβοντο.
> αὐτὰρ ὁ λαμπόμενος πυρὶ πάντοθεν ἔνθορ' ὁμίλῳ,
> ἐν δ' ἔπεσ' ὡς ὅτε κῦμα θοῇ ἐν νηῒ πέσῃσι
> λάβρον ὑπαὶ νεφέων ἀνεμοτρεφές· ἡ δέ τε πᾶσα   625
> ἄχνῃ ὑπεκρύφθη, ἀνέμοιο δὲ δεινὸς ἀήτης

ἱστίῳ ἐμβρέμεται, τρομέουσι δέ τε φρένα ναῦται
δειδιότες· τυτθὸν γὰρ ὑπὲκ θανάτοιο φέρονται·
ὡς ἐδαΐζετο θυμὸς ἐνὶ στήθεσσιν Ἀχαιῶν.

For they held on, close-fitted like a wall, or like a great beetling cliff, facing the grey sea, that resists the swift streams of howling gales and the swelling waves that foam against it. So the Greeks resisted the Trojans firmly and did not give way. But he [Hector], blazing with flame all over, leapt into their ranks, and he fell upon them as when a wave falls upon a swift ship, a wild wave lifted up beneath the clouds by the gale. But it is completely engulfed in foam and a fearful blast of wind roars into the sail and the sailors tremble in their hearts with fear, for they escape death by only a little. So was the spirit of the Achaeans torn within their breasts.

Here the poet moves from one simile to the other as the situation undergoes a dramatic change, and the second simile is only partially operative in the context because—although the Greeks in fact break and flee—only one man is killed by Hector.

However, in the Virgilian sequence no change takes place in the situation. Instead, the poet uses the Homeric sequence to define two different perceptions. What happens is that the aspect of the rock-simile must be defined, not from the viewpoint of Latinus, and still less from that of the impartial poet; it must be defined from the viewpoint of the warmongers: to them, Latinus' unwelcome stubbornness seems to be like a rock. But, with a nice touch of irony, the poet goes on to contrast this point of view with its opposite, as the king expresses his own sense of himself. Here the aspect of the rock-simile is modified and commented on by the new aspect of the metaphor used by Latinus, the ship helplessly driven before a storm. He then views himself—by a slight change of metaphor—as a ship already at the harbour-mouth (of death); he has nothing to lose except a happy death, and so he withdraws from attempting to govern his people.

This is the aspect, too, of the simile that defines Aeneas' appearance as he comes ashore from his ship (10.270–75),[8] or of the simile that compares Mezentius to Orion (10.763–68), or Aeneas to Athos or Eryx or father Appenninus (12.701–03). In the same series should also be placed another simile that has caused commentators trouble. As Aeneas, after hearing of the death of Pallas, rages over the battlefield killing all he meets, he is described thus (10.565–70):

8. See p. 65 above.

Aegaeon qualis, centum cui bracchia dicunt
centenasque manus, quinquaginta oribus ignem
pectoribusque arsisse, Iovis cum fulmina contra
tot paribus streperet clipeis, tot stringeret ensis:
sic toto Aeneas desaevit in aequore victor
ut semel intepuit mucro.

Like Aegaeon who, they say, had one hundred arms and one hundred hands and
fire blazed out from fifty mouths and lungs as he roared against the thunderbolts
of Juppiter with the same number of matching shields and drew the same number
of swords: so Aeneas raged victoriously over the whole plain once his sword-
blade grew warm.

One writer says about this passage: "For all this barbarity and irresistible
violence, Virgil compares Aeneas to a monstrous giant who challenges
the very might of Jupiter (565 ff.). The implication is that our hero has
exceeded the limits."[9] Even the latest commentator remarks: "It is very
significant that Aeneas, given over as he now is to rage and frenzy,
should be compared with a barbaric figure symbolising violence and
brutality."[10]

The only appearance of Aegaeon in the *Iliad* is at 1.402–05, where he
is remembered as having protected Zeus against plots by other gods.
However, the Roman poet has deliberately cast him in his role of ally to
the Giants in their assault on Juppiter. Consequently, here he certainly is
a figure for violence and barbarity. But the commentators suppose that
the poet is thereby condemning Aeneas—that is, the simile is authorially
objective and impartial. This makes no sense. The reader can be trusted to
have grasped the poet's conception of Aeneas by now, and this simile,
coming in the middle of a list of warriors slain by Aeneas, is another that
views the subject of both context and simile through the eyes of his
opponents. Aeneas seems, to the Latins in their terror, like Aegaeon. This
is a much more interesting and pointed idea than that the poet thinks of
Aeneas as behaving as if he really were Aegaeon. Here, the index of
discrepancy between context and simile that makes a reader question the
objectivity of the simile lies in the hundred arms and fifty chests that
breathe fire. These details clearly have no objective analogy in Aeneas,
only in the terrifying image of him that the doomed Latins see.

This can be contrasted with the simile that portrays Dido as Aeneas

9. Anderson (1969), p. 84.
10. R. D. Williams (1973), ad loc. (p. 359).

first sees her:[11] there the analogy of Diana is provided with multiple correspondences with the context, and these even extend to the overadequate detail of Latona's delight in seeing her daughter. A similar close integration of image and context characterises the parallel simile that compares Aeneas, as he makes his appearance to join the hunt (4.141–50), to Apollo. Both of these are truly objective similes, more ornamental and designed to appeal to a generically legitimated field than to make a visual impact. In fact, with such material the poet measures the greatest possible distance between his persona as engaged with events of the twelfth century as they happen and his persona as a craftsman of the age of Augustus. The poet's claim to a privilege that allows him to use the gods as figurative elements in his narrative belongs to the aspect of his poetic activity that sets him firmly in the age of Augustus. This is, of course, also true of the simile that compares Aeneas to Aegaeon. Such material is at the furthest remove from the fields of equally objective similes that use visual observation of everyday life, especially when it is given a more or less contemporary Roman colour, as, for instance, in the striking simile that views Juturna's erratic driving of the chariot in terms of a swallow that has flown into a rich man's house (12.473–78). Here, too, the poet measures the distance between the two aspects of his persona; however, in this case it is not in virtue of his privileged access to a field closed to ordinary men (which applies, for instance, to the field of divine machinery), but in virtue of his own observation of the world that he himself lives in.

Recognition of the objectivity of certain similes is important to the reader's judgment of certain moral situations. A good example is the simile that portrays Dido in love (4.68–73):

> uritur infelix Dido totaque vagatur
> urbe furens, qualis coniecta cerva sagitta,
> quam procul incautam nemora inter Cresia fixit
> pastor agens telis liquitque volatile ferrum
> nescius: illa fuga silvas saltusque peragrat
> Dictaeos; haeret lateri letalis harundo.

Poor Dido is on fire and wanders insanely throughout the whole city, like a deer when an arrow is shot and a shepherd, hunting with his weapons amidst Cretan woods, has transfixed it off its guard from afar and, without realising, he has left

---

11. See p. 62 above.

the flying steel in it: in its flight it traverses the woods and glades of Dicte: the deadly shaft is fixed in its side.

There are many obvious correspondences with the whole story of Dido from beginning to end, and the simile is authorially objective. The only judgment involved is that of the detached poet, sympathetic and pitying, but also tentatively apportioning responsibility in the words (70) *incautam* and (72) *nescius*. The collocation of the words, however, is paradoxical: to be caught off guard by someone who does not know of your presence is a figure that recognises the deadly intractability of love and its ever-present potential for tragedy. The attitude is appropriate to contemplation of Dido's tragedy, but it is also a view of human love that marks all of the poet's ideas on that subject from his earliest to his latest work. This simile is objective in the sense of expressing the detached poet's assessment of the situation rather than viewing it through the eyes of either individual involved.

Recognition of that same objectivity is very important in a later simile. Dido tries to get Aeneas to change his mind, even to a small extent, but in vain (441–49):

> ac velut annoso validam cum robore quercum
> Alpini Boreae nunc hinc nunc flatibus illinc
> eruere inter se certant; it stridor, et altae
> consternunt terram concusso stipite frondes;
> ipsa haeret scopulis et quantum vertice ad auras
> aetherias, tantum radice in Tartara tendit:
> haud secus adsiduis hinc atque hinc vocibus heros
> tunditur, et magno persentit pectore curas;
> mens immota manet, lacrimae volvuntur inanes.

And just as when northern gales from the Alps battle among themselves with blasts, now on one side now on the other, to uproot an oak mighty with the strength of years; a creaking is heard and leaves from high up strew the ground as the trunk is shaken; but it clings firmly to the rocks, since as high as it reaches into the winds of heaven with its top so far does it reach also with its root downward into Tartarus: not otherwise is the hero buffeted with continuous pleas on this side and on that and deeply feels the pain of love in his brave heart; his resolution remains steadfast, the tears stream down in vain.

The authorial objectivity of the simile guarantees what is otherwise hardly mentioned: Aeneas is deeply in love with Dido. He loves Carthage (281 *dulcisque relinquere terras*) and is deeply torn; he has to suppress his feelings of love as he addresses her (332) and he leaves Dido after her out-

burst (395) *multa gemens magnoque animum labefactus amore* "groaning deeply and shaken to the core by the greatness of his love." That is all that is
said of Aeneas' feelings for Dido, but the simile authoritatively enacts the
desperate inner struggle from which he eventually emerges still determined to follow what he sees as his duty. Multiple correspondences
between this simile and its context are clear to see.[12] This fact can be used
to settle an old problem: are the tears (449) Aeneas' or Dido's? The falling
of these tears corresponds to the falling of the leaves of the shaken oak[13]
and so they are Aeneas' and constitute the outward sign of the deep
division within him. The poet thus objectively affirms the power of the
love Aeneas feels for Dido.

2. Apostrophe, Epitaphs, and Authorial Comment

The devices to be examined in this section are all techniques that
permit the poet to make himself evident in his own text, and that entails a
distinction between the surface of the text, as it were, and the actual
process of composition. This distinction is also likely to involve the perception of a gap between the twelfth century, in which the narrative is
active, and a period that may be timeless or else more or less identical
with the period of the composition of the poem.

(a) *Apostrophe.*[14] At the beginning of Book 11 the poet describes
Aeneas setting up a trophy to Mars, using the armour and weapons of
Mezentius (5–11):

> ingentem quercum decisis undique ramis
> constituit tumulo fulgentiaque induit arma,
> Mezenti ducis exuvias, tibi, magne, tropaeum,
> bellipotens; aptat rorantis sanguine cristas
> telaque trunca viri, et bis sex thoraca petitum
> perfossumque locis, clipeumque ex aere sinistrae
> subligat atque ensem collo suspendit eburnum.

On a mound he set up a huge oak, with its branches cut off on all sides, and
decked it with shining armour, spoils from the leader Mezentius, a trophy to you,
mighty god of war; he attached crests bedewed with blood and the man's broken
weapons, and his breastplate struck and punctured in twelve places, and his

---

12. See West (1969), pp. 44–45.
13. Ibid., p. 45.
14. On apostrophe, see Quintilian 9.2.38–39 and 9.3.24–27. For a theoretical analysis
of the figure, see especially Culler, *Diacritics* 7 (1977): 59–69.

shield of bronze he bound to the left side and hung his ivory sword around the neck.

This detailed account of the setting up of a trophy is preceded at 10.541–42 by a brief reference to the custom:

> arma Serestus
> lecta refert umeris tibi, rex Gradive, tropaeum.

His arms Serestus collects and carries off on his shoulders as a trophy to you, King Gradivus [Mars].

The address to the god (the same in both cases) by the poet functions in part as a re-enactment of the original verbal dedication that is to be imagined as having been spoken by the dedicator and perhaps recorded in writing on the trophy as well.[15] That is, the poet uses the formal device of apostrophe to echo the actual address to the god made in the original ceremony. Such a reproduction by means of apostrophe of what amounts to a dedicatory epigram can also be seen in the account of Daedalus' arrival in Cumae (6.18–19):

> redditus his primum terris tibi, Phoebe, sacravit
> remigium alarum posuitque immania templa.

Restored to earth first at this place, he dedicated to you, Phoebus, the oarage of his wings and he founded a massive temple.

The same device is used at 6.251, where Aeneas makes sacrifice (249–51):

> ipse atri velleris agnam
> Aeneas matri Eumenidum magnaeque sorori
> ense ferit, sterilemque tibi, Proserpina, vaccam.

Then Aeneas on his own slays with his sword a black-fleeced lamb to the mother of the Eumenides and to the great sister, and a heifer to you, Proserpina.

The joint sacrifice to Night and Earth is followed by one to Proserpina, which is made more immediate by echoing the actual formula used by Aeneas. In the same way, Aeneas' sacrifice to Juno, after the Tiber has appeared to him in a dream, is reproduced by apostrophe (8.84–85):

> quam pius Aeneas tibi enim, tibi, maxima Iuno,
> mactat sacra ferens et cum grege sistit ad aram.

15. As Aeneas does at Actium (3.286–88).

⟨A sow⟩ which devoted Aeneas slaughters, making it a sacrifice for you, for you indeed, almight Juno, and sets it with its brood at the altar.

In both of these instances, the deity addressed by the poet has a very special significance in the narrative: Proserpina as queen of the Under-world where Aeneas is going, and Juno as the persistent enemy of the Trojans and—ironically, in view of the pious sacrifice—destined to con-tinue to be so. Clear here, therefore, is a particular expression of emo-tional concern on the part of the poet that is conveyed by the device of apostrophe.

A final example of this type of apostrophe comes from the account of Amata's mad careering over the countryside as she simulates the rites of Bacchus (7.385–91):

> quin etiam in silvas simulato numine Bacchi
> maius adorta nefas maioremque orsa furorem
> evolat et natam frondosis montibus abdit,
> quo thalamum eripiat Teucris taedasque moretur,
> euhoe Bacche fremens, solum te virgine dignum
> vociferans: etenim mollis tibi sumere thyrsos,
> te lustrare choro, sacrum tibi pascere crinem.

She even flew out into the woods and, pretending that it was the influence of Bacchus, ventured a greater crime and entered on a more extreme madness: she hid her daughter in the leafy mountains that she might deprive the Trojans of their marriage and delay the wedding-torches, screaming "euhoe, Bacchus!" shouting that only you are worthy of the maiden and that it is in your honour she is taking up the pliant thyrsi, that it is you she is celebrating in her dance, that it is as an offering to you she is growing her hair long.

Here the apostrophe can be seen taking its origin in the vocatives shouted by Amata and then being carried on by the vocatives that follow, now from the mouth of the poet acting, as it were, on behalf of Amata. But of course he cannot do so in any literal sense, and this example shows (what is easier to miss in the earlier examples) that the apostrophe is not only a vehicle of the poet's special emotional concern in a particular situation and with a particular deity; it also permits him to make his presence felt in the text, though not on the level of the participants who are the objects of his narrative. But his presence is always privileged, as he has access to a world which is not that of his characters, and his voice is always the voice of the poet. When he apostrophises a deity who is also being addressed by one of his characters, whether the form of the apostrophe echoes the original dedication, epigram, or prayer, he is therefore claiming a specially intimate relationship with the deity which is quite different from his character's (since the poet is not making prayer or sacrifice) and which is parallel to the easy relationship he displays with the gods in virtue of his privileged position as narrator. That is, the apostrophe momentarily and self-consciously cancels the gap between the temporality of the narrative on the one hand and that of the composition on the other: the poet assumes to himself the relationship that the twelfth-century character is made to express. The mental world of the poet that comprehends the events of the twelfth century is itself timeless and also includes the age of Augustus.

This sense of a timeless world to which events of the twelfth century are assimilated by apostrophe can be clearly seen in apostrophes of geographical places in the catalogue of Italian forces at 7.682–85:

> quique altum Praeneste viri quique arva Gabinae
> Iunonis gelidumque Anienem et roscida rivis
> Hernica saxa colunt, quos dives Anagnia pascis,
> quos, Amasene pater.

And men who inhabit elevated Praeneste and the fields of Juno of Gabii and the chill Anio and the Hernican rocks bedewed by streams, those whom you, rich Anagnia, and whom you, father Amasenus, nurture;

or at 7.797–800:

> qui saltus, Tiberine, tuos sacrumque Numici
> litus arant Rutulosque exercent vomere collis
> Circaeumque iugum, quis Iuppiter Anxurus arvis
> praesidet et viridi gaudens Feronia luco.

Those who plough your glades, Tiberinus, and the sacred bank of the Numicus and vex the Rutulian hills with their ploughs and the ridge of Circe, fields over which Juppiter of Anxur presides and Feronia who rejoices in her verdant grove;

(in the catalogue of Etruscan forces) at 10.198–201:

> Ille etiam patriis agmen ciet Ocnus ab oris,
> fatidicae Mantus et Tusci filius amnis,
> qui muros matrisque dedit tibi, Mantua, nomen
> Mantua, dives avis, sed non genus omnibus unum.

There also was Ocnus who had levied a contingent from his ancestral borders, the son of the prophetess Manto and of the Tuscan river [Tiber], he who gave walls and the name of his mother to you, Mantua, Mantua rich in ancestry, but not all of one race.

Here the names of places that echo through Roman history and (in the case of Tiberinus) through the epic itself are drawn out beyond the twelfth-century setting by the poet's apostrophe in an emotional intimacy of relationship which converts them into subjects instead of objects; this intimacy reaches a climax when the poet mentions his own hometown of Mantua, from which the poet alleges that (in spite of its being so far farther north than any other place mentioned) a contingent came to fight as allies of Aeneas.

A related type of apostrophe, also concerning an Italian place-name, opens Book 7 (1–4):

> Tv quoque litoribus nostris, Aeneia nutrix,
> aeternam moriens famam, Caieta, dedisti;
> et nunc servat honos sedem tuus, ossaque nomen
> Hesperia in magna, si qua est ea gloria, signat.

You too, Caieta, nurse of Aeneas, by your death brought eternal fame to our shores; and now your glory guards the abode and the name marks your resting-place, in great Hesperia—so far as that glory has a meaning.

Similar to this is an apostrophe in Book 5, 123 *genus unde tibi, Romane Cluenti* ("whence your family-name, Roman Cluentius"), in a list of Roman families that originated with Trojans. Both of these are indexes to the field of Roman history, and the effect of the poet's entering his own text is to cancel the gap between the twelfth century and the time of writing by drawing the characters into the timeless mental world that the poet commands.

The same effects, achieved by differing means, can be seen in the apostrophes of persons in both catalogues: at 7.734 *nec tu carminibus nostris indictus abibis, / Oebale* ("nor shall you go by unmentioned in my poem, Oebalus"), the poet directly confronts Oebalus with a promise that only the poet can fulfill. Oebalus does not appear again in the poem. Ufens, who appears on four subsequent occasions, of which the final two (12.400, 641) are his death and an important comment on it by Turnus,[16] is apostrophised more conventionally (7.744–45). Umbro, whose death is not explicitly mentioned at 10.543–44, receives a lament in terms of the pastoral pathetic fallacy (7.759–60):[17]

16. See p. 31 above.
17. For more detail, see Williams (1968), pp. 723–24.

> te nemus Angitiae, vitrea te Fucinus unda,
> te liquidi flevere lacus.

Thee the grove of Angitia, thee Fucinus with its glassy water, thee the clear waters of the lakes mourned.

At 10.185–86, Cunarus receives a poetic promise similar to that given to Oebalus. In all of these the apostrophe, though accorded to only one or two individuals, expresses the impartial pity of the poet for those destined to war, and this emotion is effectively extended over all the participants in both catalogues. The further effect, common to all these apostrophes, of closing the gap between the temporality of the narrative and that of the composition, can be seen in comparison with Anchises' review of Roman heroes in Book 6 where the apostrophes (817–86), whether to Aeneas or to those in the review, have all the effect of apostrophe for the reader, though dramatically they are real addresses made to people actually present. It is, in fact, only the drama of the review that differentiates it from the essentially similar technique in the description of the shield where the voice is the voice of the poet, there too addressing both the reader (8.676, 688, 691) and the barbarously executed Mettus (643). The example of Mettus shows the gap being cancelled by his being addressed as if he were still alive to complain.[18]

Address to the reader is very infrequent in the *Aeneid*, but it is used by the poet as the Trojans prepare to leave Carthage (4.401–15):

> migrantis cernas totaque ex urbe ruentis.
> ac velut ingentem formicae farris acervum
> cum populant hiemis memores tectoque reponunt,
> it nigrum campis agmen praedamque per herbas
> convectant calle angusto: pars grandia trudunt   405
> obnixae frumenta umeris, pars agmina cogunt
> castigantque moras, opere omnis semita fervet.
> quis tibi tum, Dido, cernenti talia sensus,
> quosve dabas gemitus, cum litora fervere late
> prospiceres arce ex summa, totumque videres   410
> misceri ante oculos tantis clamoribus aequor!
> improbe Amor, quid non mortalia pectora cogis!
> ire iterum in lacrimas, iterum temptare precando
> cogitur et supplex animos summittere amori,
> ne quid inexpertum frustra moritura relinquat.   415

18. See pp. 153–55 above.

You can see them moving out and hurrying from every part of the city. As when ants plunder a vast heap of corn, mindful of the winter, and store it in their home, a black line goes across the plain and they haul their loot by a narrow path through the grass; some heave and push monstrous grains with their shoulders, others drill the lines and discourage delay; the whole pathway is seething with activity. What feeling did you then have, Dido, as you saw such happenings, or what groans did you emit, when you looked out from the top of the citadel at the shores seething in all directions, and saw right before your eyes the sea a confusion of such shouts? Cruel Love, to what do you not force mortal hearts? She is forced a second time to resort to tears, a second time to try entreaties and humbly submit her spirit to love lest she should leave anything untried, fated to die in vain.

The invitation to the reader is expressed in the most immediate way possible by the surprising present subjunctive ("You can see, ⟨should you trouble to look⟩"): the same device is used to convey the extraordinarily vivid effect of Vulcan's representation of the ship at Actium on the shield (8.691 *credas*). The ant-simile has the detachment and humour of the poet's own voice, and so maintains the atmosphere of an address to the reader. The address to Dido links her with the viewing reader by the use of the verb (408 *cernenti*), but hers is not a detached viewing. Her separation from the union of reader, situation, and poet is marked by past tenses: only the poet can understand and communicate with her. The poet's mental world is immediately available to the reader; it is the text in front of his eyes. But the real agony of the real Dido in the twelfth century is only available to the poet, who confronts her directly with his sympathy. The reader can share the sight that she saw, but he can understand what it meant to her only from the poet's confrontation with her. The following interrogative apostrophe to *Amor* (harshly condemned by *improbe*) releases the poet from the immediate presence of Dido in the twelfth century into the timeless field of the human condition, and this makes the transition (linked by *cogis . . . cogitur*) to a detached description of Dido's humiliation. Here the poet's voice (and not Dido's)[19] should be heard in *frustra moritura*: at this point the poet foresees the future as Dido cannot, and he comments ironically on her vain hopes—she will die without accomplishing anything. Here the three successive apostrophes cancel the gap between the temporality of the narrative and that of the composition in three different ways: by the poet's addressing a contemporary reader, by his identifying with the heroine of the narrative, and by his confronting a force that is always destructive of human beings.

19. For this view, see Austin (1955), ad loc.

Justice is here done to a complex situation at the same time as the poet's voice suggests a judgment of his own.

The apostrophe to the reader here and in the description of the shield introduces a dimension into one's reading of the narrative that measures the gap between the events and the poet at the same time as it tries to cancel it. The same effect can be felt in the use of *nostris* (7.1) in the address to Aeneas' nurse. It is seen again in 7.47–49:

> hunc Fauno et nympha genitum Laurente Marica
> accipimus; Fauno Picus pater, isque parentem
> te, Saturne, refert, tu sanguinis ultimus auctor.

We hear that he was born of Faunus and the Laurentian numph Marica; Picus was father to Faunus and he reports you, Saturn, as his parent, you are the final author of his blood.

Here *accipimus* works, as it were, against the cancelling effect of the apostrophe. The poet's own voice spells out the same gap as *accipimus* when he says (7.646) *ad nos vix tenuis famae perlabitur aura* "to us a faint breath of rumour barely trickles through"; that sense of a formidable historical gap is hardly perceptible in the Homeric model for this line at *Iliad* 2.486, "But we hear only report and know nothing ourselves." The historical consciousness of the poet of the *Aeneid* is always alive in the narrative to create the gap that needs constant bridging.

Occasionally the gap lies between the immediate narrative and something that precedes rather than follows. For instance, in Book 5.495–97:

> tertius Eurytion, tuus, o clarissime, frater,
> Pandare, qui quondam iussus confundere foedus
> in mediòs telum torsisti primus Achivos.

Third was Eurytion, your brother, o most illustrious Pandarus, you who once, upon orders to break the truce, were the first to shoot an arrow into the Achaean ranks.

Here the gap that is cancelled lies between the text of Homer (*Iliad* 4.68–187), where Menelaus is wounded by Pandarus' arrow, and the text of the *Aeneid*—a gap that the poet measures and bridges on a number of occasions, outstandingly in the story of Achaemenides at the end of Book 3. The gap is closed by the poet, who, in composing the later text, shows himself aware of the earlier one by a personal entrance into his own narrative.

A slightly different gap is bridged in *Aeneid* 5.563–65:

> una acies iuvenum, ducit quam parvus ovantem
> nomen avi referens Priamus, tua clara, Polite,
> progenies, auctura Italos.

One of the lines of young men is that which in triumph little Priam leads, recalling the name of his grandfather, your distinguished offspring, Polites, destined to augment the people of Italy.

The gap here is between the immediate event of the *lusus Troiae*, designed to recall the Trojan past, and the horrible death in Troy of Polites, recounted in *Aeneid* 2.526–53. The apostrophe to the dead man brings him alive in the timeless mental world of the poet to enjoy his son's distinction. Of course, the major effect of the apostrophe here is pathos, arising from the contradiction between the apostrophe and the reader's knowledge of his death, and that same pathos is predominant in a great series of apostrophes to human beings. So it is with the apostrophe to the dead Icarus at 6.31 (contrasting with the apostrophe to Apollo at 6.18) or to the soon-to-be dead Palinurus at 5.840. The pathos arises from a contrast usually drawn between appearance (the supremely gifted artist or the confident Palinurus) and reality—often of death and its effect. On one occasion however, the effect is not pathos but irony; that is when the poet apostrophises Tarchon at 10.302 after his grandiose orders and their successful execution by every ship—except his own.

The use of apostrophe greatly accelerates in the battle scenes of Books 10 and 12, and there the poet's hatred of war distinctly comes across in the tone of pity. There is always an increase of emotional concern in these authorial invasions of the text; for instance, at 10.429–30:

> sternitur Arcadiae proles, sternuntur Etrusci
> et vos, o Grais imperdita corpora, Teucri.

There is laid low the youth of Arcadia, there are laid low the people of Etruria, and you, Trojans, o bodies that were indestructible to Greeks.

Here, as in the sacrifice of Aeneas in 6.249–51, the climax of the tricolon is reserved for apostrophe to those of most concern to the poet, as he recounts the tale of slaughter wreaked by Lausus (and cancels the textual distance from the *Iliad*).

At 10.513–15 the emotion of Aeneas after he has heard of the death of Pallas is represented by an apostrophe:

> proxima quaeque metit gladio latumque per agmen
> ardens limitem agit ferro, te, Turne, superbum
> caede nova quaerens.

He reaps all that is closest to him with his sword and, blazing, drives a path through the wide battle-line with his steel, searching for you, Turnus, arrogant from your fresh slaughter.

Here, as with those of dedication and prayer, the apostrophe represents the thought of Aeneas re-enacted by the poet.

Pallas is of special concern to the poet. As Pallas succeeds in rallying his frightened and inexperienced forces, a simile represents courage spreading like fire and ends with these words (10.410–11):

> non aliter socium virtus coit omnis in unum
> teque iuvat, Palla.

Not otherwise did all the courage of your friends unite and aid you, Pallas.

There is a foreboding pathos in the apostrophe that is picked up in the epitaphic address at the end of Pallas' story (10.507–09):

> o dolor atque decus magnum rediture parenti,
> haec te prima dies bello dedit, haec eadem aufert,
> cum tamen ingentis Rutulorum linquis acervos!

O you who will return as a great grief and yet glory to your father, this day was the first to send you to war, this same day carries you off; yet in spite of that you are leaving behind heaps of Rutulians.

The effect of the apostrophe here is certainly pathos, but it also allows the poet to combine two standards: on the one hand, the human tragedy both in the particular terms of Pallas' grieving father and in the more general pity inherent in the idea of brevity expressed by "the same day"; on the other, the heroic sense of values that could regard the tragedy as to some extent offset by the destruction wreaked by Pallas upon his enemies. The glory lies in the slaughter; Pallas and his father could feel that, but the poet insulates himself in the ambiguous tone of *cum tamen*. This moral ambiguity that allows the poet to see and express two points of view, both of which may have their own validity in particular circumstances, is a characteristic of the *Aeneid*.[20]

Once a narrow escape from death is the subject of apostrophe (10.324–30):

20. See chap. 8.

> tu quoque, flaventem prima lanugine malas
> dum sequeris Clytium infelix, nova gaudia, Cydon,
> Dardania stratus dextra, securus amorum
> qui iuvenum tibi semper erant, miserande iaceres,
> ni fratrum stipata cohors foret obvia, Phorci
> progenies, septem numero, septenaque tela
> coniciunt.

You too, unfortunate Cydon, as you kept close to Clytius, your latest delight, whose cheeks were golden with the first down, you too might have been lying pitifully cut down by the Dardan's [Aeneas'] right hand, forgetful of the love of young men you always felt, had not the close-packed cohort of your brothers, the offspring of Phorcus, seven in number, opposed themselves and hurled seven spears.

Here the surprising adjective *infelix* expresses the incompatibility of love and war; but it also expresses the destructive and dangerous nature of love for those who feel it. The concept is expanded by the implication that dying would be the only way Cydon could forget love. Cydon's love is homosexual, which ought to make it more compatible with war, but the incongruous nature of his activity is expressed both in the description of Clytius and also in the harsh contrast between *nova gaudia* and the fate that he has only just escaped. It is that escape which makes *infelix* surprising and so allows it to bear so much meaning.[21]

Also present here are generic markers of sepulchral epigram in the piquant contrasts and the apostrophe. The bitter humour of another apostrophe is similarly epitaphic (10.390–96):

> vos etiam, gemini, Rutulis cecidistis in agris,
> Daucia, Laride Thymberque, simillima proles,
> indiscreta suis gratusque parentibus error;
> at nunc dura dedit vobis discrimina Pallas.
> nam tibi, Thymbre, caput Euandrius abstulit ensis;
> te decisa suum, Laride, dextera quaerit
> semianimesque micant digiti ferrumque retractant.

You too fell on Rutulian fields, twin Larides and Thymber, identical offspring of Daucus, indistinguishable to their own parents and source of happy error. But now Pallas has given you harsh distinguishing marks. For Evander's sword cut your head off, Thymber; and your right hand, Larides, chopped off, tried to find its owner and your still-living fingers twitched and kept grasping the sword.

---

21. It is a surprise analogous to that of the poet's apostrophising Nisus and Euryalus as (9.446) *fortunati ambo*, where a depth of meaning also needs to be understood (see pp. 205–07 below).

Here the apostrophe supplies the tone of epigram, shading pity into a detachment that allows the grim joke about the twins' distinction. This sense of detachment is underlined by *suis* (instead of *vestris*), which shows the poet's awarness of an audience; and, in turn, the humour, together with the physical details, expresses the poet's horror and pity.

The siege of the camp gives an opportunity for a swift review of individual Trojans (10.118–45). Ismarus is introduced thus (139–42):

> te quoque magnanimae viderunt, Ismare, gentes
> vulnera derigere et calamos armare veneno,
> Maeonia generose domo, ubi pinguia culta
> exercentque viri Pactolusque inrigat auro.

You too your great-hearted clans beheld, Ismarus, dealing out wounds and tipping your arrows with poison, high-born from your Maeonian home, a land where men work the rich cornfields and Pactolus irrigates them with gold.

Here again the combination of detachment with a tone of melancholy and foreboding (nothing more is heard of Ismarus) comes from the epitaphic apostrophe and a theme that characterises Virgil's poetry from first to last—the sense of exile, of a man facing death in a land far from his home.

That theme is given memorable expression at the death of Aeolus (12.542–47):

> te quoque Laurentes viderunt, Aeole, campi
> oppetere et late terram consternere tergo:
> occidis, Argivae quem non potuere phalanges
> sternere nec Priami regnorum eversor Achilles;
> hic tibi mortis erant metae, domus alta sub Ida,
> Lyrnesi domus alta, solo Laurente sepulcrum.

You too the Laurentian plains saw fall, Aeolus, and cover the wide ground with your back. You lie dead whom neither the battle-lines of Argos could bring down nor Achilles, destroyer of the kingdoms of Priam. Here death brought your life's course to an end; your proud home was at the foot of Ida, in Lyrnesus was your proud home, on Laurentian soil is your grave.

This is the tone of Macaulay's fine poem on the death of a Jacobite in Italy. It combines the irony of escape from the Greeks (cf. 10.429–30) with the pathos of a grave in exile in a foreign land. The emotion is generated by the apostrophe.

This epitaph is immediately preceded by two parallel deaths (12.538–41):

> dextera nec tua te, Graium fortissime Cretheu,
> eripuit Turno, nec di texere Cupencum
> Aenea veniente sui: dedit obvia ferro
> pectora, nec misero clipei mora profuit aerei.

Neither did your right hand save you from Turnus, Cretheus, bravest of the Greeks, nor did his gods protect Cupencus when Aeneas came: he presented his breast to the spear and the delay in his bronze shield was no help to him, poor man.

The apostrophe expresses the pity for Cretheus whose death need not be elaborated upon (he is Greek because he is one of Evander's men), but the same negative formula used for Cupencus takes its emotional overcharge from the preceding apostrophe, and the ironical contrast in *dextera* and *di . . . sui* is of the essence of sepulchral epigram. The two deaths are thus united in one epigram. The contrast, which is ironical and thus no real contrast at all, is another instance of the poet's subverting any suggestion that gods are actually involved in human actions.

The recognition of the genre of sepulchral epigram in these epitaphic addresses of the poet can settle at least one problem of text (10.315–17):

> inde Lichan ferit exsectum iam matre perempta
> et tibi, Phoebe, sacrum: casus evadere ferri
> quo licuit parvo?

Then he slew Lichas, cut from his mother's womb after her death and consecrated to you, Phoebus. To what purpose was he permitted to escape destruction by steel when he was still tiny?

Here *quo* is a correction in the Palatine manuscript; most manuscripts have *quod*. If *quod* is read, then the final clause gives the reason for Lichas' being consecrated to Apollo: "because he was permitted to escape death by steel when he was tiny." Not only is this redundant since it is already expressed by *exsectum iam matre perempta*, but it also fails to do justice to the apostrophe. What was Apollo doing while Lichas was being killed? That question is posed in the words of the surprising and perfectly epigrammatic ending, and it is spoken with the detached irony of the poet's voice, as expressive of pathos as any direct attempt to evoke emotion.

In all these types of apostrophe there is clearly a special touch of pathos and pity that derives from authorial intervention. There is only one apostrophe in the battle-scenes that looks as if it might be conventional, in the manner of earlier and especially of later poets; it is at 10.402 where Rhoeteus, fleeing from Teuthras (apostrophised as *optime Teuthra*), is accidentally struck by Pallas' spear (intended for Ilus). But even here the apostrophe serves to anticipate the recovery of Pallas' forces, and Teuthras, sometimes taken by commentators to be a Trojan, should really be seen as a Greek (his name occurs at *Iliad* 5.705 in a list of those killed by Hector) and one of Evander's people. The poet intervenes to commend an ally of Aeneas, not mentioned elsewhere, who is putting his enemies to flight. There is always, too, the additional feature, seen in earlier examples, that the apostrophe cancels the gap between the temporality of the narrative and that of the composition in such a way as to refer the situation to the timeless mental world of the poet. What emerges from the poet's voice lamenting deaths of Italians and Trojans impartially is an explicit condemnation, given the fullest authority, of the tragedy of war.

(*b*) *Epitaphs.* Also in the battle-scenes are a whole series of epitaphs in which, despite the absence of apostrophe, the poet's voice may usually be recognised. These constitute a continuous dirge over man's folly and the tragedy of war. They start with the splendid epitaph on Priam, spoken by Aeneas (2.554–58). Here the tone and point of view are perfectly accommodated to the voice of Aeneas,[22] and the epitaph corresponds to the practice, common among Roman historians, of giving a brief biography (like a *laudatio*) after the death of an important individual.

Dido is allowed to speak her own epitaph (4.653–58),[23] but, as she dies, the poet devises a means for entering his text and pronouncing an epitaph of his own over her (696–97).[24]

Anchises speaks a lengthy epitaph, really a *laudatio*, over Marcellus,[25] eleven centuries before his death (6.870–86); the *laudatio*, however, is adapted to allow Anchises not only to imagine the funeral (872–74) but also to take part in the ceremonies himself (883–86).

But the epitaphic style is really heard in the battle-scenes. In the first sporadic fighting between Trojans and Italians, Galaesus is killed (7.535–39):

> corpora multa virum circa seniorque Galaesus,
> dum paci medium se offert, iustissimus unus
> qui fuit Ausoniisque olim ditissimus arvis:

22. See Appendix, sec. 1(b) for text and commentary.
23. See Austin (1955), ad loc. (pp. 188–90).
24. See below, p. 217.
25. See pp. 148–49 above.

> quinque greges illi balantum, quina redibant
> armenta, et terram centum vertebat aratris.

Around him were many bodies and also the elderly Galaesus, ⟨killed⟩ as he offered himself a mediator for peace, he who had been the single most just man and the wealthiest in Ausonian land; five flocks he had of sheep, five herds came home for him, and he turned the earth with one hundred ploughs.

The closest Homeric analogue for this is *Iliad* 6.12–17:

> Ἄξυλον δ' ἄρ' ἔπεφνε βοὴν ἀγαθὸς Διομήδης
> Τευθρανίδην, ὃς ἔναιεν ἐϋκτιμένῃ ἐν Ἀρίσβῃ
> ἀφνειὸς βιότοιο, φίλος δ' ἦν ἀνθρώποισι·
> πάντας γὰρ φιλέεσκεν ὁδῷ ἔπι οἰκία ναίων.   15
> ἀλλά οἱ οὔ τις τῶν γε τότ' ἤρκεσε λυγρὸν ὄλεθρον
> πρόσθεν ὑπαντιάσας,

Then Diomedes of the loud war-cry killed Axylus, son of Teuthranus, who dwelt in the pleasant town of Arisbe, rich in the things of this life and beloved of men; for, living in a house by the wayside, he used to entertain all. But not one of them now came forward against the enemy and saved him from miserable death. . . .

The pathos is strong in Homer, as well as the brief sense of a particular character. But the Virgilian epitaph expresses the destruction of values; it has a moral dimension, absent in Homer, which stresses peace, justice, and the kind of distinction in a community that comes from owning land and working it oneself—or at least supervising the working of it in person. War is incompatible with these moral values; within its context they lose all meaning.

In *Aeneid* 9 it is only after a long battle-account and many deaths that the poet speaks the first epitaph (771–77):

> inde ferarum
> vastatorem Amycum, quo non felicior alter
> ungere tela manu ferrumque armare veneno,
> et Clytium Aeoliden et amicum Crethea Musis,
> Crethea Musarum comitem, cui carmina semper
> et citharae cordi numerosque intendere nervis,
> semper equos atque arma virum pugnasque canebat.

After that ⟨Turnus kills⟩ Amycus the slayer of wild beasts, than whom no one was more adept at smearing weapons with his own hand and arming steel with poison, and Clytius son of Aeolus and Cretheus beloved by the Muses, Cretheus companion of the Muses, whose delight always was in poetry and the lyre and in playing tunes on his strings, always he used to sing of horses and of men's weapons and of battles.

The pathetic epanalepsis of the name of Cretheus slows the movement of the battle into the epitaphic style and the ironic contrast, perfectly suited to that genre, between being a poet inspired by war and an actual participant in war. The voice of the poet mocking himself as he too sings of battles is clear in these words.

The same strategy of completing a list of killings with an epitaph can be seen in Book 12, where Turnus and Aeneas both go on a rampage of slaughter. Aeneas kills a series of men; then Turnus (516–20):

> hic fratres Lycia missos et Apollinis agris
> et iuvenem exosum nequiquam bella Menoeten,
> Arcada, piscosae cui circum flumina Lernae
> ars fuerat pauperque domus nec nota potentum
> munera, conductaque pater tellure serebat.

He [Turnus] killed the brothers sent from Lycia and the lands of Apollo, and Menoetes, a young man who hated war—in vain, an Arcadian whose skill had been spent on the fish-filled waters of Lerna; his home was modest; he knew nothing of the rewards of attendance on the powerful, and his father planted seed in earth that he rented.

This epitaph has no Homeric analogue. Like that on Galaesus, it expresses a sense of values in concrete images: hatred of war, a modest life of hard work combining fishing and agriculture, and a contentment that sought neither influence nor possessions. This young Greek was one of Evander's people, and the epitaph contains not just the sense of values subverted by war but also the pathos of death on foreign soil far from a beloved homeland. The values expressed here are all a source of great poetic power to the writers of Virgil's own age, and they played a part, too, in Augustan ideology.

The great series of epitaphic interventions by the poet comes, however, in the crucial and most savage fighting of Book 10. Some of these have already been considered among instances of apostrophe, but others remain that are not apostrophic. An impressive series occurs in the account of Aeneas' attack on the Italians as the Etruscans are landing (308–32). Among these is the death of Cisseus (317–22):

> nec longe Cissea durum
> immanemque Gyan sternentis agmina clava
> deiecit leto; nihil illos Herculis arma

> nec validae iuvere manus genitorque Melampus,
> Alcidae comes usque gravis dum terra labores
> praebuit.

And not far off he sent down to death hardy Cisseus and monstrous Gyas, who were both laying low the battle-lines with their clubs; the weapons of Hercules did not help them then nor their strong hands nor that Melampus was their father who was the companion of Hercules during all the time that the earth provided grievous labours for him.

The epitaphic nature of this emerges by comparison with the closest Homeric analogue at *Iliad* 5.49–58:

> υἱὸν δὲ Στροφίοιο Σκαμάνδριον, αἵμονα θήρης,
> Ἀτρεΐδης Μενέλαος ἕλ' ἔγχεϊ ὀξυόεντι,   50
> ἐσθλὸν θηρητῆρα· δίδαξε γὰρ Ἄρτεμις αὐτὴ
> βάλλειν ἄγρια πάντα, τά τε τρέφει οὔρεσιν ὕλη·
> ἀλλ' οὔ οἱ τότε γε χραῖσμ' Ἄρτεμις ἰοχέαιρα,
> οὐδὲ ἑκηβολίαι, ᾗσιν τὸ πρίν γ' ἐκέκαστο·
> ἀλλά μιν Ἀτρεΐδης δουρικλειτὸς Μενέλαος   55
> πρόσθεν ἕθεν φεύγοντα μετάφρενον οὔτασε δουρὶ
> ὤμων μεσσηγύς, διὰ δὲ στήθεσφιν ἔλασσεν,
> ἤριπε δὲ πρηνής, ἀράβησε δὲ τεύχε' ἐπ' αὐτῷ.

Then Menelaus, son of Atreus, with his sharp-pointed spear killed Scamandrios, son of Strophios, devoted to hunting and a fine hunter. For Artemis herself taught him to shoot all wild animals that the woods nurture on the mountain-slopes. But Artemis the archer was of no help to him then nor his own far-shooting in which formerly he had won fame. For the glorious spearman Menelaus, son of Atreus, struck him with his spear as he fled before him, in the middle of the back between his shoulders, and drove it through his chest. Face down he fell and his armour clanged over him.

There is nothing epitaphic in the Homeric sequence, where the mention of Artemis is only descriptive and pathetic. What happens in the Virgilian passage is that the death is recounted and then the voice of the poet is heard intoning the epitaph. It is perfectly suited to the genre of sepulchral epigram that what in Homer was a reference to divine intervention and a skill owed to that fact, becomes in Virgil a significant list of qualities, introduced by the epitaphic formula, "this and this and this were of no help . . ." (belonging to the commonplaces of the genre of *consolatio*); this, when completed, also explains why the brothers used the odd weapons they did to fight—they were imitating their father's friend Hercules.

The Homeric pattern, descriptive rather than epitaphic, can be seen in the account of Acron's death at the hands of Mezentius (719–31), where the details of his background are recounted before his death.

Finally, there is the striking account of Antores' death (10.776–82):

> dixit, stridentemque eminus hastam
> iecit. at illa volans clipeo est excussa proculque
> egregium Antoren latus inter et ilia figit,
> Herculis Antoren comitem, qui missus ab Argis
> haeserat Euandro atque Itala consederat urbe.
> sternitur infelix alieno vulnere, caelumque
> aspicit et dulcis moriens reminiscitur Argos.

He [Mezentius] spoke and from a distance hurled the whistling spear. But as it flew it was deflected from the shield of Aeneas and far away it pierced the distinguished Antores between ribs and groin, Antores the companion of Hercules, who, sent from Argos, had kept with Evander and had settled in the Italian town. Unlucky, he is laid low by a wound meant for another, and, looking up at the sky, he remembers as he dies his sweet Argos.

Here again is the poetry of exile and death in a foreign land and the dying memory of home (in spite of years spent in Italy). The physiological details of the wound deliberately contrast with the quiet melancholy of the ending that is utterly conclusive in the manner of epigram. There are many Homeric analogues for a weapon missing one target and killing another, but none for this fine epitaph.

Turnus' death ends the epic, and his indignant soul has the last word; an epitaph in the voice of the poet would be inappropriate. So Turnus is, like Dido, allowed to pronounce his own epitaph before the final duel begins (12.643–49):

> "exscindine domos (id rebus defuit unum)
> perpetiar, dextra nec Drancis dicta refellam?
> terga dabo et Turnum fugientem haec terra videbit?
> usque adeone mori miserum est? vos o mihi, Manes,
> este boni, quoniam superis aversa voluntas.
> sancta ad vos anima atque istius nescia culpae
> descendam magnorum haud umquam indignus avorum."

"Am I to stand by while our homes are destroyed (that has been the one element missing in our misfortunes), and am I not to refute the charges of Drances with my sword-arm? Shall I turn tail and shall this land see Turnus running away? Is it so very bitter to die? O powers of the dead, be favourable to me since the will of the gods is turned away from me. I shall descend to you a guiltless soul, innocent of such a crime and not unworthy of my grand ancestors."

This is a perfect expression of Turnus' sense of values, but it is idealised. He has been running away and the land will see that sight again; he will be afraid to die (916) and will beg humbly for his life. But that is not how he wishes to see himself behaving, and the words have a winning nobility.

Aeneas does not die within the epic, so he too is allowed to speak his own epitaph (12.435–40).[26] Chracteristically, he thinks not of himself but of his son, to whom he wants to be a worthy example in every way— except in his *fortuna*. Aeneas does not often complain, and this bitter comment on *fortuna* recalls various occasions in Book 1 when he expressed bitterness at the burden it was his destiny to bear.[27] It is a good epitaph for Aeneas: the emphasis lies not in the least on achievement and glory but on character and behaviour. In the case of both epitaphs the accents are those of the individuals, the judgment, the poet's.

(c) *Authorial comment.* Very seldom does Virgil explicitly enter his own epic text other than as a poet commenting on his poetry (see section 3) or in apostrophe or learned remarks (such as 1.109–10) and explanations that link the twelfth century to historical Rome (such as 5.121–23 or 8.337–38, 348, and 360–61). The exclamation at 4.412 *Improbe Amor, quid non mortalia pectora cogis!* (see p. 189 above) is unusual, but there are several examples of such authorial intervention in Book 4. For instance at 65–66:

> heu, vatum ignarae mentes! quid vota furentem,
> quid delubra iuvant?

Alas! the ignorance of prophetic minds! How can prayers, how can temples help someone insane with love?

The poet has just described in detail the rites and ceremonies that Dido undertook to obtain divine approval for her love of Aeneas, ending with extispicy, to make sure that the future augured well. His entry into the text totally subverts all that, and it is hard to avoid the impression that his remarks not only suit the immediate dramatic situation but also have the effect of expressing a far more wide-ranging scepticism that calls into

---

26. See p. 14 above.
27. See section 3 below.

question both religion (including omens) and the gods themselves. For "Virgil's description here shows as usual his deep love for Italian religious tradition and his exact knowledge of its detail";[28] yet his comments doubt its validity in a common human situation and so introduce doubts about its relevance to any human situation.

A less far-reaching authorial comment is the parenthetical question of the poet as he tells how Dido sensed in advance Aeneas' wish to leave (296–98):

> At regina dolos (quis fallere possit amantem?)
> praesensit, motusque excepit prima futuros
> omnia tuta timens

But the queen (who can deceive a lover?) sensed his treachery in advance and was the first to catch the sound of the movement to come, anxious when everything was safe.

The psychological sensitivity of the phrase *omnia tuta timens* is most impressive, and the effect of the explicit authorial intervention is to make that phrase general. In fact, what authorial comments of this type do is to provide a clear index to the human condition.[29] It is significant that there are so many interventions of this type in the story of Dido's tragic love: to this poet, love is always potentially destructive, and Dido's tragedy is certainly a particular one, but it is also typical of the human condition. This fact suggests a second characteristic of such interventions: they create the impression of conveying the poet's own thoughts and opinions and not just the sentiments demanded by the immediate dramatic situation.

Both characteristics can be seen in another striking authorial intervention over the dead Pallas (10.501–05).[30] The poet's comment (501–02) is perfectly suited to the immediate dramatic situation and is referred to it in the following specific lines (503–05); it is equally suited to its function in the ring-composition, by which it is an index to the last scene of the epic. But the effect of the poet's adopting and modifying a comment that Homer put in the mouth of Zeus is both to draw attention to the modification and to lend it the authority of the poet. The explanation thereby becomes an index to the human condition and is generalised; it is also constituted

---

28. Austin (1955), p. 41. See Austin, ad loc., for this sense of *vatum ignarae mentes;* the objection of Henry, ad loc., that Virgil never uses *ignarus* with a subjective genitive has no force, since *ignarae* here is absolute. The relevant parallel is 10.501 *nescia mens hominum.*

29. See chap. 6, sec. 3.

30. See p. 87 above for text and commentary.

to create the impression of being the real view of the poet and true of human life in general.

The authority of the poet's voice is sometimes of particular importance. Two examples will suffice. After Dido has been with Aeneas in the cave the poet asserts (4.169–72):

> ille dies primus leti primusque malorum
> causa fuit; neque enim specie famave movetur
> nec iam furtivum Dido meditatur amorem:
> coniugium vocat, hoc praetexit nomine culpam.

That day was the first and original cause of death and suffering. For no longer is Dido influenced by thought of reputation or appearances; it is not a secret love she now practises. Marriage is her name for it—with the word she concealed her guilt.

The authority of the poet is crucial here in "telling" what he will later "show"—that Dido is convinced she is married to Aeneas; the poet makes it clear that she was mistaken in the conviction because she had merely convinced herself of what she wanted to believe.

The poet's authority is also important at 7.583–84:

> ilicet infandum cuncti contra omina bellum,
> contra fata deum perverso numine poscunt.

Thereupon one and all demand an unspeakable war, contrary to all omens, contrary to the declarations of the gods, under a malign influence.

The poet is not guaranteeing the value of omens or oracles with these words. His condemnation is in the word *infandum*; the other condemnations are expressed in terms of considerations that would have been judged important by the participants, were fully known to them, and also forbade the war. These lines therefore stand as an absolutely authoritative condemnation of the war, and no talk about marauding Trojans or ruthless invasion can gainsay the explicit words of the poet. It was right that the Trojans should settle in Italy and that settlement could and should have been accomplished peacefully.

3. Pessimism and Poetics

There is no reason to discount the story, told with variations in all the *Lives*, that Virgil, before he left Italy on his last journey to Greece, arranged with Varius for the *Aeneid* to be burnt should anything happen to him; then, when he returned very ill, he tried to burn it himself but could not persuade anyone to give him the manuscript. The *Aeneid* was not ready for publication, and the story suggests a degree of perfectionism in the poet that need not surprise us. But it also suggests a deep lack of confidence about the project and its success. In the event, Augustus arranged for its careful editing and publication. The poet's lack of confidence, however, remains, and recalls a similar sense (expressed especially in the prooemium to Book 3 and in the *sphragis*) that the *Georgics* might prove a failure and would have to be redressed by the *Aeneid*.[31] Suggestions of that foreboding of failure also exist in the *Aeneid*. When the poet comes to Lausus' protection of his father, he breaks off in a parenthesis (10.789–93):

> ingemuit cari graviter genitoris amore,
> ut vidit, Lausus, lacrimaeque per ora volutae.
> Hic mortis durae casum tuaque optima facta,
> si qua fidem tanto est operi latura vetustas,
> non equidem nec te, iuvenis memorande, silebo.

When he saw, Lausus groaned deeply for love of his dear father and tears rolled down his cheeks (here I shall certainly not be silent on the disaster of your harsh death and your outstanding deeds, if a long passage of time can in any way win credence for so fine an act, nor about you, young man, who deserve to be remembered) . . .

Here the apostrophe strikingly cancels the gap between the temporality of the narrative and that of the composition: the poet directly addresses Lausus. The observation virtually settles one problem in this text. From the time of Donatus (792) *tanto . . . operi* was as often interpreted to be "the *Aeneid*" as it was to be "the brave act" of Lausus. But the silence the poet refuses to permit is relevant to the moment of composition, and the credence he seeks cannot be postponed to the far-distant future. The grounds for belief are to be supplied by *vetustas* "the long passing of time," not from the moment of composition to some far-off hypothetical moment in the future, but from the moment of the act to the moment of composition about it. The idea expressed is that an unselfish sacrifice such as that made by Lausus would simply not be believed by the poet's contemporaries unless it was said to have happened a very long time ago, safely outside the limits of contemporary standards of behaviour. This is a pessimistic enough view of Virgil's own age. But there is another aspect to the expression. The poet does not promise Lausus celebration in his

---

31. See Williams (1980), pp. 251–55, 258, 263–64.

poem. He is simply promising to tell of his deed and hoping that the millennium that has gone by since it happened will win credence for it. Nowhere is the suggestion that any act of the poet can win credence for what he says. That, too, if not downright pessimistic, at least betrays a lack of confidence in the power of his poetry.

This apostrophe should be compared with the earlier address to Nisus and Euryalus (9.446–49):

> Fortunati ambo! si quid mea carmina possunt,
> nulla dies unquam memori vos eximet aevo,
> dum domus Aeneae Capitoli immobile saxum
> accolet imperiumque pater Romanus habebit.

Lucky pair! If my poetry has any power, no day shall ever take your names from the record of time, as long as the house of Aeneas shall dwell on the unshaken rock of the Capitol and a Roman father shall exercise his rule.

Nisus and Euryalus have just been horribly killed, Nisus falling dead over the corpse of Euryalus (444–45). What does the poet mean by calling them "lucky"? It seems a strange word to use of such deaths. He clearly does not mean "lucky because you will be celebrated in my poem." They are not any luckier in that respect than all others mentioned in the *Aeneid*; in any case, the designation would be insufferably patronising and complacent. When the Rutuli are about to kill Euryalus, Nisus comes out of hiding and pleads for his life (427–30):

> "me, me, adsum qui feci, in me convertite ferrum,
> o Rutuli! mea fraus omnis, nihil iste nec ausus
> nec potuit; caelum hoc et conscia sidera testor;
> —tantum infelicem nimium dilexit amicum."

"At me, at me—here I am who did it—at me direct your swords, o Rutuli. The treachery was all mine; that boy dared nothing and could not have. I call on the heavens here and the stars that watched to witness. He merely loved his unlucky friend too much."

His appeal is made in vain and Euryalus is slaughtered. The poet's comment *fortunati ambo* contradicts (430) *infelicem*; the participants and the rest of the world might judge them unlucky, but the poet sees it differently. Why? He does not say; only his implications remain. The usual interpretation seems to be that the poet recognises in the pair something of the essential spirit of Rome, and it is sometimes added that they are treated as "an example of what might be hoped for from Augustus' own perceptive youth policy."[32] Any such interpretation ignores the effect of apostrophe as Virgil uses it: to establish an immediate timeless and personal relationship between the poet and the addressee. In other words, it is personal admiration that he is expressing; hence the surprise of *fortunati*. The promise they are given is adapted by the poet to constitute an index to Roman history beyond the age of Augustus. It expresses the poet's hope that his poem will in some way be connected with the national life, and that form of promise is relevant to a pair who were, so to speak, founder-members of the Roman empire. But the fame he promises them is on his own personal terms;[33] they are not to be an example of anything except the good fortune which the poet expresses in the exclamation *fortunati ambo*. The problem of what he meant by that therefore remains.

Their enterprise failed and they were killed, though they killed many of the enemy first.[34] How, then, are they lucky? They are lucky because, loving one another, they died together. At any time Nisus could have saved himself. He chose not to, and the poet signifies that decision to have been right: Euryalus was lucky because he did not die alone and abandoned; Nisus was lucky because he did not outlive his lover, and his death on his lover's behalf was noble (in the words given to his thoughts—by the poet—as he wonders what to do: 400–01 *an sese medios moriturus in ensis / inferat et pulchram properet per vulnera mortem?* "or should he rush on their swords, intending to die, and hasten a noble death for himself by wounds?"). This may be a noble view, but it is melancholy. It has something in it of the sentiment of the chorus toward the end of *Oedipus Coloneus* (1224–27): not to be born is the best fate; but, once born, to return whence one came as quickly as possible is second best. That was the message that Silenus, captured and tortured by Midas, revealed to mortals—a story most memorably told in the *Eudemus* of Aristotle (fr. 44 Rose[3]); Virgil knew the story but adapted Silenus to a different end in *Eclogue* 6. Here the lovers are lucky because they died together before they could know the unhappiness of life. The poet's fervent appreciation is expressed in the apostrophe that cancels the gap between narrative and composition making way for his promise.

The memory of Nisus and Euryalus will last as long as the Roman empire. That duration is expressed in terms of the poem. The "house of

32. Lennox (1977), p. 342.
33. As with the epitaph on Lausus: see p. 204 above.
34. Cf. 10.509 on Pallas (p. 192 above), and see chap. 8 on the theme of moral ambiguity and the poet's attitude to the exploit of Nisus and Euryalus.

Aeneas" represents the descendants of the epic hero, Romans in general, but also the family of the Julii in particular. The "unshakeable rock of the Capitol" was shown to Aeneas by Evander in the previous book (8.347–58). Finally there is the *pater Romanus*. This is often taken to refer to Juppiter. However, this is not possible as, not only could there be no conceivable end to Juppiter's rule, but his rule is over the universe, which is not relevant to Aeneas and the Capitol. Also the Horatian phrase, often used to support this interpretation, is irrelevant. At *Odes* 3.5.12, Horace says *incolumi Iove et urbe Roma* "while Juppiter is safe and the city of Rome," but in the military context this is simply a poetic version of the ancient formula (probably occurring in the hymn of the triumphant general) *salva urbe atque arce* "while the city and citadel is safe";[35] so, in Horace, *incolumi Iove* means the Capitol, not the god. Nor is *pater Romanus* in the singular a reasonable way to refer to Roman senators. It is a way of expressing the position held by Augustus in the terms relevant to the epic, a position which had no name but was characterised by authority and responsibility. Horace asks him to remain on earth as *pater atque princeps* (*Odes* 1.2.50), and *pater* in this sense of a person who is responsible for the well-being of others is exactly how the poet uses the word for Aeneas when he goes, for instance, to fight the decisive duel with Turnus (12.697 *at pater Aeneas . . .*). So the phrase here looks to Augustus and to a succession of similar *patres* that it is hoped will be indefinitely long.

Finally, the promise is predicated on *si quid mea carmina possunt*. This structure is ambiguous in Latin, since *si quid* need not express doubt or uncertainty but simply indefiniteness. Here it could just signify modesty on the part of the poet, but there is no way of escaping the possibility that the poet is also expressing a heartfelt doubt. It is, in fact, characteristic of his style that he uses this structure in such a way that the suggestion of doubt is unmistakable as at least a part of the meaning.[36]

Here the poet is dubious about the power of his poem while he asserts that the memory of Nisus and Euryalus is worthy to live on as an example of good fortune for as long as the Roman empire itself. Because the poet (and his reader) is aware that he invented the story of the pair, the strength of his own self-doubt and his assertion of the pair's death as the epitome of good fortune are both increased.

This is a melancholy and pessimistic view of the human condition. It recalls Aeneas' surprise in the Elysian fields (6.719–21):

35. Williams (1968), pp. 366–67.
36. For further examples, see below.

> "o pater, anne aliquas ad caelum hinc ire putandum est
> sublimis animas iterumque ad tarda reverti
> corpora? quae lucis miseris tam dira cupido?"

"O father, it is conceivable that any souls should go soaring up to the daylight and again return to sluggish bodies? Why do the poor creatures feel such a terrible lust for the light?"

Commentators rightly remark that this reflects Aeneas' own sufferings. It is also consonant with the tone of his own epitaph (12.435–40). But the pessimism is more far-reaching. It is not alleviated by Anchises' reply, in which life is represented as a stage in the purification of souls; that is why they return to the world above. Eventually, like the happy few who actually achieve purification in Elysium, they will become eligible to stay there and not be compelled to return to life. In the words of Aeneas, as well as in the whole concept, there speaks the pessimism of the poet.

It resonates in a different way also in some remarkable words of Anchises at the end of the review of Roman heroes (6.847–53):

> "excudent alii spirantia mollius aera
> (credo equidem), vivos ducent de marmore vultus,
> orabunt causas melius, caelique meatus
> describent radio et surgentia sidera dicent:
> tu regere imperio populos, Romane, memento
> (hae tibi erunt artes), pacique imponere morem,
> parcere subiectis et debellare superbos."

"Others shall beat out more gracefully the breathing bronze (I am certain that they will) and shape living features from marble; they shall plead cases more skilfully, and shall mark out with their measuring-rod the paths of the heavens and shall predict the risings of the constellations (850). But you, Roman, you are to make it your task to rule the nations with your empire (these will be your arts) and to impose on peace the order of custom, to show mercy to the conquered and to bring down the arrogant by war."

This is the characteristic Roman concept of peace; a condition imposed on nations by military victories. Peace is the ideal state, but it must be supported by *mos* in the sense of "a recognised and settled pattern of behaviour." Clemency should be shown only where it is deserved. Commentators who quote this passage and then assert that Aeneas breaks his father's command at the end of the epic by not sparing Turnus are simply ignoring the temporal gap: Anchises addresses himself not to Aeneas but specifically to Romans, and the passage is a clear index to the age of

Augustus. Civilization, characterised by law and order, is Rome's contribution to mankind.

In favour of this, the other arts are abandoned to Greeks (*alii*); those
specifically mentioned are sculpture in bronze and marble, oratory, and
astronomy. What is really surprising here is the surrender of oratory to
Greece. Cicero would have been outraged. In his *Brutus* (254), he has
Brutus report Caesar's judgment that Cicero had made himself a benefac-
tor of the Roman people, in that the one area of superiority which conquered Greece could claim as hers had been taken from her, or at any rate
was now shared between her and Rome, as a result of Cicero's rhetorical
achievements. Virgil has Anchises surrender all that, and it is hard to
resist the impression that oratory here is a metonymy for epic poetry and
that, in allowing the Greeks superiority in oratory, the poet is also admitting the impossibility of his being able to rival the great Greeks in epic
poetry. In fact, the general tone of Anchises' remarks comes close to that
of the *sphragis* of the *Georgics*, where the poet declares himself *inglorius* as
compared either with farmers or with Augustus victorious on the Eastern
frontiers, and that in turn echoes the tones of pessimism about his own
poetry to be heard at the end of *Georgics* 2, in the prooemium to Book 3,
and in the myth of Orpheus toward the end of Book 4.[37]

That tone is echoed in a different way at the beginning of Book 7 in
the apostrophe to Caieta, the nurse of Aeneas. Here the comment, in the
poet's own voice (4) *si qua est ea gloria* cannot simply be interpreted (with
Conington) as equivalent to *quae magna est gloria*. The structure is again
ambiguous: it can indeed be a modestly ironical understatement, but it
also admits a different tone.[38] The words may cast doubt (as Servius
suggests) on the value of such commemoration: "if that distinction has
any meaning." This sense suits the melancholy tone of the epitaphic
apostrophe and carries the idea that to the dead such things not only
bring no consolation but literally have no meaning since death is the end
of everything. The same melancholic doubts are expressed by Aeneas as
he looks at the dead Lausus and promises him burial: (10.828) *si qua est ea
cura*.[39] The idea that burial is an empty gesture is arrogantly expressed by

37. See note 28 above.
38. Cf. Fraenkel (1945), p. 2: "while the Italian patriot rejoices at the long and glorious
history of his country's towns and monuments ('litoribus nostris . . . aeternam . . . famam . . . dedisti'), the sage, a gentle sage, not a Stoic zealot, strikes a note of mellow resigna-
tion: 'si qua est ea gloria', and this makes us see the glory of earthly things in true
perspective."
39. See p. 204 above.

Turnus over the dead Pallas: (10.493) *quisquis honos tumuli, quidquid sola-*
men humandi est, / largior "whatever distinction there is in a grave, whatever consolation in burying, I grant it generously." It is highly appropriate that the poet, having described in detail Aeneas' journey (or apparent
journey) among the dead, should himself, at the beginning of the following seventh book, express doubts that are grounded in the Epicurean
view of death as the dissolution of both soul and body and so the end of
all sensation. Aeneas is made to stop short of such total scepticism at the
beginning of Book 11, when he orders the burial of the dead, saying (23)
qui solus honos Acheronte sub imo est "since that is the only honour among
the dead." But the remark, in which a Homeric phrase is adapted and
deliberately extended, savagely undercuts the sights he was supposed to
have seen in the Underworld.[40]

In fact, in such sentiments, expressed both in the poet's voice and in
the hero's, any literal interpretation of the journey through the Underworld is further subverted. Does the poet express belief in any sort of
existence after death? I think the answer must be: certainly not. The
journey through the Underworld is a trope, metaphoric in nature, for the
hopes and fears of mankind. Every form of those hopes and fears is
represented in a pageant that allows all inconsistencies to stand unre-
solved. It also functions as a device whereby Aeneas confronts his own
past and comes to terms with it, completing his understanding of horrors
that had been left pending in the earlier text of the poem, so that his
privilege becomes retrospectively equivalent to that of the reader. Finally,
a Platonic myth is adapted to provide a synecdoche of the historical
process, as far as Rome was concerned, seen from the twelfth century
with the hindsight of the age of Augustus. That is, the journey through
the Underworld is a figurative narrative device that needs to be interpreted but commits the poet to no expression of a belief. The poem's
attitude to life (and death) is unobtrusively suggested in scattered remarks that are deliberately calculated to avoid any impression of a doctrine but are entirely consistent with Lucretius' expression of the ideas of
Epicurus.

The further question suggests itself whether the poem expresses a
belief in the gods. Here, too, I think the answer must be: certainly not.
Again a series of unobtrusive remarks is in question. When Aeneas reveals himself to Dido, he says that it is not in the power of the Trojans to
recompense her for her help or to thank her adequately; then (1.603–05):

40. See p. 161 above.

> "di tibi, si qua pios respectant numina, si quid
> usquam iustitiae est, et mens sibi conscia recti
> praemia digna ferant."

"May the gods (if any deities have respect for the dutiful, if there is any justice anywhere) and your own consciousness of doing right bring you adequate rewards."

There are various difficulties here. The correct reading in line 604 may well be the less well-attested *iustitia;* in that case the meaning is "if justice has any meaning anywhere." Whichever reading is correct, however, it is implausible to take *et mens sibi conscia recti* as part of this *si*-clause, since it makes little sense to doubt either the existence of or the value to be attached to a consciousness of doing right. The translation "as sure as there is any justice anywhere and an inward sense of what is right" does not fully bring out the difficulty, because *sibi* must mean self-consciousness and the primary reference must be to Dido. Consequently *et* must link (603) *di tibi* with *mens sibi conscia recti*, and *si qua . . . iustitiae est* is therefore a parenthesis.[41] Here again it is true that *si qua* could mean "as surely as there is . . . ," but the lack of balance between *di* and *mens sibi conscia recti* suggests that the *si qua . . .* and *si quid . . .* clauses redress that balance by doubting the reality, and certainly the relevance, of the gods. That particular kind of imbalance occurs elsewhere: for instance at 12.538–39 *dextera nec tua te . . . nec di . . . / . . . sui*, or at 11.118 *deus aut sua dextera*. In all of these passages the imbalance undercuts the significance of the gods. The expression that comes closest to that of the present passage is *Aeneid* 9.252–54:

> "quae vobis, quae digna, viri, pro laudibus istis
> praemia posse rear solvi? pulcherrima primum
> di moresque dabunt vestri."

"What rewards, what rewards, men, am I to consider worthy of being used to recompense brave deeds like these? In the first instance the gods and your own characters will give you the finest rewards."

What is meant here can be illustrated by words that Macrobius quotes from the dream of Scipio in Cicero's *de republica* (Macrobius *somn. Scip.* 1.4.2–3):

For it was this opportunity that incited Scipio to tell of his dream which he swore he had silently suppressed for a long time. Because, when Laelius complained

41. On this interpretation, see R. D. Williams (1972), ad loc.

that no statues of Nasica had been set up in public to commemorate his slaying the tyrant, Scipio, after other things, said something like this: "But although their own consciousness of their splendid deeds is the fullest reward courage receives in the view of wise men, yet that divine virtue does not look for statues set in lead or triumphant processions whose laurels wither but more lasting and more evergreen types of rewards." "What are they?" said Laelius. Then Scipio said, "Permit me, since we are now celebrating the third day of the holiday . . ." and other things by which he arrived at the exposition of his dream, demonstrating that those were the more lasting and evergreen types of rewards that he had himself seen reserved in heaven for good rulers of states. . . .

What the poet does by means of the *si qua* and *si quid* clauses is to undercut the rewards that may be reserved in heaven in favour of those that are conferred by the sheer consciousness of doing right. Human beings must be self-reliant even to the extent of finding the rewards for virtue within themselves. Aeneas here speaks to Dido; he had earlier expressed his bitter sense of the gods' lack of interest in *pietas* (378–85). There he was speaking, though he did not know it, to his mother and professed to regard her as a goddess (326–34 and 372). In other instances of the structure, the speaker is praying in a situation where there is a contradiction between what is happening and the hypothesis that there are gods who respect justice and *pietas*. So Priam, as he watches Pyrrhus slaughter his son before his eyes, says (2.535–39):

> "at tibi pro scelere," exclamat, "pro talibus ausis
> di, si qua est caelo pietas quae talia curet,
> persolvant grates dignas et praemia reddant
> debita, qui nati coram me cernere letum
> fecisti et patrios foedasti funere vultus."

"But for that crime, for such an outrageous act, may the gods—if there is any *pietas* in heaven that bothers about such things—pay you a worthy requital and render you the rewards you deserve, you who made me witness my own son's death before my eyes and contaminated a father's features with that death."

Or Dido in her anger prays for vengeance (4.382–84);

> "spero equidem mediis, si quid pia numina possunt,
> supplicia hausurum scopulis et nomine Dido
> saepe vocaturum."

"I hope that, if deities that are *pia* have any power, you will drink the full cup of punishment on the reefs that lie between and will call often on Dido by name."

Or Aneas, as he sees the ships on fire, prays (5.687–90):

> "Iuppiter omnipotens, si nondum exosus ad unum
> Troianos, si quid pietas antiqua labores
> respicit humanos, da flammam evadere classi
> nunc, pater, et tenuis Teucrum res eripe leto."

"Omnipotent Juppiter, if you have not yet conceived a hatred of Trojans to the last man, if your *pietas* as of old has any regard for human suffering, grant now that the fleet escape the flames, father, and snatch the tenuous fortunes of the Trojans from death."

In all these passages the theory is implicit that the gods should display to human beings a *pietas* "a dutifulness," corresponding to that which the human beings concerned display toward the gods. But in each case the formulation is ambiguous and provides for the possibility that the gods, in fact, have no regard for human beings.[42] However dramatically appropriate in its context each single instance is, cumulatively an authorial attitude seems to come through to the reader.

In my view, the text of the *Aeneid* enjoins a reading that is entirely consistent with the theology of Epicurus: death is the end of everything, and the gods, if they exist, are remote beings, possible objects of human contemplation, but without the slightest interest in the world of human beings and certainly never inclined to intervene in the world. The gods are a narrative device, a fiction of the poet, a synecdoche of human attempts to explain an essentially hostile universe that recognises itself as a fiction and is subverted sufficiently often by the poet to maintain that fictionality. Virgil recognises religion as a historical and even poetic element in human life, the focus of human ideals and perhaps a synecdoche of them as well as a means of perpetuating them. But the objects of religion have no other existence than in the minds of worshippers and no reality except as a synecdoche for the very large seemingly inexplicable element in human existence.

The real pessimism of the *Aeneid* lies in its views of the ultimate responsibility of human individuals both for themselves and—what is worse—for achieving such ideals of human existence as they are capable

---

42. The bitter scepticism of Aeneas should be added as he comments on the death of the just Rhipeus (2.428) *dis aliter visum;* even more bitter and far-reachingly sceptical is his comment when Coroebus tries to rescue Cassandra (2.402) *heu nihil invitis fas quemquam fidere divis!* "Alas! it is wrong for men to put any trust in gods that do not will it."

of formulating. For human beings are absolutely subject to the fact of death. The paradigmatic case is the death of Marcellus at the climax of the review of Roman heroes in *Aeneid* 6. The future beyond Augustus has collapsed. For the only thing that men can do to transcend their condition is to establish a way of life (*mos / mores*) that expresses their ideals and to try to ensure that it will become a tradition handed on from one generation to another. So Aeneas, in his epitaph, instructs Ascanius in the ways he should strive to imitate his father and also his uncle Hector (12.435–40). But at any point, as in the case of Marcellus, death may intervene most unexpectedly to ruin what seemed to be well-conceived plans. There is much less recourse against that universal condition than there is against the kind of malice and opposition of evil or misguided men which led to war between Trojans and Italians in the twelfth century and to civil war in the lifetime of the poet.

MORAL AMBIGUITIES

There are times in the *Aeneid* when the poet intervenes, in his own voice, to declare a moral position; for instance, when war breaks out between Italians and Trojans at the instigation of Turnus and Amata, he makes a definitive moral judgment—the war was wrong (7.583–84). But often Virgil presents two aspects of a complex situation and, by refraining from comment, implicitly asserts the impossibility of making an absolute moral judgment between the two. A good example of this on a small scale is the way he has Anchises present L. Junius Brutus (6.817–23):

> "vis et Tarquinios reges animamque superbam
> ultoris Bruti, fascisque videre receptos?
> consulis imperium hic primus saevasque securis
> accipiet, natosque pater nova bella moventis
> ad poenam pulchra pro libertate vocabit.
> infelix! utcumque ferent ea facta minores:
> vincet amor patriae laudumque immensa cupido."

"Do you wish to view the kings Tarquin and the proud soul of the avenging Brutus and the recovery of the fasces? He shall be the first to receive the authority of a consul and the cruel axes, and when his sons stir up revolutionary wars, he, though their father, shall summon them to punishment in defence of beautiful freedom—unfortunate man, however much later generations shall extol that deed: love of the fatherland shall prevail and a measureless desire for glory."

Brutus, revered founder of the Republic, is oddly given the adjective (817) *superbam*, which belonged by right to the last Tarquin. The word normally, but not always, has a condemnatory sense in Latin, even in Virgil.[1]

---

1. See Austin (1977), on line 817 (pp. 251–52).

However, if it used here in a good sense, it is clearly also ambiguous and (together with *saevas*) anticipates something of the tone of line 823, where the concept of patriotism unexpectedly expands to that of unbounded ambition for glory. The moral ambiguity here resides in the tension between paternal love (an emotion of keen intrest to Anchises and to Aeneas) and the requirements of patriotism. The address (822) *infelix* expresses Anchises' pity for that unhappy clash of the two imperatives, but *superbam* with *laudum immensa cupido* injects a note of disapproval of the man who interpreted the demands of patriotism with such barbarous rigour. A metonymic association is clear with M. Junius Brutus, the descendant of this man, an *ultor* too, who exhibited his patriotism by assassinating his friend Julius Caesar (condemned in the following section, 826–35). The moral ambiguity can thus be transferred from the earlier to the later Brutus in such a way as to make inevitable the appearance of Cato on the shield of Aeneas as the pillar of morality in the late Republic.[2] The excesses of both the earlier and the later Brutus can be defended in terms of patriotism and desire for fame; but there is another slant on their actions. The poet, seeing both sides, refuses to choose.

After her second impassioned address to Aeneas, Dido faints and has to be carried away by her maidservants. The narrative continues (4.393–96):

> At pius Aeneas, quamquam lenire dolentem
> solando cupit et dictis avertere curas,
> multa gemens magnoque animum labefactus amore
> iussa tamen divum exsequitur classemque revisit.

But Aeneas, obedient to duty, though he longs to soothe her pain by consoling her and to dispel her agony with words, groaning deeply and shaken to the core by the power of his love, nevertheless carries out the orders of the gods and returns to the fleet.

The trouble this account has caused commentators can be illustrated in the words of the latest:[3]

393 *pius Aeneas:* some commentators have here failed to understand the significance Virgil has put into the use of the epithet. Page, for example, says (intro. p. xix) "Virgil . . . begins the next paragraph quite placidly *at pius Aeneas* . . . ! How

2. See p. 155 above. A similar attitude to the contrast between Brutus and Cato can be seen in Horace *Odes* 1.12.33–36: see Williams (1980), pp. 13–19.

3. R. D. Williams (1972), p. 368.

the man who wrote the lines placed in Dido's mouth could immediately after-
wards speak of 'the good Aeneas etc.' is one of the puzzles of literature." But the
only possible defence for Aeneas' actions is his *pietas;* in any other capacity than as
a man of destiny he should have stayed—*pietas* is why he must leave, and Virgil
wants us to remember this. It may be that many (presumably including Page)
would wish that *pietas* had not prevailed, but it is utterly wrong to object to being
told that it has done so.

The desire to find some relief from the painful drama by assigning blame
or attempting a defence, which is a feature of the majority of commentators and writings on the episode of Dido and Aeneas, at least shows the
power of the poet's concept. But distress is inherent in the situation and is
not to be alleviated by moralising.

   The poet makes a strange assertion about Dido's death agony
(4.696–99):

> nam quia nec fato merita nec morte peribat,
> sed misera ante diem subitoque accensa furore,
> nondum illi flavum Proserpina vertice crinem
> abstulerat Stygioque caput damnaverat Orco.

For, since she was perishing neither by fate nor by a death that she deserved, but
pitifully before her time and in the fire of a sudden passion, Proserpina had not
yet taken the yellow lock from her head and condemned her to Stygian Orcus.

Cornutus (Macrobius *Sat.* 5.19.2) thought that Virgil had invented this
ritual; he was wrong, as Macrobius could show by referring to Euripides
Alcestis 74–76. That play influenced Virgil in his whole account of Dido's
suicide, and he is certainly relying on it for this theme. But, apart from an
apparent occurrence in the *Alcestis* of Phrynichus (from which Euripides
borrowed some material),[4] the ritual is not attested until Horace *Odes*
1.28.19. The ritual, that is, is literary, and it does not work in any literal
sense in Virgil's assertion, since the fact that a death happened to be
undeserved could be no reason for Proserpina's powerlessness.[5] The poet
is here making use of the ritual for an ulterior purpose. Dido was allowed
to speak her own epitaph (653–58), commemorating her achievements
and regretting the Trojan arrival. Now, in describing, from his privileged
position, a ritual act performed for Dido by a goddess, the poet creates the
opportunity to pronounce an epitaph of his own that can only come from

4. See Dale (1954), p. xii.
5. See Bailey (1935), p. 246.

him: Dido did not deserve to die; she died before her time, and she was
the victim of a sudden passion. The privileged voice of the poet speaks in
this epitaph, in pity and understanding.

The importance of this sympathy is that at a number of points Dido
seems to be, at least implicitly, condemned by the narrative. She is the
founder of a city, yet love of Aeneas brings all building activity to a halt
(86–89); it is Aeneas who will start it again (260–61). More explicit is the
comment (again in the voice of the poet) after the episode in the cave
(4.170–72);

> neque enim specie famave movetur
> nec iam furtivum Dido meditatur amorem:
> coniugium vocat, hoc praetexit nomine culpam.

For Dido is no longer affected by appearance or reputation and no longer does she
have her mind on a concealed love: she calls it marriage, with that word she
concealed her guilt.

Here Dido is shown to be concealing culpable activity by representing it to
herself (with perfect sincerity) as marriage.[6] Dido is convinced that she is
married to Aeneas; the poet dissociates himself from that view. What the
poet's final epitaph accomplishes is similar in function to the scheming of
the goddesses (90–128): Dido is the victim of a passion she could not
resist; what that passion causes her to do must be judged culpable, but
essentially she is innocent. The poet explicitly contradicts her own self-
condemnation (547). The goddesses are a figure for the irresistibility of
passion; the poet's epitaph picks up that theme and makes it authoritative. This enforces retrospective judgment on all that Dido has done—
from her anger, rhetoric, and madness, to her suicide.

Retrospective judgment is also enforced in the case of Aeneas. The
goddesses say nothing of his falling in love with Dido; Juno's pitiless and
sarcastic comment is: (4.103) *liceat Phrygio servire marito* "let her be a slave
to her Phrygian husband." Marriage is what Juno plans, and she takes
Aeneas for granted. Venus says nothing of Aeneas. The goddesses are
externalisations of the loves of Dido and Aeneas: Dido will be trapped
and destroyed; Aeneas will be trapped but will eventually struggle free.
That harsh struggle has to be interpreted by retrospective judgment in the
case of Aeneas;[7] but, when the struggle is over, he can sleep (554–55),
while Dido lies in wakeful agony (522–53). Their situations are oddly

6. On the interpretation, see Williams (1968), pp. 379–80.
7. See chap. 3, sec. 2 above.

similar: both exiles, both to be founders of new states, both in love with one another. There the clash arises; for Aeneas is able to fight down his own love in favour of his vision of a new city. Whereas Dido does not realise until far too late that this love is something to be fought against; by then there is no way out for her but suicide, since she can only be ruined personally and politically by Aeneas' departure.

The account concentrates on Dido, leaving the point of view of Aeneas to emerge at a late stage and fragmentarily. This poetic strategy is justified, since Dido will only be present in the narrative for a short time; Aeneas will last to the final line of the epic, and so retrospective judgment is always possible in his case. The final meeting in the Underworld (6.450–76) does nothing to change the circumstances: Aeneas is still in love with Dido (455 *dulcique adfatus amore est*) but still explains himself in the old terms (of imperatives from gods) that she cannot understand; Dido says nothing and absolutely rejects Aeneas, reunited now with her former husband and restored to the dignity of *univira*. What Virgil has done in the episode of Dido and Aeneas is to present two utterly opposed points of view that cannot possibly be reconciled and yet must be if tragedy is to be averted. Each needs to be understood on its own terms and, understood in that way, each is right and the other appears to be wrong. It is this kind of moral ambiguity which interested the poet—and is inherent in the human condition.

Dido is presented as a most attractive character from first mention; it is hard, however, to imagine a character better designed to be a villain than Turnus. He is bloodthirsty and lives for battle. He is also self-centred, to such a degree that he fails to take advantage of a major strategic opportunity because he cannot bear to share the stage with anyone else. When he is foolishly admitted through the gates of the Trojan camp, he kills everyone within reach (722–55); then the poet explicitly enters his own text to comment (9.756–61):

> Diffugiunt versi trepida formidine Troes.
> et si continuo victorem ea cura subisset,
> rumpere claustra manu sociosque immittere portis,
> ultimus ille dies bello gentique fuisset.
> sed furor ardentem caedisque insana cupido
> egit in adversos.

The Trojans turn and scatter in all directions, trembling and frightened, and if the thought had there and then occurred to the victor to break the bars apart and let his allies in through the gates, that would have been the final day for the war and for that people. But battle-fury and a crazy lust for slaughter drove him hotly against his enemy.

The same neglect of strategy—though less self-centred—also characterises his behaviour after Camilla has been killed (11.901–05),[8] where again *furens* is the explanatory adjective. But already in Book 11 there is a sense of another way of looking at Turnus. It begins in the lengthy confrontation with Drances. There is an interesting contradiction here because the instinct for realism and compromise in Drances' speeches is clearly commendable; yet the poet introduces Drances with extreme prejudice at lines 122–23 and even more so at 336–41. The contradiction between Drances' sensible proposals and his thoroughly unpleasant character (he pursues an unremitting vendetta against Turnus) serves to undercut the sincerity of his moderate views and compels some sympathy for the downright singlemindedness of Turnus (characterised though it is by *violentia*).

The sympathy for Turnus is steadily increased throughout Book 12 in a series of similes and scenes that demonstrate how justified are his fear of Aeneas and his growing sense of doom. That growth of sympathy, however, is not constant: his instinctive cruelty and barbarity is deliberately revealed, for instance, in the detail of cutting off his enemies' heads and displaying them on his chariot (511–12). Nevertheless, sympathy reaches one climax at the point where news of the attack on Latinus' city reaches him and he can no longer deceive himself (12.665–68):

> obstipuit varia confusus imagine rerum
> Turnus et obtutu tacito stetit; aestuat ingens
> uno in corde pudor mixtoque insania luctu
> et furiis agitatus amor et conscia virtus.

Turnus was deeply shaken, confused by the changing picture of events, and stood gazing speechlessly. In that one heart there was a turmoil of deep shame and madness mingled with grief and love driven wild by frenzy and a consciousness of his own valour.

This analysis was to supply a model for later European literature to the extent that "mixture of motives" has become a psychological cliché with us. The concept is explored in full for the first time in this passage, and it is used to reveal a man in whom, though evil may predominate, it is mixed with good. Here *conscia virtus*—that self-conscious pride in one's

8. See p. 37 above.

reputation for valour—wins the struggle and Turnus goes to face Aeneas. The motive may be self-centered but the decision is noble and (in a way that would have had no relevance to Turnus) right. This makes way for the final climax of the duel, in which a series of similes and echoes from *Iliad* 22 suggests viewing Turnus as a Hector (and Aeneas as an Achilles).[9] But while that strategy allows the poet to win special sympathy for Turnus, it also enables him to measure the distance between Turnus and Hector, particularly in two ways.[10] First, Hector is frightened when he catches sight of Achilles and runs away from him; but, deceived by Athene into stopping, he fights bravely to the death. Turnus' fear of Aeneas is not only constant and becomes paralysing, but it extends beyond Aeneas to death, for Turnus is afraid to die (916). Second, in consequence of this, whereas Hector in his last request to Achilles asks only for burial and, when refused, is magnificently contemptuous of Achilles, Turnus, pretending to make the same request of Aeneas, in reality is begging for his life and, in the hope of gaining his request, humbles himself before his conqueror (930–38). The allusion to the Homeric scene allows Virgil not only to win sympathy for Turnus but also to define him by comparison with the model of Hector, thus modifying the sympathy.

This strategy is clearly deliberate. Nothing would have been easier for the poet than to sharpen the portrait of Turnus as a bloodthirsty villain who richly deserved the death that came to him. Did the poet, then, in modifying his portrait, intend to condemn the lethal act of Aeneas? Many modern commentators are sure that he did; for instance:

the question which confronts the critic of the epic's final book is whether Aeneas, as he comes face to face with this composite of past antagonisms [Turnus], maintains the standard of reason and restraint he has hitherto called his own. That the answer must be negative appears only after careful consideration of the book's events as seen through the poet's imagination. [Putnam (1965) 156]

by the book's end Dido's revenge could be called complete because Aeneas by bringing death to Turnus, becomes a victim of that very unreason which hitherto he had done his best to shun. [ibid. 162]

It is Aeneas who loses at the end of Book XII, leaving Turnus victorious in his tragedy. [ibid. 193]

The reaction he wants to prompt is plain. We must condemn the sudden rage that causes Aeneas to kill Turnus when he is on the point of sparing him—and when

9. See chap. 7, sec. 1.
10. For details, see chap. 5, sec. 3 above.

his death no longer makes sense, for Turnus has acknowledged defeat. . . . The killing Turnus cannot be justified, this is beyond doubt the judgment expected of us. It is of course intolerable, from the point of view of plot construction, that Turnus should be left alive. But if he is a competent poet, aware of the implications of his own fiction, Virgil must make Aeneas' action both psychologically plausible and forgivable: we cannot be invited to condemn the poem's hero at the very climax of the poem. [Quinn (1968) 273]

The conclusion to be drawn from this last quotation seems to be that either Virgil was not a competent poet or that the reader is not meant to condemn Aeneas. But quotations of this kind could be repeated many times from writings of the last fifteen years. Even the latest editor, more moderate in his judgment, says:[11] "But the fact remains that the reader expects Aeneas to show mercy . . . and is profoundly disquieted when he does not." This judgment, however, should be questioned, since what creates expectation in the last quarter of Book 12 is the constant appeal by the poet's text to *Iliad* 22. It seems more justifiable to say that the reader expects Turnus to die; the narrative tension is directed to the question: how?

A good deal is also made of Aeneas' irrational state: he is (12.946–47) *furiis accensus et ira/terribilis* "fired with fury and terrifying in his anger." The latest editor comments on this:[12] "at the last Aeneas falls a victim to the violent passions (*furor* and *ira*) against which he has so long been struggling with partial success." This statement is more moderate than most, but it still moralises in Stoic and even modern categories. Aeneas hates war and all that goes with it (especially 11.110–11), but he is sometimes forced to fight, though he foresees the horror of it and places the blame squarely on Turnus (8.538 *quas poenas mihi, Turne, dabis* "what a penalty you will pay me, Turnus"). The only way a good man can go into battle and kill is by having *furor* and *ira* aroused in him.[13] Consequently, Aeneas' state at the moment he kills Turnus is merely the state necessary for that act; the question is whether he is justified in being driven to that point. All that can be said on this subject is that the poet, by a careful ring-composition, has done his utmost to make Aeneas' state of mind understood and able. Aeneas remembers Pallas and regards Turnus as a criminal (947–49):

11. R. D. Williams (1973), p. 503.
12. Ibid. on 12.946–47 (p. 508).
13. See Thornton (1976), Appendix A.

> tune hinc spoliis indute meorum
> eripiare mihi? Pallas te hoc vulnere, Pallas
> immolat et poenam scelerato ex sanguine sumit.

"Are you, decked in the spoils of my people, to be saved from me? Pallas with this wound, Pallas sacrifices you and exacts the penalty on your criminal blood."

The killing is regarded by Aeneas as being done not by him but vicariously by Pallas, it is a religious duty (*immolat*), and Turnus is being made to pay the penalty for a crime. It will not do to ignore or subvert Aeneas' words by saying, for instance, "He may claim that Pallas 'immolates' Turnus, but the metaphor cannot conceal the identity of the real killer."[14] The verb *immolare* is also used of the youths captured by Aeneas and destined as a sacrifice to the shade of Pallas (10.519), and then of Aeneas' killing of Haemonides just after hearing of Pallas' death (10.541). All three uses of the verb concern Aeneas' duty to avenge Pallas. The point of reference by which this must be judged is Achilles' need to avenge Patroclus. Aeneas is a twelfth-century man, and this vengeance was laid upon him as a sacred duty by his relationship with Pallas (expressed in the Roman terms of *contubernium*) and explicitly demanded in the message sent to him by Evander (11.177–81). There is a further element: Turnus is paying the penalty for a criminal act (*scelus*).[15] This cannot be the slaying of Pallas as such, but the fact that Turnus more than anyone was responsible for making Latinus break his oath and ties of hospitality and so was the prime instigator of a war condemned explicitly by the poet's own voice at 7.583–84 and implicitly in the penalty with which Turnus is threatened (8.538).[16] Aeneas recognises the crime; Pallas demands the penalty for it: the two themes of punishment and vengeance are made to coincide.

What the poet has done with this ending has been to make as difficult as possible, in moral terms, the problem of whether to kill Turnus or spare him. Not only has Turnus been made more sympathetic, but, unlike Hector, he has expressly raised that issue by begging for his life. Aeneas is made to feel the problem acutely (12.938–41):

---

14. Anderson (1969), p. 84.

15. Among those punished in Tartarus are (6.612–13) *quique arma secuti / impia*; cf. Latinus' words as he lists the crimes he has been compelled to commit through his love for Turnus and the persuasion of Amata: 12.31 *arma impia sumpsi*. The crime is Turnus'.

16. See pp. 87–93 above.

> stetit acer in armis
> Aeneas volvens oculos dextramque repressit;
> et iam iamque magis cunctantem flectere sermo
> coeperat . . .

Aeneas, stood, fierce in his armour, ⟨restlessly⟩ moving his eyes,[17] and he restrained his sword-arm. Turnus' words had just begun to win him over as he
hesitated more and more, when . . .

The instinct to spare his enemy is not characteristic of twelfth-century
man, who felt no moral dilemma in such circumstances. But Aeneas does,
and when his anger takes over it is not anger for himself but for someone
else. Servius shows how a reader was intended to consider this: "The
whole thrust of the passage is towards the glory of Aeneas. For in that he
thinks of sparing his enemy he is shown to be *pius;* and in that he kills him
he wears the badge of *pietas.*"

Another interesting and important feature of this scene needs to be
taken into account. At the point in Book 10 where the ring-composition
which this scene closes was begun, the poet entered his text in his own
voice to condemn Turnus for a common human blindness to the necessity
of moderation in success.[18] The implication is that, if Turnus had acted
differently (that is, if he had not stripped the belt from Pallas), Aeneas,
too, would have acted differently (that is, he would have spared Turnus'
life). There are two elements in Aeneas' relationship with Turnus. The
first may be called political: Aeneas must fight and defeat Turnus if the
Trojans are to find a home in Italy; defeat of Turnus in single combat
would settle the whole war in accordance with a historical Roman
custom, applied anachronistically here by the poet.[19] The second element, however, is personal: Aeneas owes to Evander the duty of avenging the death of Pallas; the eight youths taken prisoner by him were a
surrogate for that sacrifice. The two elements are kept separate in the last
scene. The second, in fact, made its last previous appearance early in
Book 11 in the message from Evander to Aeneas (177–81), delegating the
duty of killing Turnus to him. Since then Aeneas' sole concern has been
political, and throughout Book 12 his aim in staging the single combat
with Turnus has had that motive—the making of peace and the ensuring
of an alliance between Trojans and Italians. When Turnus pleads for his
life, he points out to Aeneas that he has now achieved those aims; his

17. On the meaning of this phrase, see Anderson (1971), pp. 58–65.
18. 10.501–05.
19. See pp. 102–03 above.

anger is therefore no longer necessary (936–38). It is this consideration, together with a basic instinct for clemency, that gives Aeneas pause and tempts him to spare Turnus' life. It is only when the second element— long since dormant—is accidentally brought to life for him by the sight of Pallas' belt that anger flares up and he commits the act of sacrifice that has been required of him. This is the reason for his saying that not he but Pallas immolates Turnus and exacts the penalty for his crime.

What the poet has done here is to show, as in the episode of Dido, two totally incompatible points of view and to understand but not pass judgment on them. For, from the point of view of Turnus and his friends, there is no reason why Aeneas should not spare him—the war has been settled in favour of the Trojans. But for Aeneas that would mean forgetting the death of Pallas as well as the breaking of the *foedus,* and there lay the dilemma for him: as an un-Homeric character he wishes to spare the life, but as a twelfth-century hero his duty will not let him spare the man once Turnus' earlier act of folly reminds him of it. Nothing could be more false to this sense of moral dilemma and refusal to pass judgment than to say: "The reaction he wants to prompt is plain. We must condemn the sudden rage that causes Aeneas to kill Turnus."

The way in which the character of Turnus is treated has its parallel in Mezentius: he is presented as a tyrant who committed unspeakable atrocities and was a *contemptor divum;* yet, when his son is killed, the poet allows an unsuspected nobility of character to appear. This is not used to raise the slightest question in Aeneas' mind about sparing him. That question can only occur to Aeneas when the war is over; till then, so Mezentius himself says (900–02), it is kill or be killed. But it does make his death more painful, and suggests not only the poet's hatred of war but also his aversion to easy moral condemnation. Such moral ambiguities lie at the heart of life for Virgil. Another can be seen in the incompatible viewpoints of Trojans and Latins: to the Trojans, Italy is their destined land; to the Latins, the Trojans are violent and illegal usurpers. Neither side is right—except to itself and in its own terms. That dilemma is never resolved but is often posed, especially in Book 7 and in the council of the gods in Book 10. It could have been resolved by decisive action on Latinus' part; but he too is morally ambiguous—his views (like those of Drances) are just and sensible, but his character is weak and vacillating and pregnant with tragedy for his people. The poet introduces the moral ambiguity to trouble the reader; it is only resolved by the pragmatic verdict of history. But it is not resolved within the immediate terms of the poem.

Judgment about the episode of Nisus and Euryalus that led to the death of both is equally divided. One set of critics condemns the actions of the pair as dangerously reckless: "as a miniature tragedy, it emphasises human error and the penalty that characters must pay for their mistakes, and this Virgil stresses repeatedly in IX–XII";[20] Nisus' plan to carry a message to Aeneas is only a pretext. One critic even asks about this episode: "If Rome admires these acts, if these are the values it holds forth to men—we recall Brutus killing his sons, Tullus rousing men to arms, Augustus conquering distant peoples—where exactly is the quality of its civilization?"[21] Others take the poet's apostrophe (9.446) *fortunati ambo* as indicating his admiration and, for instance, assert: "Here they are now, the youth upon which the Aeneadae will depend for their future, willingly presenting themselves at this crucial moment for a most crucial task. In this episode Virgil is presenting in another form the optimism for the future of Rome which he elsewhere divulges through prophecy and ecphrasis."[22]

As in the Homeric account of the corresponding episode in *Iliad* 10, the purpose of the exploit does not, as it is first formulated, include slaughter of the enemy. Nisus says (9.192–96):

> "Aenean acciri omnes, populusque patresque,
> exposcunt, mittique viros qui certa reportent.
> si tibi quae posco promittunt (nam mihi facti
> fama sat est), tumulo videor reperire sub illo
> posse viam ad muros et moenia Pallantea."

"Everyone, both people and elders, demands that Aeneas be summoned and that men be dispatched to report what has really happened. If they promise you what I demand (for the glory of the deed is enough for me), I think I can find at the foot of that hillock a path to the walls and fortifications of Pallanteum."

Militarily the plan is sound, but the twelfth-century heroic ethic intrudes in the requirement of specified rewards—not for himself, however, but for Euryalus. Patriotism is modified by a consideration important to the heroic world. When they take the plan to the elders in council, Nisus points out that the Rutulians are sprawled in drunken sleep and that there is a way through, known to him. He then says (240–45):

20. For example, Duckworth (1967), p. 147.
21. Fitzgerald (1972), p. 127.
22. Lennox (1977), p. 342.

"si fortuna permittitis uti,
quaesitum Aenean et moenia Pallantea,
mox hic cum spoliis ingenti caede peracta
adfore cernetis. nec nos via fallit euntis:
vidimus obscuris primam sub vallibus urbem
venatu adsiduo et totum cognovimus amnem."

"If you allow us to make use of this good luck to seek Aeneas and the fortifications of Pallanteum, you will soon see us back here with booty and great slaughter
done. And the track causes us no uncertainty as we go: on frequent hunting-trips
we have caught sight of the outskirts of the city from down in hidden valleys and
we have come to know the whole of the river."

The obvious meaning of this is that spoils and the killing of the enemy are
as important as the military purpose. A recent commentator objects to
this interpretation: "Nisus is trying to convince his listeners to win permission to leave the camp. . . . They are not interested in the safe return
of Nisus and Euryalus, except insofar as it would mean that Aeneas had
been apprised of the situation. Still less are they interested in any booty
which the two could win. If nos[23] equals Nisus and Euryalus, then 242 f.
must be admitted to be completely out of step with what the argument
requires, and otherwise receives, and with what the *ductores Teucrum
primi* desire. Is this the thoughtful and logical Nisus of 184–196 and
199–206? Could we really expect the leaders not to notice, or fail to ad-
monish such a glaringly irrelevant and reckless statement of intent?"[24]
But this treats the speech as if it were a historical document and one could
go behind the actual words to the real occasion.

   After Diomedes and Odysseus frighten the information they want
out of Dolon, they brutally murder him and set off to kill and loot on the
basis of the information. On their return they display their loot and boast
of having killed fourteen men (*Iliad* 10.558–63). This possibility of loot and
slaughter had not been mentioned during the discussion with Nestor that
preceded the expedition. The raid on the Thracians is actually suggested
by the miserable Dolon, because they are newcomers, unguarded, and
have magnificent equipment. What Virgil does is to show how naturally
loot and slaughter were indisputable concomitants of any military exploit
that was to bring fame to the perpetrator. So Nisus includes that element
in his proposal and it is accepted without question by the elders. It is not

23. To be understood as the subject of *adfore*.
24. Lennox (1977), p. 338.

possible to escape this implication by taking *nos* to include Aeneas,[25] for not only is such an extension not demanded by the run of the text, but there is no attempt to confine the looting and slaughter to the period after the mission has been accomplished.

It is recognised that this episode is unique in the *Aeneid*. The latest commentator says of it:[26] "The first half is remarkably direct and straightforward in diction, quite without the usual density of Virgilian imagery and overtone; the speeches are simple in phraseology, on occasion naive. Ascanius and Euryalus speak their thoughts ingenuously: the Homeric atmosphere of chivalry and bravery and princely behaviour is not modified or advanced in Virgil's usual manner, but directly transplanted. The episode is made to depend on its immediacy and its context: it is less sophisticated than any other part of the poem." One might quibble here over the Homeric atmosphere's being "directly transplanted," but this is generally a perceptive comment on the episode's peculiarity. Its value to the poet was that it provided him with the opportunity to expose the psychology of the heroic ethic, especially in the introductory conversation between Nisus and Euryalus.

That conversation begins abruptly with Nisus saying (9.184–85):

> "dine hunc ardorem mentibus addunt,
> Euryale, an sua cuique deus fit dira cupido?"

"Do the gods set this passion in men's minds, Euryalus, or does each man's terrible desire become a god to him?"

He goes on to say that he longs to do some great deed and has a plan. The abruptness of the question shows that Nisus has been pondering the problem. This question is often interpreted in terms of free will and determinism, and here it is certainly made by the poet to operate on the reader in such a way as to subvert any idea of divine determinism.[27] But it also has a significance in the immediate drama. Another commentator, denying any question here of free will and determinism, says: "It is certain that Virgil wants us to believe that Nisus' contemporaries thought that in some form or other the young man had been inspired by the gods: for thus Aletes exclaims when he hears Nisus' proposal:

> "di patrii, quorum semper sub numine Troia est,
> non tamen omnino Teucros delere paratis,

25. As Lennox does, loc. cit.
26. R. D. Williams (1973), p. 291.
27. On this, see p. 25 above.

> cum talis animos iuvenum et tam certa tulistis
> pectora."

["Gods of our fathers, under whose influence Troy always lies, you are after all not preparing to destroy the Trojans completely since you have given us such spirit in our young men and hearts so reliable".][28]

The same commentator says of this: "Not until Aletes enthusiastically responds to this proposal is Nisus convinced that it is a plan stirred in him by the gods rather than some base and destructive passion which ought to be stoically controlled."[29] But this is to confuse rhetoric and life. Aletes' prayer is the rhetoric of the situation and entails no serious religious interpretation. He goes on to wonder what suitable rewards he can offer, and that is what Nisus is really wanting to hear (194–95). Nisus' original question functions dramatically as an indication of his apprehension: his desire is "terrible" because it is focused on an exceedingly dangerous enterprise. The poet has formulated the question in such a way that it also functions for the reader outside the immediate context, suggesting that men's behaviour, especially in war, is indeed determined, but from within themselves; it is a measure of what the heroic ethic of the twelfth century really meant as seen by the privileged poet. The apprehension of Nisus is further expressed in his words, in reply to Euryalus' determination to accompany him, in which he suggests that things may (as they often do) go wrong, due either to chance or to a god (207–18). The effect of this can be measured against the Homeric analogue where Diomedes wants someone to accompany him, but only because two are better than one and a man on his own can be hesitant and make mistakes (*Iliad* 10.224–26). The words of Nisus foreshadow disaster, especially if Euryalus goes with him.

   The addition of loot and slaughter to the formulation of the plan (240–45) and the tacit acceptance of this by the elders bring out the ambiguity of the situation as well as expanding on the sense of (185) *dira cupido*. Fame is measured by the number of dead bodies. The poet recognised that as the twelfth-century attitude in his epitaph on Pallas (10.509),[30] and in authorial foreshadowing of the tragic end of this enterprise. Ascanius gives the pair all sorts of messages for his father (9.312–16):

28. Lennox (1977), p. 334 (I have added the translation).
29. Ibid., p. 340.
30. See p. 192 above.

                                     sed aurae
               omnia discerpunt et nubibus inrita donant.
               Egressi superant fossas noctisque per umbram
               castra inimica petunt, multis tamen ante futuri
               exitio.

But the breezes snatch them all away and distribute them without issue to the
clouds. They made their way out, climbed over the defenses and through the
darkness of the night made for the enemy camp, destined, however, first to bring
death to many.

The two elements of the enterprise are here separated out: the messages
were not to reach Aeneas; (the pair was destined to die) but only after
killing many of the enemy. The highly elliptical *tamen ante* conveys a
complex sense by a mere change of tone. The camp of the enemy is as far
as they will get; there the temptation to loot and slaughter will ruin the
rest of the enterprise. That killing is assimilated to the slaughter of the
Thracians by Diomedes and Odysseus by the use of the same simile of the
starving lion in an unguarded sheepfold (339–41; *Iliad* 10.485–86), but the
horror is greatly increased by physical details. It is an unnecessary slaughter in strictly military terms: Nisus drives a broad path through the enemy
(323): Euryalus is supposed to guard him, but he too gets carried away by
blood-lust (342–43). At last Nisus' apprehension surfaces (9.353–56):

                        breviter cum talia Nisus
               (sensit enim nimia caede atque cupidine ferri)
               "absistamus" ait, "nam lux inimica propinquat.
               poenarum exhaustum satis est, via facta per hostis."

. . . when Nisus briefly spoke like this (for he sensed that they were being carried
away by an excessive lust for slaughter): "Let us desist, for hostile dawn approaches. A sufficiency of vengeance has been exacted, a path has been cleared
through the enemy."

This is the epitome of the heroic ethic: killing the enemy was the exaction
of deserved vengeance. What is new here is the sense in Nisus of a proper
limit; the theme will be expressed in the poet's own voice in respect to
Turnus (10.502). The poet then lists the loot they did not take, before he
describes Euryalus' donning of the fatal helmet, with an authorial intervention in (364) *nequiquam* (it was in vain)—he is unthinking and it will
betray him (374 *prodidit immemorem*).

     Two points of view are expressed here and left unresolved. The first
concerns the danger threatening the Trojans and the value of getting a

message to Aeneas: everyone wanted that (192–93) and it is given priority in all the discussions. The other recognises that no twelfth-century hero could possibly resist the opportunity to "exact vengeance" on the enemy when it was presented to him. The poet shows how the two points of view turn out to be incompatible, but he refuses to pass judgment. His aim is understanding, and he transcends the delivery of a verdict by his apostrophe in the paradoxical words (446) *fortunati ambo*. He sees the pair as lucky, not in terms of the immediate situation or even in providing an exemplary model of any sort whatever to historical Romans, but in appealing to criteria inherent in the human condition itself, a timeless point of view that will be valid as long as Latin continues to be understood— that is, as long as Rome itself lasts (448–49).

All of the morally ambiguous situations analysed above express a clash between opposing viewpoints that the poet refuses to resolve. Sometimes, as in the case of Dido and Aeneas, that clash is timeless and is inherent in the human condition as such. The refusal of the poet to deliver a verdict recognises the fact that such clashes cannot be resolved except to the satisfaction of partisans. There is no conceivable moral system by which either side is absolutely right; each has its own justification in its own terms, and the tragedy consists in the fact that those sets of terms hardly intersect at all. What is needed is human understanding. At other times the clashes represent a conflict between the twelfth century and the age of Augustus, or, rather, between the poet's understanding of twelfth-century attitudes and his own sensibility, whether or not that is to be regarded as characteristic of the age of Augustus. The plea of Turnus to be spared appeals to a humanitarian revulsion from slaughter and a sense of the value of even the least promising life. Aeneas' final act must be seen and understood within the moral imperatives of the twelfth century, which at times he has uniquely transcended. These moral ambiguities, therefore, bridge the gap between the field of the narrative and either that of the age of Augustus or that of the human condition as such. They belong to, and are characteristic of, the very technique of composition itself.

9 IDEAS AND THE EPIC POET

During the last half-century two totally opposed views about the relationship of the *Aeneid* to the times in which it was written have come to be current: on the one hand, it is seen as a clear case of propaganda for Augustan ideology; on the other, it is interpreted as a point of view hostile to Augustus and all he stood for. Here are some characteristic quotations:

(*a*) The character of the epic hero is neither splendid nor striking. That was not intended. The perpetual guidance lavished upon the hero is likewise repugnant to romantic notions. Aeneas is an instrument of heaven, a slave to duty. "Sum pius Aeneas," as he stamps himself at once. Throughout all hazards of his high mission, Aeneas is sober, steadfast and tenacious: there can be no respite for him, no repose, no union of heart and policy with an alien queen. Italy is his goal—"hic amor, haec patria est." And so Aeneas follows his mission, sacrificing all emotion to *pietas*, firm in resolution but sombre and a little weary. The poem is not an allegory; but no contemporary could fail to detect in Aeneas a foreshadowing of Augustus. [Syme (1939), pp. 462–63]

(*b*) But there is of course a broader problem that we have hardly touched upon so far in this book. That is the justification of Virgil's "ideological" viewpoint, the extent to which his poetry may or may not be vitiated by his Augustan "propaganda," if indeed we can use so unkind a term without question-begging. First of all, it seems quite plain that Virgil was himself a convinced Augustan. He was clearly inspired by his theme: he believed in his own "ideology." He really saw in Augustus the type of man who could bring peace out of fratricidal war, order from anarchy, self-control from selfish passion, in a sense, an "age of gold" from an age of iron. [Otis (1963), p. 389]

232

(c) Virgil seems to say here [in the final scene], if we judge correctly, that Aeneas—and through him Augustus—can never fulfill in fact the ideal conditions of empire, where force and freedom must be fused into a fortunate amalgam. [Putnam (1965), pp. xiii–xiv]

(d) The purpose of the *Aeneid* is clear enough. The poem commemorates a great victory, the battle of Actium, which came soon to symbolize the end of decades of bloody civil war.

(e) The ideal contemporary reader we postulated earlier would take it for granted that somehow or other, Aeneas was Augustus.

(f) If the Aeneas of Book 4 suggests Julius Caesar or Mark Antony, the Aeneas of Book 12 points plainly to Augustus; and the portrait is hardly a flattering one. [Quinn (1969), pp. 22; 54; 253]

(g) The thought of this intelligent, sensitive, reflective poet, at the height of his powers and in the maturity of his later years, subscribing to a limited political program as the basis of his epic—surely that is artificial and mind-boggling. It is also degrading. [Di Cesare (1974), pp. viii–ix]

From propaganda for Augustus to propaganda against Augustus is an easy step for the attitudes expressed by these quotations (and many, many more examples of both points of view could be adduced). Both extremes require several strategies of interpretation: for instance, a literal and partial reading of the poem, and a conviction that an ideology is either being expressed or attacked (by another ideology, of course). The inadequacy of seeing Aeneas as "an instrument of heaven"[1] or of interpreting the poem as a commemoration of the battle of Actium can be demonstrated, and one purpose of this book has been to attempt that demonstration. It is perhaps harder to demonstrate the violence that is done to the text of the *Aeneid* by excavating some kind of "ideology" out of it.

The attempt, however, should start from a distinction between ideas and ideology. It is simple enough to list the major elements in the ideology of Augustus (as we can detect it in the pronouncements of his *res*

---

1. Carlsson (1945) quotes Sellar's characterisation of Aeneas as (115) "a passive instrument in the hands of destiny," and later puts his own view thus (131): "Aeneas is of a thoroughly passive nature and not at all a man driven on by any impulse of his own or by any 'divine' power within him towards personal development or energetic action."

gestae). But what ideas are expressed in the *Aeneid*? It is easy to sense that many complex ideas are there expressed, but indirectly and in such a way that they bear no clear relevance to Augustan ideology. Again the criteria by which an ideology is judged are expedience, usefulness, practicability, effectiveness, and so on. Ideas, on the other hand, are powerful sources of poetic energy and emotion, neither of which has the slightest relevance to ideology, and their quality is judged by their capacity to generate that combination of intellectual and emotional power. In short, there are many ideas in the *Aeneid* and no ideology.

A further strategy of interpretation is needed even by those who proclaim that the *Aeneid* is not an allegory. This is to regard Aeneas as in some way symbolic of Augustus; another way of formulating this thesis is to say that Aeneas is a forerunner of, or that he foreshadows, Augustus. But either formulation involves an unwelcome consequence. For if Aeneas is to be a symbol for, or even to foreshadow, Augustus, then the time-span of the *Aeneid* is in some way symbolic of the time-span of Roman history as a whole down to, and including, the age of Augustus. But the poet has made every effort to show that point of view decisively mistaken. For the major indexes that relate the immediate field of the *Aeneid* to Roman history as a whole and to the age of Augustus in particular all have a peculiar feature: they are so designed as to suggest a continuum of history that is in the most important ways Roman, extending from the late twelfth century B.C. to the time of the poem's composition. The first of them (Juppiter's prophecy at 1.257–96) is actually designed to constitute an exemplary chronological framework that establishes the time of Aeneas as an integral part of Rome's earliest origins.

What generates poetical excitement in the *Aeneid*—and no doubt did so in its poet—is that sense of the magical and inspiring story of the origins of a state which was destined in the poet's time to include under its rule almost all of the known world. Antiquity in general may have been unencumbered by anything like the modern "idea of progress" (though there has recently been argument against this idea),[2] but Romans viewed their own state as evolving gradually over a very long period of time and thus, in this (as in other respects) quite different from other ancient states that sprang into existence, like Athene, full-grown from the head of Zeus. The idea is well formulated by Cicero in words he puts into the mouth of Scipio Africanus the younger. Scipio is telling how much he learned from the great Cato (*de republica* 2.2):

2. See Nisbet (1980), pp. 10–46.

is dicere solebat ob hanc causam praestare nostrae civitatis statum ceteris civitatibus, quod in illis singuli fuissent fere quorum suam quisque rem publicam constituisset legibus atque institutis suis, ut Cretum Minos, Lacedaemoniorum Lycurgus, Atheniensium, quae persaepe commutata esset, tum Theseus tum Draco tum Solo tum Clisthenes tum multi alii, postremo exsanguen iam et ia-centem doctus vir Phalereus sustentasset Demetrius, nostra autem res publica non unius esset ingenio sed multorum, nec una hominis vita sed aliquot con-stituta saeculis et aetatibus.

He used to declare that the constitution of our state was superior to all other states for the reason that in them it was virtually one man in each case who had founded the state on his own laws and institutions, as Minos did for Crete, Lycurgus for Sparta, for Athens (whose constitution had often been changed) at one time Theseus, then Dracon, then Solon, then Cleisthenes, then many others, finally when it was bloodless and prostrate that scholarly man, Demetrius of Phalerum, had revived it. But our state had been founded not by the genius of one man but of many, nor in one man's lifetime but over several centuries and the ages of many men. . . .

Then Scipio undertakes to "demonstrate our state to you both at its birth and in its years of growth and when it became adult and firm and strong" (*de republica* 2.3). The metaphor of the gradual growth of a human being is used to express the concept.

Scipio, however, starts with Romulus in the eighth century. What Virgil does is to start the whole process with Aeneas, and the nature of Aeneas' contribution is made clear in the speech of Juppiter in Book 1. It is not just the settling of the Trojans in Italy, but (1.264) *moresque viris et moenia ponet* "he shall found a way of life and fortifications for them." The contribution of behaviour is at least as important as that of the physical buildings designed to protect the state. The concept is used by Anchises to define the nature of Roman civilization (6.852): *pacique imponere morem* "to impose a settled way of life on peace." The poetical interest of Aeneas lies in the vision of a man who is a Homeric hero yet is also a primitive colonizer and possesses elements of behaviour, of morals, of values that mark him out from all his surroundings as a proto-Roman. In many ways, then, Aeneas is a man of the twelfth century, and in certain situations of stress where other standards cannot be applied, he is shown to revert to the pattern of behaviour of a Homeric hero. That is why he is void of interest if one regards him as a symbol of Augustus or even as a forerun-ner of him (except in the most literal and limited way). The poetical excitement of Aeneas lies in the concept and creation of an individual who belongs to one world but has visions of another that are so far in advance of his time that he cannot help but be torn between them. Augustus—together with all good Romans at all times—has inherited a moral tradition from the past that is specifically Roman; the index of the shield at the end of Book 8 is designed to bring out that aspect of the tradition. It is exactly those qualities, expressed in the valuation placed on *pax*, *fides*, *libertas*, *pietas*, and *virtus*, that are to be seen, at times dimly, in the character of Aeneas and also, to some extent, in that of Evander and his people. But the *mores* established by Aeneas are not Trojan; that is guaranteed by Juppiter's promise to Juno (12.834). They are phenomena of the frontier spirit of a man who has to rely on himself, discover his own values, and invent a system of behaviour that responds to the situation in which he finds himself. But they are also related to what is best in Italian values, even if this does not come through explicitly in the action of the *Aeneid*, since there the Italians are enemies of the Trojans. In fact, those *mores* come closest to what is suggested about the Italian age of Saturn, though more by Evander (8.314–36) than by Latinus (7.202–04). After that age there was a decline, the leading characteristics of which were war and greed (8.326–27). It is to the prelapsarian state of Italy that the ideal and somewhat instinctive *mores* of Aeneas and of Evander are related.

Somewhere at the basis of all ideology, at whatever remove, are ideas, though they lose blood and life when translated into an ideological programme. Consequently, it is possible to abstract ideas from the *Aeneid* and assert that they are relevant to the ideology of Augustus; and then to take the further step of claiming that the *Aeneid* supports the political programme of Augustus. But this is as much a travesty of a subtle and complex text as to assert the opposite: that the ideas of the *Aeneid* are conceived in such a way as to throw doubt on any hopes invested in Augustus, if not to attack his ideology directly. It is, in fact, very hard to say what the ideas of the *Aeneid* are, and some violence and over-simplification are done to the text just by attempting to do so. The reason for this is that the ideas are inherent, unstated; they emerge from the changing patterns of the narrative as underlying assumptions that possess all the more power for not being formulated. But the apprehension of these ideas is an important source of emotional power in the text.

For instance, the value of peace becomes an insistent note in the second half of the *Aeneid*. It becomes clear in the portrait of idyllic peace in Italy during the reign of Latinus in the first half of Book 7. This is, in fact, an irony, since the reality is far from peaceful, as will become evident, and the ideal of peace is more convincingly exhibited among Evander and his people. The ideal is given powerful expression by Aeneas when the Italian embassy comes to ask a truce for burial of the dead (11.108–11):

> "quaenam vos tanto fortuna indigna, Latini,
> implicuit bello, qui nos fugiatis amicos?
> pacem me exanimis et Martis sorte peremptis
> oratis? equidem et vivis concedere vellem."

"What stroke of undeserved ill-fortune, Latins, enmeshed you in such a war that you shun our friendship? Do you ask me for peace on behalf of the dead and those cut down by the chance of war? I should for myself certainly have wanted to grant it to the living also."

A different view is suggested by Turnus at the climax of his contemptuously angry speech to Allecto disguised as an old temple-attendant (7.444):

"bella viri pacemque gerent quis bella gerenda"

"War and peace will be conducted by men whose business it is to conduct war."

Here peace is subordinated to war in the main clause by the use of *gerere*, a verb meaning "to wage" and naturally associated with *bellum*; in the subordinate clause peace is omitted altogether. The sentence, by its structure, portrays a man who lives for war. That will be a major element in the portrait of Turnus; it is the opposite with Aeneas. That constant sense of peace as the essential condition for the ideal life colours the tragedy of Books 7–12 and underlies the frustration of Aeneas.

But this peace is not the peace of Augustan ideology, the *parta victoriis pax* (*res gestae* 13). Peace in the poet's sense is an absolute value. Its nature, paradoxically, emerges most clearly in another leading idea of the poem, hatred of war. For war destroys the values of peace. That idea is poignantly expressed in the first death of the Italian war when the poet speaks an epitaph over Galaesus, killed (7.536) *dum paci medium se offert*, while he was trying to mediate for peace.[3] It comes out in the constant pity of the poet, expressed in descriptions of horrible deaths and in the recurring epitaphs and apostrophes. War transforms character, so that Aeneas reverts to the type of Homeric hero, speaking in a loathsome way for instance, to Tarquitus (10.557–60):

> "istic nunc, metuende, iace. non te optima mater
> condet humi patrioque onerabit membra sepulcro:
> alitibus linquere feris, aut gurgite mersum
> unda feret piscesque impasti vulnera lambent."

"Now lie there dead, frightening man. Your fine mother will not lay you in the

3. See p. 197 above.

earth or weigh down your limbs with an ancestral tomb. You will be left for wild birds, or the wave will carry you sunk in its tide and ravenous fishes will lick your wounds."

The words are a combination of what Odysseus says to Socus (*Iliad* 11.450–55 "ravenous birds") and Achilles to Lycaon (21.122–35 "fishes"). Even the attractive Pallas, whose noble speech to his followers precedes his *aristeia* (10.369–78), is then shown perpetrating horrors (380–425) before he is himself slain.

War is seen to be almost an absolute evil—but not quite, because the poet recognises that there are times when a man has no choice but to fight, as Aeneas must, after doing all that he can to prevent war. In the same way, it seems to be suggested, Augustus had no possible option but to fight Antony and Cleopatra at Actium (8.678–713). The ideal society is free from war, and so the climax to Juppiter's great speech shows war eliminated by Augustus (1.293–96). But there the poet is clearly thinking mainly of civil war, and it is above all at this kind of war that his hatred is directed; for that reason the Italian war is portrayed as a sort of civil war. There is some tenuous connexion with Augustan ideology and the ceremony of closing the gate of Janus; it was closed three times by Augustus—in 29 B.C., in 25 B.C., and on one later, unknown occasion (*res gestae* 13)—and the multiple closures indicate its propaganda value. But it is only a tenuous connexion, and a far more Augustan attitude is shown in sentiments such as those of Horace in *Odes* 3.2, lauding war against foreigners as the gymnasium of patriotism.

Another idea of the epic is the value placed on tradition, or *mos* and *mores*, on the concept of settled custom. But of its nature tradition cannot be established and maintained by one man. There must be like-minded successors. Aeneas is shown in the poem establishing a way of life that depends on a series of values virtually unknown to the heroic world. The tradition is handed on to his son, who is to imitate him (12.435–40), and so on. It is to that sense of a settled tradition broken by civil war that Augustus appealed when he wrote, early in his *res gestae* (8.5): "By new laws passed on my proposal I brought back many exemplary practices of our ancestors that were perishing in our time and I myself have handed on to posterity for imitation exemplary practices in many fields." But because no man is exempt from death such a tradition can be unexpectedly broken; the paradigmatic case of this in the *Aeneid* is the dirge performed over the dead Marcellus, designated successor to Augustus. The sense not only of the inevitability of death but also of its unpredictability is one source of the considerable tone of pessimism that pervades the epic. In consequence, all human planning is frail and every tradition uncertain. The more confident Roman, and still more Augustan, attitude is put into the mouth of Anchises (6.852) *pacique imponere morem* "to impose on peace a settled way of life." That attitude is explicitly stated; the other, left to be inferred, is more powerful.

Similarly left to be inferred is another idea basic to the epic: it concerns the problem of human free will versus necessity. Is the writer of quotation (*a*) on p. 232 above right in talking about "the perpetual guidance lavished upon the hero" and Aeneas as "an instrument of heaven"? The poet uses the gods as a figure by which the problem of free will can be accommodated. But what emerges from the epic is that men are conscious of their freedom of will at the moment of action; it is only the privileged poet who has the vantage point capable of seeing a pattern in history and of understanding that what did happen could not have happened otherwise. The problem, in fact, is not a problem: there are just two points of view that cannot coincide. The noble speech of Pallas to his followers has just been mentioned; it is a fine expression of the dilemma (10.369–78):

> "quo fugitis, socii? per vos et fortia facta,
> per ducis Euandri nomen devictaque bella
> spemque meam, patriae quae nunc subit aemula laudi,
> fidite ne pedibus. ferro rumpenda per hostis
> est via. qua globus ille virum densissimus urget,
> hac vos et Pallanta ducem patria alta reposcit.
> numina nulla premunt, mortali urgemur ab hoste
> mortales; totidem nobis animaeque manusque.
> ecce maris magna claudit nos obice pontus,
> deest iam terra fugae: pelagus Troiamne petemus?"

"Where are you running away to, my friends? ⟨I beseech⟩ you by the brave deeds, by the name of our leader Evander and the wars won by him and by hope that now arises to rival my father's fame, do not put your trust in your feet. A path must be hacked through the enemy by steel. Where the press of men thrusts there most densely, through there does your glorious country demand you and your leader Pallas back. No divine powers oppress us; we are mortals oppressed by a mortal enemy: we have the same number both of souls and of hands as they. See! the tide imprisons us with the great barrier of the ocean, there is no land left for running away: is it the sea we are to make for, or Troy?"

The Homeric analogue to this, the speech of Ajax to his troops as the Trojans reach the Greek ships (*Iliad* 15.733–41), makes no mention of gods. The poet of the *Aeneid* uses the gods in the following narrative, but Pallas knows nothing of that. What emerges clearly here is the isolation of man, his total self-dependence, his responsibility for his own acts and their consequences. There are no gods to help or hinder; they are a poetic device for expressing the hindsight of history.

Another powerful idea operative throughout is that moral judgments have no necessary claim to absolute right or wrong (see chapter 8). Here again the gap between the temporality of the narrative and that of the composition operates. For in the twelfth century the poet represents both sides as thinking in their own terms and each judging itself to be justified; in the age of Augustus can he look back and see that two totally incompatible sets of criteria were operating, between which judgment could only be made, if at all, on a third set of terms unknown to the actors, and so, from their point of view, arbitrarily. The poet witholds judgment, and his integrity has the effect not only of generating emotion but also of making a reader see such moral dilemmas as a feature not of one time or place but of the human condition as such. The technique—it is close to what Keats called "negative capability" (defined as "capable of being in uncertainties, mysteries, doubts, without any irritable reaching after fact and reason")—creates a depth and range that is beyond the easy certainties of other poets.

There is a further aspect to moral ambiguity that has not yet been touched on. For there is a distinct contradiction, though it remains always implicit and unobtrusive, between the poet's hatred of war and the laudation of Augustus as a conqueror. It is always a voice other than the poet's that pronounces the laudation: at 1.289–96 it is Juppiter; at 6.791–800 it is Anchises; and at 8.722–28 it is the workmanship of Vulcan. In the first of these statements, Augustus will wage the war to end all wars, but the emphasis here is heavily on the cessation of civil war; in the second, the laudation is of extension of the empire as such and the fear with which Augustus is already regarded in the twelfth century by potential enemies; in the final passage, it is laudation of his sheer conquest of peoples from all over the world. The principle is voiced by Anchises (6.851–53): Rome's arts are those of government, the imposition of law and custom, clemency to the humbled, and the crushing of the arrogant by war. The poet recognises two standards in somewhat the same way as he recognises that fame is due to Pallas for the slaughter of enemies at the same time as he grieves over his death (10.507–09). There is a moral ambiguity between the valuation of peace (and hatred of war) and admiration for the greatness of Rome. For ultimately, greatness is owed to, and to some extent measured by, military power. The fame of Greece derives from the arts of peace; they are the poet's arts, and so he dissociates himself from the expression of what he nevertheless recognises to be a fact of life by using voices other than his own. The two points of view cannot be reconciled; they can only be expressed and judged on their own terms. This is the essence of moral ambiguity—and of poetic integrity.

This dichotomy of irreconcilable points of view can also be regarded as measuring the gap between the two secondary fields of the epic: the field of Roman history and the age of Augustus on the one hand, and, on the other, the field of the human condition in a hostile universe. The general ideas that lie at the basis of the epic are related to the latter field. It is to be noticed that these ideas are inherent; they are never expressed as such and can only be distantly apprehended by the reader. The themes that focus on Augustus, on the other hand, are stated explicitly. They have a relationship to the major elements of Augustan ideology, but, because of the way in which the poet puts those themes in the mouth of privileged persons (gods and Anchises), he dissociates himself from direct implication in their expression. An interesting exception to this can be seen in Book 8. For Evander, when he conducts Aeneas about the site of future Rome, gives expression to a way of life that was certainly idealised in the age of Augustus—the life of simple virtue in natural surroundings (8.337–69). Here the poet deliberately enters the text in his own voice to point the contrast with contemporary Rome (348–50 and 360–61). This is a theme that lies at the very roots of the *Georgics*, and it seems likely that the ideas that underlay certain aspects of Augustan moral reform excited the poet's sympathetic imagination in a way that military greatness and political goals did not. Hence, at this point the two fields of the human condition and the age of Augustus intersect.

The association of the primary field of the poem with that aspect of the secondary field which is the age of Augustus suggests that one of the poet's basic concepts was this: the ideals of human existence that can be poetically shown to have been implicit in the first beginnings of the Roman state in the twelfth century are only now, at last in the age of Augustus, coming to be realised. The proposition is optative. It is no propaganda for a particular regime but a poetical vision, disappointed and betrayed in reality, yet the hallmark not only of an age (and shared by other poets of the time) but also of the historical vision of a great poet.

However, it is questionable whether this exactly is the final impression left on the reader. It seems, rather, as if the poet used the twelfth century to some extent to redress the present and in Aeneas, contrary to what most commentators now assert, created a figure closer to the ideal in one important respect than any contemporary Roman could be. For Aeneas at no point shows interest in the kind of fame that is acquired by military prowess. Quite the opposite: he does everything possible to avoid war and shows every sign of sharing the poet's hatred of it. The *pax Augusta* was recommended on no such grounds; patriotism and conquest were as closely linked as in Horace *Odes* 3.2. Anchises puts the Augustan point of view not only in (6.853) *debellare superbos* but in his stated purpose in the review of Roman heroes (6.718, 806–07, and 889)—to inflame Aeneas with pride in the fame to come from Roman military superiority. There is no sign that anything of the kind played any part in Aeneas' motivation. He can revert to being a Homeric hero when frustrated in his better plans, but his real soul is laid bare more surely in the account of the Greek destruction of Troy or in his tears elicited by the Trojan scenes on Dido's temple (1.459–65)—tears quite different from the dramatic tears of Odysseus when he hears the ballad of Demodocus (*Odyssey* 8.83–95), which were the Homeric model for the poet—when he says (1.461–62):

> sunt hic etiam sua praemia laudi;
> sunt lacrimae rerum et mentem mortalia tangunt.

Even here great deeds receive their rewards, there are tears for what happens and mortal sufferings touch the heart.

This is a fine index to the secondary field not of Roman history but of the human condition, and it is true that Aeneas in relation to all he takes a part in is linked as often to that aspect of the secondary field as to the age of Augustus. It is as though, in spite of apparent optimism about the age of Augustus, the poet's natural pessimism was so great that in the end human achievement, its significance and certainly its permanence, is called into question, especially in the face of the fact of death. Aeneas wondering how the blessed dead could ever want to come to life again is a synecdoche for the poem's judgment on man and his universe. Such indexes again and again enforce a judgment that measures ideals not by the terms of Rome's national self-interest and self-esteem but by the requirements of the human condition itself.

If this is true, then it helps to support the answer given to the other general problem faced by this book: to choose between two rival readings of the *Aeneid* (see p. 2 above). The conclusion clearly suggested by this examination of the epic is that the world of Aeneas is to be viewed as a part of the real world of human experience, and that the poet is not giving a direct account of the constitution of the universe when he uses the concepts of Fate and the gods; on the contrary, those concepts are figurally active (mainly in a metaphorical mode) in the narrative and are to be distinguished from authorially guaranteed beliefs. The poet does not express beliefs directly, but instead a sense of deep pessimism is conveyed about the capacity of human beings to attain ideals in a universe that is essentially hostile. The hope that is constantly expressed in the formulation of such ideals is pitifully vulnerable to the very nature of the human condition.

APPENDIX
SIGNS OF CHANGES OF PLAN IN THE *AENEID*

The *Life of Virgil* by Donatus has an interesting account of the way the poet went to work on his *Aeneid:*

After first shaping the *Aeneid* in prose and distributing it over twelve books, he began to compose it bit by bit as each detail caught his fancy, and taking nothing in order. Also, so that there should be nothing to hold back his inspiration, he left some passages incomplete, others he propped up, as it were, with very tenuous lines that he said jokingly were being inserted as supports to hold the work up until the solid pillars should arrive. The *Bucolics* took him three years, the *Georgics* seven, and the *Aeneid* eleven years.

There is no reason to doubt the general authenticity of this description of Virgil's procedure. It was doubtless passed on through oral tradition by friends, and the detail of the "props" is dramatically confirmed by the so-called "half-lines" which are quite obviously the result of composing passages here and there, without, at the time of composition, any clear idea of the way in which each separate passage would eventually be incorporated into a continuous narrative. They can be found in every book: Book 12 has only one; Books 6 and 11 have two each; Books 1 and 8 have three each; Book 4 has five; Books 7, 9, and 10 have six each; Books 3 and 5 have seven each; and Book 2 has ten. Most of them occur at the end of a speech or paragraph; a few introduce a speech. The pattern clearly shows the difficulty of linking (both at beginning and end) already composed sections together. There were certainly many more which are now concealed by the poet's success in devising seamless transitions; those which remain need not indicate any unusual difficulties at those points, but only the random working habits of the poet and the fact that death cut short his efforts.

This method of composition was bound, in spite of the prose digest of the *Aeneid*, to promote changes of plan both large and small. It is the aim of this Appendix to consider the artistic effect of some of these, especially in the first six books. There is inevitably an element of speculation in this procedure since the poet has been surprisingly successful at covering his tracks, but some observations that are not purely speculative are worth making.

1. The Narrative Technique of Book 2

The artistic success of Book 2, where Aeneas takes over the narration from the poet, presents quite a contrast with Book 3 and is worth analysing from this point of view. A series of elements in the narrative, ranging from style to subject matter, are relevant to the analysis.

(*a*) *The character of the narrator.* Aeneas, unlike Virgil, was a man of the twelfth century and, also unlike Virgil, had both lived through and played an active role in the events that led to Troy's destruction. His emotional involvement in those past events has already been recounted in the poet's own voice as he told of Aeneas' feelings at seeing the pictures in Dido's temple (1.450–93). Such a man would naturally relate those events from a different perspective from that of the poet. The challenge presented by this προσωποποιία or *fictio personae* (Quintilian 9.2.29–37) was to represent that difference by means of the narrative technique in such a way that a reader might actually hear a new voice and sense a different character. Aeneas expresses his feelings immediately (3–13):

> "infandum, regina, iubes renovare dolorem,
> Troianas ut opes et lamentabile regnum
> eruerint Danai, quaeque ipse miserrima vidi   5
> et quorum pars magna fui. quis talia fando
> Myrmidonum Dolopumve aut duri miles Vlixi
> temperet a lacrimis? et iam nox umida caelo
> praecipitat suadentque cadentia sidera somnos.
> sed si tantus amor casus cognoscere nostros   10
> et breviter Troiae supremum audire laborem,
> quamquam animus meminisse horret luctuque refugit,
> incipiam."

"You ask me, queen, to bring alive again an unspeakable pain—how the Greeks destroyed the splendour of Troy and its pitiable kingdom—most heart-rending things that I myself both witnessed (5) and of which I was a large part. What soldier of the Myrmidons or of the Dolopes or of hard-hearted Ulysses, in the telling of such a tale, could hold back from tears? And now dank night falls headlong from the sky and the setting stars urge sleep. But if your desire is so great to learn of our disasters (10) and briefly hear of Troy's final trial, though my spirit shivers at the memory and has started back from the grief, I shall begin."

The pathetic fallacy closely prefigures the speaker's feelings and recalls Henry James' striking formulation: "a landscape is a state of mind." This narrator is not the poet; this is someone for whom Ulysses and the followers of Achilles and Neoptolemus are still alive, and, enemies though they have been and still are, could scarce forbear to weep. The force of such personal emotion, marking Aeneas as an authentic eye witness, is supported by one further statement of his own feelings. As he tells of the serpents coming ashore to attack Laocoön, he says (204) *horresco referens* "I shiver with fear as I tell of it." He returns once more to the theme of an agony so great that mere words or tears cannot do it justice as he recounts the brave effort to fight the Greeks (361–62):

> "quis cladem illius noctis, quis funera fando
> explicet aut possit lacrimis aequare labores?"

"Who could in telling of it unfold all the disaster of that night, the deaths, or who could with his tears keep pace with our agonies?"

It is characteristic of poets of this period that by a very restrained use of a stylistic or technical touch (sometimes a single instance) they manage to create the suggestion of an effect, which the reader must generalise over the whole of the relevant context. The effect of these expressions of emotion by Aeneas—emotion generated in Troy and relived in Carthage—is to cancel the gap between the actual events and their narration; Aeneas, and his audience, are reliving the actuality of his experiences.

This unique character of the narrator, once established, is sustained by various adaptations of the narrative technique and of features of epic style throughout the book.

(b) *"Showing" and "telling."*[1] When the poet "tells," it is in virtue of his omniscient authority. But when Aeneas tells, it is the expression of hindsight, and this opens the possibility of a particularly striking form of dramatic irony. Aeneas now knows from bitter experience what the meaning of the wooden horse really was, and his opening words tell the whole story from this vantage point (13–24). This is then contrasted with

---

1. On this distinction, see p. 17 above.

the happy holiday spirit in Troy after the Greek's apparent departure (25–39); but there are ironic touches. The Trojans gaze at (31) *innuptae donum exitiale Minervae* "the deadly gift of the virgin Minerva"; and, when Thymoetes proposes to bring the horse into the city, Aeneas remarks aside (34) *sive dolo seu iam Troiae sic fata ferebant* "whether by treachery or whether the fate of Troy was already moving in that direction." Another aside from hindsight comes with Sinon's dramatic (60) *hoc ipsum ut strueret Troiamque aperiret Achivis* "for this very stratagem—to open up Troy to the Greeks." Then, as he is about to let Sinon tell his own convincing story, he introduces it with the ironic words (65–66):

> "accipe nunc Danaum insidias et crimine ab uno
> disce omnis."

"Now hear the treachery of the Greeks and learn about all of them from the villainy of one."

The second section of Sinon's story is introduced with a bitterly ironic comment (105–07):

> "Tum vero ardemus scitari et quaerere causas,
> ignari scelerum tantorum artisque Pelasgae.
> prosequitur pavitans et ficto pectore fatur."

"Then we are truly ablaze to learn and to find out the reasons, ignorant of crimes of such magnitude and of Greek cunning. He continues, shivering with fear, and speaks with lying heart."

Finally, Sinon ends and Aeneas sums up, again from bitter hindsight (195–98):

> "Talibus insidiis periurique arte Sinonis
> credita res, captique dolis lacrimisque coactis
> quos neque Tydides nec Larisaeus Achilles,
> non anni domuere decem, non mille carinae."

"With such treachery and skill in perjury on Sinon's part the affair was believed, and there were taken prisoner by guile and crocodile tears those whom neither the son of Tydeus nor Achilles of Larisa nor ten years subdued nor a thousand ships."

Here dramatic irony is used to place a sort of epitaph on Troy into the mouth of Aeneas,[2] well before its fall in terms of the temporality of the

---

2. The rhetoric of "incapable of destruction by Greeks" is repeated in the authorial epitaphs on Trojans in 10.429–30 and on Aeolus in 12.542–47 (see pp. 191 and 194 above).

narrative (though not of the "composition"). The tone of these comments from hindsight is a dramatic bitterness that reaches a climax as Aeneas vividly describes the Greek fleet sailing back by night to Troy, and Sinon opening the wooden horse (257) *fatisque deum defensus iniquis* "under the protection of the unjust decrees of the gods." Aeneas later learns that the gods are against Troy and on the side of the Greeks (604–23).

All of the irony in Aeneas' telling, derived from hindsight, is focused on the moment when he actually witnesses the horrific result of Greek treachery; this is the point at which there is no longer a gap between his perception within the temporality of the narrative on the one hand and within that of the "composition" on the other. The moment is introduced by dramatic telling as Aeneas recounts the din of war and the screams that gain in volume while he is still asleep (298–301). He wakes, climbs to the roof; a simile takes over the narrative (see below p. 253), and this comment follows (309–10):

> "tum vero manifesta fides, Danaumque patescunt
> insidiae."

"Then ⟨the reality of⟩ our trust is revealed, and the treachery of the Greeks stands naked."

Since perception and knowledge now coincide, there is no irony in the eye-witness account that follows; but there is one further striking instance of "telling" derived from hindsight (554–58):

> "haec finis Priami fatorum, hic exitus illum
> sorte tulit Troiam incensam et prolapsa videntem
> Pergama, tot quondam populis terrisque superbum
> regnatorem Asiae. iacet ingens litore truncus,
> avulsumque umeris caput et sine nomine corpus."

"This was the end of Priam's destiny, this was the death that carried him off by fate, as he witnessed the burning of Troy and the collapse of Pergamum, once the proud ruler over so many peoples and lands of Asia. There he lies, a huge trunk on the sea-shore, and the head is torn from its shoulders and the body is without a name."

This is an epitaph on Priam, with the epitaphic contrast between glorious past and shameful present mirrored in the movement from past to present tense, which suggests that, at the very time Aeneas is speaking, the body is still lying nameless on the shore. The basis for the final clauses lies in hindsight, but, unlike the epitaph on Troy (195–98), the solemnity of this statement contains no irony, and so also serves as an epitaph on the

whole of the Trojan past for which Priam is the symbol. Aeneas' world—
and so his narrative—from this point on contracts to himself and his
immediate family.

(c) *Stylistic control of the viewpoint.* In no book of the *Aeneid* is the
exclamatory particle *ecce* used so often. The majority of the examples in
other books are either a mere gesture in narrative, without any implication of surprise, or else (when they occur in speeches) they are a verbal
gesture, corresponding to a real gesture, again with no element of surprise. There are perhaps nine examples in the whole of the *Aeneid*, excluding Book 2, where *ecce* is calculated to re-enforce surprise at a turn of the
narrative. In contrast with this, all eight examples in Book 2 occur at
crucial junctures in the narrative (57, 270, 403, 682; *ecce autem* 203, 318,
526, 673). This distinguishes Aeneas from the poet as a narrator who is
recreating a recent experience as an eye-witness. In the mouth of the poet
the particle is deliberately mannered and self-conscious; Aeneas uses it to
re-enact his own immediate surprise.

Another effect of the controlled use of *ecce* is to substantiate the
presence of a listening audience whose surprise is being evoked. That
audience is directly addressed in the person of Dido, its most conspicuous
member, as the climax of the narrative approaches. After Aeneas has just
described Troy filled with triumphant Greeks and fire, he says (506) *For-
sitan et Priami fuerint quae fata requiras* "Perhaps you may also be asking
what happened to Priam at the end." His detailed eyewitness account of
Priam's death follows.

There are two notable apostrophes in Aeneas' tale of Troy. The first
comes at a dramatic moment as Laocoön's spear quivers and echoes within the wooden horse (54–56):

> "et, si fata deum, si mens non laeva fuisset,
> impulerat ferro Argolicas foedare latebras,
> Troiaque nunc staret, Priamique arx alta maneres."

"And if the decrees of the gods, if our own wits had not been against us, he had
inspired us to deface the hiding-place of the Greeks and Troy would now be
standing, and you, high citadel of Priam, would still be in existence."

This is the kind of apostrophe that converts an object into a subject and
thereby establishes a particular kind of emotional intimacy with it. Here
the gap between the temporality of the narrative and that of the "composition" is not so much cancelled as measured by the combination of

emotive apostrophe with the keen sense of what might easily have been if only something quite simple had been different. Here Aeneas also expresses that frequent sense of men as solely responsible for their own destinies by placing on the same level "decrees of the gods" and "the wits" of human beings;[3] the "gods" are demoted to a mere trope of explanation, bitterly and immediately exchanged for the real cause.

The other apostrophe is equally emotional and bitter (424–30):

> "ilicet obruimur numero; primusque Coroebus
> Penelei dextra divae armipotentis ad aram
> procumbit; cadit et Rhipeus, iustissimus unus
> qui fuit in Teucris et servantissimus aequi
> (dis aliter visum); pereunt Hypanisque Dymasque
> confixi a sociis; nec te tua plurima, Panthu,
> labentem pietas nec Apollinis infula texit."

"Thereupon we are overwhelmed by numbers, and first Coroebus fell by the sword-arm of Peneleus at the altar of the warlike goddess [Athene]; there fell also Rhipeus, far the most just of all among the Trojans and finest champion of what is fair (the gods thought differently); there perished both Hypanis and Dymas, shot by their friends; and neither your infinite devotion nor the head-band of Apollo protected you, Panthus, as you fell."

Here the bitterness grows from the ironic aside on Rhipeus' goodness, unappreciated by the gods, to the failure of his *pietas* and his insignia as priest of Apollo to be of any help to Panthus. The very existence of the gods and certainly their relevance to mankind are called into question.[4]

When the poet enters his own text in apostrophe, the emotional quality of that entrance is conditioned by a detachment that derives from the gap, which is marked at the same time as it is cancelled, between the twelfth century and the age of Augustus. There is no such detachment in the apostrophes of Aeneas, largely because the corresponding gap of no more than seven years hardly exists for the eyewitness as he relives the scenes, and so the emotional quality is much more intense. This fact especially permits the lively expression of a surprising depth of bitterness that convincingly measures the distance between Aeneas and Virgil as narrators.

The same bitterness and irony characterise the one "authorial" in-

---

3. See chap. 7, sec. 3.
4. See previous note.

tervention by Aeneas. He lists those who joined him to fight the Greeks
(339–46):

> "addunt se socios Rhipeus et maximus armis
> Epytus, oblati per lunam, Hypanisque Dymasque
> et lateri adglomerant nostro, iuvenisque Coroebus
> Mygdonides—illis ad Troiam forte diebus
> venerat insano Cassandrae incensus amore
> et gener auxilium Priamo Phrygibusque ferebat,
> infelix qui non sponsae praecepta furentis
> audierit!"

"There join me as comrades Rhipeus and Epytus, most stalwart in battle, chanc-
ing to meet me in the moonlight, and both Hypanis and Dymas gather at my side
and the young man Coroebus, son of Mygdon—he had by chance come in those
days to Troy, on fire and out of his mind with love for Cassandra, and as son-in-
law he was trying to help Priam and the Trojans; unfortunate man that he did not
listen to the warnings of his inspired bride!"

The comment is telling derived from hindsight, and from that source it
acquires an ironic bitterness that easily distinguishes the immediate personal involvement of Aeneas as narrator from Virgil. The emotional depth
of that distinction is dramatically used when Aeneas reveals that he is
ashamed of having survived the fall of Troy (431–34):

> "Iliaci cineres et flamma extrema meorum,
> testor, in occasu vestro nec tela nec ullas
> vitavisse vices, Danaum et, si fata fuissent
> ut caderem, meruisse manu."

"Ashes of Ilium and funeral flame of my people, I call on you to witness that as
you collapsed I avoided no weapons nor perils from the Greeks, and that, if it had
been my destiny to fall, I earned death by my deeds."

This immediately follows the list of deaths of which Panthus' is the climax.
In the roll-calls by the poet in the second half of the *Aeneid* only a small
proportion of those named are mentioned again (usually epitaphically).
But only one out of the list of those who joined Aeneas (339–46) is not
mentioned in the bitter reprise (424–30) as having been killed. This is the
setting for the anxious and shame-faced appeal by Aeneas for belief in his
courage. It strikingly underlines both the immediacy to him of the events
he narrates and his own sense of the very particular audience he is
addressing. The goal of his narrative differs from that of the poet; he is
almost a witness speaking before a jury in his own defence.

(d) *Similes.*[5] The figure of simile allows the epic poet to enter his own text and make his voice heard. Consequently, careful adaptation is needed when the poet ceases to be the narrator. There is no such adaptation in Books 9–12 of the *Odyssey* when Odysseus takes over the narrative from Homer: the voice is still the voice of Homer. But in *Aeneid* 2 the similes are carefully managed to convey a different voice. There are nine similes in the book, all of them striking. When the poet indulges in the figure, he emphasises the gap between the temporality of the narrative and that of the composition. But there is no such gap—or only in a negligible sense—between Aeneas' speaking and the events he narrates. The material of the similes is therefore restricted; they are all drawn from the world of nature: two concern floods; two, snakes; and one each the sacrifice of an ox, a wolf-pack, storm-winds, doves in a storm, and a felled tree. The list recalls familiar Homeric material for similes; what is remarkable, however, is that only four (304–08, 379–81, 471–75, and 496–99) have Homeric models that are at all close. This is largely due to the adaptation of the similes to a voice other than Virgil's.

Two remarkable similes bracket Aeneas' description of Troy's destruction. The first comes as he wakes, hears, and goes to view it (301–08):

> "clarescunt sonitus armorumque ingruit horror.
> excutior somno et summi fastigia tecti
> ascensu supero atque arrectis auribus asto:
> in segetem veluti cum flamma furentibus Austris
> incidit, aut rapidus montano flumine torrens
> sternit agros, sternit sata laeta boumque labores
> praecipitisque trahit silvas: stupet inscius alto
> accipiens sonitum saxi de vertice pastor."

"The sounds gradually become clear and the clash of arms grows terrifying; I am shaken from sleep and climb right up to the highest point of the roof and stand with ears pricked, as when flame falls upon a cornfield during a raging south-west storm, or a torrent marauding with its mountain-swollen stream destroys fields, destroys ripe crops and the toil of oxen and sweeps woods away headlong, the bewildered shepherd, hearing the sound from the high pinnacle of a rock, is struck dumb."

The other comes after Venus' revelation that the destruction of Troy is actually being carried out by the gods (624–31):

5. See chap. 7, sec. 1.

"Tum vero omne mihi visum considere in ignis
Ilium et ex imo verti Neptunia Troia;
ac veluti summis antiquam in montibus ornum
cum ferro accisam crebrisque bipennibus instant
eruere agricolae certatim; illa usque minatur
et tremefacta comam concusso vertice nutat,
vulneribus donec paulatim evicta supremum
congemuit traxitque iugis avulsa ruinam."

"Then indeed I saw all Ilium collapsing into the flames and Troy built by Neptune being upturned from the bottom; even as when farmers vie with one another to uproot an ancient ash on the mountain-tops that has been chopped with steel and frequent ⟨blows of⟩ axes, it threatens all the time and, with its foliage trembling, sways as its top is shaken, until, little by little overcome by its wounds, it groans for the last time and, torn up, deals destruction all across the ridge."

The function of both similes is similar: both are in secondary language and substitute for a primary context that is not otherwise explained. So Aeneas describes neither his feelings as he sees the Greeks victorious in the streets nor the physical destruction of Troy. The structure of the similes is designed to support that function. First, there is no reprise. The preceding lines provide the ground for the simile, but, by the time it is finished, the narrator has passed on to another stage of the narrative. Second, there is a gap between the introductory lines and the simile; the assertion of similarity is not between what is described in those lines and the simile, but between something that has to be read back into those lines from the simile and the simile itself. In the first passage, Aeneas describes only his attentiveness in the arresting picture of the dog with ears pricked (303 *arrectis auribus*); what he witnesses and the emotions aroused thereby must be read back from the simile. In the second passage, Aeneas only mentions the collapse of Troy into the flames and expands that with the metaphor of the whole city being upturned from the bottom; this metaphor leads to the simile which concretely enacts, in a way that must be read back into the introductory lines, the single fall of each tall building.[6] Third, both similes are structurally and syntactically complete in themselves, and independent. In the first, the shepherd, who is only an extra and ornamental detail in the Homeric model (*Iliad* 4.452–55), acts the part of Aeneas and takes the place of a reprise ("So I was thunderstruck . . ."). The second is so independent that a recent

6. See West (1969), p. 41.

editor felt obliged to comment: "The simile is left in the air, as in iv.402 ff., where an unfinished line has also just preceded . . . ; Virgil has plainly not worked out the completion of the picture preceding 620."[7] This is not justified. What happens here and at 4.402–07 (and at 6.707–09) is that the simile is made to coalesce with the context in such a way that its terms take the place of those that belong to the context, and *ac veluti* is to be understood (by analogy with a structure like *ac si* "even if") as meaning "even as." The effect is the same as with the earlier simile: an unspoken context must be reconstructed by the reader.

Both similes occur at crucial moments of truth for Aeneas, and this fact is signalled verbally by *tum vero* "then in truth," which is used to lead out of the first simile (309) and to introduce the second (624). This use of a simile to substitute for vital but unspoken elements in the context was learned by Virgil from Catullus, and the second simile bears some similarity to the simile in Catullus 64.105–111, where the picture of a tree uprooted by a tornado enacts, at the same time as it takes the place of, a description of the Minotaur's death at the hands of Theseus.[8]

The simile at 416–19 is unique in Book 2 because it uses traditional "poetic" material. It compares the attack of the Greeks, after Cassandra has been rescued, to three winds conflicting (corresponding to the three groups of Greeks);[9] it ends (418–19):

> "stridunt silvae saevitque tridenti
> spumeus atque imo Nereus ciet aequora fundo."

"The forests howl and foamy Nereus goes wild with his trident and stirs the waters from the bottom of the sea."

The last detail, starting from the rage of the Greeks (413 *ira*), moves out into authorial material, achieving for a moment both a sense of superhuman forces at work in the world and a distance from the harsh reality that are characteristic of the poet-author rather than of the actor-narrator. In neither Homeric analogue (*Iliad* 16.765–69 is closer than 9.4–7 but still quite remote) does a deity play any part, and the distance is increased by the mannered rococo detail of the trident. The simile is substituted for a description of the fighting which, in fact, marks the end of Trojan resistance. The sense of desperation is increased by the deliberately distancing mannerism of the simile. As with the two similes previously exam-

7. Austin (1964) on line 626 (p. 240).
8. Williams (1980), pp. 48–49.
9. West (1969), pp. 40–41.

ined, this too has its connexion with what precedes. When it ends, Aeneas has already (420) moved on to another detail.

There is one simile in Book 2 that has the conventional return to the context as well as the lead-in connecting with what precedes. This is at 378–82 where Androgeos suddenly realises that he is not among Greek friends but Trojan enemies:

> "obstipuit retroque pedem cum voce repressit.
> improvisum aspris veluti qui sentibus anguem
> pressit humi nitens trepidusque repente refugit
> attollentem iras et caerula colla tumentem,
> haud secus Androgeos visu tremefactus abibat."

"He froze with shock and checked his foot together with his voice, as a man who has trodden into the ground a snake unseen among prickly thorn-bushes, putting his weight on it, and suddenly terrified recoils as it lifts high its rage and swells its bright blue neck; not otherwise did Androgeos, terrified at the sight, try to get away."

The Homeric analogue at *Iliad* 3.33–35 is not close and has none of the detailed observation of reciprocal movement. Also, in Homer the man gets away (as Paris got away from Menelaus). But in Virgil the traveller's death is to be understood and the simile takes the place of a description of Androgeos' death, which is only inferred from Coroebus' donning his weapons and armour (391–93). His implied death is to be read back into the simile. The formality of the simile, despite its extreme speed and economy, halts the narrative and serves to mark the death of Androgeos as exemplary. In the same way, Coroebus becomes exemplary for Trojans as they disguise themselves as Greeks; but such snake-like treachery can only work for Greeks, not for the ancestors of Romans.

Another snake-simile has only a very remote analogy in *Iliad* 22.93–95, where Hector is like a snake as he waits for Achilles to approach. The Virgilian simile depicts the son of Achilles (469–75):

> "Vestibulum ante ipsum primoque in limine Pyrrhus
> exsultat telis et luce coruscus aena;
> qualis ubi in lucem coluber mala gramina pastus,
> frigida sub terra tumidum quem bruma tegebat,
> nunc, positis novus exuviis nitidusque iuventa,
> lubrica convolvit sublato pectore terga
> arduus ad solem, et linguis micat ore trisulcis."

"Before the very entrance-hall and right in the palace doorway Pyrrhus is triumphant, shining in his weapons and a sheen of bronze: as when a snake, which frosty winter has been harbouring swollen beneath the ground, comes out into daylight after feeding on poisonous plants; now, renewed with its skin sloughed off and shining with youth, lifting its breast raised high to the sun, it coils its slippery back and flashes its forked tongue in and out of its mouth."

This simile takes the place of a description of Pyrrhus (including his braggart insolence now that his father is dead).[10] It, too, lacks a reprise and is focused on the two preceding lines; by the time it is finished, Aeneas has gone on to enumerate his retinue (476). The description is as much psychological as physical, and the context must be fleshed out by the reader's sympathetic imagination.

Pyrrhus and his men burst in (494–500):

> "fit via vi; rumpunt aditus primosque trucidant
> immissi Danai et late loca milite complent.
> non sic, aggeribus ruptis cum spumeus amnis
> exiit oppositasque evicit gurgite moles,
> fertur in arva furens cumulo camposque per omnis
> cum stabulis armenta trahit. vidi ipse furentem
> caede Neoptolemum geminosque in limine Atridas."

"A path is carved out by violence; the Greeks break down the entrance and, rushing in, butcher those there and fill every corner with their soldiery. Not so, when a foaming river, breaking its banks, has flooded and with its tide over-whelmed the barriers set in its path, does it swoop in a mass crazily upon the fields and sweep herds together with their steadings over the whole plain. With my own eyes I saw Neoptolemus crazed with butchery and the twin sons of Atreus at the entrance-way. . . ."

Negative similes are very unusual: that is, the poet confesses the inability of his imagination to invent an adequate analogy by asserting the inadequacy of what has occurred to him. It differentiates this simile from Homeric analogues like *Iliad* 5.87–91 (which are, in any case, only remote). The simile is adapted to the mouth of Aeneas both by its abrupt opening and by its highly unusual ending in the middle of a line (at the caesura). It is thus closely integrated into the context. Like the others examined, it too is linked only with what precedes; by the time it ends, Aeneas is elaborating his authenticity as an eye-witness, and describing the bloodlust of Pyrrhus (Neoptolemus); but he makes an unexpected link with the simile in the word (499) *furentem*.

The remaining three similes are very brief and make conspicuous

10. To be transferred from the simile to the context (where it is unspoken); see West (1969), p. 42.

use of the technique of coalescing with the context (already seen, especially in 626–31 and 496–99). None has any close Homeric analogue. The first comes as Laocoön is attacked by the sea-serpents (222–26):

> "clamores simul horrendos ad sidera tollit:
> qualis mugitus, fugit cum saucius aram
> taurus et incertam excussit cervice securim.
> at gemini lapsu delubra ad summa dracones
> effugiunt saevaeque petunt Tritonidis arcem."

"At the same time he raises frightful screams to the stars, such as are the bellowings when a wounded bull has fled the altar and has thrown off the ill-aimed axe from his neck. But the twin serpents glide off and escape to the highest temple and make for the citadel of cruel Athene. . . ."

Here *qualis mugitus* (accusative plural) picks up *clamores . . . horrendos* in such a way as to require the verb *tollit* to be mentally repeated: "like the bellowings a bull raises. . . ." As it were, *clamores* is emended into *mugitus* to enable the simile. The death of Laocoön is not described but implied, just as the ultimate death of the bull is only implied. Here again, simile and context are mutually supportive, and effectively the simile enacts the death of Laocoön.

Aeneas addresses a band of Trojans who cluster round him and inspirits them to fight the Greeks (355–60):

> "sic animis iuvenum furor additus. inde, lupi ceu
> raptores atra in nebula, quos improba ventris
> exegit caecos rabies catulique relicti
> faucibus exspectant siccis, per tela, per hostis
> vadimus haud dubiam in mortem mediaeque tenemus
> urbis iter; nox atra cava circumvolat umbra."

"Thus recklessness was injected into the young men's spirits. Then, as marauder wolves in the black cloud ⟨of night⟩, when incessant torture in their bellies drives them blindly and cubs left behind await them with parched throats, through weapons, through enemies we make our way to no uncertain death and hold our way through the centre of the city; black night wings round us with enveloping darkness."

Here *per tela, per hostis* is common both to simile and to context, so that the simile is collapsed into a context with which it shares many other terms.[11]

Finally, Hecuba and her daughters take refuge at the altar (515–17):

11. See ibid., p. 43.

> "hic Hecuba et natae nequiquam altaria circum,
> praecipites atra ceu tempestate columbae,
> condensae et divum amplexae simulacra sedebant."

"Here Hecuba and her daughters sat in vain around the altar, like doves dropping headlong down in a black tempest, huddled together, clasping the images of the gods."

Here *condensae* belongs both to simile and to context and *sedebant* has to be read into the simile: the doves are to be pictured dropping sheer down to perch in safety.

In all of these similes the gap between the temporality of the narrative and that of the "composition" is cancelled to the greatest extent possible by various devices that integrate simile and context. The result is to achieve as close an identity as possible between narrator and participant: that is, Aeneas as narrator does his best to avoid coming between his audience and the events he narrates. This effort can be seen also in the aspect of the similes he is made to use. There is no sign in Book 2 of the tripartite division of aspect that is needed to account for similes in other books.[12] With one possible exception, all the similes of Book 2 view the situation from the vantage point of the "author": that is, they carefully mirror the point of view of a narrator who is also an eye-witness and whose subjective emotions are in every instance involved. The one possible exception is the mannered simile of the winds in conflict (416–19); but there the speaker deliberately distances himself authorially from a scene that is too painful to paint in its full reality.

(e) *Reported speeches.* The detached and omniscient poet has no more difficulty than a dramatist in reporting speeches by his characters at whatever length seems appropriate. Indirect speech is very infrequent in epic (and not very common even in historiography); the actual words are more dramatic and function as an important means of revealing character and emotion. But when the poet is reporting a two-book-long speech by Aeneas, who is in turn reporting speeches he has heard (and at least once such a speech itself reports a speech by someone yet further removed),[13] tactful restraint is called for. With the exception of Sinon's, the speeches in Book 2 are modest in length. Of some nineteen speeches, fifteen are less (most, considerably less) than ten lines long. Those that exceed that

---

12. See chap. 7, sec. 1.
13. When Sinon recalls the actual words of Calchas (116–18).

limit have a special importance. Panthus (following the dream-vision of Hector) reveals the death of Troy and Trojans to Aeneas in solemn tones (324–35). The very important instructions by Aeneas on leaving Troy, which are to lead to Creusa's death, take fourteen lines (707–20), as does the prophecy given by Creusa's ghost to Aeneas (776–89).

A twenty-seven-line speech by Venus (594–620) is crucial in the poet's strategy for motivating and justifying Aeneas' abandonment of Troy,[14] and most of the speech is her description of what she sees as the gods destroy Troy. Another equally important speech in that strategy only occupies twelve lines. After Venus' revelation of the hopelessness of Troy's predicament, Aeneas puts his father's safety first, before that of either wife or son (635 *quem tollere in altos / optabam primum montis primumque petebam* "him above all I wanted to carry up into the high mountains and him above all I was looking for"). A crucial test comes for Aeneas when Anchises refuses to leave. It enables the poet to show Aeneas as not just a proto-Roman in his regard for the *pater familias* but also a brave Homeric hero. He abandons wife and son and rushes off to die in battle, taking at least some Greeks with him; like his father, he too will die with Troy. Anchises' speech seems short for the weight it has to carry, but the poet has made Aeneas introduce the actual words with a line and a half of indirect speech, suggesting that Anchises' words were, in fact, very much longer.

Sinon's speech is divided into three sections, separated by accounts of audience reaction (77–104, 108–44, 154–94). The effect of allowing Aeneas to report such long speeches is that he impersonates Sinon for the moment, as he tells the highly romantic and exciting story of the Greek camp seen by a supposed eye-witness whose life was in constant danger. With such dramatic material it is easy for the reader to catch the change of voice as Aeneas impersonates the plausible liar; his actual words were essential to be effective.

(f) *Fate and the gods.* Nothing more clearly distinguishes Aeneas from the poet than his view of Fate and the gods. To the omniscient poet these concepts were explanatory tropes. But Aeneas is far more ordinarily human in his expression of them. To him, for instance, Fate is a way of looking at events that have happened at a time before their occurrence; it constitutes a sufficient explanation of their happening, though he can speculate on other causes. So, when Thymoetes proposes bringing the

14. It is also a late insertion into the text: see below.

horse inside the walls, it may be either because he was treacherous or because the Fate of Troy was already moving in that direction (34). Similarly, Aeneas says that Troy might now be standing if destiny or Trojan wits had not gone awry (54). There is something almost colloquial about this easy way of talking from hindsight. It is close to the way in which Aeneas uses the idea of divine intervention to explain something that he does not trouble to account for further. Thus, after leaving Venus, he can miraculously make his way home safely, (632) *ducente deo* "under divine guidance"; or he says that something confused his mind so that he lost Creusa; (735–36) *male numen amicus / confusam eripuit mentem* "a thoroughly unfriendly deity confused and deprived me of my senses"; and when she is lost (745) *quem non incusavi amens hominumque deorumque?* "What god or man did I fail to blame in my madness?" The gods function in such expressions as they do in casual curses or blessings.

Closely related, and just as characteristic of the tone of Book 2, is a series of bitter outbursts that use the gods to express the same bitterness at being let down that Aeneas expresses in Book 1 after he has been carried off to Africa by a storm: there he introduces himself bitterly to Venus (378) *sum pius Aeneas*—his *pietas* is of no account. In Book 2 he refers to Sinon as (257) *fatisque deum defensus iniquis* "under the protection of an unfair destiny." As the Trojan luck turns, he explains (402) *heu nihil invitis fas quemquam fidere divis* "alas! no man is allowed to trust in unwilling gods." On the death of Rhipeus, he comments (428) *dis aliter visum* "the gods thought otherwise," a deeply bitter remark. When Anchises refuses to leave, Aeneas bitterly remarks (659) *si nihil ex tanta superis placet urbe relinqui* "if the gods are decided that nothing be left of so great a city." It is exactly the same bitterness toward the gods that Anchises presents as his reason for not leaving Troy (641–49).

Such ways of conceptually making use of Fate and the gods are characteristic not only of Aeneas but of other characters as well; but they are far removed from the figurative manipulations of the poet. Thus they not only differentiate Aeneas in Book 2 from the poet, but they also show him to be an ordinary human being in a hostile universe. The way in which he uses the "pathetic fallacy" in Book 2 is related to this: just as the gods are against the Trojans, so is Nature, and she is consequently in league with the enemy, defending them and lulling Aeneas into inappropriate relaxation (254–59 and 268–69); Nature is opposed even to the recounting of disturbing events (7–8). But Aeneas is not just an ordinary human being. He is privileged in a particular way, in that he has a goddess for a mother and is also subject to visitations, especially from the dead, who are themselves privileged. Consequently, he can represent Venus revealing to him that the gods are destroying Troy (604–20); he is obedient to her revelation (it justifies his abandoning Troy), but he is vague about what he actually saw (621–23) and quickly moves into his own perception of Troy's physical destruction (624–31).[15] The visitations by Hector (268–97) and above all by Creusa (771–94) reveal a duty to him whose obligations are to outweigh all other considerations. This capacity to know the truth in a way that ordinary men cannot is a mark of Aeneas' privilege; it is paralleled in a limited way in Book 2 by the privilege of the priest Panthus, who, in virtue of his office, can tell Aeneas (326–27) *ferus omnia Iuppiter Argos / transtulit* "cruel Juppiter has handed everything over to Argos." Book 2 is crucial to the poet's conception of Aeneas as different from other men in the specific feature that he carries within him a sense of a destiny imposed on him from without in a vague, undefinable way; that sense of destiny constitutes his duty.

2. The Peculiarities of Book 3

This convincing narrative technique that identifies Aeneas as a totally different personality from the poet is disrupted in many ways in Book 3. There are many features that strike a reader as authorial and dissonant with Aeneas as narrator. For instance, the episode of Achaemenides, unknown to the Aeneas legend and designed to link the *Aeneid* with the *Odyssey,* is recounted at length in a mannered style of grandiose rhetoric[16] that is not only out of place in the mouth of Aeneas but is even uncharacteristic of the poet of the *Aeneid* (the swiftly moving concreteness of the Cacus episode in 8.185–275 can be contrasted). The episode is largely Aeneas' report of Achaemenides' own description; this can be contrasted with Aeneas' report of Sinon's account of his own adventures, where vivid concreteness conveys a sense of a real but macabre situation in the Greek camp (though it is admittedly fiction). There are, in fact, a number of signs that, at the time of composition, the poet thought of the Achaemenides episode as spoken in his own voice. The Trojans suddenly see a figure like a Robinson Crusoe coming out of the woods (588–95):

"Postera iamque dies primo surgebat Eoo
umentemque Aurora polo dimoverat umbram,

15. See chap. 2, sec. 2.
16. See the comments of R. D. Williams (1962), pp. 181–204.

> cum subito e silvis macie confecta suprema
> ignoti nova forma viri miserandaque cultu
> procedit supplexque manus ad litora tendit.
> respicimus. dira inluvies immissaque barba,
> consertum tegimen spinis: at cetera Graius,
> et quondam patriis ad Troiam missus in armis."

"The following day was already rising up with the appearance of the Morning Star and Aurora had moved apart the damp curtain of night in the sky when suddenly from the woods emerged an extraordinary shape of an unknown man, wracked with the final stages of emaciation and pitiable in his dress, and he stretched forth his hand in supplication toward the shore. We stare back. A dreadful squalor and an unkempt beard, a garment sewn together with thorns; yet in all else he was a Greek, and once upon a time had been sent off to Troy in the armour of his fathers."

Here the mannered poeticism of the description of daybreak is authorial and does not suit Aeneas. But far worse is the explanatory comment on the man's Greekness and the pathos of "once upon a time." Those features destroy the bated-breath suspense that is proper for a narrative by Aeneas, but they are perfectly appropriate in the mouth of the poet who can artistically achieve the suspense and at the same time, in virtue of his authorial detachment, subvert it with an omniscient aside that anticipates what Achaemenides himself is about to say (613–15). The force of (595) *quondam* is pathos, the pathos of the contrast between a pitiful present and a grand past; in Aeneas it comes from hindsight, but here it is far from the tactful use of hindsight that characterised Book 2.

Another authorial feature arises from Achaemenides' self-introduction as (613) *sum patria ex Ithaca, comes infelicis Vlixi* "My homeland is Ithaca and I was in the company of ill-starred Ulysses." That is certainly how a Greek would view Odysseus. But Aeneas ends this section of his voyaging with these words (690–91):

> "talia monstrabat relegens errata retrorsus
> litora Achaemenides, comes infelicis Vlixi."

"Such were the shores Achaemenides pointed out as he sailed along them again, having wandered past them in the opposite direction—he who was in the company of ill-starred Ulysses."

The repetition of the self-description in the mouth of Aeneas could only be ironical, and that is totally alien to his tone. But in the mouth of the poet it has pathos and closes a section with something close to ring-composition, expressing instead of the normal Trojan hatred for Odysseus, the detached sympathy of the poet for a human being.

There are two further examples of an authorial sympathy that is inappropriate in the mouth of Aeneas. Achaemenides has no sooner finished speaking than Polyphemus comes in sight (658–61):

> "monstrum horrendum, informe, ingens, cui lumen ademptum.
> trunca manum pinus regit et vestigia firmat;
> lanigerae comitantur oves; ea sola voluptas
> solamenque mali."

"A horrific monster, ugly, enormous, with his eye destroyed. A lopped pine guides his hand and steadies his footsteps; woolly sheep surround him—they are his one joy and solace in his misery."

The pathos derives from Polyphemus' speech to his beloved ram in *Odyssey* 9.447–60; there Odysseus reports the speech but feels no pathos himself. Here too the sympathy is the poet's. It is echoed as the Trojans look back from their ships (677–81):

> "cernimus astantis nequiquam lumine torvo
> Aetnaeos fratres caelo capita alta ferentis,
> concilium horrendum: quales cum vertice celso
> aeriae quercus aut coniferae cyparissi
> constiterunt, silva alta Iovis lucusve Dianae."

"We see the Aetnean brothers standing frustratedly with savage eye, holding their heads high into the skies, a frightful gathering, such as are sky-high oaks or cone-bearing cypresses as they stand upon a lofty ridge, a tall forest sacred to Juppiter or a grove of Diana."

The terrifying sight is modified by the sympathetic (677) *nequiquam* and all but negated by the serene poeticism of the simile. The brothers are no more fearful now than tall trees on a mountain ridge. This is the only simile in Book 3, and it echoes the voice of the poet, not that of Aeneas, as does the shift to a sympathic tone.

The immediately preceding section of Book 3 (506–87) also shows more signs of the poet than of Aeneas. Night (like Dawn in 588–89) is described in a mannered phrase (512) *necdum orbem medium nox Horis acta subibat* "nor was Night, drawn by the Hours, yet at the mid-point of her circuit." This ornate personification, essentially Greek, is as inappropriate in the mouth of Aeneas as the detailing of the stars observed by Palinurus that follows it (515–19). A further incongruity, if spoken by Aeneas, is the caution expressed by (551) *si vera est fama* when the adjective *Herculeus* is attached to the gulf of Tarentum; such learning is the poet's. Much worse, however, in the mouth of Aeneas as he speaks to Dido and her company is the long manneristic description of Aetna (570–87), a piece of pure Hellenistic rococo, complete with authorial account of the legends used to explain the volcano, introduced by (578) *fama est . . .* "legend has it that. . . ." When that account was composed, the poet was thinking of his own interests and was not projecting himself into the personality of a different narrator.

The same can be said of the preceding speech of Helenus (374–462). Both stylistically and metrically, the impression conveyed is of a ponderous solemnity and a long-winded repetitiousness that are as unsuited to the personality of the narrator as they are to the occasion. The interest in details of religion (403–09 and 433–40), of prophetic ritual (441–60), and of legendary monsters that make a connexion with the world of the *Odyssey* (410–32, Scylla and Charybdis) is authorial. This is quite clear both in the account of Scylla and Charybdis and also in the description of what happens in the Sibyl's caves. The Trojans do not have to endure the monsters, so this is the author's only opportunity for a poetic treatment of them; and the method of counsulting the Sibylline oracle used in Book 6 is totally different, so that here the poet indulges his own poetic interests in the other type of consultation, which is done by lots. In style, subject matter, and length (89 lines) the speech shows indifference both to the character of the supposed narrator and to any sensitivity on his part to the special audience whom he addresses.

The book ends with a very successful evocation of Aeneas' personally felt grief at his father's death, expressed especially in an apostrophe to his father which in its pathos, really serves its purpose of cancelling the gap between the temporality of the narrative and that of the "composition." The sensitivity with which the figure is used here draws attention to much less convincing examples that occur earlier. At 118–20 Aeneas describes Anchises making sacrifice (119) *taurum Neptuno, taurum tibi, pulcher Apollo* "of a bull to Neptune, and a bull to you, handsome Apollo"; here the apostrophe re-enacts the verbal dedication to Apollo,[17] but in a way that is purely formal and authorial. At 369–72 Aeneas recounts how Helenus led (371) *meque ad tua limina, Phoebe* "me to your threshold, Phoebus," where the apostrophe might be interpreted as implying an

17. See chap. 7, sec. 2(a).

expression of gratitude to Apollo for his guidance, and at least it is personal. Far worse are a couple of examples in the passage immediately preceding the death of Anchises where apostrophe is used in inane geographical addresses to the water-nymph Arethusa (696) and to the city of Selinus (705), which seem to exist purely for metrical convenience. This passage is marked by another example of the authorial (694) *fama est* "legend has it that . . . ," and a further instance of *quondam* that is quite inappropriate in the mouth of Aeneas. The Trojans are sailing past Acragas (703–04):

> "arduus inde Acragas ostentat maxima longe
> moenia, magnanimum quondam generator equorum."

"Then Acragas, perched high up, shows its huge walls from afar, once upon a time the parent of great-hearted steeds."

The point of view expressed by *quondam* is that of the poet living in the age of Augustus and not that of the supposed narrator in the twelfth century.

What all of this suggests is that Book 3 went through a stage in which the poet conceived of himself rather than Aeneas as the narrator. There are other traces of this stage. For instance, as the Trojans sail away from the Cyclops, they suddenly realise they are making for Scylla and Charybdis (684–86):

> "contra iussa monent Heleni, Scyllam atque Charybdim
> (inter utramque viam leti discrimine parvo)[18]
> ni teneant cursus; certum est dare lintea retro."

"The orders of Helenus are a warning against their holding course toward Scylla and Charybdis, there being only a small distance between both paths that lead to death: it is decided to turn the sails in the opposite direction."

So the lines appear in all manuscripts and ancient commentaries, with the exception of Servius Auctus who alleges that "others read *teneam*." This is an obvious emendation, but the consensus of the manuscripts means that the poet certainly wrote *teneant*. If so, he was certainly the narrator. Why did he not make the easy alteration? The theme is a mere repetition of the incident when the Trojans first approached the Strait of Messina and

---

18. There is no good reason to emend 685: *discrimine parvo* is an ablative absolute and the idea is that, by taking the track to one side, one would fall victim to Scylla, while the track to the other side would deliver one to Charybdis; there is just a very narrow path that holds dead centre between those two deadly tracks, with no margin for error on either side.

Anchises gave a sudden warning to turn back (558–63). Consequently, the poet may have marked 684–86 for deletion and not bothered to accommodate the lines to the changed narrator. This is certainly a possible explanation also for the three lines that Servius Auctus alleges were found circled in the margin of Virgil's text.[19] Two lines explain that the Trojan fleet is being carried by the storm round the Peloponnese and past Malea; these lines are out of place in Aeneas' mouth, since he is explaining that even Palinurus does not know where they are (202); but they are perfectly appropriate as an explanatory comment from the omniscient poet. The third line, with verbs in the first-person plural, belongs to Aeneas but is repetitious in the present text. Of course, the lines could be a mere forgery or a quotation from some other poet; but, if the poet had accommodated this storm-passage to another narrator, those lines would have caused him trouble, and he may well have marked them for deletion.

Another odd sequence of sentences occurs after the Penates have appeared to Aeneas (172–78):

> "talibus attonitus visis et voce deorum
> (nec sopor illud erat, sed coram agnoscere vultus
> velatasque comas praesentiaque ora videbar;
> tum gelidus toto manabat corpore sudor)   175
> corripio e stratis corpus tendoque supinas
> ad caelum cum voce manus et munera libo
> intemerata focis."

"Shaken by such appearances and the voice of gods (nor was that deep sleep, but I felt that I recognised their faces in my presence and their garlanded hair and their features right before my eyes; then cold sweat flowed from my whole body), I raised myself quickly from the bed and stretched my hands, palms upturned, and my voice to heaven and made offering of pure sacrifice at the hearth."

Complex parenthesis is a frequent feature of Virgilian style,[20] but here the stop after *videbar* and the link made with *tum* is so weak as to suggest the remnants of an authorial account, imperfectly accommodated to Aeneas, in which the poet may have intended to delete line 175. (Its content is already expressed in line 172.)

19. Between lines 204 and 205; they are:

hinc Pelopis gentes Maleaeque sonantia saxa
circumstant, pariterque undae terraeque minantur;
pulsamur saevis et circumsistimur undis.

20. See Williams (1968), pp. 730–32.

An awkward problem was presented by the need for Aeneas, when he became the narrator, to give adequate treatment in his account to the actions and feelings of participants other than himself. This problem is skillfully met in Book 2: during the episode of the wooden horse, Aeneas is an observer of a crowd's reaction (39 *vulgus*); when Sinon suddenly appears, Aeneas watches the young men crowd around him (63–64 *Troiana iuventus*), but then he joins the group (74 *hortamur*, 105 *ardemus*, 145 *damus et miserescimus*); Priam next takes over (146–51), but at the end of Sinon's speech the epitaphic judgment is pronounced with hindsight (195–98). When the sea-serpents arrive, Aeneas joins everyone in running away (212 *diffugimus*), but he distances himself to sum up the general opinion (228–33), while joining in carrying out the fatal decision (234 *dividimus . . . pandimus*; 244 *instamus*; 249 *velamus*). With the vision of Hector the narrative becomes personal and singular until Aeneas is joined by others; but the scene at Priam's palace is viewed at a distance and the narrator only introduces himself at the end (559). From there on he is the centre of the narrative.

The problem was certainly more difficult in Book 3, as there are three participants whose continuous interaction needs adequate treatment: Aeneas, Anchises, and the Trojans in general. The result seems sometimes unnecessarily disturbing in some mixed sequences of first persons singular and plural and third persons plural: for instance, (71) *deducunt . . . complent*; (72) *provehimur*; (78) *huc feror*; (83) *iungimus . . . subimus*; (84) *venerabar*; (90) *fatus eram*; (93) *petimus*; (100) *cuncti . . . quaerunt*. In this passage it is odd that Aeneas performs the religious rites (84), while Anchises interprets the oracle (102–20). It is followed by this sequence: (124) *linquimus . . . volemus*; (128) *nauticus exoritur . . . clamor*; (129) *hortantur socii . . . petamus*; (131) *adlabimur*; (132) *molior*; (133) *voco*; (134) *hortor*; (137) *dabam*; (144) *hortatur pater*. The mixture of persons becomes really bizarre at 207–10:

> "vela cadunt, remis insurgimus; haud mora, nautae
> adnixi torquent spumas et caerula verrunt.
> servatum ex undis Strophadum me litora primum
> excipiunt."

"The sails come down, we rise on the oars; there is no delay, the sailors straining churn the foam and sweep the blue sea. The shores of the Strophades first give me shelter when I am saved from the deep."

This strange sequence can be contrasted with the coherence of 234–37:

> "sociis tunc arma capessant
> edico, et dira bellum cum gente gerendum.
> haud secus ac iussi faciunt tectosque per herbam
> disponunt ensis et scuta latentia condunt."

"Then I gave instructions that my men are to take up their weapons and that war must be waged on the horrific group. They do exactly as ordered and dispose swords hidden among the grass and lay by concealed shields."

Here Aeneas makes a distinction between himself, with whom responsibility for saving his countrymen lies, and those who look to him for leadership. A similar distinction can be seen in 259–67:

> "at sociis subita gelidus formidine sanguis
> deriguit: cedidere animi, nec iam amplius armis,
> sed votis precibusque iubent exposcere pacem,
> sive deae seu sint dirae obscenaeque volucres.
> et pater Anchises passis de litore palmis
> numina magna vocat meritosque indicit honores:
> 'di, prohibete minas; di, talem avertite casum
> et placidi servate pios.' tum litore funem
> deripere excussosque iubet laxare rudentis."

"But in my men their blood freezes, chilled with sudden terror; their spirits fell, and they insist that we no longer use weapons but seek peace with vows and prayers, whether the creatures be goddesses or horrible disgusting birds. And father Anchises, his hands stretched out from the shore, calls upon the great gods and proclaims due sacrifices: 'Gods, ward off dangers from us; gods, avert a catastrophe like that and graciously save us who are your devotees.' Then he bids them free the cable from the shore and unfurl and pay out the sheets."

Here Aeneas shows his authority as leader being rejected by his men, and in the crisis Anchises takes charge. There is a psychologically convincing integration of the three very different participants. But, in what follows, the text returns to a mixed sequence of persons (272–93) that is generally characteristic of the book as a whole and that could well be the result of a narrative originally conceived as the poet's but sporadically altered to accommodate it to a narrative by Aeneas. This would be very difficult to make convincing because the coherent psychological viewpoint of a participant would not have controlled the original composition and could only be introduced at random. Typical of the resulting uneasy alternation are lines 192–95:

> "Postquam altum tenuere rates nec iam amplius ullae
> apparent terrae, caelum undique et undique pontus,
> tum mihi caeruleus supra caput astitit imber
> noctem hiememque ferens, et inhorruit unda tenebris."

"After the ships held the deep and no land was any longer in sight, just sky on all sides and on all sides sea, then a black cloud stood over my head, bringing on darkness and storm and the sea grew rough with the blackness. Instantly the winds churn the water and huge seas arise, we are scattered and tossed over the vast tide."

Here the specification of *mihi* is very odd, in a way that the corresponding singular at 5.10 (where this passage is simply repeated) is not, since there the poet-narrator's gaze (and the reader's) is on Aeneas as he looks back at Dido's burning pyre (though he does not realise what it is); and the concentration of the storm on him simply continues the sense of oppression that dominates *Aeneid* 4. But the storm of Book 3 has no special significance for Aeneas in particular. The word *mihi* reads like a mechanical gesture towards a narrator who is also a participant.

The opening of Book 3 also makes a strange impression if read continuously with the ending of Book 2, which is highly personal and conveys an intense awareness of the character of the narrator. This is how Book 3 opens (1–12):

> "Postquam res Asiae Priamique evertere gentem
> immeritam visum superis, ceciditque superbum
> Ilium et omnis humo fumat Neptunia Troia,
> diversa exsilia et desertas quaerere terras
> auguriis agimur divum, classemque sub ipsa   5
> Antandro et Phrygiae molimur montibus Idae,
> incerti quo fata ferant, ubi sistere detur,
> contrahimusque viros. vix prima inceperat aestas
> et pater Anchises dare fatis vela iubebat,
> litora cum patriae lacrimans portusque relinquo   10
> et campos ubi Troia fuit. feror exsul in altum
> cum sociis natoque penatibus et magnis dis."

After it was decided by the gods above to destroy the state of Asia and the undeserving people of Priam, and proud Ilium fell and the whole of Troy, built by Neptune, was smoking rubble, we were driven by portents from the gods to seek far-off regions of exile and uninhabited lands and we worked hard to build a fleet right beneath Antandros and the peaks of Phrygian Ida (6), in the dark as to where fate was pointing, where we should be allowed to settle, and we collected manpower. Scarcely had the first of summer begun and father Anchises was giving orders to set our sails to fate,[21] when in tears I left the shores of my fatherland and its ports (10) and the plains where Troy stood. I was carried an exile out to sea with my men and my son, the household deities and the great gods.

There are a number of reasons for surprise here. First is the grandiose and impersonal tone, which contrasts strikingly with the ending of Book 2 and suggests the voice of the poet far more than that of Aeneas. Second, the bitterness expressed in *Priamique evertere gentem / immeritam visum superis* goes beyond analogous expressions of bitterness by Aeneas in Book 2. Here, placed in a subordinate clause, it has a casual, off-hand air if spoken by Aeneas, and, if put in conjunction with the statement in the main clause (5) *auguriis agimur divum*, it becomes downright cynical. However, both the grandiose tone and the explicit condemnation of the gods would make quite a different impression if the lines were spoken in the voice of the poet: the detached omniscience of the poet allows him a privileged view that can comprehend decisions of the gods which, from the human point of view, are unjust and arbitrary, while yet recognising that such apparent injustice does not deprive the gods of their right to continue guiding and ordering human affairs. That these lines were originally composed to be spoken by the poet is strongly suggested by the extraordinary syntax of lines 8–11. The structure of *vix* and the pluperfect indicative followed by a copula, rather than a temporal conjunction, to introduce a subordinate clause is quite frequent in Virgilian composition (e.g., 2.692–93); the sense is equivalent to "scarcely had . . . than. . . ." What is strange here is that the structure must be *vix . . . inceperat . . . et . . . iubebat . . . cum . . . relinquo. . .* ; that is, an inverted *cum*-construction (i.e., "He had climbed the hill when he saw the enemy") follows two coordinated verbs, one pluperfect and one imperfect, linked by *et*. The sequence is extremely awkward and abrupt from the imperfect indicative action of Anchises to the historic present used by Aeneas of his own action. Further, the normal effect of an inverted *cum*-construction is to express surprise at an unexpected event, but nothing of that effect is appropriate here. It looks as if line 9 belonged to an original version intended for the voice of the poet, while line 10 was composed to express the autobiographical emphasis of Aeneas as narrator of his own past. In fact, here too the awkward immediate juxtaposition of verbs in the first-

---

21. That is, to let Fate decide our course by following whatever wind happened to blow.

person plural with those in the first-person singular may be explained by a re-writing designed to accommodate to the character of Aeneas a narrative originally spoken by the poet.

This hypothesis would account for the various features that surprise on a reading that proceeds continuously from Book 2 to Book 3. It would also explain another oddity. Toward the end of Book 2 the ghost of Creusa reveals to Aeneas that he must make his way to Hesperia and the Lydian Tiber and there found a kingdom. However, Book 3 proceeds on the assumption that the Trojans do not know where in the world they may settle. They try Thrace but are warned off. They consult Apollo and go to Crete; but this turns out to be a misunderstanding. Then the Penates finally reveal Italy as the destined goal, and after that the only obstacles are those of nature and geography. The contradiction is sharpened by the opening lines of Book 3 because, whereas it could be held that Creusa's revelation need not be regarded as decisive in itself but requiring both confirmation and explanation, the tone of those lines goes much too far in uncompromising assertion of ignorance. It is, in fact, as though only the omens presented to Anchises (2.679–704) were in the mind of the poet as he wrote these lines and not the prophecy of Creusa. The force of the contradiction would be considerably lessened if Book 3 had been designed to precede Book 2—in fact, to be the opening book of the epic. Additional distance would be put between the two accounts, as the earlier would be in the poet's voice and would represent a viewpoint quite different from that of Aeneas.

The other serious contradiction in Book 3 is in the scene of eating the tables in Book 7.107–34. The prophecy of eating the tables was a fixed feature of the Aeneas legend and was assigned to various sources, to Juppiter of Dodona, to Venus, or to the Erythraean Sibyl.[22] It was certainly an invention of Virgil's to attribute it to the Harpy Celaeno (3.247–57). In her mouth it is a hostile prophecy, and she emphasises the suffering implied in it. But when the omen is fulfilled, Aeneas attributes it to Anchises and quotes his exact words (7.124–27); however, in Anchises' mouth, the prophecy takes on a totally different tone and denotes not suffering but hope, because the place where it is fulfilled is destined to be the site of Aeneas' city. The fulfillment will be the sign for Aeneas to recognise the end of Trojan sufferings (126–32), and so Aeneas rejoices and gives thanks in various ceremonies. That attribution looks as if it was the poet's original conception.

22. References in R. D. Williams (1962), pp. 107–08.

The whole episode of the Harpies seems to be a later insertion in an already composed text. The most striking indication of this is the peculiar way in which the Trojan arrival at Actium is described (3.278–80):

> "Ergo insperata tandem tellure potiti
> lustramurque Iovi votisque incendimus aras,
> Actiaque Iliacis celebramus litora ludis."

"So, having finally gained the land we had not expected to reach, we performed lustral ritual to Juppiter and set the altars blazing with our offerings and we crowd the shores of Actium with Trojan games."

The word *insperata* is explained thus by the most recent editor: "because they have been sailing through Greek seas, and have just passed the most dangerous area of all, the islands around Ithaca (282–83)."[23] This is quite unconvincing, not only because there is no sign that the Trojans fear (as distinct from hate) Ulysses, but far more because Actium also is still in Greek territory. The word *insperata* here is different from (509) *optatae . . . telluris;* there the Trojans have reached a "longed-for land" because from it they can see Italy and there is only a short journey across (507). The sense of *insperata* "that they did not expect to reach" can be illustrated by the use of *optata . . . harena* at 1.172. There the Trojans had not longed for the African shore because it was African; in fact, it was the last place they wanted to be, but any shore was better than the sea after the storm they had suffered. Similarly, the much stronger *insperata* means that the Trojans had not expected to survive a storm. But the storm in question at 3.194–208 has been adapted by the poet to explain a Trojan landing on the Strophades and to ground the consequent adventure with the Harpies. It was originally intended to carry the Trojans past Malea and along the western Peloponnese almost to Actium. Virgil inserted lines 209–69 in an already composed text but omitted to correct the implication of a storm in the word (278) *insperata.* This suggestion of a later composition, designed for Aeneas as narrator, is supported by the observation made above of the success with which Aeneas, in the Harpy episode as distinct from elsewhere, co-ordinates his own actions as commander with those of his men on the one hand and of Anchises on the other.

The Harpy incident was introduced by Virgil into the Aeneas legend from the *Argonautica* of Apollonius Rhodius. Two other incidents, unknown to the Aeneas legend before Virgil, seem likely to have been

23. Ibid., p. 112.

introduced by him at a late stage precisely to provide authentic emotional eye-witness experiences for Aeneas. The first is the strange incident of Polydorus (22–57). The basis for the account is the *Hecuba* of Euripides, and it is told in a convincingly personal way by Aeneas, with description of his emotional reaction (29–30) and a unique address that shows for once in Book 3 his consciousness of a live audience; as he reaches the climax of horror, he asks rhetorically of his audience (39) *eloquar, an sileam?* "Should I tell it all or should I keep silent about it?" It is also notable that in this account there is a very well-managed passage of "telling" which, as in Book 2, derives from Aeneas' own hindsight (49–57), and it is introduced by a finely pathetic (49) *quondam* "at one time." It ends with another entry of Aeneas' own personality as he reflects on the greed of humankind (56–57):

> "quid non mortalia pectora cogis,
> auri sacra fames?"

"To what excesses do you not compel the hearts of men, accursed hunger for money!"

This recalls the poet's own entry into his text at 4.412, in a similar reflection on the inordinate power of Love.[24]

The other incident that may be regarded as a later composition is a significant part of the visit to Buthrotum (294–505). That visit was certainly a well-established part of the Aeneas legend. In the account of Dionysius of Halicarnassus (*Roman Antiquities* 1.51), the Trojans landed in Ambracia and it was Anchises who went to Buthrotum. Aeneas marched inland to Dodona and met Helenus there; he also, according to Varro (quoted by Servius on 3.256), consulted the oracle of Juppiter and was there told the prophecy of eating the tables. What has no part in the tradition before Virgil is the meeting between Aeneas and Andromache that is structured to surround the meeting with Helenus (294–345 and 482–91). This poignant scene, described with convincingly personal emotion by Aeneas, has its basis in Euripides' *Andromache* and *Troades*. Its character as a later composition is borne out not only by the extraordinary contrast in narrative viewpoint and style between the scene with Andromache and that with Helenus, but also by the somewhat contrived insertion of Andromache into the farewell-scene, in which she gives presents to Ascanius (482–91). Her presence there is motivated by the narrator

---

24. See chap. 7, sec. 2(a).

in the oddly abrupt comment in parenthesis (484) *nec cedit honore* "and she does not take second place in showing regard." The portrait of Andromache, who lives totally in the past in a make-believe Troy, gives the opportunity for a fine self-portrait by Aeneas of the opposite attitude— that of a man who has a mission to found a truly new state for his people in a far-off land. It is notable that it is only in this effective speech that in all of Book 3 oblique reference is made to the prophecy of Creusa (495, 500); and this should probably be seen as another sign of later composition.

The final passage that is certainly a later composition is this (707–15):

> "hinc Drepani me portus et inlaetabilis ora
> accipit. hic pelagi tot tempestatibus actus
> heu, genitorem, omnis curae casusque levamen,
> amitto Anchisen. hic me, pater optime, fessum
> deseris, heu, tantis nequiquam erepte periclis!
> nec vates Helenus, cum multa horrenda moneret,
> hos mihi praedixit luctus, non dira Celaeno.
> hic labor extremus, longarum haec meta viarum.
> hinc me digressus vestris deus appulit oris."

"After this the port and joyless shore of Drepanum receives me. Here, beaten by so many storms of the sea, alas! I lose Anchises, who brought relief in every worry and every disaster. Here, dearest father, you abandon me, alas! saved in vain from such terrible dangers. Neither the prophet Helenus, though he warned me of many fearful things, predicted grief like this, nor did deadly Celaeno. This was my final trial, this was the finishing-point of long journeying; after I had departed from here a god drove me upon your shores."

The deeply personal tone of the emotion expressed by the son for his father comes out strongly by contrast with the authorial tone of the preceding section, which is quite unsuited to Aeneas. It also brings out an ambiguity in the figure of Anchises in Book 3.[25] One aspect of his role takes its lead from line 9 *et pater Anchises dare fatis vela iubebat*. So, on several occasions Anchises surprisingly gives orders, without any suggestion that he consults Aeneas. One of the strangest is when Aeneas is being advised by Helenus; Anchises orders the fleet made ready to sail (472–73). Another is when Anchises gives the order to come about and avoid sailing past Scylla and Charybdis (558–60). It is natural that An-

---

25. For a different treatment of the character of Anchises, see Lloyd (1957).

chises should interpret omens and oracles and perform ritual and perhaps even (as Priam did for Sinon) assure Achaemenides of Trojan protection, but the technical details of leadership are—and should be—Aeneas'. This is what those who gathered to accompany him were made to say specifically (2.796–800):

> "atque hic ingentem comitum adfluxisse novorum
> invenio admirans numerum, matresque virosque,
> collectam exsilio pubem, miserabile vulgus.
> undique convenere animis opibusque parati
> in quascumque velim pelago deducere terras."

"And here to my astonishment I find that a great number of new companions have gathered together, both women and men, a people bonded together for exile, a pitiable mass. They have come together from everywhere ready and willing with their resources for any land toward which I shall choose to mount an expedition over the sea."

This is a mandate for Aeneas; Anchises is frail and dependent, loved and respected, consulted when appropriate, but no leader. That view of Anchises is prepared in the final part of Book 2, and it clashes to some extent with what may have been an earlier concept in an authorially spoken Book 3 (conceived as Book 1). It is to the earlier concept of Anchises that the attribution of the prophecy about eating the tables belongs. The later version of that prophecy (as it was argued to be above) is alluded to in the equally late subjective expression of loss over the death of Anchises at the end of Book 3 (713). The change from the earlier to the later concept can be regarded as an important aspect of the change of narrator from poet to participant, since the role of leader, with dependent father, enhances the impact of Aeneas' subjective narrative.

The poet takes over the narrative in his own voice again at the end of the book with these words (716–18):

> Sic pater Aeneas intentis omnibus unus
> fata renarrabat divum cursusque docebat.
> conticuit tandem factoque hic fine quievit.

Thus father Aeneas with everyone closely attentive all alone recounted the destiny imposed by the gods and explained his wanderings. Finally he fell silent and making an end here was quiet.

The idiom *omnibus unus* emphasises excellence (e.g., 1.15) or uniqueness in some respect (e.g., 2.743) or one against all (e.g., 10.691). Here it is otiose; the poet simply uses a convenient metrical tag provisionally to fill a gap. This needed a revision that it did not receive.

What has been suggested here (not for the first time) is that at one time the book had been composed for the voice of the poet to open the epic. Later the plan was changed and the book revised to accommodate it to narration by Aeneas. The details of that revision cannot be demonstrated, but it will not have been simply a matter of shifting the person of verbs. Consequently, it is not relevant to object to the hypothesis by issuing a challenge, as, for instance, the latest editor has done: "It must be stressed that there is no possibility whatsoever that the bulk of Book III is a third-person narrative slightly rewritten into the first person. If anyone thinks that it is, let him try to write it back again into the third person, adding the subjects *Aeneas, Teucri*, etc. where necessary."[26] The revision must have cut deep into the existing text and much must have been discarded. For instance, there is no use of the divine machinery in the book in the way in which that framework is used when the poet has charge of the narrative. On the other hand, the absence of Venus, for instance, may have been forced upon the poet. In spite of Aeneas' claim to Venus in 1.381–82

> "bis denis Phrygium conscendi navibus aequor,
> matre dea monstrante viam data fata secutus"

"With twice ten ships I climbed the Phrygian seas, following the destiny assigned to me, with my goddess-mother leading the way,"

she makes only a single, purely textual entrance in Book 3 when, at line 19, Aeneas makes sacrifice *Dionaeae matri* "to my mother, daughter of Dione." It may have been difficult to make her active in the text of Book 3 in view of the constant presence of Anchises. But her entrance in Book 2 is certainly a later conception (see below), and the poet may have had ideas for introducing her into Book 3 too.

What can be detected as a weakness is a general failure, subject to specific, carefully designed exceptions, to alter the point of view convincingly from that of the poet to that of a major participant. Book 2 is wonderfully successful in this. Of course, it was easier to view the highly concentrated, very dramatic events of the few hours in which Troy was destroyed through the eyes of a participant than the somewhat repetitive stages of a voyage around the Mediterranean. But Polydorus, the

---

26. R. D. Williams (1962), p. 2 n. 2. Contrast Crump (1920), pp. 16–40.

Harpies, Andromache, and the death of Anchises are some measure of what could be achieved.

3. The Funeral of Anchises

Book 5 in its present form is a neatly structured ring-composition, with Aeneas and Palinurus opening the book and Palinurus and Aeneas closing it. The opening is carefully devised to motivate the major theme of the book, the funeral-games of Anchises. An account of funeral-games had become a generic marker of epic, originating with the games at the funeral of Patroclus in *Iliad* 21. The highly emotional and subjective nature of Aeneas' account of his father's death at the end of Book 3 was designed to relieve the poet of the necessity for any facts about the old man's death or burial. Anchises is the only personage in antiquity whose funeral-games were held on the first anniversary of his funeral rather than at the funeral itself. The device was contrived so that the poet could take over the account of the games and avoid the implausibility of making Aeneas subject Dido to a detailed description. The lyrical outburst of Aeneas at his father's death and the curious storm at the beginning of Book 5, which compels a return to Drepanum, are thus both designed to achieve the separation of Book 5 from Book 3. But there are oddities that point to a different original conception.

When Aeneas pours a libation at the tomb of Anchises, he says (80–83):

> "salve, sancte parens, iterum salvete, recepti
> nequiquam cineres animaeque umbraeque paternae.
> non licuit finis Italos fataliaque arva
> nec tecum Ausonium, quicumque est, quaerere Thybrim."

"Hail, divine father, again I say hail, ashes gathered in vain and spirit and ghost of my father. I was not permitted in your company to search for the territory of Italy and the fields decreed by fate nor Ausonian Tiber (whatever that is)."

Ancient commentators wanted to punctuate after (80) *iterum* on the ground that this was the second time Aeneas was addressing his dead father—he had already done so at the funeral. But the structure *salve . . . iterum salvete . . . .* , emphasising the repetition of the call, is well attested in such contexts; while the notion that Aeneas is asserting that he had already done this before is very odd. This difficulty, however, pales before *recepti nequiquam cineres*. This was taken by Servius to refer to the rescue of Anchises when Troy was burning, and it still remains the favoured explanation. But, while Anchises is certainly portrayed as weak and dependent at the end of Book 2, it is exaggerated to call him "ash." Nor is it convincing that *recepti* should be genitive singular: "ashes of the man I rescued in vain." Still less can the words refer to the legend of the violation of Anchises' tomb by Diomedes. Nor is it plausible that *recepti* should mean "restored to me" (i.e., "through the fact that I have returned here"). The phrase most strongly suggests a constant epitaphic theme: the idea that the funeral rites, though of course obligatory, are vain and empty—in the sense that they do nothing real for the dead person. So Anchises himself, as he imagines that he is conducting the funeral of Marcellus, ends by saying (6.885–86) *et fungar inani/munere* "and I shall complete the empty ritual." At 6.213 the poet speaks of the funeral rites of Misenus as performed *cineri ingrato* "for the ungrateful ash," a variation on the same theme. But, if that is the meaning, then the words are far more appropriate to the real funeral and not to an anniversary celebration.

Once that possibility emerges, various considerations support it. For instance, when Aeneas declares that there will be games, he says (64–65):

> "praeterea, si nona diem mortalibus almum
> Aurora extulerit radiisque retexerit orbem"

"Besides, when the ninth dawn shall have lifted up her kindly light for mortals and shall have uncovered the world with her rays . . ."

Roman funeral rites lasted for nine days. But that idea, too, suits the real funeral rather than its anniversary. Again, the Trojan women, before they burn the fleet, are mourning Anchises (613–15):

> at procul in sola secretae Troades acta
> amissum Anchisen flebant, cunctaeque profundum
> pontum aspectabant flentes.

But far away, set apart on the lonely sea-shore, the Trojan women were mourning the loss of Anchises and all of them gazed with tears on the deep sea.

It turns out that Beroe has absented herself because she was not allowed to be present at the ceremony and offer due sacrifice to Anchises (650–52). That Roman custom whereby women were excluded from the funeral ceremony is also better suited to the occasion of the real funeral than of its anniversary.

Another consideration can be added here. The real complaint of the women is this (615–17):

> heu tot vada fessis
> et tantum superesse maris, vox omnibus una.
> urbem orant, taedet pelagi perferre laborem.

"They all express one and the same idea: alas, that there remain so many straits for them, worn out as they are, and so much expanse of sea; they beg for a city, they are tired of enduring the toils of the ocean."

It is clearly more convincing that they should feel like this after six years of continuous voyaging than after a long stay in Carthage and a brief sea-passage to Sicily. That is, the whole dramatic situation suggests the occasion of Anchises' death at the end of Book 3 and not its anniversary a year later. This is confirmed by the words of Iris, who has disguised herself as Beroe (623–29):

> "o miserae, quas non manus" inquit "Achaica bello
> traxerit ad letum patriae sub moenibus! o gens
> infelix, cui te exitio Fortuna reservat?
> septima post Troiae excidium iam vertitur aestas,
> cum freta, cum terras omnis, tot inhospita saxa
> sideraque emensae ferimur, dum per mare magnum
> Italiam sequimur fugientem et volvimur undis."

"'O pitiable women,' she says, 'in that a Greek band did not drag you in wartime to death beneath the walls of your fatherland! O unfortunate people, for what death is Fate preserving you? Now the seventh summer is coming round since the fall of Troy and we in our voyaging have measured out all the seas, all lands, so many threatening shoals and skies while we run over the great ocean in pursuit of an Italy that recedes and are tossed upon the waves.'"

When Dido asked Aeneas to tell his story, she said (1.753–56):

> "immo age et a prima dic, hospes, origine nobis
> insidias' inquit 'Danaum casusque tuorum
> erroresque tuos; nam te iam septima portat
> omnibus errantem terris et fluctibus aestas."

"Come, my friend, and right from the beginning tell us of the treachery of the Greeks and the disasters of your friends and your wanderings; for it is now the seventh summer that carries you in your wandering over all lands and all seas."

The wording of the two passages is close enough to suggest that in composing the Dido-passage (which is late because it treats Book 2 and 3 as told by Aeneas), the poet plundered the passage from Book 5, perhaps intending to cancel or re-write the latter section. But however that may be, what emerges from the conjunction of both passages is that the poet imagined the Trojans in Carthage a short time after the death of Anchises and that he therefore composed Book 5 with the real funeral of Anchises, not its anniversary, in mind.

4. The Death of Palinurus

The only serious discrepancy in Book 6 is closely connected with Book 5. Palinurus is drowned at the end of Book 5; Aeneas then meets him in the Underworld in Book 6, but the account that Palinurus there gives of his own death bears little resemblance to the poet's account in Book 5. The discrepancies are such as to make it certain that the two accounts were composed independently and never received the necessary revision. It is clear, too, that the account in Book 5 is the later, composed to form a ring-composition with the opening of the book (also a late composition).

The death takes place during a calm in the account of Book 5, but during a storm in Book 6; the god Sleep is the murderer in Book 5, divine intervention is explicitly denied in Book 6; in Book 5 Aeneas thinks the death is an accident, due to over-confidence on the part of Palinurus (which is ironically contradicted by the privileged poet's account), but in Book 6 he asks what god was the perpetrator; in Book 6 Palinurus says that he swam for three days and on the fourth reached Italy, but there is only one day's gap between the events at the end of Book 5 and the meeting with Palinurus. But the most interesting discrepancy concerns geography. In Book 5 the Trojan fleet is sailing from Drepanum in Sicily to Cumae, half-way between the Straits of Messina and the Tiber. However, in Book 6 Palinurus tells Aeneas that the accident happened (338) *Libyco nuper cursu*. These words would most naturally mean "on the recent voyage to Libya," but in no way could a voyage from Drepanum to Carthage be relevant to a man's swimming ashore on Cape Palinurus (unless the ship had already made considerable progress toward Cumae before being blown back to Africa by the storm). Consequently, the adjective *Libyco* must have the unusual function of designating the point of origin of the voyage and not its destination. Furthermore, when that conclusion is reached, it can be said in support of it that when a ship sailing to Cumae is blown off course so badly that it ends up near Carthage, that cannot properly be described as a "voyage to Libya."

So, when the poet composed an account of Palinurus' death for the victim's own mouth in Book 6, he was thinking in terms of a voyage from

Carthage to Cumae, more or less non-stop. That is, the situation in that part of Book 6 envisages no return to Sicily, and so, when the poet composed this account of Palinurus, he assumed that the funeral-games for Anchises and the burning of the ships had already taken place before the storm carried the Trojans to Carthage.

This hypothesis makes sense of another discrepancy in Book 6. When the ships are burned in Book 5, Aeneas loses heart and is strengthened in his purpose first by Nautes, then by Anchises (724–39). In that speech Anchises prescribes the voyage to Italy and foretells the war there; but he bids Aeneas first come and visit him in Elysium. When they meet there Anchises says (6.687–94):

> "venisti tandem, tuaque exspectata parenti
> vicit iter durum pietas! datur ora tueri,
> nate, tua et notas audire et reddere voces!
> sic equidem ducebam animo rebarque futurum
> tempora dinumerans, nec me mea cura fefellit.
> quas ego te terras et quanta per aequora vectum
> accipio! quantis iactatum, nate, periclis!
> quam metui ne quid Libyae tibi regna nocerent!"

"So you have come at last! And that devotion of yours, relied on by your father, has won out over the difficult road! I am allowed to see your face, my son, and to hear that well-known voice and answer it! That was just what I kept turning over in my mind and thought would come to pass, and I counted off the time, nor did my anxious hope deceive me. What lands you have been to, what seas you have traversed for me to receive you here! What dangers, my son, stormed round you! How frightened I was that the kingdom of Libya would injure you in some way!"

Of course, Anchises appeared to Aeneas on other occasions than that in Book 5, as Aeneas goes on to say (695–96), but the poet has clearly linked the two passages. In the present arrangement there is only a day or so between them, and it makes more sense of the poet's purpose if the passage in Book 5 had been composed for the immediate aftermath of Anchises' actual funeral and before the storm carried Aeneas off course to Libya.

5. The Effect of the Changes of Plan in Books 1–6

The conclusion to be drawn from all that has been said in this appendix is that the poet's early conception of the first half of the *Aeneid* envisaged an ordering of the material in which the substance of Book 3 came first; it ended with the death of Anchises and was followed by the substance of Book 5. Both of these books were told in the poet's voice, as was the next book, the present Book 1; then followed Books 2, 4, and 6 more or less as they exist now.

There was good artistic sense in deciding to put Book 3 first. Its strategy is of a man, exiled from his country, gradually coming to realise more and more clearly that he has a special destiny to found a new state in a particular region. The many prophecies in the book create a unifying series of thematic anticipations right at the beginning of the epic. A further motive may have been a desire to avoid the structural weakness of the *Odyssey*, in which the lengthy tale of his wanderings by Odysseus totally disrupts the Telemachus-plot. Certainly a proper limit had to be placed on the account given by Aeneas, and it must have been at the point when the poet decided to give the narrative of Book 3 to Aeneas that he was compelled to devise the stratagem of giving Anchises his funeral-games a year after the funeral, for Aeneas could not be allowed to give Dido a detailed account of the games. As it is, the account in Book 3 of events that purportedly were spread over six years has been telescoped into a series of exemplary incidents, with the stages between left vague and the passage of time unmeasured but organised to convey the impression of continuous movement.

But the change of plan had a more important purpose. It made Carthage as central to the first half of the *Aeneid* as Lavinium is to the second, with a unity that starts from Juno's love of the city (1.12–32) and extends through the first four books; Dido's pyre overshadows Book 5, and her rejection of Aeneas in Book 6 precedes his initiation into the future greatness of Rome. Consequently, Dido pervades the first six books as powerfully as Turnus does the second. A much less concentrated, much more historical, and even antiquarian epic would have resulted from placing Books 3 and 5 first.

Parts, at any rate, of Book 1 were composed after the decision to change had been made, since, for instance, the number of ships is undiminished by the burning (381, 383, 393) and Aeneas is invited by Dido to recount both the fall of Troy and his wanderings (754–55).

Book 2 was little altered, but there was one important change. The forger who had the idea of making Aeneas attack Helen[27] inserted his product into a passage that probably ran like this (564–66, 589–91):

---

27. On this forgery, see Goold (1968). I am not persuaded by the opposing thesis, most ably advocated by Austin (1961); see also his edition (1964), pp. 217–28.

"respicio et quae sit me circum copia lustro
(deseruere omnes defessi, et corpora saltu   565
ad terram misere aut ignibus aegra dedere)
cum mihi se, non ante oculis tam clara, videndam
obtulit et pura per noctem in luce refulsit   590
alma parens . . ."

"I am looking back and searching to see what forces I have to support me (they have all deserted me in exhaustion and either flung their weak bodies to the ground by leaping or thrown them into the flames), when my sweet mother presented herself to may gaze—never previously so clearly—and shone with a pure light through the darkness . . ."

Though complex parentheses are a feature of Virgil's style,[28] they were easy victims of misunderstanding, and this, together with the mention of Helen by Venus (601), inspired the forgery and gave it a foothold. But the introduction of Venus at this point was certainly a later insertion by the poet into a text that ran continuous from the parenthesis (565–56)—which, of course, would not then have been a parenthesis—to 632–33:[29]

"descendo ac ducente deo flammam inter et hostis
expedior: dant tela locum flammaeque recedunt."

"I climb down and, with the guidance of a god, make my way amidst the flames and the enemy: weapons give way before me and the flames fall back."

When the poet composed this he had no idea in his mind that Venus had appeared to Aeneas. Here Aeneas is simply under generalised divine protection; he is saved, unlike his companions, and explains it by saying that he led "a charmed life."[30] His use of the concept of divine protection corresponds to his general attitude toward the gods as the poet makes him express it in Book 2. But he was privileged in one special way: he had a goddess for his mother. The poet made use of this privilege to present Aeneas as irresistibly compelled to abandon Troy and to have regard for his family and himself.

This intervention by Venus, however, raises the question as to why she does not appear in Book 3. This discrepancy is parallel to the discrepancy created by Creusa and has the same origin. The special mission for

28. See note 20 above.
29. On this, see Körte (1916).
30. The phrase (632) *ducente deo* was composed without any idea of specifying a particular god (and certainly not Venus). For the similar vague and ambiguous use of *deus* at 7.498, see p. 23 above.

which it was Aeneas' duty to abandon Troy was merely outlined in the appearance of Hector's ghost (2.289–95). It is not directly mentioned in Venus' speech, except insofar as she reveals that the destruction of Troy is willed by the gods. It becomes more positive with the omens presented to Anchises, since they convince him that the gods decree the abandonment of Troy and intend a promising future for Trojan survivors (701–04). The climax only comes with Creusa's revelation not only of the fated abandonment of Troy but of a specific geographical goal and a destined future (2.777–84). This serves a double purpose. First, it is the final justification for Aeneas' leaving Troy. But it also makes authoritative for Aeneas' audience, especially Dido, that he has a destiny (elsewhere than in Carthage), revealed to him in some detail, which it is his duty to see fulfilled. Both the appearance of Venus and the revelation of Creusa certainly imposed further adaptation of Book 3 on the poet, which he had no time to make.

The composition of Books 1–6 was made difficult for Virgil by the existence not only of the *Odyssey* but also of various versions of a quite detailed legend of Aeneas' progress from Troy to the Tiber, covering a number of years. A further advantage the poet derived from his rearrangement was that the time-scale of that half of the epic was essentially narrowed from seven years to a few months. There was no similar difficulty in the composition of Books 7–12, since the legend was much less precise and predecessors were almost negligible (Ennius probably treated this part of the story very briefly). Consequently, there is a unity that easily survives considerable complications of plot, and the *Iliad* is sufficiently distant for the poet to be able to make full use of it as a soundingboard. The only place at which a change of mind shows through the artistry of the narration is the description of the past history of Camilla (11.535–94). This is now, a little oddly, put into the mouth of Diana, but a series of references to herself in the third person (537–38, 566, 582–83) are dissonant with the character of Diana as narrator and suggest that the passage may have been composed for the poet's voice to come at the introduction of Camilla in the review of Italian troops, perhaps between lines 811 and 812.

SELECT BIBLIOGRAPHY

The following abbreviations are used:

AJP	*American Journal of Philology*
AUMLA	*Journal of the Australasian Universities Language and Literature Association*
CJ	*Classical Journal*
CQ	*Classical Quarterly*
CSCA	*California Studies in Classical Antiquity*
GRBS	*Greek, Roman, and Byzantine Studies*
HSCP	*Harvard Studies in Classical Philology*
JRS	*Journal of Roman Studies*
Mus. Helv.	*Museum Helveticum*
PCPS	*Proceedings of the Cambridge Philological Society*
RhM	*Rheinisches Museum*
TAPA	*Transactions of the American Philological Association*

Anderson, W. S. "Vergil's second *Iliad*." *TAPA* 88 (1957): 17–30.
_____. *"Pastor Aeneas:* on pastoral themes in the *Aeneid*." *TAPA* 99 (1968): 1–17.
_____. *The Art of the* Aeneid. Englewood Cliffs, N.J., 1969.
_____. "Two passages from Book 12 of the *Aeneid*." *CSCA* 4 (1971): 49–65.
Austin, R. G. *P. Vergilii Maronis* AENEIDOS: *Liber Quartus* (Oxford: Clarendon Press, 1955); *Liber Secundus* (Oxford: Clarendon Press, 1964); *Liber Primus* (Oxford: Clarendon Press, 1971); *Liber Sextus* (Oxford: Clarendon Press, 1977).
_____. "Virgil *Aeneid* 2.567–88." *CQ* 55 (1961): 185–98.

Bailey, Cyril. *Religion in Virgil.* Oxford: Clarendon Press, 1935.

Benario, Herbert W. "The tenth book of the *Aeneid.*" *TAPA* 98 (1967): 23–36.

Binder, G. *Aeneas und Augustus: Interpretationen zum 8. Buch der Aeneis,* Beiträge zur klassischen Philologie 38. Meisenheim am Glan, 1971.

Bömer, Franz. "Studien zum VIII. Buche der Aeneis." *RhM* 29 (1944): 319–69.

Boyancé, Paul. *La Réligion de Virgile.* Paris, 1963.

Boyle, A. J. "The meaning of the *Aeneid:* A critical inquiry." *Ramus* 1 (1972): 63–90 and 113–51.

Buchheit, Vinzenz. *Vergil über die Sendung Roms: Untersuchungen zum Bellum Poenicum und zur Aeneis, Gymnasium* Beiheft 3. Heidelberg: Winter, 1963.

Büchner, Karl. *P. Vergilius Maro: der Dichter der Römer.* Reprinted from Pauly-Wissowa viii A, Stuttgart 1955.

Camps, W. A. *An Introduction to Virgil's* Aeneid. Oxford: Oxford University Press, 1969.

Carlsson, Gunnar. "The hero and Fate in Virgil's *Aeneid.*" *Eranos* 43 (1945): 111–35.

Clausen, Wendell. "An interpretation of the *Aeneid.*" *HSCP* 68 (1964): 139–47.

Commager, Steele, ed. *Virgil: A Collection of Critical Essays.* Englewood Cliffs, N.J., 1966.

Conington, John, and Nettleship, Henry. *The Works of Virgil: The Aeneid.* Vols. 2 and 3. London, 1883, 1884.

Crump, Marjorie. *The Growth of the Aeneid.* Oxford: Basil Blackwell 1920.

Culler, Jonathan. "Apostrophe." *Diacritics* 7 (1977): 159–69.

Dale, A. M. *Euripides* Alcestis. Oxford: Clarendon Press, 1954.

d'Anna, Giovanni. *Il problema della composizione dell'Eneide.* Rome, 1957.

Di Cesare, Mario A. *The Altar and the City: A Reading of Vergil's* Aeneid. New York: Columbia University Press, 1974.

Duckworth, G. E. "The significance of Nisus and Euryalus for *Aeneid* 9–12." *AJP* 88 (1967): 129–50.

Fitzgerald, G. J. "Nisus and Euryalus: A paradigm of futile behaviour and the tragedy of youth." In *Studies in Honour of Harold Hunt,* pp. 114–31. Amsterdam, 1972.

Fordyce, C. J. *Aeneidos Libri vii–viii.* Oxford: Oxford University Press, Glasgow University Publications, 1977.

Fraenkel, Eduard. "Vergil und die Aithiopis." *Philologus* 87 (1932): 242–48.

———. "Some aspects of the structure of *Aeneid* VII." *JRS* 35 (1945): 1–14.

———. "*Urbem quam statuo vestra est,*" *Glotta* 33 (1954): 157–59.

_____. "Zum Text von Aeneis 6.852." *Mus. Helv.* 19 (1962): 133–34.

Galinsky, G. K. *Aeneas, Sicily, and Rome.* Princeton: Princeton University Press, 1969.

Gercke, Alfred. *Die Entstehung der Aeneis.* Berlin: Weidmann, 1913.

Goold, G. P. "Servius and the Helen episode." *HSCP* 74 (1968): 101–68.

Gow, A. S. F., and Page, D. L. *The Greek Anthology: The Garland of Philip.* 2 vols. Cambridge: Cambridge University Press, 1968.

Greene, Thomas M. *The Descent from Heaven: A Study in Epic Continuity.* New Haven and London: Yale University Press 1963.

Guillemin, A. M. *Virgile.* Paris, 1951.

Heinze, Richard. *Virgils epische Technik.* Leipzig and Berlin, 1915.

Henry, James. *Aeneidea.* 5 vols. London, Dublin, and Meissen, 1873–92.

Heyne, C. G., and Wagner, G. P. E. *Virgilii Opera.* 4th ed. in 5 vols. Leipzig and London, 1830–41.

Horsfall, Nicholas. "Numanus Remulus: Ethnography and propaganda in *Aen.* ix. 598 f." *Latomus* 30 (1978): 1108–16.

Hügi, M. *Vergils Aeneis und die hellenistische Dichtung.* Bern and Stuttgart, 1952.

Jackson Knight, W. F. *Roman Vergil.* 2d ed. London, 1966.

Johnson, W. R. "Aeneas and the ironies of *pietas.*" *CJ* 60 (1965): 360–64.

_____. *Darkness Visible: A Study of Vergil's* Aeneid. Berkeley: University of California Press, 1976.

Klingner, Friedrich. Virgil: *Bucolica, Georgica, Aeneis.* Zurich and Stuttgart, 1967.

Knauer, G. N. *Die Aeneis und Homer.* Hypomnemata, Vol. 7. Göttingen, 1964.

_____. "Vergil's *Aeneid* and Homer." *GRBS* 5 (1964): 61–84.

Körte, Alfred. "Zum zweite Buch von Vergils Aeneis," *Hermes* 51 (1916): 145–50.

Lennox, Peter G. "Virgil's night-episode re-examined (*Aeneid* ix.176–449)." *Hermes* 105 (1977): 331–42.

Little, D. A. "The death of Turnus and the pessimism of the *Aeneid.*" *AUMLA* 33 (1970): 67–76.

Lloyd, Robert B. "On *Aeneid* III, 270–280." *AJP* 75 (1954): 288–99.

_____. "Penatibus et magnis dis." *AJP* 77 (1956): 38–46.

_____. "*Aeneid* III: A new approach." *AJP* 78 (1957): 133–51.

_____. "*Aeneid* III and the Aeneas legend." *AJP* 78 (1957): 382–400.

_____. "The character of Anchises in the *Aeneid.*" *TAPA* 88 (1957): 44–55.

Mackay, L. A. "Three levels of meaning in *Aeneid* VI." *TAPA* 86 (1955): 180–89.

_____. "Achilles as a model for Aeneas." *TAPA* 88 (1957): 11–16.

_____. "Hero and theme in the *Aeneid.*" *TAPA* 94 (1963): 157–66.

Moskalew, Walter. *Formular language and poetic design in the* Aeneid. *Mnemosyne*, suppl. vol. 73 (1982). Leiden, Brill.

Nettleship, Henry. "Suggestions introductory to a study of the Aeneid." In *Lectures and Essays*, 1st ser., pp. 97–142. Oxford: Clarendon Press, 1885.

Nisbet, R. G. M., and Hubbard, Margaret. *A Commentary on Horace:* Odes *Book 1.* Oxford: Clarendon Press, 1970.

Nisbet, Robert. *History of the Idea of Progress.* New York: Basic Books, 1980.

Norden, Eduard. *Ennius und Vergilius.* Leipzig, 1912.

_____. *P. Vergilius Maro: Aeneis Buch VI.* Leipzig and Berlin, 1927.

Otis, Brooks. *Virgil: A Study in Civilized Poetry* Oxford: Clarendon Press, 1963.

Pease, A. S. *P. Vergili Maronis Aeneidos Liber Quartus.* Cambridge, Mass.: Harvard University Press, 1935.

_____. *M. Tulli Ciceronis de Natura Deorum.* 2 vols. Cambridge, Mass.: Harvard University Press, 1955–58.

Perret, J. *Les origines de la légende troyenne de Rome.* Paris, 1942.

Pöschl, Viktor. *Die Dichtkunst Virgils.* Innsbruck-Wien, 1950. Translated by Gerda Seligson as *The Art of Vergil: Image and Symbol in the Aeneid.* Ann Arbor: University of Michigan Press, 1962.

Putnam, M. C. J. *The Poetry of the Aeneid.* Cambridge, Mass.: Harvard University Press, 1965.

Quinn, Kenneth. *Virgil's Aeneid: A Critical Description.* London, 1968.

Reed, Nicholas. "The Gates of Sleep in *Aeneid* 6." *CQ* 23 (1973): 311–15.

Segal, C. P. "*Aeternum per saecula nomen:* The Golden Bough and the tragedy of history." Part 1, *Arion* 4 (1965): 617–57; Part 2, *Arion* 5 (1966): 34–72.

Sellar, W. Y. *The Roman Poets of the Augustan Age: Virgil.* 3d ed. Oxford: Clarendon Press, 1897.

Sparrow, John. *Half-Lines and Repeitions in Virgil.* Oxford: Clarendon Press, 1931.

Steiner, H. Rudolf. *Der Traum in der Aeneis.* Noctes Romanae: Forschungen über die Kultur der Antike, edited by W. Wili. Bern and Stuttgart, 1952.

Stinton, T. C. W. " *Si credere dignum est:* some expressions of disbelief in Euripides and others." *PCPS* n.s. 22 (1976): 60–89.

Syme, Ronald. *The Roman Revolution.* Oxford: Clarendon Press, 1939.

Thornton, Agathe. *The Living Universe: Gods and Men in Virgil's* Aeneid Dunedin: University of Otago Press, 1976.

West, David. "Multiple-correspondence similes in the *Aeneid*." *JRS* 59 (1969): 40–49.

_____. "Virgilian multiple-correspondence similes and their antecedents." *Philologus* 114 (1970): 262–75.

Williams, Gordon. "Some aspects of Roman marriage ceremonies and ideals." *JRS* 48 (1958): 16–29.

_____. *Tradition and Originality in Roman Poetry*. Oxford: Clarendon Press, 1968.

_____. *The Third Book of Horace's* Odes. Oxford: Clarendon Press, 1969.

_____. "Horace *Odes* 1.12 and the succession to Augustus." *Hermathena* 118 (1974): 147–55.

_____. *Change and Decline: Roman Literature in the Early Empire*. Berkeley: University of California Press, 1978.

_____. *Figures of Thought in Roman Poetry*. New Haven and London: Yale University Press, 1980.

Williams, R. D. *P. Vergili Maronis AENEIDOS. Liber Quintus*. Oxford: Clarendon Press, 1960. *Liber Tertius*. Oxford: Clarendon Press, 1962.

_____. *Virgil. Greece and Rome*, New Surveys in the Classics No. 1. Oxford: Clarendon Press, 1967.

_____. *The Aeneid of Virgil: Books 1–6*. New York: Macmillan, 1972.

_____. *The Aeneid of Virgil: Books 7–12*. New York: Macmillan, 1973.

Wilson, J. R. "Action and emotion in Aeneas." *Greece and Rome* 16 (1969): 67–75.

Wlosok, Antonie. *Die Göttin Venus in Vergils Aeneis*. Bibliothek der klassischen Altertumswissenschaften, n.s. 2, vol. 21. Heidelberg: Winter, 1967.

_____. "Vergil in der neueren Forschung." *Gymnasium* 80 (1973): 129–51.

INDEX OF PASSAGES
DISCUSSED

Apollonius Rhodius, *Argonautica:*
  1.1243–49: 174
  2.278–83: 168–70
  2.799–805: 103–04
  3.291–95: 83, 126–27
  4.1062–65: 127

Augustus, *res gestae:*
  3.1–2: 150
  8.5: 238–39
  13: 137, 146, 238
  34.1–2: 156

Cicero, *de re publica:*
  6.13: 55–56
  6.16: 56

Euripides, *Alcestis*, 74–76, 217–18

Homer:
Iliad:
  4.141–47: 61
  4.273–83: 166–67
  5.49–58: 199
  6.12–17: 197
  6.146–49: 66
  6.506–11: 82–83
  12.277–89: 60–61
  12.433–35: 126
  14.267–69: 124–25
  15.263–68: 83
  15.585–91: 175–76
  15.618–29: 178–79
  16.433–38: 158–59
  17.198–208: 87–88
  21.26–32: 100–01

22.159–61: 89
22.188–93: 168–70
22.199–201: 173
22.209–13: 89–90
22.337–43: 91
22.356–60: 91
23.173–83: 115–16
Odyssey:
  19.560–69: 47–48

Lucretius, *de rerum natura:*
  1.1–49: 39
  2.167–83: 39
  6.68–79: 39

Macrobius, *Commentary on Dream of Scipio:*
  1.4.3: 15, 211–12

Virgil:
Aeneid 1:
  6–7: 133
  33: 133
  71–75: 125
  108–11: 133
  148–56: 70–72, 125, 133–34, 166
  263–96: 138–42
  314–17: 69–70
  441–93: 93–94
  461–62: 242
  490–93: 68–69
  498–504: 62, 181
  603–05: 15, 210–11
  607–10: 40–41
  650–55: 67–68
  753–56: 280–81

GENERAL INDEX